A TASTE
OF
SOUTH
CAROLINA

BY THE PALMETTO CABINET

SANDLAPPER
PUBLISHING, INC.
Orangeburg, South Carolina

A TASTE OF SOUTH CAROLINA

First printing........................1983
Second revised printing......1984
Third Printing......................1985
Fourth printing....................1986
Fifth printing........................1989
Sixth printing.......................1992
Seventh printing.................1995

Published by
Sandlapper Publishing Co., Inc.
Orangeburg, South Carolina

PRINTED IN THE UNITED STATES OF AMERICA

Cover photograph © 1995 Robert Clark

Royalties realized from the sale of A
TASTE OF SOUTH CAROLINA will be
spent to further the beautification of the
Mansion Complex—which includes the
South Carolina Governor's Mansion, the
Lace House, and the Boylston House
and Gardens—through the Governor's
Mansion Foundation.

Library of Congress Cataloging-in-Publication Data
Main entry under title:

A Taste of South Carolina.

   Includes index.
      1. Cookery, American—South Carolina. 2. South
Carolina—Description and travel.   I. Palmetto Cabinet
(Columbia, S.C.)
TX715.T21356   1983   641.59757   85-14573
ISBN 0-87844-064-X

Printed in the USA by

WIMMER
The Wimmer Companies, Inc.
Memphis

INTRODUCTION

The Palmetto Cabinet was organized in 1975 to allow the wives of legislators the opportunity to become better acquainted.

The membership of the Palmetto Cabinet consists of the wives of the members of the General Assembly or women members of the General Assembly, the wives and daughters of the present and former Governors, and wives of the constitutional officers of the State or women elected to these offices. Members of the Palmetto Cabinet remain eligible for membership through annual dues after their connection with State government is terminated.

The Cabinet's monthly luncheon meetings feature programs designed to stimulate cultural awareness and promote fellowship among the members. Special emphasis is given to assisting with physical improvements to buildings and grounds in the Governor's Mansion Complex.

The Palmetto Cabinet had an illustrious beginning and looks forward to years of successful service.

Mrs. H. Parker Evatt
PRESIDENT, 1983-1984

The Palmetto Cabinet wishes to thank

the many South Carolinians who contributed recipes to this cookbook: its own Cabinet members, Legislators, Governors, U.S. Senators, Congressmen, and Constitutional Officers. We regret that space limitation precluded the use of all the contributions.

A special section is dedicated to the Governor's Mansion, the stately home of South Carolina's first family. Recipes were collected from eight governors and their wives by Mrs. Richard W. Riley.

The remaining sections provide historical sketches of each of South Carolina's forty-six counties, the State House, and historical homes in the state. The Institute for Southern Studies, University of South Carolina, assisted in the compilation of this material. Mrs. Frank McGill contributed the illustrations of historical places.

"Menus for Every Occasion" offers menus suitable for various types of entertaining, including selection of the proper wine. Mr. Lee Ruef, assisted by Mr. John Carrington, loaned his expertise on wine to complete this section.

Also included are "quantities to allow" and "food measurements" to help determine exact measurements needed for a particular dish or meal, thereby avoiding waste and accumulation of leftovers.

The editorial staff takes special note of the contributions of Mrs. Christie Zimmerman Fant of the S.C. Department of Archives and History, the many county historical societies, the Clemson University Extension Service, the Governor's Mansion Commission, Mrs. Lois T. Shealy, and the officers and members of the Palmetto Cabinet for their support and tireless efforts in the publication of this book.

Mrs. Robert N. McLellan
EDITOR

Mrs. Herbert Kirsh
Mrs. Nick A. Theodore
ASSOCIATE EDITORS

CONTENTS

RECIPES

BRIEF HISTORIES OF SOUTH CAROLINA COUNTIES

6

ILLUSTRATIONS
SOME OF SOUTH CAROLINA'S OLDEST BUILDINGS

THE GOVERNOR'S MANSION

For nearly the first two hundred years of its existence, South Carolina did not have an official residence for its chief executives. Colonial governors either rented or purchased homes in Charleston, which served as the capital of South Carolina from 1670 until 1790.

In 1868 Governor James L. Orr persuaded the General Assembly to convert the former officers' quarters of the abandoned Arsenal Academy into a governor's residence. The remodeling of the "two two story tenements" into one dwelling cost approximately $4,000.00. Since there was a common wall, the conversion was not too difficult. Still, the building was not very comfortable as three governors chose not to live in the "mansion." Beginning in 1879, the Governor's Mansion has been occupied by all of the state's chief executives.

By 1946 it was structurally unsound and there was a serious move to abandon the residence for quarters more "in keeping with the dignity of the high office of the Chief Executive of the great State of South Carolina." Major repairs were made in the 1950s and 1960s.

In 1965 the Governor's Mansion Commission was formed to oversee the maintenance and beautification of the Mansion. This group, and its fund-raising counterpart, the Governor's Mansion Foundation, have succeeded far beyond the hopes of their first members.

It is the aim of the Commission to make the Mansion and its allied properties, the Lace and Boylston houses, indicative of the history of the entire state. The furnishings in the Mansion help tell the story of the more than 300 years of South Carolina history. Handsome 18th century Charleston-made pieces are at home with later 19th century upcountry ones. Museums across the state have been generous in lending items from their collections for use in the Mansion.

Among the furnishings of note are the silver from the battleship South Carolina, the upcountry-made secretary of Governor Francis W. Pickens, the "new colonial" style dining room furniture which is the only documented furniture purchased specifically for the Mansion, a pair of rare pastel portraits by Henrietta Johnson, and the Bernard Baruch chandelier in the large drawing room.

The eclectic nature of the furnishings in the Mansion is deliberate. It reflects the history and taste of more than three centuries of South Carolina lifestyles. And, most importantly, it underscores the fact that the Mansion is a home, not a museum.

The Governor's Mansion of South Carolina is open to its citizens and to other visitors on a regular basis. Because of the often hectic schedules that we place on our first families, it is recommended that advance arrangements be made by calling or writing the Mansion.

THE FAMILY DINING ROOM

The Family Dining Room in the Governor's Mansion features wallpaper taken from the Bolyston House. The scenic wallpaper is a 1910 edition of an 1830's wallpaper using the original wood blocks. It is hand-blocked. It was installed during the administration of Governor Richard W. Riley.

The Governor's Mansion

BUTTER NUT BRIE

Serves 25 to 30   Governor and Mrs. Richard W. Riley, 1978 -

1-1/4 cups butter, softened   Pinch salt
2   1-3/4 ounce packages pecan   Cayenne pepper to taste
     chips   2   4-inch wedges fully ripened
5 - 6 tablespoons cognac   chilled Brie
Dash of lemon juice

Combine the first 6 ingredients, mixing well. Remove crust from one cheese wedge. Cover top of wedge with butter mixture; chill about 5 minutes. Remove from refrigerator. Remove crust from remaining cheese wedge. Place on top of first wedge and coat top and sides with butter mixture. Place in refrigerator. About 1 hour before serving, remove from refrigerator and let stand at room temperature so cheese will achieve full flavor. Serve with fresh fruit and crackers.

CAVIAR DIP

Yield: 1 cup   Governor and Mrs. Richard W. Riley, 1978 -

6   ounces whipped cream cheese   1-1/2 tablespoon chopped fresh dill
3   ounces sour cream   Pinch of pepper
1   tablespoon lemon juice   2   ounces red or black caviar
1   teaspoon grated onion

Mix together the cream cheese and sour cream. Fold in remaining ingredients, except caviar. Add caviar last and refrigerate until needed. Serve with toast points.

SMOKED OYSTER LOG

Governor and Mrs. Richard W. Riley, 1978 -

1   3-3/4 ounce can smoked oysters 1/2 cup chopped parsley
16   ounce cream cheese, cold   1/2 cup chopped walnuts

Drain oysters. Shape 1/2 of the cream cheese on waxed paper into a log 15x2-inches. Top with drained oysters. Shape remaining cream cheese into a 12x2-inch strip and place on top of oysters. Tuck in ends. Roll and press seams, using waxed paper to ease rolling. Roll in parsley and walnuts. Chill until serving. Serve with crackers or party rye.

SALMON PÂTÉ

Yield : 2 cups   Governor and Mrs. Richard W. Riley, 1978 -

1	16-ounce can red salmon	2	teaspoons grated onion
1	8-ounce package softened	1	teaspoon horseradish
	cream cheese	1/4	teaspoon salt
1	tablespoon lemon juice	1/4	teaspoon liquid smoke

Mix all ingredients together well. Can be put into a crock or shaped into a loaf and rolled in parsley or pecans. Serve with stoned wheat crackers or wheat thins.

MARINATED SHRIMP

Governor and Mrs. Richard W. Riley, 1978 -

2	pounds large boiled shrimp, peeled, cleaned and chilled	1	tablespoon dill weed
		1	teaspoon garlic salt
2	cups red wine vinegar	1	teaspoon salt
1	tablespoon sugar	1	teaspoon pepper
1	tablespoon dry mustard	1-1/2	cups oil

Mix all the marinade ingredients with a whisk in a large bowl. Add shrimp and one sliced onion. Marinate overnight. Drain marinade before serving. Serve in a glass bowl on ice. Save the marinade in a glass jar in the refrigerator. It will keep for approximately 2 weeks and can be used to make more shrimp.

BRIOCHE

Serves 10 to 12   Governor and Mrs. Richard W. Riley, 1978 -

4	cups flour	1/4	teaspoon salt
1/2	cup sugar	2	packages yeast dissolved in 1/2 cup water
5	eggs, at room temperature		
2/3	cup soft butter		

In a large bowl mix together yeast, flour, sugar, butter and salt. Make a well in dry ingredients and add eggs, one at a time. If dough is too heavy, add more egg. Knead, cover and refrigerate at least 10 hours. When ready to bake, remove and shape 2/3 of dough into medium balls and remaining 1/3 into small balls. Place large balls in well-greased brioche, tart or muffin pans. Cut gash in center of each and place small ball in opening.. Let rise. Brush with beaten egg to which 1/4 teaspoon salt has been added. Bake at 375 degrees for 12 minutes for small brioche and 15 to 18 minutes for large brioche. With a spatula carefully loosen from side of pans, then remove.

BUTTERMILK DINNER ROLLS

Yields: 15 rolls

Mrs. Richard W. Riley (Tunky)
Wife of Governor Riley, 1978 -

1	package yeast (1 tablespoon)	2-1/2	cups plain flour
1	cup warm buttermilk	1	teaspoon baking powder
1	tablespoon brown sugar	1	teaspoon salt
1/4	teaspoon soda	3	tablespoons melted butter

Dissolve yeast in buttermilk. Stir in sugar and soda. Let this bubble. Sift together flour, baking powder and salt. Stir 1 cup of this into buttermilk and then stir in melted butter. Slowly add remaining flour. Knead in the rest. Put dough in greased bowl and let rise until double. Punch dough down and turn out. Roll to 14x6-inch rectangle. Cut into 1-inch strips. Twist ends in opposite directions and tie in a knot. Cover with towel and let rise until nearly doubled. Bake at 425 degrees for 15 to 20 minutes.

SPOON ROLLS

Yields: 2 dozen

Mrs. James B. Edwards (Ann)
Wife of Governor Edwards, 1975-1978

1	package dry yeast	1/4	cup sugar
2	cups very warm water	1	egg
1-1/2	sticks of margarine, melted	4	cups self-rising flour

Place yeast in warm water. Melt butter and cream in sugar in large bowl. Add beaten egg. Add yeast and water mixture to the above. Add flour. Mix well. Place in air-tight bowl and keep in refrigerator. To bake, drop by spoonful into greased muffin tins. Bake at 350 degrees for 30 minutes or until brown. Keeps for one week in the refrigerator. (Using mini-muffin tins make the rolls very attractive.)

CREAM OF CARROT SOUP

Serves 6 to 8

Mrs. Richard W. Riley (Tunky)
Wife of Governor Riley, 1978 -

2	cups chicken stock	Salt to taste
1	pound carrots, sliced thinly	1/4 teaspoon white pepper
2	potatoes, diced	1/4 teaspoon curry powder
1	large onion, diced	1/2 teaspoon cardamon
	Whipping cream	

Cook carrots, potatoes and onions in chicken stock until tender. Remove vegetables and pureé them in a blender or food processor. Return vegetables to chicken stock and add cream to thin soup to proper consistency. Add salt, pepper, curry powder and cardamon. Serve hot. Can be garnished with blanched green peas.

CAULIFLOWER SOUP

Serves 6

Mrs. Richard W. Riley (Tunky)
Wife of Governor Riley, 1978 -

1/2 medium cauliflower, divided in floweretes	2 medium potatoes, thinly sliced
Salt and white pepper	4 to 5 cups cream
4 tablespoons butter	2 tablespoons chopped parsley

Blanch the cauliflower in boiling, salted water for 2 minutes. Drain. In a heavy-bottomed Dutch oven melt 2 tablespoons butter, and add the potatoes. Press a piece of foil on top. Cover and cook gently, stirring occasionally, until potatoes are soft. (Do not allow them to brown, the soup should be light in color.) Add the milk, cauliflower, salt and pepper. Cover and let simmer 15 to 20 minutes until vegetables are tender. Purée the soup in a blender. Add more cream if necessary. The soup should be creamy, but not thick. Serve hot with croutons floating on top.

CREAM OF MUSHROOM SOUP

Serves 4 to 6

Mrs. Richard W. Riley (Tunky)
Wife of Governor Riley, 1978 -

1-1/2 pounds fresh mushrooms	6 tablespoons flour
9 tablespoons butter	6 cups chicken stock
2 finely chopped shallots or scallions	2 egg yolks
Salt, white pepper	3/4 cups heavy cream

Sauté 1/2 mushroom caps and reserve for garnish. Sauté remaining finely chopped mushrooms and onions. Set aside. Melt 5 tablespoons butter. Remove pan from heat and stir in flour. Cook over low heat 1 to 2 minutes, stirring constantly. Remove from heat, cool, slowly stir in stock. Return to heat and cook until thickened. Stir in onions and mushrooms. Cook 15 minutes. Purée soup and return to pot through a strainer. Whisk yolks and cream together. Whisk in hot soup, 2 tablespoons at a time, up to 1/2 cup. Then slowly whisk egg/cream back into soup. Bring to a boil; boil 30 seconds, stirring constantly. Remove from heat. Season with salt and pepper. Add reserved sliced mushrooms and serve. Asparagus may be substituted. Cook asparagus until tender. Reserve tips for garnish.

PEACH CHUTNEY

Yields: 4 pints

Mrs. Richard W. Riley (Tunky)
Wife of Governor Riley, 1978 -

4	quarts chopped fresh peaches	1	quart vinegar
1/2	cup chopped onion	2	tablespoons ground ginger
1/2	cup pecans	1/4	cup mustard seeds
1	clove garlic, chopped	3	cups brown sugar
1	pod hot pepper	2	teaspoons salt
1	cup raisins		

Mix all ingredients. Cook until thick, stirring frequently. Pour into hot, sterilized jars. Seal immediately.

WATERMELON PICKLE

Mrs. Richard W. Riley (Tunky)
Wife of Governor Riley, 1978 -

1	watermelon rind	1	ounce whole cloves
1	quart vinegar	1	vial of lime, available from drug
5	pounds sugar		stores
1	ounce stick cinnamon		

Peel all rind from watermelon. Slice off all of the red. Cut in squares and soak overnight in lime water. Drain liquid and cover with water. Cook 2 hours. Drain again, and cook slowly in syrup made of vinegar, sugar and spices. Seal in jars immediately.

COLD PASTA SALAD

Serves 6

Governor and Mrs. Richard W. Riley, 1978 -

1	pound elbow macaroni, cooked	1/2	cup mayonnaise
2	stalks celery, sliced	1/2	cup sour cream
1/2	cup chives, chopped	2	tablespoons red wine vinegar
3	sliced tomatoes		Salt
3	julienne carrots		White pepper
1	bunch broccoli, tops only, steamed lightly		

Place vegetables and macaroni in a large bowl. Mix together the mayonnaise, sour cream and vinegar. Season to taste and toss with the pasta. Refrigerate until serving time. This salad is particularly attractive if made with macaroni made from carrots and spinach, if available.

FRUIT SALAD

Serves 6   Governor and Mrs. Richard W. Riley, 1978 -

1	honeydew melon, peeled and cubed	1	quart fresh blueberries
1	cantaloupe, peeled and cubed	1	cup crème fraîche or yogurt
1	pineapple, peeled and cubed	2	tablespoons honey
1	quart fresh strawberries	1	tablespoon raspberry vinegar

Toss fruits together. Combine dressing ingredients, serve over fruit and sprinkle with sunflower seeds.

BALLSDAM PLANTATION TOMATO ASPIC

Mrs. Robert E. McNair (Josephine)
Wife of Governor McNair, 1965-1971

1	package gelatin	1/2 cup sliced green olives
V-8 juice (1-2/3 cups)		1/4 cup chopped bell pepper
1/2 cup chopped celery		1/4 cup chopped onion

Dissolve gelatin in small amount of cold water. Heat V-8 juice, mix in gelatin and stir thoroughly. Add other ingredients. Place in casserole dish, and allow to congeal in refrigerator. To serve, cut into squares, place on lettuce leaf and top with mayonniaise.

LA MOUSSELINE DE POISSON

(Fish Mousse with Herbed Mayonnaise)
Mrs. Richard W. Riley, (Tunky)
Wife of Governor Riley, 1978 -

1	pound fish fillets (such as trout, flounder, red snapper, pike or salmon)	**HERBED MAYONNAISE:**
3	eggs	2 egg yolks
Salt and pepper		1 whole egg
Nutmeg		1 tablespoon Dijon mustard
1	pound (1-1/2 cups) heavy cream	Pinch salt
		White pepper to taste
		1/4 cup fresh lemon juice
		2 cups corn oil
		1/2 teaspoon dill.weed or tarragon

Using steel blade, process fish of your choice. When smooth, remove to a bowl set over a container of ice cubes. With wooden spoon, work the fish well, then add the eggs, one at a time, working well after each addition.

15

THE GOVERNOR'S MANSION

Add salt, pepper and nutmeg to taste. Add the cream by tablespoons, working mixture until fluffy. Turn into heavily buttered fish mold. Place in a bain-marie and bake at 375 degrees for 10 to 15 minutes for individuals or 25 minutes for fish mold. Serve unmolded with HERBED MAYONNAISE: Combine egg yolks, egg, 1/2 of the lemon juice and salt and pepper in the bowl of a food processor. Process until mixed thoroughly. Dribble in oil slowly and stop the processor as soon as all oil is worked into the egg mixture. Add the dill or tarragon and check the seasoning. Add remaining lemon juice if necessary. Mayonnaise may be kept refrigerated in a glass jar for at least 5 days. Serve at a SUMMER DINNER BUFFET.

BRISKET ROAST

Mrs. James B. Edwards (Ann)
Wife of Governor Edwards, 1975-1978

One flat brisket, not rolled and not already pickled for corn beef. Sprinkle both sides of brisket generously with pepper, Lawry's Seasoning Salt, paprika, parsley flakes, onion or garlic salt. Place in roasting pan and sprinkle the top with one package of dry Lipton Onion Soup mix. Add 2 cups water (you may need to add more as necessary). Cook covered for 30 minutes at 400 degrees; reduce heat to 300 degrees and cook for 2-1/2 hours. May turn once. Serve with rice, using the delicious gravy over the rice. Or leave the roast in the gravy overnight and slice thinly for a COCKTAIL PARTY.

SHRIMP STEW

Serves 10

Ambassador John C. West
(Governor 1971-1975)

5	pieces streak of lean bacon	1-1/2 teaspoons Worcestershire sauce
3	medium chopped onions	2 tablespoons white wine
3	tablespoons browned flour	2 cups small creek shrimp
	(shake in skillet over flame)	Salt and pepper
2-1/2 cups water		

Fry bacon and add chopped onions to grease. Add browned flour to make gravy. Add water and other seasonings. Simmer until thick. Add shrimp, and more water if necessary, and serve on grits.

EGGS MORNAY

Serves 6 to 8   Mrs. Richard W. Riley (Tunky)
                                   Wife of Governor Riley, 1978 -

12   hard boiled eggs, chopped   3/4 to 1 cup milk
1   large onion, minced and sauteed 1/2 cup grated fresh Parmesan cheese
8   tablespoons butter   Salt and pepper to taste
6   tablespoons flour

Melt butter in a sauce pan. Whisk in flour, and stir constantly for 2 minutes.
Remove from heat and whisk in milk. Add 1/4 cup cheese and return to heat
until cheese melts. Season to taste. Toss eggs and onions in the sauce. Put into buttered baking dish and top with remaining cheese. Sprinkle with paprika. Bake at 350 degrees 10 to 15 minutes until cheese browns and dish is hot.

CHEESE SOUFFLÉ

Serves 6 to 8   Mrs. Richard W. Riley (Tunky)
                                   Wife of Governor Riley, 1978 -

8   slices white bread, trimmed   1/8 teaspoon pepper
2   cups Cheddar cheese, grated   1/2 teaspoon mustard
3   cups milk   1/2 teaspoon Worcestershire sauce
4   eggs, well beaten   Onion salt or minced onion, to taste
3/4 teaspoon salt

Arrange 4 slices bread in greased 8x8-inch pan. Sprinkle with 1 cup cheese.
Add 4 more slices bread and cover with another cup of cheese. In a bowl,
mix the last 7 ingredients and pour over bread and cheese, top with 1/2
stick butter, mash with a fork and refrigerate overnight. Bake at 375 degrees for 40 to 60 minutes, or until very brown.

WILD GAME

The favorite pastime of the McNair family is a visit to Bob's boyhood home,
Ballsdam Plantation. We especially enjoy the hunting season and want to
share several wild game recipes of Annie Beauford, who was born and raised
there.

THE GOVERNOR'S MANSION

BALLSDAM PLANTATION ROASTED WILD DUCK
Governor Robert E. McNair, 1965-1971

Dress and clean duck; stuff with sliced apple and peeled onion. Salt, pepper and rub the duck with bacon drippings. Line roasting pan with tin foil. Cover bottom of roaster with 1 cup water. Place duck in roaster, with 1 strip of bacon on top. Close tin foil tightly over duck and cook at 350 degrees until tender. Uncover and continue to cook until skin is brown.

BALLSDAM PLANTATION FRIED QUAIL
Governor Robert E. McNair, 1965-1971

Dress and clean quail; rub with salt and pepper. Dip in milk, then roll in flour. Fry in deep fat until bird is brown all over. Remove from fat. When desired number of quail have been browned, pour off top grease and make gravy. Place quail back into gravy and cook slowly for 30 minutes.

BALLSDAM PLANTATION VENISON ROAST
Governor Robert E. McNair, 1965-1971

Slowly boil one venison roast in salt water until tender and medium well done. Let the water boil down, but keep enough for gravy. Cooking time 2 hours. Add flour and pepper to stock for gravy. Cut up onion, place in the pot with the roast. Cook, covered, slowly until well done. Approximately 1 hour.

BALLSDAM PLANTATION SWEET POTATO SOUFFLÉ
Mrs. Robert E. McNair (Josephine)
Wife of Governor McNair, 1965-1971

3	cups cooked mashed sweet potatoes	1/2	cup melted butter
		1	egg, well beaten
1	cup sugar	1	teaspoon vanilla

TOPPING:
1/2 cup packed brown sugar   2-1/2 tablespoons melted butter
1/4 cup flour   1/2 cup chopped pecans

Mix the first 5 ingredients with electric mixer and place in casserole dish. Combine topping ingredients, mixing thoroughly. Boil to melt; it will be thick. Drop from pan and spread over potatoes. Prepare one day ahead and refrigerate. Remove from refrigerator one hour before cooking. Bake 35 minutes at 350 degrees.

MOTHER'S FRESH FRUIT AMBROSIA

Mrs. Rober E. McNair (Josephine)
Wife of Governor McNair, 1965-1971

Use equal amounts of:

Fresh oranges, using only the pulp and juice

Green seedless grapes

Fresh grated coconut

Chopped pecans

Prepare and refrigerate overnight. Before serving cut up equal amount of bananas and add to ambrosia.

APPLE CRUNCH

Serves 8   Senator Ernest F. Hollings (Governor 1959-1963)

6 cups apples, cut up	1 egg, beaten
1 cup flour	1/4 teaspoon salt
1-1/2 cups sugar	1/3 cup butter
1 teaspoon baking powder	Cinnamon and nutmeg for topping

Place apples in greased 9-inch square baking dish. Combine dry ingredients. Mix in egg and sprinkle mixture evenly over apples. Pour melted butter over top and sprinkle with cinnamon and nutmeg. Bake at 350 degrees for 50 to 60 minutes. Serve at room temperature with ice cream, yogurt or sour cream.

CRÈME BRÛLÉE

Serves 6   Senator Ernest F. Hollings (Governor 1959-1963)

3 cups heavy cream	6 tablespoons sugar
1 teaspoon vanilla	Brown sugar
6 egg yolks	Ice

Heat heavy cream with vanilla in top of double boiler. Beat egg yolks until light and creamy. Slowly stir warm cream into egg mixture. Return to double boiler and cook until custard coats the spoon. Put in serving dish and place in refrigerator to set. Cover top with sifted brown sugar until no custard shows. Put dish in large container filled with ice and place under broiler until sugar melts (caramelizes), but watch it closely!

ZUCCHINI STUFFED WITH ALMONDS AND CHEESE

Serves 6   Mrs. Donald S. Russell (Virginia)
Wife of Governor Russell, 1963-65

3 8x2-inch zucchini	1/2 to 2/3 cups dry fine crumbs from
Salt and pepper to taste	any sweet bread
1/4 cup finely minced onion	2 ounces grated Swiss cheese
1-1/2 tablespoons cooking oil	1 large egg, beaten
2-1/2 ounces ground almonds	3 pinches powdered cloves
1/2 cup heavy cream	3 tablespoons butter melted

Wash, trim ends and halve zucchini lengthwise. Parboil until tender-crisp, drain. When cool, scoop out center pulp and arrange shells in buttered casserole. Chop pulp. Put oil in skillet and sauté onion, covered, until clear. Uncover, raise heat and stir in zucchini flesh and cook for several minutes. Add 1/3 cup bread crumbs, all but 3 tablespoons of the cheese and the egg. Mix thoroughly. Season to taste and add cream, almonds and cloves. Fill each half with stuffing and shape into a dome. Mix together remaining bread crumb and cheese and sprinkle over each shell. Dribble butter over top. Bake in upper third of a 400 degree oven for 25 to 30 minutes until bubbling hot and browned on top. Serve from baking dish.

ANNIE'S DATE-NUT CAKE

Mrs. Robert E. McNair (Josephine)
Wife of Governor McNair, 1965-1971

2 cups self-rising flour	3/4 cup milk
4 eggs	1 tablespoon vanilla
1/2 pound butter	3 cups chopped pecans
1 cup sugar	2 8-ounce packages pitted dates,
1/2 cup Crisco oil	chopped

Using electric mixer, start with 1 cup flour. Add all ingredients except dates and nuts. Put dates and nuts in remaining cup of flour and mix. With a fork, fold into cake mixture. Bake in buttered pan for approximately 1 hour at 350 degrees. Test with straw. When cake has cooled, wrap in tin foil with cut up apples on top and around sides of the cake.

CREAM PUFFS

Yields: 10 to 12 large puffs   Governor and Mrs. Richard W. Riley, 1978 -
       36 to 40 small puffs

1   cup water
6   tablespoons butter,
    cut into pieces
1   teaspoon sugar

Pinch each salt and nutmeg
1   cup sifted plain flour
4   large eggs
Preheat oven to 425 degrees

Bring water to a boil with next 4 ingredients added. Boil slowly until butter is melted. Remove from heat and pour in all the flour at one time. Beat vigorously with a wooden spoon several seconds. Then beat over moderately high heat 1 to 2 minutes until mixture leaves the sides of the pan and the spoon forms a mass and begins to film the bottom of the pan. Remove from heat; make a well in center of paste. Break egg into the center and beat until well-absorbed. Continue beating in rest of eggs, one by one. Beat longer. Squeeze paste onto buttered cookie sheets in mounds 2-inches in diameter and 1-inch tall. Space 2-inches apart. Flatten with brushed-on egg, to which 1/2 teaspoon water has been added. Bake at 425 degrees 20 minutes, then reduce heat to 375 degrees for 10 to 15 minutes. Remove puffs from oven and make a 1-inch slit in each. Return to hot (OFF) oven, with door ajar, for 10 minutes. Pull out any damp centers and allow to cool. Delicious filled with MOCHA FILLING. For hors d'oeuvres, omit sugar and add 1 teaspoon salt and 1/8 teaspoon pepper.

MOCHA FILLING

1   cup sugar
5   egg yolks
2/3 cup sifted flour
2   cups boiling milk

1   tablespoon butter
3   ounces melted semi-sweet
    chocolate
2   tablespoons coffee

Beat sugar into yolks into a ribbon. Beat in flour. Slowly pour in boiling milk. Bring to a boil over moderately high heat. (As sauce boils it will get lumpy, but will smooth out as you beat it.) After boiling, beat over moderately low heat 2 to 3 minutes. Do not scorch. Remove from heat. Blend in butter, chocolate and coffee. Cut tops off Cream Puffs and fill each one with mocha filling. Garnish with shaved chocolate.

DIETER'S DELIGHT

Judge George Bell Timmerman, Jr.
Governor 1955-1959

Unsweetened grapefruit sections   Sliced bananas
Sliced apples

Mix all three together for a delightful, non-fattening dessert.

PÂTÉ BRISÉE

Governor and Mrs. Richard W. Riley, 1978 -

3	cups flour	2	sticks butter, frozen and chopped
1	teaspoon salt	6	tablespoons chilled shortening
Pinch of sugar		2/3	cup ice water

Process flour, salt and sugar. Add butter and shortening. Process again and add water. Rest for at least 2 hours before using. Makes 2 pie shells. Freezes well. Press into individual tart shells and bake at 350 degrees until lightly brown. Cool and fill with LEMON BUTTER. (Fill just before serving, or pastry will become soggy.)

LEMON BUTTER

6	eggs	3/4	cup lemon juice
2	egg yolks	2	tablespoons lemon rind
2	cups sugar	1	cup butter, melted

Beat sugar into eggs and yolks. Add juice and rind and melted butter. Put over simmering hot water. Stir until thickened. (Approximately 15 minutes.) Cool in pot of cold water, stirring as it cools.

PECAN PIE

Serves 8

Senator James Strom Thurmond
Governor 1947-1951

1	cup chopped pecans	3	eggs
1	cup dark brown sugar	1/8	teaspoon salt
1	cup light corn syrup	1	teaspoon vanilla flavoring
1	9-inch pastry shell (uncooked)	1	tablespoon melted butter

Beat eggs until light, add sugar gradually, then syrup, salt, vanilla and pecans. Pour into pastry shell and cook approximately 60 minutes in preheated oven at 360 degrees. Crust should be light brown.

Because of its geographical location at the intersection of two major inter-state highways, its access via a two-county jetport and its possession of numerous international industries, many have come to regard Spartanburg as the "crossroads of the New South."

Indians were followed in the sixteenth century by the first known white men, Spanish explorers, who cut a swath some 200 miles inland from their post at Port Royal to the foot of the Appalachian Mountains.

The Scotch-Irish settlers who came into the rugged area in the mid-1700s depended on game for their livlihood, as had their Cherokee predecessors. Their austere surroundings called for Spartan characteristics, thus the name of "Spartanburg" for the county which was formed in 1785. A rebel band of backwoodsmen fought during the Revolutionary War as the "Spartan Rifles." A number of skirmishes took place in the county but the most memorable occurred on January 17, 1781 when Gen. Daniel Morgan and his forces defeated Col. Banastre Tarleton at a drovers' campsite known for its commodious cowpens (now in Cherokee County).

The last fifty years have brought an economic turnaround to Spartanburg. Peaches, cattle, and grape industries have replaced cotton in importance. The county has become the fresh peach capital of the world, sometimes producing more than the entire state of Georgia (which calls itself the "Peach State"). The beauty of the peach blossoms in the spring and the not-so-distant Appalachian Mountains provide an interesting contrast to the increasingly diverse industries which dot the highways. Textile-related businesses remain dominant but an international flavor has crept into the community with the expansion of various European based industries.

Although it was not created until 1897, Cherokee County sits squarely on historic territory which formerly belonged to Spartanburg, Union and York counties. Its early history, therefore, overlaps with that of its neighbors.

Two important Revolutionary War battles are recalled in the land which came to Cherokee County. In the northwest corner lies Cowpens National Battlefield, site of a devastating British defeat in January 1781. On the opposite side of the county, straddling the York County line, sprawls the 4,000 acre Kings Mountain National Military Park which marks the turning point of the southern military tide in favor of Patriot forces (October 1780). Both battles are well known and much studied by military historians.

The economy of Cherokee County is primarily agricultural with cotton and peaches giving the area its identity. The success of cotton as a staple crop led to the establishment of cotton mills. Gaffney became a textile town as well as the home of a summer peach festival which celebrates its prosperous fruit production.

The county seat is named for Michael Gaffney who founded a tavern and store in 1820 at the intersection of Grindal Shoals and Cherokee Ford roads. This emerging town, first known as Gaffney's Crossroads, was incorporated in 1875. Today it is located in the geographical center of the county and is joined by high-speed Interstate 85 to other major cities.

Outside Gaffney is the eastern terminus of S.C. route No. 11, known as the Cherokee Foothills Scenic Highway, which begins its 130 mile arc through scenic piedmont South Carolina, rejoining I-85 at the Georgia line. The very name of the meandering highway symbolizes much about the county: "Cherokee" for its early namesake Indian tribe; "Foothills" for its proximity to the Appalachian mountains; "Scenic: for its view of peaceful peach orchards and historic battlefields.

WALNUT GROVE PLANTATION

Walnut Grove Plantation originated with a grant from King George III in 1763 to Charles Moore, who built the manor house about 1765. The plantation is now open to the public and is located on U. S. 29 and 221.

beverages

BRANDY ALEXANDER

Serves 2   Mrs. Woody M. McKay (Nancy)

1-1/2 ounces brandy   1/2 ounce Triple Sec
3/4 ounce crème de cacao   1/2 pint vanilla ice cream

Place ingredients in blender. Add 2 or 3 pieces ice. Pour into brandy glasses and sprinkle with nutmeg.

CHRISTMAS EGGNOG

Serves 25   Mrs. Heyward E. McDonald (Sylvia)

24 eggs, separated   1 quart whipping cream
2 cups sugar   2 quarts milk
1 quart bourbon   1 quart vanilla ice cream
1 pint brandy

Beat egg yolks and sugar until thick. Add bourbon and brandy, stirring constantly. The liquor cooks the eggs. Add the cream and milk and continue whipping. Break up the ice cream and add. Beat the egg whites until stiff and fold into mixture. Refrigerate at least 1/2 hour before serving. Sprinkle lightly with nutmeg. At Christmas, tie tiny red and green velvet ribbons on the handles of punch cups. Use a fresh wreath around a punch bowl.

VARIATION: Mrs. H. E. Pearce, Jr. (Jo)

Omit whipping cream and use 3 quarts milk. Decrease sugar to 1-1/2 cups. Omit ice cream and add 2 to 4 quarts commercial eggnog. Sprinkle with nutmeg.

JAMAICAN COFFEE

Mrs. William Cork (Helen)

1 ounce Grand Marnier   Whipped cream
1 ounce Kahlua   Lime wedge
Coffee to fill cup   Sugar

Moisten rim of cup with lime wedge and coat with sugar. Add Grand Marnier, Kahlua and coffee. Top with whipped cream.

KAHLUA

Yield: 1/2 gallon   Mrs. James B. Stephen (Ginger)

2   ounce jar instant coffee   2-1/2 cups boiling water
        (any kind)   1   pint brandy
3-1/2 cups sugar   2   teaspoons vanilla

Dissolve coffee in boiling water. Add sugar. Mix, but do not cook. Let cool. Add brandy and vanilla. Store in dark airtight bottle in a cool dark place for about one month.

HOT BUTTERED RUM

Yields: 25 cups   Mrs. John C. Land, III (Marie)

1   pound butter, softened   1   quart vanilla ice cream softened
1   pound light brown sugar   Light rum
1   pound powdered sugar   Whipped cream
2   teaspoons ground cinnamon   Cinnamon sticks
2   teaspoons ground nutmeg

Combine first 5 ingredients and beat until light and fluffy. Add ice cream, stirring until well blended. Spoon into a 2 quart freezer container; freeze. To serve a group, thaw slightly; or, for individual servings, just remove needed amount and refreeze. Place 3 tablespoons butter mixture and one jigger rum in a large mug. Fill with boiling water. Stir well. Top with whipped cream and serve with a cinnamon stick. Good in winter served around the fire. Can be stored in freezer and used for individual servings.

SHERRY COOLER

Serves 12   Mrs. Peden B. McLeod (Mary Waite)

1   can frozen lemonade   3   cans water
1   can sherry

Freeze for several hours (in a large bowl). Before serving, remove, and let thaw until frappé consistency.

WHISKEY SOUR PUNCH

Yields: 16 cups   Mrs. John I. Rogers, III (Carolyn)

1   small orange   1   fifth bourbon, blend, or Scotch
3   6-ounce cans frozen lemonade   Whiskey
        concentrate, thawed   1   32-ounce bottle club soda, chilled
3   cups orange juice   2   trays ice cubes

Prepare orange as garnish by thinly slicing and fluting edges; set aside. In punch bowl combine undiluted lemonade concentrate and remaining ingredients; mix well. Garnish with the orange slices.

BANANA FRUIT PUNCH

Serves 30
Mrs. Judson Busbee (Mae)
Mrs. Jarvis Klapman (Arlene)

3-1/2 cups sugar
6 cups water
3 cups pineapple juice
2 cups orange juice

Juice 2 lemons
3 large or 4 small bananas, mashed
1 two-liter bottle ginger ale or 7-Up

Dissolve sugar in water. Add other ingredients, except the ginger ale. Freeze this for about twenty-four hours in a 6 quart container with a lid. Remove from freezer and thaw to a slush, about 2 to 3 hours before serving time. Mash out any lumps with a potato masher. Add ginger ale when ready to serve.

APPLE SUNSHINE PUNCH

Mrs. I. S. Leevy Johnson (Doris)

4 cups unsweetened apple juice
2 cups pineapple juice (unsweetened)
1 cup orange juice
1/4 cup lemon juice

Combine, garnish with fresh mint, orange slices or cherries.

CRANBERRY PUNCH

Yields: 50 5-ounce servings
Mrs. Parker Evatt (Jane)

3 cups sugar
1 gallon water
64 ounces cranberry juice
32 ounces apple juice

1-1/2 cups lemon juice
2 cups orange juice
2 cups strong tea

Bring sugar and water to a boil; cool. Mix the next 5 fruit juices with sugar water. Chill. If desired, a part of this recipe may be frozen into an ice ring in order to not dilute punch with an ice ring melting in a punch bowl. 2 quarts of chilled ginger ale may be added to punch.

CRANBERRY — CHAMPAGNE PUNCH

Serves 50
Mrs. H. E. Pearce, Jr. (Jo)

4 oranges, sliced thin
2 cups sugar
1 bottle orange wine cocktail, if available (1/2 cup brandy may be used instead)
6 quarts cranberry juice
4 quarts champagne
Grapes

Mix oranges, sugar and wine. Steep overnight. Pour mixture over block of ice with grapes and fill punch bowl with cranberry juice and champagne, adding extra as needed.

COFFEE PUNCH

Mrs. William Cork (Helen)

12 cups double strength coffee   3   quarts vanilla ice cream
    (2 teaspoons instant to 1   1   quart chocolate ice cream
    cup water)   1   pint whipping cream
1   pint chilled milk   3   teaspoons vanilla

Break ice cream into small pieces. Drop into cool coffee. Spread whipped cream throughout punch and grate bitter chocolate on top.

VARIATION: Mrs. J. P. Gardner, Jr. (Pam)

Omit chocolate ice cream and milk and add 1 quart cream whipped with 5 tsp. vanilla and 5 tbls. sugar and 2 qts. vanilla ice cream in punch bowl and pour 1 gal. strong, chilled coffee over it and mix well. 50-60 servings.

HOT HOLIDAY PUNCH

Yields: 26 punch cup servings   Mrs. M. Judson Busbee (May)

1   cup lemon juice, fresh   1   teaspoon whole cloves
2   cups orange juice, fresh   1   stick cinnamon
2   cups unsweetened pineapple   1/2   cup sugar
    juice   1/2   gallon apple cider

Pour all juices into a large enamel or stainless steel pan. Tie cloves and cinnamon in a small cotton or cheese cloth bag and add to the fruit juices. Bring to a simmering boil over medium heat. Cover pan and allow mixture to simmer for 2 hours. Dissolve sugar in hot wassail before removing from heat. Serve hot in mugs or punch cups.

VARIATION: Mrs. Nick A. Theodore (Emilie)

Let 2 each cloves and cinnamon sticks steep in 2 cups water. Add 12 ounces apricot nectar, 1 cup orange juice, 4 cups each apple and pineapple juice, 1 can frozen lemonade and 3/4 to 1 cup sugar.

COLD PUNCH

Serves 40   Mrs. John M. Rucker (Harriet)

1   large can pineapple juice   1   pint syrup (2 cups sugar + 1 cup
1   large can frozen orange juice   water)
1   bottle real lemon   2   quarts ginger ale

Mix and serve.

BEVERAGES

HOT SPICED PUNCH

Yields: 30 cups · Mrs. John C. Land, III (Marie)

2	quarts unsweetened pineapple juice	1	tablespoon whole allspice
2	quarts cranberry cocktail		2 to 4 cinnamon sticks, broken into pieces
1	quart cold water	2	large lemons, thinly sliced
2/3	cup dark brown sugar (packed)		

Mix pineapple juice, cranberry cocktail and water into the bottom of a 30 cup electric coffee pot. Put brown sugar, allspice and cinnamon in basket of coffee pot and perk until pot stops automatically. Check the brown sugar to be sure that it is dissolved. Garnish each cup with a lemon slice. Makes your house smell like Christmas!

SPARKLING STRAWBERRY PUNCH

Serves 25 · Mrs. John C. Land, III (Marie)

2	10-ounce packages frozen, sweetened strawberries	1	28-ounce bottle club soda, chilled
1	6-ounce can frozen lemonade	1/4	cup sugar
1-4/5 quart bottle Rosé wine, chilled		Orange slices and fresh strawberries for garnish	
2	28-ounce bottles ginger ale, chilled		

In blender, at high speed, blend strawberries and lemonade (undiluted). Pour mixture into large punch bowl. Add wine and remaining ingredients; except garnishing fruit. Stir punch until sugar is dissolved. Add garnish and just enough ice to keep cold. Ladies favorite at tea.

ORANGE JULIUS

Mrs. William Cork (Helen)

1	6-ounce can frozen orange juice	1/2	cup sugar
1	cup milk	1	teaspoon vanilla
1	cup water		10 to 12 ice cubes

Blend 30 seconds. Serve immediately.

INSTANT SPICED TEA

Mrs. H. E. Pearce, Jr. (Jo)

1	small jar Lipton instant tea	2	small packages unsweetened
1	27-ounce jar Tang		Wylers lemonade
1-1/2	cups sugar	2	teaspoons cinnamon
1	large package lemonade	1	teaspoon ground cloves
	with sugar	1/2	teaspoon ground ginger

Mix thoroughly, adding more sugar, if desired. Add 2 teaspoons mixture to a teacup of boiling water.

INSTANT COCOA

Mrs. I. S.Leevy Johnson (Doris)

2	cups powdered milk	1	cup powdered sugar
1/4	cup cocoa		Dash salt

Combine and store in air-tight container. Use 4 tablespoons of mix per cup of boiling water. Add whipped cream or marshmallows. VARIATION: For a richer taste, add 1/3 cup non-dairy cream or 1 or 2 tablespoons malted milk powder.

RUSSIAN TEA

Yields: 2-1/2 quarts   Mrs. B. E. Thrailkill (Peggy)

2	quarts water	1-1/4	cups sugar
1	12-ounce can orange juice	5	regular size teabags
1	16-ounce can pineapple juice	2	teaspoons whole cloves
1/2	cup ReaLemon	2	sticks cinnamon

Put cloves and cinnamon in a teaball and bring to a boil in water. Remove from heat, add teabags for 5 minutes. Add juices and sugar and bring to a boil again. Leave spices in juice for 30 minutes.

INSTANT RUSSIAN TEA

Mrs. I. S. Leevy Johnson (Doris)

3/4	cup instant tea with lemon	1-1/2	cups sugar
1	package lemon twist	1	teaspoon cinnamon
2	cups Tang	2	teaspoons ground cloves

Combine. Store in air-tight container. Use 2 teaspoons per cup of hot water.

WASSAIL

Serves 16   Mrs. Parker Evatt (Jane)

6	inches stick cinnamon	6	cups apple cider
16	cloves (whole)	2	cups cranberry cocktail
1	tablespoon allspice (whole)	1/4	cup sugar
3	medium oranges, studded with cloves		

Tie cinnamon, cloves and allspice in cheesecloth. Combine juices with sugar. Add oranges and spices. Simmer, covered, for 20 minutes. A wonderful hot drink traditionally served at Christmas but delicious anytime during cold weather. Makes house smell great!

FRESH PEAR ICE

Yields: 1 gallon   Mrs. Robert M. McLellan (Doris)

2	cups sugar	4	cups puréed fresh ripe pears or
4	cups water		fruit of your choice
1/2	cup lemon juice		

Make a syrup of sugar and water over hot heat. Peel and slice the pears, put in blender and add to the syrup immediately to keep them from turning dark. Cool, add lemon juice and freeze in ice cream freezer. Serve with or without pear brandy or just a small liqueur glass of Calvados or Champagne at a formal dinner between dishes of great richness such as a fish or fowl course and a meat course to clear the palate and to help make room for the rest of the dinner. Raspberry Sherbet laced with champagne is a favorite aperitif.

ORANGEBURG COUNTY

Around 1735 a small group of Swiss farmers left Charleston traveling up the Edisto River into the backcountry, searching for land suitable enough to begin life in the new world. They stopped along the river and began a settlement which eventually grew into the thriving community of Orangeburg. The success of the early Swiss settlers soon lured other immigrant groups to the area. Germans, English, and Scotch-Irish families established small farms in the territory. Originally known as Saxe Gotha, the early Orangeburg district was one of the largest and most important commercial centers during the early colonial period.

Many events crucial to the outcome of the Revolution occurred in Orangeburg. The British maintained a large garrison in the district throughout the war. In 1781, when the British hold on the state began to weaken, the town was liberated by the forces of General Sumter. The retreating British army made an attempt to fall back on the city of Charleston where ships were waiting to take the troops to reinforce Lord Cornwallis in Virginia. The British were caught at Eutawville and the battle which followed helped determine the outcome of the war.

Prosperity returned to the area after the war. Primarily an agricultural community, Orangeburg was home to some of the finest plantations in the state.

During the modern era Orangeburg has emerged as one of the state's leading educational centers and tourist attractions. Claflin College, the oldest black college in the state, and South Carolina State College serve the educational needs of students from all over the state. Edisto Gardens attracts visitors from around the country. In the eastern corner of the county the Santee State Park offers excellent recreational facilities. Visited by over a million people a year the Santee resort is the number one tourist attraction in the state.

Modern Calhoun County was among the last group of counties organized by the state legislature at the turn of the century. Supporters of the county had been lobbying the legislature for years but controversy over Calhoun's proposed borders stalled its creation until 1908. Portions of Lexington and Orangeburg were combined to make the new county which was named in honor of John C. Calhoun.

The first settlements in the area occurred around 1735. Families of Swiss-German immigrants traveling up from Charleston settled in the county along the banks of the Congaree River.

During the Revolution the county was a crossroads for both the British and American armies. Frances Marion and "Light Horse" Harry Lee operated in the county. The British maintained a sizable garrison at Belleville plantation on the Congaree. Named Fort Motte in honor of the family who owned the plantation, the garrison was a key stronghold in the British western line of defense. Lee attempted to drive the invaders from the home in 1781 but was unsuccessful. Mrs. Motte, the mistress of the plantation, was so anxious to see the British leave her property, that she persuaded Lee to burn them out of her home. The British, convinced of the Americans determination, promptly surrendered. The blaze in the Belleville mansion was quickly extinguished and Mrs. Motte and her family moved back into their liberated home.

During the Civil War the Calhoun area was raided by a detachment of Federal cavalry from Sherman's advancing army. The economy of the area was shattered by the events of the war. It was not until after the depression that Calhoun County began to re-emerge as a major economic force in the state.

Although still a major crop in the area, cotton has recently been surpassed by soybeans. A pioneer in the development of the crop, Calhoun County is now the leading producer in the state on a bushel per acre basis. The county is also known for its horses. Numerous thoroughbred farms in the county have been responsible for producing some of the finest racing champions in the country.

DORCHESTER COUNTY

In 1897, Dorchester County was created from portions of Colleton and Berkeley Counties. It takes its name from the seventeenth century settlement on the east side of the Ashley River established by Congregationalists who named the town for their home in Massachusetts. A small village persisted from 1696 to 1752, when the Congregationalists abandoned Dorchester in a body to follow their minister to a more congenial spot in Georgia. The tabby ruins of the old Congregational Church and Fort Dorchester, built to defend the settlement, are now preserved in a state park where visitors may see various relics found in archeological digs.

The county seat of St. George was the center of trade when it was established in 1788 as part of St. George's County. Another Dorchester town is Summerville. Known as "Flower Town" this beautiful town was first founded in 1847 as a resort for planters. At one time there was a town ordinance forbidding the cutting of any pine trees, even those on private property. Generations of devoted gardeners have helped Summerville maintain its striking beauty as camellias, azaleas, and wisteria bloom in turn against the dark backdrop of the pines.

The whole county is known for its beauty, especially Middleton Place Gardens, begun by Henry Middleton, future president of the Continental Congress, in 1741. Arthur Middleton, son of Henry and a signer of the Declaration of Independence, added to the gardens and is buried on the place. One of the most outstanding features of Middleton Place Gardens, that took 100 slaves 10 years to complete, are the twin Butterfly Lakes that are at the foot of the terraces that slope toward the Ashley River.

THE DONALD BRUCE HOUSE

The Donald Bruce House was built in 1780, when Orangeburg was the location for a large camp of recruits. Today the Bruce House can be seen at Middlepen Plantation, two miles north of Orangeburg on U.S. 301.

appetizers

MINIATURE CREAM PUFFS

Yields: 70   Mrs. Robert Helmly (Vera)

1   cup boiling water   1   cup plain flour, sifted with 1/2
1/2 cup butter   teaspoon salt
4   eggs

Heat oven to 400 degrees. Heat water and butter to rolling boil in saucepan. Stir in flour. Stir vigorously over low heat until mixture forms a ball, about 1 minute. Remove from heat and beat in eggs thoroughly, one at a time. Beat until smooth. Drop dough by slightly rounded teaspoonfuls onto ungreased baking sheet 2-inches apart. Bake about 25 minutes or until puffed, golden brown and dry. Remove from baking sheet and allow to cool. Slice top and fill with chicken salad or other filling, then replace top. Puffs may be frozen (unfilled). The day before you plan to serve them, fill with salad and refrigerate in covered dish. Place filled puffs on cookie sheet and bake in 350 degree oven for about 5 minutes to "crisp" them. Filling will not be warmed. Dip stuffed edge into chopped parsley.

TIROPETES
(CHEESE TRIANGLES)

Yields: 40 Triangles   Mrs. Nick A. Theodore (Emilie)

4   eggs, well-beaten   1   pound fila pastry
1   8-ounce package cream cheese 1/2 pound butter, melted
1   pound Feta cheese

Beat eggs with electric mixer until fluffy. Add cream cheese and continue beating until well-blended. Remove bowl from mixer. Crumble Feta cheese with fork, and combine with egg mixture. Cut fila 6x12-inches. For each triangle, brush half the fila with melted butter; fold over other half of fila to make a strip about 3 inches in width. Brush with butter. Place 1 teaspoon cheese mixture at one end of each strip, folding strip diagonally until triangles are formed. Brush tops with melted butter, and place on ungreased baking sheet. Bake in oven at 375 degrees for 20 minutes, or until golden. Serve warm. To freeze, place unbaked butter triangles in plastic container, separating layers with wax paper, and place in freezer. When ready to serve, place frozen triangles on ungreased pan and bake. May be frozen for at least 2 months.

SPANAKOPITA
(SPINACH PITA)

Serves 8 to 12   Mrs. Nick A. Theodore (Emilie)
Or 50 to 60 Triangles

2	pounds spinach, finely chopped	2	tablespoons olive oil
1	tablespoon salt		Dash of salt and pepper
1	pound Feta cheese, crumbled	15	fila pastry
1	small onion, chopped fine	1/2	pound butter, melted
4	eggs, slightly beaten		

Wash spinach, and chop very fine. Sprinkle with 1 tablespoon salt and allow to stand 15 minutes. Squeeze spinach to remove excess moisture. (This is a very important step in making a good filling.) Combine with cheese, onion, eggs and olive oil. Season to taste. Arrange 9 fila, which have been brushed with butter, in a greased 10x5-inch pan and cover with spinach filling. Cover with 6 fila over all, brushing each with melted butter. Seal edges to retain filling. Brush top with melted butter. Bake in 350 degree oven for 45 minutes.

FILLING II

3	10-ounce packages frozen chopped spinach	1	small onion, chopped fine
		3	tablespoons olive oil
1	8-ounce package cream cheese	1	teaspoon chopped dill, optional
1	pound Feta cheese	1	teaspoon salt
1/2	cup grated Romano cheese, optional	1/4	teaspoon pepper
		4	eggs

Allow spinach to stand at room temperature to defrost completely (do not soak in water). Squeeze dry and combine with remaining ingredients.

SPINACH TRIANGLES

Spinach filling I or II   1   cup butter, melted
1/2   pound fila pastry

Prepare spinach filling; wrap by teaspoonfulls in fila, as directed in Tiropetes (cheese triangles). (See index.) Serve warm.

ARTICHOKE SPREAD

Yields: 2-1/2 cups   Mrs. Isadore E. Lourie (Susan)

1   14-ounce can artichoke hearts   1   cup mayonnaise
    drained and broken into   3/4 teaspoon garlic salt
    small pieces   Parmesan cheese for top
1   cup grated fresh Parmesan cheese

Squeeze out all the juice from the artichoke pieces and mix with remaining ingredients. Spoon into a lightly greased 3 cup shallow baking dish (one that the spread can be served in). Sprinkle with additional Parmesan cheese on top and bake at 350 degrees for 20 to 40 minutes or until golden brown on top. Serve hot with Triscuits, Melba Toast rounds, or other crackers.

BEER CHEESE SPREAD

Yields: 1-3/4 cups   Mrs. J. P. Gardner (Pam)

2   cups shredded natural sharp   1/2 teaspoon dry mustard
    Cheddar cheese   3   drops Tabasco sauce
1   8-ounce package cream cheese   1   tablespoon chopped chives
1/4 cup beer   1   teaspoon chopped pimento

Combine cheddar cheese, cream cheese, beer, mustard and Tabasco sauce. Mix well until blended. Stir in chives and pimento. Great on Melba Rounds or your favorite cracker.

HOT CRAB SPREAD

                                        Mrs. T. Ed Garrison (Juanita)

1   8-ounce cream cheese   1   teaspoon lemon juice
1   tablespoon milk   Dash Worcestershire
1   6-1/2-ounce can crab meat   Salt and pepper to taste
2   tablespoons green onion   1/3 cup toasted sliced almonds
1/2 teaspoon horseradish

Blend well. Spoon into ovenproof dish; sprinkle top with sliced almonds. Bake at 375 degrees for 15 minutes. Serve hot with crackers or party size rye bread.

BACON CRISPS

                                        Mrs. T. W. Edwards, Jr. (Dottie)

1   box Waverly crackers   1   pound very thin bacon

Slice bacon in half and wrap half pieces bacon around crackers; place on cookie sheet and bake at 200 degrees until bacon is done. Let stand to crisp. To freeze; bake and let cool, wrap in foil and pull out when company drops in. Place, frozen, in slow oven and heat. Drain on paper towels.

APPETIZERS

BROCCOLI BALLS

Yields: 65 balls   Mrs. Herbert Kirsh (Suzanne)

2	10-ounce boxes frozen chopped broccoli, cooked and drained	3/4	cup butter, melted
		1/2	cup grated Parmesan cheese
2	cups herb bread stuffing mix	1	tablespoon garlic salt
2	onions, finely chopped	1	teaspoon pepper
5	eggs, beaten	1/2	teaspoon thyme

Mix ingredients well and chill 2 hours. Put a little oil on hands and form balls, using 1 tablespoon mixture for each, and bake on lightly greased baking sheet at 350 degrees for 20 to 30 minutes. These can be frozen and kept in plastic bags. Bake frozen at 350 degrees for 35 minutes and serve with cocktail picks and hot mustard sauce, if desired.

VARIATION: Mrs. Mona Chapman

Substitute frozen spinach instead of broccoli and make spinach balls.

CHEESE BALL

Serves 20   Mrs. J. M. Cooper (Melba)

1	pound sharp Cheddar cheese	1	clove garlic, crushed or
1	pound cream cheese		Garlic salt
1/2	pound Roquefort or Bleu cheese	2	teaspoons Worcestershire sauce
1	small onion, grated		

With all ingredients at room temperature, mix well. Shape into 2 medium balls or 4 logs. Roll the balls into a mixture of your choice or leave as is. Serve chilled with an assortment of crackers.

DRIED BEEF CHEESE BALL

Serves 10   Mrs. Alex S. Macaulay (Maria)

1	2-1/2-ounce jar dried beef, shredded	2	tablespoons green pepper
		2	tablespoons green onion, finely chopped
1/4	cup sour cream		
1	8-ounce cream cheese		Nuts, chopped

With all ingredients at room temperature, mix well. Shape into ball and roll in nuts.

CHEESE BISCUITS

Yields: 62   Mrs. Marion H. Kinon (Reba)

1/2 pound sharp New York cheese,   1   stick butter, softened
       grated   Red cayenne pepper
1-1/2 cups self rising flour

Cream together all ingredients. Make into a roll 1-1/2 inches in diameter and
10 inches long. Refrigerate or freeze. Slice into thin wafers. Place on cookie
sheet. Top with pecan half or brown sugar. Bake 25 to 30 minutes at 250
degrees. Do not brown or they will be bitter.

MELTAWAY CHEESE PUFFS

                                        Mrs. Robert C. Lake, Jr. (Carolyn)

1   loaf unsliced white bread   2   egg whites
1   stick butter   1/4   pound sharp cheese, grated
3   ounces cream cheese

Melt cheese and butter in double boiler. Beat the egg whites until stiff. Cut
bread with electric knife into 1-inch cubes. Fold egg whites into cheese and
dip bread cubes into mixture until they are covered. Chill on cookie sheet.
Bake at 400 degrees about 20 minutes or until brown. These may be frozen
on a cookie sheet and stored in a plastic container. For a different taste, add
a little scraped onion or bacon crumbs on top with paprika.

CHEESE STRAWS

Yields: 12 dozen   Mrs. Ramon Schwartz (Rosa)

1   pound New York State very   3-1/2 cups cake flour
       sharp cheese, grated finely   1/2   teaspoon salt
3   sticks butter   1/4   teaspoon red pepper (rounded)

Have cheese and butter at room temperature. Sift flour with salt and pepper
3 times. Blend butter and cheese. Add flour. Put in cookie press, using the
star pattern. Using the press, line up the dough lengthwise for the full length
of an ungreased cookie sheet, approximately 1/4-inch apart. There is enough
dough for 3 cookie sheets. Take floured knife and cut each length into 5
pieces, pushing them slightly apart. Cook at 350 degrees until edges are
slightly brown, approximately 10 to 15 minutes. Cool, take out with spatula.
Will keep frozen a long time.

APPETIZERS

CHEESY HOT QUICHE SQUARES

Yields: 12   Mrs. William N. Cork (Helen)

8 eggs	4 cups shredded Monterey Jack cheese
1/2 cup all-purpose flour	1-1/2 cups cottage cheese
1 teaspoon baking powder	1/4 cup chopped jalapeño peppers
3/4 teaspoon salt	

Beat eggs 3 minutes. Combine flour, baking powder and salt; add to eggs and mix well. Stir in cheese and peppers. Pour into a greased 9x13x2-inch baking pan; bake at 350 degrees for 30 to 35 minutes. Let cool 10 minutes; cut into squares.

CURRY CANAPÉS

Mrs. D. H. Wilkins (Susan)

1/2 pound cheddar cheese, coarsely grated	1 bunch green onions, chopped
1-1/2 10-ounce bottles ripe olives, chopped	1 cup mayonnaise
	1 teaspoon curry powder

Mix all ingredients well. Refrigerate. To serve, place on tray and serve with Melba rounds or crackers of your choice. Can be served hot by spreading cheese mixture on crackers and heating at 425 degrees for a few minutes until bubbly. Keeps for weeks in refrigerator.

DILL ROLL-UPS

Yields: 36 to 48   Mrs. Herbert Kirsh (Suzanne)

6 slices fresh white bread or whole grain bread	3 ounces cream cheese, softened
	6 whole medium dill pickles

Trim crusts from bread, spread with cream cheese. Place pickle on bread and roll up jelly roll fashion. Chill for several hours. When ready to serve, slice each roll into 6 or 8 slices, about 1/4-inch thick.

HOT MUSTARD DIP

1/2 cup dry mustard	1/2 cup boiling pineapple juice
1-1/2 cups boiling water	

Stir until it becomes a smooth paste. Keep refrigerated and serve at room temperature.

CLEMSON HOUSE OF LEUNG CHINESE EGG ROLLS

Serves 6   Mrs. Robert N. McLellan (Doris)

1/2 head cabbage, shredded	Dash freshly ground pepper
1 stalk celery, chopped	1 teaspoon sugar
1 5-ounce can bamboo shoots, chopped	1/8 teaspoon peanut butter
	1/8 teaspoon monosodium glutamate
4 to 6-ounces ground pork or beef	2 eggs, beaten separately
1 teaspoon salt	6 egg roll wrappers

Bring a big pot of water to a boil. Add the cabbage, celery and bamboo shoots. Turn off heat. When water stops boiling, drain vegetables. Saute meat and add salt, pepper, sugar, peanut butter and MSG. Add egg and blend together. Pour into a bowl, add the vegetables and mix well. Place a handful of stuffing in the center of each wrapper. Brush the inside edges with beaten egg. Fold bottom corner edge over filling, fold two sides in over filling, and then turn the other side over and roll to seal. Place sealed side down on wax paper. Deep-fry egg rolls, sealed side down, at 320 degrees in hot oil for 8 minutes. Take out, drain on paper towels, and let cool. Refrigerate until ready to use or freeze them. When ready to use, deep fry egg roll, sealed side down, in hot oil at 320 degrees for 8 more minutes. Serve hot with HOT MUSTARD DIP and SWEET AND SOUR SAUCE: (See Page 42 for HOT MUSTARD DIP)

SWEET AND SOUR SAUCE

1 whole lemon, sliced	4 soup spoons tomato sauce
4 cups water	1 teaspoon Worcestershire sauce
1/2 cup white vinegar	1 cup sugar
1 teaspoon salt	2 or more soup spoons corn starch
3 or 4 drops red food color	2 or more soup spoons cold water

Bring 4 cups water to a boil; add lemon slices and boil 4 minutes. Remove lemon slices, discard, and add vinegar, food color and Worcestershire to lemon water. Bring to a boil and add sugar, salt and tomato sauce and continue to cook until it comes to a boil. Turn off heat. Make a paste of the cornstarch and cold water and add to the sauce. Stir until mixture is thick and transparent. Keep refrigerated and reheat when ready to serve.

HAM MOUSSE

Serves 8   Mrs. Larry A. Martin (Susan)

1/2	pound boiled ham	1	tablespoon Dijon mustard
1/4	pound butter	1-1/2	tablespoons unflavored gelatin
1	cup whipping cream	1/2	cup Madeira
1	tablespoon salt	1	cup chicken broth
1	teaspoon white pepper	1/4	cup Cognac

Put ham through the meat grinder, using finest blade. Combine ham and butter in a bowl, mixing well. Blend in cream; stir vigorously. Add salt, pepper and mustard. Soften gelatin in Madeira. Bring broth to a boil, remove from flame and add gelatin, stirring to dissolve. Cool. Add to the ham. Check seasoning. Mix well with Cognac and pack in a 1-1/2-quart mold. Refrigerate. Unmold and serve with rice crackers or dark bread.

HAM ROLLS

Yields: 80   Mrs. Robert C. Lake, Jr. (Carolyn)
                                      Mrs. David E. Turnipseed (Cindy)

1/2	pound soft margarine	1	small onion grated very fine OR
3	tablespoons poppy seed	2	tablespoons onion flakes
3	tablespoons prepared mustard	4	packages dinner rolls (20 per
1 to 3 teaspoons Worcestershire sauce			package)
3	tablespoons poppy seeds (opt.)	5	ounces Swiss cheese, sliced fine
		1	lb. boiled or baked ham

Mix together the first 6 ingredients and spread filling on both sides of sliced dinner rolls. Fill rolls with a thin piece of ham and sliced Swiss cheese. Wrap with foil and heat until mixture is melted. These can be frozen before heating.

VARIATION: Mrs. Mona Chapman

For 30 HAM BISCUITS, decrease mustard to 2 teaspoons, poppy seeds to 2 tablespoons and butter to 1/2 cup. Use 30 Pepperidge Farm party rolls, 30 slices smoked ham and 30 slices Swiss cheese.

HAM ROLL-UPS

Yields: 80   Mrs. James B. Stephen (Ginger)

1	8-ounce package cream cheese	1	teaspoon horseradish
2	tablespoons evaporated milk	1/4	cup chopped pecans
2	tablespoons chopped parsley	10	slices boiled packaged ham
1	teaspoon grated onion		

Mix first 6 ingredients. Spread on ham. Roll up like a jelly roll. Wrap and refrigerate until serving time. Cut in 1/2-inch slices. Hold with toothpicks.

VARIATION: Mrs. Robert N. McLellan (Doris)

Omit horseradish and pecans. Add dash cayenne and salt to taste. Spread generous amount on sliced dried beef or wafer-thin slices of pastrami. Roll and cut in 1/2-inch slices. Fasten with toothpicks and serve cold.

SCALLOPS RAMAKI

Yields: 24   Mrs. Robert N. McLellan (Doris)

Boiling water		24	whole water chestnuts (optional)
12	slices bacon	2	tablespoons soy sauce
24	scallops	1/2	cup white wine

Pour boiling water over bacon and let stand 5 minutes; drain and dry. Stretch the bacon as long as you can and then cut each slice in half. Wrap around a water chestnut and a scallop and secure with a toothpick. Cover with the soy sauce and wine in a shallow pan. Marinate for several hours. Remove and put in a 350 degree oven until bacon has cooked. Remove toothpicks and replace with fresh or plastic ones. Serve hot

OYSTERS ROCKEFELLER

Senator Horace C. Smith

1	cup milk	1	tablespoon cracker meal
1	heaping tablespoon flour	3	tablespoons sherry wine
1/4	teaspoon dried mustard		Black pepper
1/4	teaspoon nutmeg	1-1/2	teaspoons salt
1	cup onion, grated well	1	14-ounce package frozen spinach,
2	tablespoons butter		cooked and drained
1	pint oysters, drained	1/2	teaspoon sugar
1	tablespoon cornstarch		

Add all the ingredients, except the oysters, to the cooked spinach. Let set for one day. Add oysters and bake in casserole at 400 degrees for 30 minutes. Serve with saltine crackers.

PÂTÉ DE FOIE GRAS

Mrs. Larry A. Martin

1 pound chicken livers	1/2 cup softened butter
Chicken broth	1/2 teaspoon dry mustard
2 teaspoons salt	2 tablespoons finely minced onion
Pinch cayenne	1 tablespoon dry sherry

Bring livers to boil in chicken broth barely to cover and simmer covered for 15 to 20 minutes. Drain and put through finest blade of food chopper. Mix this with salt, cayenne, butter, mustard and onion. Blend well, add dry sherry; pack the mixture in a crock and chill in refrigerator. You may freeze. This pâté substitutes very well for the imported pâté de foie gras.

MARINATED MUSHROOMS

Serves 6   Mrs. T. Ed Garrison (Juanita)

2 pounds fresh mushrooms	Salt
1/2 cup chopped onion	1/4 teaspoon tarragon, crushed
1 clove garlic, minced	1 cup white wine
1/4 cup chopped parsley	1/2 cup white vinegar
2 bay leaves	1/4 cup olive oil
1/8 teaspoon freshly ground pepper	1 tablespoon lemon juice

Trim ends of mushroom stems and wipe clean with a damp towel. Combine in a large heavy saucepan with the rest of the ingredients and bring to a boil. Reduce heat and simmer 8 to 10 minutes, or until tender, stirring several times. Refrigerate and serve on toothpicks. Will keep two weeks under refrigeration.

STUFFED MUSHROOMS

Serves 6 to 8   Mrs. James B. Stephen (Ginger)

20 large fresh mushrooms	1/2 cup soft breadcrumbs
1 clove garlic, minced	1/2 cup grated Parmesan cheese
1/4 cup olive oil	1 tablespoon dried parsley flakes

Clean mushrooms and remove stems and chop. Sauté stems and garlic in oil until tender; remove from heat. Stir in remaining ingredients; spoon into mushroom caps. Place in shallow baking dish and bake at 350 degrees for 20 to 25 minutes.

HOT BROCCOLI DIP

Serves 30   Mrs. Hicks Harwell (Nancy)

2	10-ounce packages frozen chopped broccoli, thawed	1	teaspoon Worcestershire sauce
1	onion, chopped	6	ounces sharp cheese, grated
2	tablespoons margarine	1	large can sliced mushrooms
1	teaspoon salt		Large chafing dish

In a heavy saucepan on medium heat sauté onion in margarine until tender. Add salt, Worcestershire, cheese and mushrooms. Stir until cheese melts. Add broccoli last, on medium heat, and cook about 10 minutes or until hot through and through. Serve from a chafing dish on the buffet table with wheat thins or any cocktail cracker.

CLAM DIP

Yields: 1 pint   Mrs. Herbert Kirsh (Suzanne)

1	13-ounce package cream cheese	1-1/2	teaspoons lemon juice
1	cup sour cream	2	tablespoons chopped green onions
1/2	teaspoon salt		
1/8	teaspoon cayenne pepper	2	10-1/2-ounce cans minced clams, drained
1/2	teaspoon garlic powder		
		1	tablespoon chopped parsley

Blend cream cheese and sour cream. Add next 6 ingredients and mix well. Chill 1 hour. Garnish with parsley. Serve with your favorite crackers or chips.

SPINACH DIP

Yields: 3 cups   Mrs. Robert L. Helmly (Vera)
                                               Mrs. William J. McLeod (Sara)
                                            Mrs. John I. Rogers, III (Carolyn)

1	10-ounce package frozen chopped spinach, thawed and drained	1	8-ounce can water chestnuts, drained and chopped
1	1-5/8-ounce package Knorr dry vegetable soup mix	1	cup sour cream
		1	cup salad dressing
		1/3	cup chopped green onions

Mix all ingredients. Cover and refrigerate at least 8 hours. Serve with your favorite crackers, Bugles, or as a dip for raw vegetables.

APPETIZERS

CURRY DIP

Yield: 1 cup   Mrs. Donald H. Holland (Betty)

1   cup mayonnaise   1   teaspoon curry powder
1/2 teaspoon Accent   1/2 teaspoon celery salt
1/2 teaspoon garlic powder

Mix all ingredients and blend well. Chill and serve with raw vegetables.

VEGETABLE DIP

Mrs. Parker Evatt (Jane)

1/2 pint sour cream   1   tablespoon parsley flakes
1   cup mayonnaise   1   tablespoon Beau Monde
3   ounces cream cheese   seasoning
1   tablespoon grated onion   1   tablespoon dill seed

Mix all ingredients and refrigerate overnight to allow flavors to blend. Serve with raw vegetables.

DREW'S TACO DIP

Mrs. Nick A. Theodore (Emilie)

1   pound ground beef   1   can chopped green chilies
1   small onion, grated   1   bell pepper
1   6-ounce can tomato sauce   1   8-ounce cream cheese
1/4 bottle catsup   1/2 cup Parmesan cheese

Sauté onion and meat, add tomato sauce, catsup, green chilies and bell pepper. Cook. Add cream cheese and Parmesan cheese. Serve in chafing dish with Doritos.

JALAPEÑO DIP

Mrs. Robert N. McLellan (Doris)

1   pound Velveeta cheese   Juice from jalapeño peppers
1/4 pound sharp Cheddar cheese   1   pint mayonnaise (not salad
1   large onion   dressing)
6 to 8 jalapeño peppers   Chafing dish

Grind or finely cut first 4 ingredients. Combine all ingredients in saucepan and heat. Serve in chafing dish with Fritos and Doritos. Keeps well in refrigerator.

SHRIMP DIP

Mrs. W. B. Hawkins (Sarah)

1   4-1/2-ounce can shrimp, mashed   1-1/2 tablespoons lemon juice
1   8-ounce carton sour cream   2   tablespoons grated onion
1   pint mayonnaise   Dash Worcestershire sauce

Mix all ingredients and chill for several hours.

LOBSTER DIP

Serves 6   Mrs. Dick Elliott (Anne)

2   8-ounce packages cream cheese   2   teaspoons sugar
1/2   cup mayonnaise   Dash salt
1   clove garlic, crushed   2   cups lobster or shrimp, cut up
2   teaspoons grated onion   6   tablespoons Sauterne
2   teaspoons prepared mustard   Chafing dish

Melt cheese over low heat. While stirring, blend in mayonnaise, garlic, onion, mustard, sugar and salt. Stir in lobster or shrimp in wine. Heat through. Pour in chafing dish. Serve hot with Triscuits. Can be made ahead but add wine right before serving.

GUACAMOLE

Serves 6 to 8   Mrs. Walter Bristow, Jr. (Stewart)

2   pounds ripe avocados   1/2   pound tomatoes (about 2
1/4   cup lemon juice   medium sized)
1/4   cup minced onion   5   tablespoons finely chopped green
1/4   cup chopped fresh cilantro   chilies
     (coriander leaves)   1-3/4 teaspoons salt

Cut the avocados in half lengthwise, remove the pits, and scoop out the meat. In a medium-sized bowl, mash the avocado with a silver fork or wooden spoon. Add the lemon juice, onions, and cilantro. Coarsely chop the tomatoes and add them to the avocado, along with the chilies and the salt. Stir everything together thoroughly and serve chilled with fried tortilla chips.

PEPPER JELLY TURNOVERS

Yields: 2 or 3 dozen   Mrs. Robert N. McLellan (Doris)

1   5-ounce jar Old English cheese   2   tablespoons water
1/2 cup butter   1   4-ounce jar hot pepper jelly
1   cup flour

Cut cheese and butter into flour. Quickly stir in water and shape into a ball. Refrigerate overnight. Roll out dough very thin and cut with a biscuit cutter in 2-inch circles. Place 1/2 teaspoon pepper jelly in center of each circle. Fold over and crimp edges with a fork. Bake at 375 degrees for 10 minutes. Turnovers may be frozen before or after baking. Reheat before serving. Turnovers may be filled with orange marmalade or your choice of marmalade. Dust with powdered sugar for serving with morning coffee.

SEAFOOD MOLD

Serves 40   Mrs. Horace C. Smith (Dot)

1   pound cooked shrimp, sliced   1   tablespoon chives
    if large   1   cup celery, finely chopped
1   7-1/2-ounce can crab meat,   3   hard boiled eggs, chopped
    picked and drained   1   package gelatin
Juice of 1 lemon   1   cup boiling water
1   cup mayonnaise   Dash Tabasco
2   bouillon cubes (chicken or   1/2 teaspoon onion juice
    beef)   Dash red pepper
1/2 teaspoon Worcestershire sauce   1/4 teaspoon salt

Dissolve gelatin and bouillon in boiling water. Mix all ingredients and pour into a lightly oiled fish mold. Chill. Unmold onto a serving platter and use olive for eye; garnish with parsley. Serve as a spread with crackers.

CHUTNEY SAUSAGE BALLS

Yields: 65 to 70   Representative Ginger Crocker

2   1-pound packages hot sausage   2   8-ounce bottles chutney
2   cups sour cream   1/2 cup sherry (optional)

Roll sausage into small cocktail size balls, no more than 1-inch in diameter, and bake at 350 degrees for 15 minutes. Combine sour cream and chutney in a double boiler. Put into chafing dish with warmed sausage balls and serve with toothpicks. Garnish with chopped green onions with tops.

SHRIMP MOLD

Serves 25   Mrs. Nick A. Theodore (Emilie)

2   4-1/2-ounce cans Blueplate   1   cup mayonnaise
    shrimp, drained and mashed   1/2   cup minced onion
1   8-ounce can minced clams,   1   cup celery, chopped fine
    drained (reserve juice)   1   teaspoon lemon juice
1   package gelatin   Tabasco to taste
1   8-ounce package cream cheese,   Salt to taste
    softened   Pepper to taste

Soak gelatin in clam juice. Cream mayonnaise and cream cheese. Blend in shrimp, clams, onion, celery, lemon juice and seasonings. Blend in gelatin mixture last. Pour into lightly oiled mold and refrigerate to congeal. Unmold on serving tray with an assortment of crackers.

CRAB MOUSSE

Yields: Two 4-cup molds   Mrs. Ben Hornsby (Esther)
                                           Mrs. Marion Kinon (Reba)

2   envelopes unflavored gelatin   1   cup chopped green onion
1/4 cup cold water   1   cup chopped celery
1/2 cup boiling water   Juice of 1 lemon
1   8-ounce package cream cheese,   1   tablespoon Worcestershire sauce
     softened   Dash Tabasco
1   10-1/2-ounce can cream of   1/2 cup stuffed olives, sliced
     mushroom soup   2   6-1/2-ounce cans Harris white
1   cup mayonnaise   crab meat or 1 pound fresh
                                          crab meat

Soak gelatin in cold water. Add boiling water. In mixing bowl mix cream cheese with mushroom soup. Add remaining ingredients. Add gelatin, mix all together, and place in molds. (May be molded in a loaf pan and sliced for a luncheon.) Makes 6 dozen tiny muffin pan molds for canapes or two 4-cup molds. Chill. Unmold on serving plate and serve with Triscuits, Sesame Melba Rounds or crackers of your choice.

PARTY MEAT BALLS

Yields: 85   Mrs. Nick Theodore (Emilie)

1	pound ground pork	2	teaspoons salt
1	pound ground veal	2	tablespoons margarine
2	cups soft bread crumbs	1	10-ounce jar apricot preserves
2	eggs	1/2	cup Kraft Hickory Smoked
1/2	cup finely chopped parsley		Barbecue sauce
1/4	cup packed brown sugar		Chafing dish

Combine meats, bread, eggs, onion and seasonings. Mix lightly and shape into balls. Brown in margarine. Place in casserole. Combine preserves and barbecue sauce and pour over meat. Bake 30 minutes at 350 degrees. Before serving bring to room temperature. Reheat on top of stove. Serve hot from a chafing dish with wooden or plastic toothpicks.

TERIYAKI MEATBALLS

Yields: 100   Mrs. John C. Land, III (Marie)

3	pounds lean hamburger	1-1/2	teaspoons ground ginger
1	cup Kikkoman soy sauce	2	cloves garlic, chopped
1/2	cup water		Chafing dish

Mix together soy sauce, water, ginger and garlic and set aside. Form hamburger into tiny meatballs, no more than 1-inch in diameter. Place in large flat roasting pan. Pour sauce mixture over meatballs and cook one hour, uncovered at 275 degrees. Put in chafing dish and serve warm with cocktail picks.

YUMMY MEATBALLS

Yields: 2 dozen   Mrs. Jarvis R. Klapman (Arlene)

1	pound ground beef	2	tablespoons oil
1/3	cup dry bread crumbs	1/3	cup Prime Choice Steak sauce
2	tablespoons Prime Choice	2	tablespoons light brown sugar
	Steak sauce	2	tablespoons margarine
1	egg		

Mix together the beef, breadcrumbs, egg and 2 tablespoons steak sauce. Shape into 1-inch balls and brown in oil in a skillet. Drain fat from the skillet. Combine 1/3 cup steak sauce, brown sugar and margarine with the meatballs in the skillet. Simmer, covered, until done, about 15 minutes. Serve hot from a chafing dish with toothpicks.

SOUTHERN FRIED BUFFET DRUMETTES

Cocktail buffet dish; Serves 10 to 12   Mrs. Robert N. McLellan (Doris)
(For an entree the recipe may be made with one 2 to 3-pound chicken, cut for frying.)

24	drumettes (first joint of chicken wing)	1	teaspoon garlic salt
1	cup buttermilk		Salt to taste
1	egg	2	tablespoons pepper
1	tablespoon Accent	2	cups flour
			Corn oil to fill skillet halfway

Season the chicken with salt. Beat egg, milk, Accent and garlic salt together. Put the flour in a brown paper bag, add pepper and mix well. Dip each peice of chicken into milk and egg mixture, then shake it in the prepared flour. Repeat this procedure for a thick crust. Add chicken to hot oil and fry on medium high on one side for 10 or 15 minutes (10 minutes for thin white meat, 15 minutes for thick dark meat and boney pieces). Turn over and cook for 10 minutes longer. Turn the chicken only this one time. Do not cover. If chicken gets too brown before the first 15 minutes are up, turn the burner to medium low, but turn back to medium high for last 10 minutes. Drain on paper towels. If using this recipe for the entree, drain the grease off; leaving about 1/4 cup in pan, with the crusty bits left in skillet to make a MILK GRAVY, if desired. Turn to high, add 4 tablespoons flour, stir well, add 1 cup milk and 1 cup water. Remove pan from stove unit. Stir well to desired consistency. Salt and pepper to taste. Leave on low until ready to use. The real secret of making smooth gravy is to blend flour thoroughly with fat or with cold liquid before combining it with hot liquid.

STUFFED DATES

Mrs. Herbert Kirsh (Suzanne)

10	ounce box pitted dates	4	tablespoons honey
	Walnut halves	1	cup coconut, shredded or flaked

Stuff each date with a walnut. Dip each date in the honey and roll in coconut. Put on a foiled-lined dish, cover with plastic warp and refrigerate.

GLAZED NUTS

Representative Joyce C. Hearn

1	egg white	3/4	cup brown sugar
1	teaspoon vanilla	4	cups pecans

Beat egg white very stiff; add sugar and vanilla. Stir in nuts. Cook at 250 degrees for 30 minutes. Turn off oven and let stay in oven for 30 more minutes.

APPETIZERS

FANCY PEANUTS·

Serves 6 to 8   Mrs. R. M. Kenan (Sinclair)

2   cups raw peanuts, shelled   1   cup water
1   cup sugar

Stir in heavy saucepan on medium high until nuts are glazed and all water is gone. Pour onto cookie sheet and cook at 325 degrees 20 minutes. Stir once. Store in air-tight container.

TOASTED PECANS
Representative Joyce C. Hearn

8   ounces pecan halves   Salt
1/2 stick margarine

Place pecans in shallow pan in a 200 degree oven. When pecans take on a shiny appearance, add melted margarine. Stir to coat pecans and salt to taste. After stirring, place pecans back in oven and let stay until oven cools.

MELBA GRAPEFRUIT SECTIONS
Serves 4   Mrs. William N. Cork (Helen)

2   grapefruit, cut in half   Maraschino cherries
2   tablespoons sugar   Butter
1/2 teaspoon cinnamon

Cut a thin slice from the bottom of each half to balance grapefruit. Cut around every section close to the membrane (fruit should be completely loosened from the shell). Remove core from each half; dot grapefruit halves with butter. Combine 2 tablespoons sugar with 1/2 teaspoon cinnamon; sprinkle over grapefruit halves. Place on broiler rack or in a shallow baking pan; broil 4-inches from heat for about 8 minutes or until heated through and bubbling. Garnish with stemmed maraschino cherries, if desired.
Variation: Cover with orange marmalade or honey.

SEVECHI
Serves 20   Mrs. Alex Macaulay (Maria)

1   quart firm white fillet fish   3   hot peppers, chopped fine
Juice of 6 limes   2   onions, chopped fine

Cut fish into small thumbnail size pieces. Mix chopped peppers and onions with lime juice and pour over fish pieces. Marinate for 3 to 4 hours on counter and then refrigerate until ready to use. Serve with saltine crackers or serve in individual appetizer dishes on shredded lettuce with REMOULADE SAUCE, SHRIMP COCKTAIL SAUCE, or SOUTH CAROLINA LOW COUNTRY DRESSING. (See Page 55 and Page 58)

ARTIFICIAL STRAWBERRIES

Mrs. Herbert Kirsh (Suzanne)

2/3 cup Eagle Brand Milk
2-2/3 cups flaked coconut
        (2 3-1/2-ounce cans)
1   3-ounce package strawberry
        gelatin
1/2 cup blanched almonds,
        ground fine

1/2 teaspoon almond or strawberry
        extract
Red food coloring (enough for desired
        color)
Tube of green cake decorator for
        leaves (or make your own)

Mix together milk, coconut, 3 tablespoons gelatin, almonds, extract and food coloring. Chill for short time. Shape into strawberries and let stand at room temperature for a few minutes. Roll in remaining gelatin. Add leaves and refrigerate.

REMOULADE SAUCE

Yields: 3 cups

1/2 cup celery
1/2 cup green onions
3   cloves garlic
1   sprig parsley
1/3 cup tarragon vinegar
1   cup olive oil

2   tablespoons paprika
1/4 to 1/2 teaspoon cayenne pepper
1/2 teaspoon salt
3   tablespoons Creole or Dijon pre-
        pared mustard
2   heaping tablespoons prepared
        horseradish

Grind all vegetables very fine. Combine ground vegetables and rest of ingredients in a blender and whip thoroughly. Chill several hours before serving.

SHRIMP COCKTAIL SAUCE

Yields: 1 cup

Combine 1 (12-ounce) bottle Heinz Chili Sauce, 1 tablespoon creamed horseradish, 1 tablespoon Worcestershire sauce, 1 teaspoon lemon juice and freshly ground pepper. Serve with boiled shrimp. Season with more horseradish, if desired.

GIVE ME A VEGETABLE GARDEN
(NOT A ROSE GARDEN!)

Serves 25   Cookbook Committee Selection

Large Wicker basket		2	pounds cherry tomatoes
Large red cabbage		4	medium cucumbers and 2
10 or 12-inch round loaf of bread			zucchini
Large shell		2	pounds large mushrooms, fluted
Large wooden bamboo skewers		2 to 3	red and green pepper strips
Large grapefruit		2	medium cauliflower
2	big turnips	2	bunches broccoli
1	pound large radishes	3	cups dip
2	pounds jumbo scallions	3	pounds carrots
3	pounds celery		

TURNIP DAISIES: Slice the turnip 1/4 inch thick. Cut daisies with a cookie cutter. Place a small carrot slice in the center. A dab of dip will hold them in place or stick on long bamboo skewers. RADISH FANS: Place a long thin radish on its side and make thin slices almost but not quite through the radish. RADISH TULIPS: Beginning at top of radish, cut 4 thin slices of peel almost to the bottom, making 4 petals. RADISH ROSES: Cut a thin slice off the bottom and top of a round radish. Make 8 cuts across the radish almost to the bottom, cutting first through the middle, then through each half and finally through each quarter. Place the radish fans, tulips and roses in ice water to open. CARROT CURLS: Peel, cut long thin slices, roll up and soak in ice water. CELERY AND ONION BRUSHES: Cut through green ends of each in 8 to 10 places, soak in ice water. SCALLION FLOWERS: Cut through white bulb in 8 to 10 places, soak in ice water 1 to 2 days and they will spread out like gorgeous flowers. FLUTED VEGETABLES: Cut carrots, zucchini, turnips, and cucumbers in sticks or slices with a french-fry cutter. (Holds the dip better than plain vegetable sticks.) TO ASSEMBLE BASKET: Line a large, pretty wicker basket with lettuce and fill it with uncooked decorative vegetables, cherry tomatoes, fluted mushrooms and pepper strips. Surround with 3 cups of several dips to dunk the edible vegetables. Scoop out a red cabbage deep enough for a small dish to fit it. Turn back some of outside leaves to curl attractively. Fill dish with dip. Fill a large shell with a seafood dip. Scoop out bread from inside round loaf, leaving only shell. Fill with another dip. Have 3 different dips in 3 colors. The colors look magnificent. Take the largest grapefruit you can find, cover entirely with parsley, secure parsley to grapefruit with hairpins (toothpicks will not work). Put some of the decorative vegetables on long wooden bamboo skewers just before party and insert in grapefruit. This could serve as the centerpiece for your table. YOUR VEGETABLE GARDEN CENTERPIECE AND BASKET ARE COMPLETELY EDIBLE!

WATERMELON BASKET

Serves 24   Cookbook Committee Selection

1 large 12-pound watermelon	2 medium honeydew melons
3 1-pint baskets strawberries	2 pounds grapes
1-1/2 medium pineapples	Mint to garnish
2 medium cantaloupes	Plastic party picks

Outline the top opening to make a shell and handle. Use a sharp knife and cut an X through the end tops of the watermelon to relieve the pressure inside. Cut along the shell and handle for opening. Scoop out watermelon balls, leaving the shell about 1-inch thick. Reserve watermelon fruit and balls to add to other fruit. Fill the watermelon shell with the canteloupe and honeydew balls, grapes, pineapple pieces and reserved watermelon. Garnish with mint, if desired. Serve with plastic party picks.

LIVER PÂTÉ

Yields: 3-1/2 cups   Cookbook Committee Selection

1/4 pound plus 2 tablespoons butter	3/4 teaspoon salt
2 large onions, chopped	1/4 teaspoon each pepper and thyme
1-1/2 pounds chicken livers	2 whole canned pimentos, cut in
2 hard boiled eggs, mashed with	very thin strips
a fork	Toasted and buttered small bread
1 tablespoon brandy	rounds
4 tablespoons whipping cream	

In a medium skillet over moderate heat, melt 3 tablespoons butter, or chicken fat. Sauté onions 5 to 7 minutes until soft and lightly browned. Place onion in a blender or food processor fitted with the metal blade. In the same skillet, melt 3 tablespoons butter. Sauté livers over high heat 5 to 8 minutes, turning until they are browned outside but a slight pink inside. Add livers to onions; add mashed eggs. Add 2 tablespoons cream. Process until smooth. If mixture is too thick to blend, add more cream. Place pate mixture in a small bowl and cool completely. Bring remaining butter to room temperature. Stir it into the cooled pate. Add brandy and season to taste, making certain that mixture is well flavored. Refrigerate until chilled. Shape chilled pate into a football, if desired. Place a pimento strip down to middle center. Place 3 pimento strips across the top of pimento strip on top to simulate laces. Football may be refrigerated up to 5 hours. Or spoon pate into a crock or small bowls. May be refrigerated in a crock or bowl up to 2 days, or frozen. Before serving pate, bring to room temperature. Serve with bread rounds, or Sesame seed Melba toast rounds surrounding the pate.

SOUTH CAROLINA "LOW COUNTRY" DRESSING

1	pint mayonnaise		Tabasco sauce
12	ounce bottle chili sauce	1	teaspoon steak sauce
2	tablespoons India relish	2	tablespoons grated onion
2	tablespoons Worcestershire sauce	1	teaspoon lemon juice
			Salt, freshly ground pepper

Blend all ingredients and season to taste. NOTE: This sauce is excellent for a seafood cocktail, on grapefruit salad, or as a dip for raw vegetables.

SWEDISH MEATBALLS

Yields: 4 dozen   Mrs. Robert N. McLellan (Doris)

2	cups bread crumbs	2-1/2	teaspoons salt
1/2	cup milk	1/4	teaspoon pepper
1-1/2	pound ground beef	1/2 to 1	teaspoon ground nutmeg
1	onion, finely chopped	2	teaspoon paprika
6	tablespoons butter	1	teaspoon dry mustard
		3	eggs, beaten

Soak bread crumbs in milk about 5 minutes. Squeeze dry and add meat. Sauté onions in 2 tablespoons butter; add onions and remaining ingredients to meat mixture. Shape into 48 small balls; brown in 4 tablespoons butter in a large skillet until they are browned and cooked all the way through, about 10 minutes. Remove the meatballs as they are cooked and place in a large bowl.

SAUCE

1/4	teaspoon crushed garlic	1	cup bouillon
4	tablespoons flour	1	cup water
2	teaspoons tomato paste	1	teaspoon auromatic bitters (opt.)
1	teaspoon beef concentrate	1	cup sour cream

Add garlic to drippings in skillet, blend in flour, tomato paste, beef concentrate, bouillon and water. Stir over low heat until thickened; add sour cream and serve hot from a chafing dish with wooden picks. Also delicious served over rice as a main meal. May be refrigerated several days or frozen, but do not add sour cream until you reheat. Before serving, bring to room temperature. Reheat on top of stove. Add sour cream and serve.

FISH MOUSSE WITH SHRIMP SAUCE

Serves 16 to 20 in buffet   Cookbook Committee Selection

4	pounds white fish fillets, weight without bones (such as haddock, halibut, sole or flounder)	Freshly ground white pepper Cayenne Butter Shrimp sauce
8	egg whites	Parsley
5	cups heavy cream	Twists of cucumbers
Salt		

Preheat oven to 375 degrees. Put fish through grinder, then slowly work in the egg whites. Puree in a blender a little bit at a time; work in cream, and puree in blender again until fish flesh is completely smooth. Season to taste with salt, pepper and a pinch of cayenne. Butter 2 8-cup, 7-inch deep, fish molds or loaf pans. Pour in mousse and put molds in a pan or pans of simmering water reaching halfway up side of dish. Put a buttered piece of wax paper over mold, buttered side down, to prevent top from becoming crusty, and bake in a 375 degree oven for about 25 minutes, until a knife inserted in center comes out clean. Unmold onto a platter and serve with SHRIMP SAUCE, garnished with parsley and twists of cucumber. May be served hot or cold with the hot sauce.

SHRIMP SAUCE

8	tablespoons butter	Salt	
8	tablespoons flour	Freshly ground white pepper	
4	cups milk, boiling	1	pound shrimp, cooked, peeled and deveined
1/4	cup tomato juice	2	tablespoons chopped fresh dill or 2 teaspoons dried
Dry sherry			

Melt butter in a heavy-bottomed saucepan. Stir in flour and blend well over medium heat for about 2 minutes, stirring carefully to avoid burning. Add milk and continue cooking over medium heat until thickened, stirring constantly. Color sauce with no more than 1/4 cup tomato juice. Remove from heat and season to taste. Stir in shrimp and dill.

SALMON MOUSSE

Serves 10   Cookbook Committee Selection

2   envelopes unflavored gelatin   1/4   cup finely chopped celery
    softened in 1/2 cup cold   1   teaspoon Tabasco sauce
    water   1/2   teaspoon paprika
1   cup hot sour cream (do not   1   teaspoon salt
    boil)   White pepper to taste
1   cup mayonnaise   2   teaspoons capers, rinsed and
2   15-1/2-ounce cans salmon,   chopped fine
    drained, or 1-1/2-pounds   1   cup whipping cream
    poached fresh salmon   3   tablespoons grated onion
2   tablespoons lemon juice

Oil a 6-cup fish mold, set aside. Add softened gelatin to hot sour cream. Cool. Remove skin and bones from salmon; discard. Flake well or chop fine; set aside. Stir into the cooled sour cream gelatin the mayonnaise, lemon juice, onion, Tabasco sauce, paprika, salt, pepper, celery and capers. Stir salmon into gelatin mixture. When mixture begins to congeal, fold in the cream, whipped. Pour into prepared mold. Cover with plastic wrap and refrigerate until set or up to 2 days. May be frozen up to 2 weeks. To unmold mousse, run the tip of a table knife around the edges, dip bottom of mold in warm water and invert onto platter. Decorate with slices of pimiento and black olives. Serve with DILL SAUCE and crackers.

DILL SAUCE

Yields: 1-1/2 cups

1   cup sour cream   3   tablespoons brown sugar
1-1/2 tablespoons white vinegar   2 to 3 tablespoons chopped fresh dill
1-1/2 tablespoons Dijon Mustard   or 2 teaspoons dry dill

Mix all ingredients and blend well. Refrigerate several hours or up to 1 week.

THE STATE HOUSE

The present State House in Columbia is the third official building. The first one was built in Charleston during the 1750s and burned in 1788. James Hoban designed the new capitol building in Columbia. It was a raised classical structure with lines very similar to those of the White House in Washington, D. C. And, well they should be, for after a visit to Columbia in 1791 President George Washington asked Hoban to come north to help design the new federal city of Washington. The young architect went.

Because of the growth of state government, the Hoban-designed capitol was too small by the 1850s so a larger structure was authorized by the General Assembly. J. R. Niernsee was hired to design and construct the new State House. The cornerstone was laid on 15 December 1851 and the basic structure was virtually complete when war broke out in 1861.

During the Union occupation of Columbia in February 1865, the old State House was burned as was the temporary wooden interior of the new building. Given the depressed state of the South Carolina economy, it was several years before the State House was made fit for occupancy. During the interim, the General Assembly met in the chapel at the University of S. C.

When the legislature moved into the State House, it was hardly complete. The granite shell was simply roofed over and the building had a ramshackle, barn-like appearance. The grand steps, colonnaded porticoes and a classically-inspired central tower were left off. The capitol grounds were surrounded by a white-washed fence.

Although the exterior was rather rough looking, the interior was completed in high Victorian style. The exuberance characteristic of that period is most notice-able in the lobby and the old State Library rooms just off the lobby.

There is an abundance of stone work throughout the State House. Marble floors and stone walls not only provided a dignified setting for the General Assembly, but also a fireproof building for the housing of the state's records. Until the 20th century, many valuable documents were stored on the first floor of the capitol.

At the turn of the century, the exterior of the State House was completed. Granite Corinthian columned porticoes on both the North and South fronts now received visitors at the top of a flight of stone steps. The planned classical tower was not built and in its stead a dome was constructed.

Like its executive counterpart, the Governor's Mansion, the State House reflects the more than three centuries of South Carolina's history. Traditions and artifacts from the colonial and antebellum past are still in use today. Most notable of these are the Mace of the House of Representatives which was made in England for the South Carolina Commons House of Assembly and the Sword of State used in the Senate. Throughout the building are portraits and statues of men and women who helped shape not only South Carolina's history, but that of the South and the Nation.

THE STATE HOUSE

Cherokee artifacts and nuclear reactors live harmoniously together in Pickens County. Sandwiched between urban Greenville County and rural Oconee County, Pickens serves as a buffer traversed, symbolically, by the Cherokee Foothills Scenic Highway (route No. 11), which connects points of historic and natural significance in the upstate.

Born as a county in 1826, the 529 square mile area had earlier been part of short-lived Washington District and then old Pendleton District. Named for Gen. Andrew Pickens, who had lived in the vicinity, the new county was bounded by the Saluda River on the east, Keowee River on the west, Anderson County on the south and the mountainous North Carolina state line on the north. The terrain embraced fertile valleys which proved productive for corn, hay, grain, cotton and fruits.

The northern reaches of Pickens County boasts two spectacular mountains: Table Rock and Sassafras.

John C. Calhoun and his family had more than a little bearing on Pickens County. His plantation, Fort Hill, became the site of Clemson University when his son-in-law, Thomas G. Clemson, bequeathed the acreage to the state for an agricultural college in 1889. The small town bore the name of "Calhoun" until 1943 when it was changed to that of the growing educational institution.

Past and present are complementary in Pickens. The turn-of-the century County Gaol reminiscent of a Gothic castle with its crenelated turret, has been restored to house the Pickens County Museum for History and Art. Keowee-Toxaway Park, one of the youngest in the state park system, occupies territory once at the center of the lower Cherokee nation. It proudly displays Indian relics unearthed by archeologists before the flooding for Lakes Keowee and Jocassee. The county's past has laid a strong foundation for its present and future.

Manufacturing and industry have played a key role in the history of Greenville County from its first settlement. When Richard Pearis established a trading post and grist mill at the falls of the Reedy River in the 1770s, he had no way of foreseeing the industrial mecca the area would become two centuries later. Early woolen and cotton mills along the rivers were quite successful, laying the foundation for the county's twentieth century designation as "Textile Center of the World."

The county, which took its present shape in 1776, was once an integral part of Cherokee Indian territory. In fact, the boundary line which divides Greenville from Spartanburg County formerly served as the eastern boundary between the Cherokee Nation and the Province of South Carolina. Stretching lengthwise some 50 miles along the Saluda River, the Piedmont county is bounded on the north by Blue Ridge mountains which create a climate some have called the "most delightful in the world."

If Richard Pearis is Greenville's "biological" father, then Vardry McBee (1815-1864) may be considered its "Godfather." The court house town - first known as Pleasantburg - took on an air of permanency through McBee's gifts of land for the first four churches and two academies; his construction of a mill; and his overtures to attract both Furman University and a railroad to the village. Permanent and summer residents made other contributions to growth and stability. The Old Record Building, a graceful brick Millsian structure on Main Street, served as the county's courthouse until 1855.

Verdant natural and mountain beauty are well rooted in Greenville, hence, the name of the county. The names of certain mountain peaks conjure up visions of their contour: Hogback, Glassy and Caesar's Head.

Joel R. Poinsett may have designed a picturesque stone bridge adequate for 1820 traffic, but Interstate 85 is more symbolic of fast paced modern life in this most populous county. Greenville is an urban area, highly industralized, but with few of the environmental and social ills that often follow such progress. Indeed, it has been singled out for commendation: a healthful blend of technical and artistic, agricultural and industrial, past and future.

HAGOOD GRIST MILL

Hagood Grist Mill with water wheel, built about 1830, is currently under restoration. It is located on U. S. 178, two miles north of Pickens near Tamassee.

breads

ANGEL BISCUITS

Yields: 4 dozen biscuits   Mrs. Dick Elliott (Anne)

1   yeast cake or 1 package yeast
    dissolved in 1/2 cup luke-
    warm water
2   tablespoons lukewarm water
5   cups plain flour
1   teaspoon soda

3   teaspoons baking powder
2   tablespoons sugar
1   teaspoon salt
1   cup shortening
2   cups buttermilk

Sift flour with dry ingredients. Cut in shortening, add buttermilk and yeast mixture, mixing well. Roll dough out on lightly floured surface. Cut with biscuit cutters. Bake on greased sheet in pre-heated 400 degree oven about 12 to 15 minutes. The dough will keep a week in the refrigerator.

BO-J'S BISCUITS

Mrs. Herbert Kirsh (Suzanne)

2   cups self-rising flour, sifted
2   teaspoons baking powder
2   tablespoons confectioners sugar

1/3   cup Crisco
1   cup buttermilk

Mix as for regular biscuits. Bake on greased sheet in a pre-heated 425 degree oven until brown.

BUTTERMILK BISCUITS

Yields: 12 large or 24 small   Mrs. Robert N. McLellan (Doris)

2   cups sifted flour
1/2   teaspoon baking soda
2   teaspoons baking powder

1   teaspoon salt
1/4 to 1/2 cup cold shortening
1   cup cold buttermilk

Sift dry ingredients together and cut in shortening until mealy. Add milk and mix quickly. Knead very lightly on a floured board. Pat to 1/2-inch thickness and cut with floured biscuit cutter. Place in greased pan close together for crust on top and bottom only; put far apart if crust is desired on sides also. Bake at once in 450 degree oven for 12 minutes or until brown. If using self-rising flour, cut in 2/3 cup shortening and enough buttermilk to form a stiff dough. Omit baking powder and soda.

BANANA BREAD

Mrs. Jarvis Klapman (Arlene)
Mrs. Woody M. McKay (Nancy)

1	cup butter	1/2	cup chopped nuts
1	cup sugar	2	cups self-rising flour (or plain
2 to 3 eggs			with 1 teaspoon soda)
2 to 4 mashed bananas		1	teaspoon vanilla, optional

Cream butter and sugar, add eggs one at a time and beat well after each addition. Add mashed bananas and vanilla. Mix nuts with flour and add to the mixture. Bake in loaf pan for 1 hour at 350 degrees.

BEER BREAD

Yield: 1 loaf

Mrs. John C. Land, III (Marie)

4	cups self-rising flour	1	14-ounce bottle beer, room
4	heaping tablespoons sugar		temperature

Mix flour and sugar in large mixing bowl. Stir in beer and mix only until blended. Pour into a greased and floured loaf pan. Cover loosely with foil and bake at 400 degrees for 20 minutes. Remove foil and bake 20 minutes more. Cool slightly before slicing.

ENGLISH MUFFIN BREAD

Yields: 3 1-pound loaves

Mrs. E. S. Lake (Sarah)

3-1/2 cups self-rising flour		1/2	cup oil
2	packages dry yeast	2	eggs
1/4	cup sugar		Cornmeal
1-1/4 cups very hot tap water			

Measure flour, yeast, and sugar into a large bowl. Add very hot tap water and mix until sugar dissolves. Beat until smooth, about 2 minutes, with electric mixer or 300 strokes by hand. Blend in oil and eggs. Add flour to make a stiff batter. Beat until batter is smooth and elastic, about 2 minutes. Cover and let rise in warm place (80 to 85 degrees) until light and bubbly, about 1 hour. Stir down. Divide into 3 well greased and cornmeal dusted 1-pound coffee cans, 4-inches in diameter. Cover and let rise in warm place until doubled, about 40 minutes. Bake in a pre-heated 375 degree oven for 15 to 20 minutes or until done. Let cool completely in coffee cans. Invert and shake to remove loaves.

BREADS

CHEESE BREAD

Serves 8   Mrs. T. Ed. Garrison (Juanita)

1 loaf unsliced French bread	1/4 cup butter
1 cup grated cheddar cheese	1/2 teaspoon Worcestershire sauce

Cut the bread in 1-inch slices to the lower crust. Mix the cheese, butter and Worcestershire sauce and spread on each slice. Push the bread together and wrap in foil. Heat in a 350 degree oven until cheese and butter have completely melted, about 20 minutes.

CRANBERRY BREAD

Yield: 1 loaf   Mrs. W. B. Hawkins (Sarah)

2 cups plain flour	2 tablespoons shortening
1 cup sugar	3/4 cup boiling water
1-1/2 teaspoons baking powder	1 beaten egg
1/2 teaspoon soda	1 cup chopped pecans
1 teaspoon salt	1 cup sliced cranberries
Juice and grated rind of 1 orange	

Sift the flour and dry ingredients together. Combine orange rind, juice, shortening and boiling water. Blend into the flour mixture. Add egg, pecans and cranberries and mix well. Pour into greased loaf pan and bake at 350 degrees for 1 hour. Freezes well.

MONKEY BREAD

Mrs. Alex S. Macaulay (Maria)

1-1/2 yeast cake, OR	4 tablespoons sugar
2 packages dry yeast	1 teaspoon salt
1 cup milk, heated to lukewarm	1/2 cup melted butter(not margarine)
	3-1/2 cups sifted flour

Dissolve yeast in lukewarm milk. Stir in sugar, salt and butter. Add flour and beat well. Let rise to almost double in bulk. Punch down and roll out on lightly floured board to 1/4-inch thickness. Cut in about 2-inch pieces: round, diamond or square. Dip each piece in melted butter. Pile in buttered bundt pan until half full. Let rise to double in bulk. Bake at 400 degrees for 30 minutes or until golden brown. Serve loaf uncut; let people pull off whatever amount they wish. It is already buttered, so no bread and butter plate is needed. It is always a favorite. It freezes well and may be reheated. Great toasted.

PALMETTO PUMPKIN BREAD

Yields: 2 loaves   Mrs. E. Crosby Lewis (Cleo)

1-1/2	cups sugar	14	ounces flour
1	teaspoon soda	1/2	cup oil
1/4	teaspoon baking powder	2	eggs
3/4	teaspoon salt	1	cup canned pumpkin
1/2	teaspoon ground cloves	1/2	cup water
1-1/2	teaspoons nutmeg	1/2	cup chopped nuts
1/2	teaspoon cinnamon	1/2	cup chopped dates

Preheat oven to 350 degrees. Grease 2 small loaf pans and line with waxed paper. Sift dry ingredients together. Add the oil, eggs, pumpkin and water to dry ingredients. Mix with a mixer on medium speed until well blended. Stir in nuts and dates. Bake at 350 degrees for 1 hour or until center springs back when tested.

QUICK BREAD

Senator Nell Smith

2	cups self-rising flour	6	tablespoons mayonnaise
1	whole cup milk		

Mix all ingredients well. Pour into greased muffin pan or drop on cookie sheet. Cook approximately 10 minutes at 425 degrees. Best served piping hot.

VARIATION: Mrs. Horace C. Smith (Dot)

Reduce mayonnaise to 3 tablespoons and add 1 tablespoon vinegar. Stir and spoon into greased muffin tin. Bake at 425 degrees for 20 minutes.

ZUCCHINI BREAD

Yields: 2 loaves   Mrs. Nick Theodore (Emilie)

1	cup brown sugar	1	tablespoon vanilla
2	cups white sugar	3	cups flour
3	eggs	1-1/2	teaspoons soda
1	cup oil	1-1/2	teaspoons baking powder
1	teaspoon salt	1-1/2	cups nuts, chopped
2	cups grated zucchini	1	cup raisins

Cream sugars, eggs, vanilla and oil. Add grated zucchini and mix well. Sift together flour, baking powder, soda and salt. Add to zucchini mixture, mixing well. Flour raisins before adding or they will sink to bottom. Add nuts. Place in 2 greased and floured loaf pans. Bake 350 degrees for 1 hour.

RYE BREAD

Yields: 2 loaves   Mrs. Robert N. McLellan (Doris)

2	cups buttermilk	2	tablespoons caraway seeds
1	package active dry yeast or cake compressed yeast	2	cups all-purpose flour, sifted
		2	teaspoons salt
2/3	cup molasses	2	cups rye flour, sifted
1/4	cup melted shortening or salad oil	2	cups wheat flour, sifted

Heat buttermilk to lukewarm (heating may cause milk to separate, but this is normal and will not affect the final product); sprinkle or crumble in yeast, stir to dissolve. Stir in molasses, salad oil and caraway seeds. Sift all-purpose flour with salt; mix with rye and whole wheat flours. Stir into milk mixture slowly, beating well after each addition. Turn out onto floured board, cover with inverted mixing bowl and let rest 10 minutes. Remove bowl. Knead dough until very smooth, 10 to 15 minutes. Place in greased bowl. Turn dough over to bring greased side up or brush top with soft shortening, cover with clean towel. Let rise in warm place (85 degrees) free from draft, about 1 to 1-1/2 hours or until doubled in bulk. (Rye bread takes longer to rise than white bread.) Punch dough down; turn out onto floured board, cut in half. Shape each half into a long loaf and place in greased and floured 10-1/4x3-5/8x2-5/8-inch pans, (or into a round loaf, place on greased baking sheets) cover with damp towels. Let rise in warm place (85 degrees) free from draft, about 1 hour or until doubled in bulk. With sharp knife, slash a cross 1/4-inch deep into top of each loaf. Bake in a moderate 350 degree oven for 50 to 60 minutes.

STRAWBERRY BREAD

Mrs. R. L. Altman (Nancy)

3	cups plain flour	1	8-ounce package cream cheese, cut into small pieces and separated
1	teaspoon baking soda		
1/2	teaspoon salt		
1	tablespoon ground cinnamon	1	cup chopped nuts
2	cups sugar	3	well beaten eggs
1	cup vegetable oil	2	10-ounce boxes frozen sliced strawberries, thawed

Combine dry ingredients and nuts. Mix together eggs, oil and strawberries and add to dry ingredients. Mix well. Mix cream cheese pieces into batter. Pour into 2 9x5-inch well greased and floured loaf pans. Bake at 350 degrees for 1 hour or until tester comes out clean. Cool for 15 to 20 minutes before removing from pan. Cut when thoroughly cool with sharp knife. Freezes well.

SOUR CREAM CORNBREAD

Serves 6   Mrs. Mona Chapman

1	cup self-rising cornmeal	1	cup sour cream
2	eggs	1/2	cup salad oil
1	8-3/4-ounce can cream style corn		

Combine the ingredients and pour into a greased 9-inch pan. Bake at 400 degrees about 30 minutes.

APPLESAUCE MUFFINS

Yields: 42 muffins   Mrs. R. L. Altman (Nancy)

1/2	cup margarine, softened	1-3/4	cups self-rising flour
1/2	cup sugar	1/4	cup margarine, melted
2	eggs	1/4	cup sugar
3/4	cup applesauce	1/4	teaspoon ground cinnamon

Cream margarine and sugar. Add eggs, one at a time, beating well. Blend in applesauce. Stir in flour until just moistened. Spoon into greased miniature muffin pans, filling 2/3 full. Bake at 425 degrees for 15 minutes or until done. Remove from pan immediately and dip muffin tops in melted butter. Combine 1/4 cup sugar and cinnamon and sprinkle over top of each muffin.

BRAN MUFFINS

Yields: 3 to 4 dozen   Mrs. Mona Chapman; Mrs. William Cork (Helen)
                   Mrs. Dick Elliott (Anne); Mrs. John I. Rogers, III (Carolyn)

Makes a large quantity but keeps in the refrigerator for an unlimited amount of time.

3	cups All Bran	1	pint buttermilk
1	cup boiling water	2-1/2	cups flour
1/2	cup melted shortening	2-1/2	teaspoons soda
1-1/2	cups sugar	1	teaspoon salt
2	eggs, beaten		

Put one cup of bran in boiling water and let set. Mix shortening, remaining bran, sugar, eggs and buttermilk. Sift together flour, salt and soda. Combine all together. Grease muffin tins and fill 2/3 full. Bake at 400 degrees for 15 to 20 minutes. Keep remaining batter in refrigerator for up to 6 weeks.

VARIATION: Mrs. Marion H. Kinon (Reba)

Add 1 cup raisins, 1 teaspoon vanilla and 1/2 cup chopped nuts.

BREADS

JIFFY CORN SPINACH BREAD

Yields: 9 big squares   Mrs. Nick Theodore (Emilie)

1 package Jiffy corn bread mix	1 cup sharp cheddar cheese, grated
4 eggs	1/2 cup cottage cheese
1 small grated onion	3/4 stick butter or margarine
1 package chopped spinach, thawed	

Mix all ingredients together. Put in an 8-inch square pan. Bake at 400 degrees for 30 minutes.

BEER MUFFINS

Yields: 24   Mrs. D. H. Wilkins (Susan)

4 cups Bisquick	1 can beer
2 tablespoons sugar	

Heat oven to 400 degrees. Mix all ingredients and beat 1/2 minute. Fill 24 hot greased muffin tins 2/3 full. Bake about 15 minutes. Serve warm.

SWEET POTATO NUT MUFFINS

Mrs. James Craven (Beverly)

1 cup cooked, mashed sweet potatoes	1/2 tablespoon soda
2 eggs	2 tablespoons baking powder
1 cup sugar	1 teaspoon salt
1/2 cup milk	1 teaspoon cinnamon
2 cups sifted flour	1/2 teaspoon nutmeg
	1 cup nuts, chopped

Combine sweet potatoes, eggs, sugar and milk. Add flour and other ingredients. Mix; do not use electric mixer. Batter will be lumpy. Bake in muffin tins, at 350 degrees for 20 minutes or until muffins spring back at touch.

WHEAT MUFFINS

Senator Nell Smith

2-1/2 cups flour	4 tablespoons butter
6 teaspoons baking powder	1 cup milk
1 teaspoon salt	2 eggs
6 tablespoons sugar	

Cream butter and sugar. Add eggs and beat well. Add flour and milk, Bake at 400 degrees about 20 minutes.

HOT ROLLS

Yields: 6 to 8 dozen rolls   Mrs. Parker Evatt (Jane)

3/4	cup sugar	2	envelopes yeast
2	sticks margarine	1	cup lukewarm water
2	teaspoons salt	2	eggs, beaten
1	cup water	6	cups unsifted flour

Heat sugar, margarine, salt, and 1 cup water and stir to melt margarine. Cool to lukewarm. Dissolve yeast in 1 cup lukewarm water; add to above mixture. Add eggs. Stir in flour. Cover with wax paper and refrigerate several hours or overnight. Roll out on heavily floured board (dough will be sticky; flour heavily as you roll out). Cut with biscuit cutter, place a small pat of margarine on roll, fold in half and place about 1-inch apart on greased pan. Let rise about 2 hours in warm place. Bake at 375 degrees about 15 minutes. Dough will keep several days in refrigerator.

REFRIGERATOR ROLLS

Yields: 2 dozen rolls   Mrs. B. L. Hendricks, Jr. (Carolyn)

1/2	cup shortening	1	egg, beaten
1	cup hot water	2	packages dry yeast
2	teaspoons salt	4	cups flour
1/4	cup sugar		

Pour hot water over shortening, sugar and salt. Blend and cool. Add beaten egg. Sprinkle yeast on lukewarm water and stir until dissolved. Combine with egg mixture, add flour, and blend well. Cover and place in refrigerator at least 4 hours, preferably overnight. Use a large bowl, for dough will rise. Dough will keep in refrigerator for a week to 10 days. About 3 hours before serving, roll into desired shape, using only enough extra flour for easy handling. Place on greased cookie sheet and allow to rise at room temperature, about 3 hours or until double in bulk. Bake at 375 degrees for about 15 minutes or until brown.

SOUTHERN POPOVERS

Yields: 1 dozen   Mrs. William Cork (Helen)

1-1/2 cups all-purpose flour	3	eggs, slightly beaten
1-1/2 cups milk	1/2	teaspoon salt

Combine all ingredients in blender and blend until smooth. Place well-buttered muffin tins in oven at 450 degrees for 3 minutes or until a drop of water sizzles when dropped in them. Remove tins from oven; fill two-third's full with batter. Bake at 450 degrees for 30 minutes; reduce heat to 300 degrees, and bake an additional 10 to 15 minutes. Serve immediately.

BREADS

NATALIE'S REFRIGERATOR ROLLS

Mrs. Rembert C. Dennis (Natalie)

1	stick margarine	2	eggs
1/2	cup sugar	2	packages yeast
1	teaspoon salt	1/2	cup warm water
1	cup sour cream	4	cups plain flour

Mix melted margarine, sugar, salt, and sour cream; add eggs, yeast, and flour and blend together. Let rise until mixture is doubled in bulk. Turn out on slightly floured board and knead. Put into greased bowl; grease lightly the top of the dough and cover. Place in refrigerator until ready to use. When needed, form into desired shape. Brush with margarine and let rise. Bake in 350 degree oven about 20 minutes. Use Natalie's Refrigerator Rolls to make 30 CINNAMON ROLLS:

CINNAMON ROLLS

1	recipe Natalie's Refrigerator Rolls	1/2	cup sugar
		2	teaspoons ground cinnamon
6	tablespoons butter, melted, divided	1/2	cup raisins or currants

Divide dough into 2 parts. Refrigerate 1 part and roll other part into a rectangle approximately 8x15-inches and 1/4-inch thick. Brush lavishly with 4 tablespoons butter, then sprinkle with a mixture of the sugar and cinnamon. Scatter raisins over dough and roll up like a jelly roll along the 15-inch side, pinching edges to seal. Cut in 1/2-inch segments and place in greased round cake pans. Brush tops with remaining butter and allow to rise until double in bulk. Bake at 450 degrees until brown on top (10 to 15 minutes). Repeat with remaining dough or use it to make caramel rolls or refrigerator rolls.

ORANGE-CARAMEL ROLLS

Serves 8 to 10   Mrs. Nick Theodore (Emilie)

1	tablespoon butter, softened	1/2	teaspoon cinnamon
1/2	cup orange marmalade	2	10-ounce cans flaky buttermilk biscuits
2	tablespoons pecans, chopped fine		
1	cup firmly packed brown sugar	1/2	cup melted butter

Grease bundt pan with 1 tablespoon butter. Place marmalade in bottom of pan and spread. Sprinkle with nuts. In small bowl combine sugar and cinnamon. Separate biscuits. Dip in butter, then in sugar mixture. Stand biscuits on edge in pan, spacing evenly. Sprinkle with remaining sugar and butter. Bake in center of oven 350 degrees for 30 to 40 minutes or until brown. Cool upright in pan for 5 minutes, invert into serving plate.

74

VIRGINIA SPOON BREAD

Serves 8   Mrs. Verne Smith (Jean)

1	cup cornmeal	1	cup boiling water
2	cups milk	1	teaspoon salt
1-1/2	tablespoons butter, melted	2	eggs
2	teaspoons baking powder		

Scald cornmeal with boiling water; add milk slowly to prevent lumping. Add salt, baking powder, well-beaten eggs, and butter to cornmeal mixture. Pour into a 2-quart buttered baking dish and bake 45 minutes at 375 degrees. Serve hot with butter.

WAFFLES

Mrs. Robert C. Lake, Jr. (Carolyn)

3	cups sifted self-rising flour	2	cups milk
2	teaspoons sugar	4	eggs, separated
2/3	cups melted butter or margarine		

Beat the egg yolks 1 minute, using No. 8 speed; add the milk, and beat for 1 minute longer. Add the sifted dry ingredients to this mixture at No. 4 speed, and beat for a minute longer at No. 8 speed. Add the melted shortening, and beat for 15 seconds at No. 8 speed or until the mixture is thoroughly blended. Fold in stiffly beaten egg whites at No. 1 speed.

EASY YEAST ROLLS

Yields: 5 dozen   Mrs. Thomas L. Hughston (Jeanne)

Pour 1 cup boiling water over 1/2 teaspoon salt and 2 sticks butter. Cool to lukewarm. Add 2 eggs and mix with mixer. Add mixture of 1 package yeast dissolved in 1 cup lukewarm water. Then add 7 cups sifted plain flour. Let rise overnight in refrigerator. The next day knead slightly with flour, roll out and cut with biscuit cutter. Fold in half and place in pan. Brush tops with melted butter. Let rise in warm place 2 hours. Bake at 350 degrees until tops brown, about 10 to 15 minutes. These can be browned slightly and frozen to use as brown and serve rolls. (If you don't have a warm place for rising turn your oven to 400 degrees for one minute only and then turn it off. It should have reached a temperature between 80 and 100 degrees. Put dough in oven and place a pan of hot water on oven floor before closing the door.)

Chesterfield was originally settled by small farmers from Virginia, North Carolina, and Pennsylvania around 1750. Later the area became part of the Cheraw District and in 1785 it was organized as Chesterfield, named in honor of Earl Chesterfield, British statesman and diplomat.

The county is rich in history and tradition and has played a prominent role in the development of South Carolina since the colonial period. The county was once the homeland of the Pee Dee and Cheraw Indian tribes. During the Revolution the town of Cheraw was used as a supply base for Cornwallis' British troops. St. David's Church served as a hospital for the British garrison.

A careless soldier set off an explosion in one of the storage buildings and the blast leveled a major portion of the town. To honor those who made sacrifices during the war, residents of Chesterfield erected a memorial on the grounds of St. David's Church. Dedicated in 1867, this Confederate Memorial was the first monument commemorating the "lost cause" built in the south.

Railroads built through the county replaced the Pee Dee River as the principal trade routes for area farmers. Timber re-emerged as an important industry and lumber produced from area saw mills began being sold to builders throughout the South. Cheraw known by many as the "most beautiful town in Dixie" is visited annually by hundreds of vacationers.

Since the early colonial period Marlboro County has been one of the state's strongest and most productive agricultural communities. The traditions of hard work, careful management, and wise land use policy, which are evident in the county today, were hallmarks of the county's first settlers. In 1736 Welsh Baptists from Delaware and Pennsylvania established a community near present day Society Hill called Welsh Neck. The success of that settlement spread and soon other immigrants, mostly Scotch-Irish from Pennsylvania, began entering the area. Many families crossed the Pee Dee and headed into the area now known as Chesterfield County.

The county was named for John Churchill, Duke of Marlboro, 18th century British politician, military hero and direct ancestor of Winston Churchill, Britain's World War II Prime Minister. The Blenheim community takes its name from the Marlboro ancestral home in England.

The first county seat was established on the north bank of Crooked Creek at Evans Mill later known as Winfieldsville. The nearby swamp made living in the Winfieldsville unhealthy and in 1818 the official county seat was moved to Bennettsville. Agriculture continued to flourish in the county throughout the 19th century. Cotton dominated all other cash crops in the area and by 1927 Marlboro County was ranked among the top five cotton producing regions in the country.

Today Marlboro County continues to advance economically with the rest of the state. Agriculture continues to dominate the life style of the county. Tobacco and soybeans have replaced cotton as the principal crops in the area and timber cut from the rich Marlboro forests provides building materials to suppliers throughout the South. The rich Pee Dee traditions that run deep in the area provide Marlboro County with a distinctive link to its fascinating past.

DARLINGTON COUNTY

Until the 1730's Indians of the Cheraw Nation were the lone inhabitants of the area today known as Darlington County. Welsh settlers began locating in the county by 1737. These early pioneers from Delaware and Pennsylvania established their first community at Welsh Neck in present day Marlboro County. Across the river in Darlington County these settlers built a boat landing and trading post. From this vantage point on the Pee Dee, settlements began to spread into the backcountry. Good land in the region drew settlers to the county and by 1776 there were four small communities in the district.

The county territory was originally part of the Cheraw District. In 1785 when the state legislature redrew the judicial boundaries Darlington was created. The new county was without a suitable site for the county seat. A decision was finally made to locate the county court house at the geographic center of the district. The area was marked off and a site on John King's plantation was designated as the location for the court house. The first court house was built in 1791 and burned in 1806. Although no proof ever surfaced, local residents at the time believed that an old woman whose case was due to be heard during the next court session set fire to the building in order to do away with incriminating evidence. A new court house was built but this one also burned in 1866. A new structure was erected in 1870 which was eventually replaced in 1903 by the present court house.

Agriculture, as it does today, dominated the early life of the county. Cotton and corn were the principal crops and numerous plantations operated in the area. The county was spared from most of the destruction of the Civil War and many of the antebellum mansions which once housed the planters of the county are still standing. Tobacco was introduced into the area in the 1880's and by the end of World War I the flue cured leaf had become the largest cash crop in the county.

Today the calm and easy pace of the county only gives way to the excitement of major stock car racing. Home of the Rebel 500 and the Southern 500, the Darlington Raceway is a major attraction on the racing circuit. Today the races at the Darlington speedway are attended by millions of fans from throughout the country. Along with the tobacco produced in the county, stock car racing has brought Darlington major national attention.

In 1910, the citizens of the Northernmost section of Marion County won a 15 year battle to form their own county. It began when the State Constitution Committee of 1895 reduced the acreage requirements for new counties and ended when the residents of Marion voted to split the county.

At that same election, voters chose to name the new county Dillon rather than Pee Dee. The Dillon family had been a permanent family in the area since the nineteenth century. William Dillon, an Irish merchant, settled in Marion County in the mid-eighteenth century. His son, James W. Dillon, moved in the northern portion of the county and became a merchant. The settlement that began around his store took the name of its leading citizen.

Like its parent county of Marion, Dillon is largely an agricultural community. Until the 1890s when low prices forced many farmers to diversify, cotton was the favored crop in the area. Some farmers began experimenting with a crop that was popular with its North Carolina neighbors - tobacco, which became the leading crop. During the depression 82% of the farmers were tenants and were forced to raise this cash crop rather than foodstuffs. Life for many residents improved greatly in 1938 when U.S. Representative John McMillan sent a telegram to his home county announcing that electricity would be available to farms through the REA.

Manufacturers of products using deviations from cotton, such as cotton seed oil, were attracted to Dillon County. When highway 301 from Washington to Florida was routed through the county in 1922, it brought the beginnings of another profitable industry for Dillon - tourism. For many modern Florida-bound travelers on I-95, the now legendary "South of the Border," with its thematic architecture is their only exposure to South Carolina.

Close to the border of North Carolina, a state with more stringent marriage laws than South Carolina, Dillon has become the leading marriage center. In 1974-75 over 6,000 licenses were granted, at $4.00 each for a license. That's big business for the county.

ST. DAVID'S EPISCOPAL CHURCH

St. David's Episcopal Church was the last church built in South Carolina under George III. In 1780 the 71st Highlanders used old St. David's for their headquarters. Built in 1768 the church is in Cheraw.

soups and sandwiches

HOUSE SPLIT PEA SOUP

Serves 8   Cookbook Committee Selection

1	pound dried split peas	2	carrots, coarsely chopped
1-1/2 to 2-pounds shank or butt		1	potato, coarsely chopped
	end of smoked ham	1	teaspoon thyme
3	quarts water	Salt, freshly ground pepper	
3	large onions, coarsely chopped	4	knockwurst, sliced
1	leek, sliced	1	tablespoon Hickory smoked salt
2	celery ribs, coarsely chopped		(optional)
1/4	cup chopped parsley		

If the peas require soaking, soak overnight in water to cover. Drain before starting the soup. Combine the ham with the peas and 3 quarts water in a 6-quart heavy pot. Bring to a boil, reduce heat, and cook 30 to 40 minutes, skimming frequently. Add the onions, leek, celery, carrots and potato. Add thyme, season to taste, and simmer slowly, uncovered, about 5 hours or until very thick, stirring occasionally. Remove the ham, cut into pieces and return to the soup with the sliced knockwurst 30 minutes before serving. Add the optional smoked salt and stir in parsley. Serve with whole-grain bread and sweet butter.

BROCCOLI BISQUE

Serves 8   Mrs. William Cork (Helen)
                                                Mrs. W. B. Hawkins (Sarah)

1-1/4 to 1-1/2 pounds fresh		2	tablespoons butter
	broccoli flowerets, trimmed	1	teaspoon salt
	OR	1 to 2 teaspoons curry powder	
2	packages frozen chopped	Dash pepper	
	broccoli	2	tablespoons lime juice
2	13-3/4-ounce cans chicken	8	lemon slices
	broth	1/2	cup dairy sour cream
1	medium onion, quartered	1	tablespoon snipped chives

Place broccoli in a large saucepan. Add broth, onion, butter, salt, curry powder and pepper. Bring to boiling. Reduce heat and simmer, covered, for 8 to 12 minutes or until just tender. Place half the broccoli and broth mixture at a time in blender container. Cover and blend until smooth. Repeat with remaining broccoli mixture. Stir in lime juice. Cover and refrigerate at least 4 hours. Ladle into small bowls. Top with a lemon slice, then a spoonful of sour cream, and a sprinkle of chives.

BEAUTIFUL EASY BISQUE

Serves 8   Mrs. J. P. Gardner, Jr. (Pam)

2   cups flaked canned crab or   2   10-3/4-ounce cans split pea soup
      lobster meat   2-1/2 cups cream or milk
6   tablespoons sherry   Salt and pepper to taste
2   10-3/4-ounce cans condensed tomato soup

Soak crab or lobster in sherry for 10 minutes. Combine soups and simmer until hot. Stir in cream or milk; add crab or lobster. Heat thoroughly, but do not allow to boil. Season with salt and pepper. Garnish with tiny shrimp.

OYSTER BISQUE

Serves 4   Representative T. W. Edwards, Jr.

2 to 4 tablespoons butter   1/2   cup cream
1/2   teaspoon grated onion   1/2   teaspoon salt
1 to 1-1/2 pints oysters with liquid 1/8   teaspoon pepper
1-1/2 cups milk   2   egg yolks, beaten

Saute butter and onions lightly in top of double boiler, over hot water. Add oysters, milk, cream, salt and pepper. When oysters float, and milk is hot, remove from heat and pour a small quantity over egg yolks. After mixing, add them slowly to the hot bisque. Heat slowly for 1 minute, but do not boil. (You can hold over hot water in a double boiler until ready to serve.) Garnish with chopped parsley.

SENATE BEAN SOUP

Yields: 4-1/2 quarts   Cookbook Committee Selection

1   pound dried beans (navy or   1   cup chopped onion
          great northern)   1   cup chopped celery
1-1/2 to 2 pounds shank or butt   2   cloves minced garlic
          end of smoked ham   Salt
3   medium potatoes, cooked   Freshly ground pepper
          and mashed

Wash and soak beans overnight in a large kettle. Next morning, add ham and simmer about 2 hours, or until beans begin to mush. Add remaining ingredients and simmer 1 hour. Remove ham; cut up meat, and return to soup. Season to taste. Can be frozen and reheated.

BORSCHT

Serves 4   Mrs. Alex S. Macaulay (Maria)

1	cup coarsely grated cabbage	1/2	teaspoon sugar
1	cup boiling water		Salt, freshly ground pepper
2	tablespoons butter	1 to 1-1/2 tablespoons fresh lemon
1/2	medium onion, finely chopped		juice
1	1-pound can whole or julienne	1/4	cup dry white wine
	beets		Sour cream
2	cups chicken stock		Snipped fresh dill (optional)

Cook the cabbage in the boiling water for 10 minutes. Melt the butter in a 3-quart heavy-bottomed saucepan, and cook the onion over low heat until translucent but not browned. Drain the beets, reserving the juice, and shred finely if using whole beets. There should be 2 cups of shredded beets. Add the chicken stock to the onion, and bring to a boil. Add the cabbage and the water in which it was cooked. Add the shredded beets, 1/2 cup reserved beet juice, sugar, salt and pepper to taste, and simmer over low heat for 10 minutes, skimming occasionally. Remove the pan from the heat, and add the lemon juice and wine. Return to the stove and bring just to the boiling point. Remove and chill thoroughly. Serve in punch cups with a bowl of sour cream to spoon over and snipped dill. Note: This borscht is equally delicious served hot, immediately after the final heating.

CREAM OF BROCCOLI SOUP

Mrs. Dill Blackwell (Margaret)

4	cups chopped broccoli (can include stems, peeled and sliced thin)	4	tablespoons butter
		2-1/2	cups water or stock
		2	cups milk
1	cup broccoli flowerets (put aside)	1/2	cup sour cream (or evaporated milk)
1-1/2 cups chopped onion		1/2	cup buttermilk (if desired)
1	medium green bell pepper, chopped	1	bay leaf
			Thyme or basil to taste

Sauté onions in butter with bay leaf until tender. Add bell pepper, chopped broccoli, water or stock and salt to taste. Cook until broccoli is tender but still bright green (about 10 minutes). Purée in blender or food processor until smooth. Whisk in sour cream or evaporated milk. Add buttermilk just before serving. Steam broccoli flowerets just until tender. If serving right away, combine flowerets with soup, and add buttermilk. If holding, to serve later, put broccoli flowerets in soup bowls, and pour soup over them when ready to serve. Can be topped with a dollop of sour cream and a little chopped parsley or onion.

CONSOMMÉ'

Serves 6   Mrs. E. Crosby Lewis (Cleo)

1-1/2 quarts beef stock, strained   1/2 pound lean beef, coarsely
1   carrot, sliced   chopped
1   onion, minced   2   egg whites, lightly beaten
2   celery stalks, sliced   Salt and pepper
1/2 cup Madiera or sherry

Place all of the ingredients in a pan. Stirring constantly, bring the mixture
to a boil over medium high heat. Stop stirring just as the boil is reached.
Cover the pan and simmer over low heat for about 45 minutes. Skim off any
matter on the surface of the bouillon. Line a large strainer with several thick-
nesses of cheesecloth and ladle the consomme' through it. Return to pan.
Add wine and correct seasoning. Bring to boil to evaporate the alcohol.

CAROLINA CORN SOUP

Serves 8 to 12   Mrs. Robert N. McLellan (Doris)

1/4 cup butter   1   egg, beaten
1/4 cup finely chopped onion   1-1/4 teaspoon salt
3   cups fresh or frozen corn   1/2 teaspoon white pepper
4   cups half-and-half

Melt the butter, add the onion and sauté until soft, but not brown. Add the
corn and cook for 5 minutes, but do not brown. Add cream and beaten egg.
Cook until mixture begins to boil, stirring constantly, about 3 minutes. Season
to taste. Let cool slightly, put in a blender and whip until creamy. Strain and
reheat. Ladle from a tureen into demitasse cups with cheese straws (see index) to
munch on. May be served cold.

CRAB CHOWDER

Serves 6   Mrs. Woody McKay (Nancy)

1/2 cup chopped onion   18   ounce can cream style corn
1/2 cup chopped celery   2   tablespoons chopped pimento
1   tablespoon margarine   1/4 teaspoon salt
3   cups milk   1/2 teaspoon thyme
1   10-ounce can cream of   1   bay leaf
     potato soup   1/4 cup sherry
17 1/2-ounce can crab meat   1/2 cup chopped parsley
     (or fresh 1 pound)

Sauté onions and celery. Cook all ingredients (except sherry and parsley) 15
minutes. Stir in sherry and remove bay leaf. Garnish with parsley.

CLAM CHOWDER

Serves 6 to 8   Representative T. W. Edwards, Jr.

4   tablespoons butter   3   6-1/2-ounce cans clams, strained
1   large chopped onion   (reserve liquid and add water
3   tablespoons flour   to make 3 cups)
2   cups raw diced potatoes, peeled 4   cups milk

Sauté onion in butter. Add flour, stirring constantly for 1 minute. Add clam juice water and milk, and stir until blended. Add potatoes and cook until tender. Add clams and heat thoroughly. Season to taste.

CRAB SOUP

Serves 6   Mrs. J. E. Kinard, Jr. (Ellen)

1   7-1/2-ounce can Harris white   1   10-3/4-ounce can shrimp soup
      crab meat   1-1/2 cups milk
1   10-3/4-ounce can pepperpot   1/4 cup dry sherry
      soup
1   10-3/4-ounce can chicken gumbo soup

Combine soups and milk; stir in crab meat. Cook over low heat until almost boiling, stirring often. Add sherry before serving.

MANNING CRAB SOUP VIA MARYLAND

Serves 4   Mrs. John C. Land, III (Marie)

8 to 10 steamed crabs, outer shell,   2   28-ounce cans tomatoes
      devils fingers, etc. removed.   1   large onion
      Leave on small legs and claws   8   slices bacon
      and leave meat in cartilage,   2   cups water (or more for right
      but break crab in half down   soup consistency)
      the middle.   Seasoning to taste
1   16-ounce package frozen mixed vegetables, or cut-up fresh vegetables
      as you would use in vegetable soup

Fry bacon until crisp, remove from pan and sauté onions in renderings. Add water and simmer 10 minutes; add frozen mixed vegetables or fresh vegetables as you would to vegetable soup. Add juice of tomatoes and broken-up whole tomatoes. Boil until vegetables are cooked; drop crabs into soup and simmer on low for 20 minutes. Add seasonings according to how much you already seasoned the crabs. This is served in bowls with spoons, but it is proper to pick up the crab and pick it with your fingers.

SHE-CRAB SOUP

Serves 6   Mrs. L. Edward Bennett (Peggy)

1/2	stick margarine or butter	1/4	teaspoon black or white pepper
1-1/2	tablespoons flour	1	teaspoon Worcestershire sauce
1	quart milk		Salt to taste (Lawry's Seasoned Salt)
1	pint cream	1	pound white crab meat
2	tablespoons grated onion	2	tablespoons dry sherry
1/4	teaspoon mace or nutmeg		

Melt butter in heavy saucepan or top of double boiler and blend with flour until smooth. Blend in onion. Add milk, gradually, stirring constantly. Add cream and all other seasonings except sherry. Cook slowly until hot. Add crab meat. When hot and slightly thickened, add sherry and serve. NOTE: If unable to obtain she-crabs, crumble yolk of hard boiled egg in bottom of soup bowls before serving.

CURRIED CARDINAL CUP

Serves 9 to 10   Mrs. Heyward E. McDonald (Sylvia)

2	10-3/4-ounce cans tomato soup	2	cans water
2	10-3/4-ounce cans pea soup	1/2	teaspoon salt
1	10-3/4-ounce can consommé	1	tablespoon lemon juice
1	tablespoon parsley flakes	1	teaspoon curry

Bring to boil. Reduce heat and simmer, covered, for 30 minutes. Add curry. Sprinkle with parsley. I like serving my guests something to sip before they go to the buffet table. I serve this from a tureen (or pot on stove) into demitasse cups.

GAZPACHO

Serves 6 to 8   Mrs. J. P. Gardner, Jr. (Pam)

3-1/2	cups tomato juice	1/4	cup red wine vinegar
1-1/2	cups cucumber chunks	1/3	cup onion, cut up
1	small green pepper in chunks	2	slices white bread
2	cloves garlic, minced		Salt, pepper and Tabasco sauce to
3	tablespoons olive oil		taste

Blend all ingredients in blender. Refrigerate. The color of Gazpacho should be exploited. Serve this soup in crystal as it gives a glow to the table. Ladle into punch cups with a cucumber slice.

CLEMSON HOUSE OF LEUNG EGG DROP SOUP

Serves 4   Mrs. Robert McLellan (Doris)

8	cups clear chicken broth	4	teaspoons corn starch
1	teaspoon salt	1/8	cup cold water
1	teaspoon sugar	1	drop yellow food color
1/4	teaspoon monosodium glutamate	2	eggs, beaten

Bring the first four ingredients to a boil. Add corn starch mixed with cold water to thicken. Add food color. Before serving, add the beaten eggs, but do not stir. Remove from flame. Serve at once in individual soup bowls. Garnish with chopped green onion and a generous amount of CHINESE NOODLES: Cut egg roll wrappers or skins (buy in the produce section) in half and slice in 1/4-inch thick strips. Drop in 340 degree hot oil in a deep fry pan. When the skins come to the top of the oil, the noodles are cooked. Remove and put on paper towels.

GARLIC SOUP

Serves 6   Mrs. T. W. Edwards, Jr. (Dottie)

2	large heads peeled garlic cloves, chopped roughly	Pinch	saffron
2	quarts boiling water	3	egg yolks
2	teaspoons salt	1/4	cup olive oil
2	whole cloves		Parsley
1/4	teaspoon sage		French Bread slices, hard-toasted
1/4	teaspoon thyme	1	cup grated Swiss or Parmesan cheese
1/2	bay leaf		

Place the garlic and seasonings in a saucepan of boiling water and boil slowly for 30 minutes. Correct seasonings. Beat the egg yolks in a soup tureen for a minute until they are thick and sticky. Drop by drop, beat in the olive oil as for making a mayonnaise. Just before serving, beat a ladleful of hot soup into the egg mixture by droplets. Gradually strain in the rest, beating, and pressing the juice out of the garlic. Garnish with parsley. Serve immediately, accompanied by the bread and cheese.

RICH BROTH FOR WEAKNESS, X-RAY'S AND ULCERS
Cookbook Committee Selection

Cut a 4-pound round steak in cubes. Place in a 1/2 gallon Mason glass jar and screw top on. Place jar in a deep container of water to cover 3/4's of jar. Set on stove. When water boils, turn to low and leave 6 to 8 hours. Keep adding water to container as it cooks down. Strain. Discard meat. Serve 1/4 pint broth at a serving. Salt if needed. If not having X-Ray's, you may not want to strain, but discard meat.

LEMON SOUP
Serves 4   Mrs. Dill Blackwell (Margaret)

4	14-1/2-ounce Swanson's chicken broth	1/3	cup rice
1/2	cup finely grated carrots	2	egg yolks
Chopped parsley sprigs		Juice of one large lemon	

Wash rice in several waters and drain well. Add carrots and parsley to chicken broth and bring to a boil. Slowly add rice. Simmer 30 minutes. Beat egg yolks with lemon juice thoroughly. Slowly add about one cup of hot stock to lemon-egg mixture. Reduce heat on stock to low and add lemon-egg broth mixture when boiling has stopped. Stir to prevent curdling.

SIX HOUR FRENCH ONION SOUP
Serves 8 to 10   Mrs. Robert N. McLellan (Doris)

1	stick butter	1-1/3 to 3 tablespoons salt	
3	pounds purple onions, peeled and thinly sliced	8 to 10 thick slices French bread, toasted	
10	cups water	2	cups freshly grated Swiss or Parmesan cheese
6	beef bouillon cubes		

Cook the onions slowly with the butter in two heavy-bottomed, 4-quart covered saucepans, for 15 minutes. Add the water and beef bouillons. Bring to a boil, stirring frequently. Reduce the heat to simmer. Cover and simmer for 5 hours. Add the salt and continue cooking for 1 more hour. May be frozen or refrigerated for two days at this point. (Do not oversalt as it may be too salty when reheated.) To serve, reheat onion soup on top of stove. Preheat the oven to 400 degrees. Ladle the soup into individual bowls before adding the toasted French bread to each, and sprinkle it generously with the cheese. Bake the soup in the middle of the oven for 10 to 15 minutes, or until the cheese bubbles.

QUICK FRENCH ONION SOUP

Serves 4   Representative Lloyd Hendricks

3 onions, sautéed (don't brown)	Onion powder to taste
2 cans beef broth bouillon	Celery seed to taste
Oregano to taste	Tabasco sauce to taste
Garlic powder to taste	

Add the onions, seasonings and Tabasco sauce to the bouillon and cook for approximately 1/2 hour. Put into soup bowls and put toasted sour dough bread slices on top with Mozzarella cheese. Bake 10 minutes at 400 degrees.

OLD FASHIONED POTATO SOUP

Serves 6   Mrs. Robert C. Lake, Jr. (Carolyn)

4 medium potatoes, diced	1 tablespoon salt
1 large onion, diced	1/4 teaspoon pepper
1/2 cup celery, diced	8 slices bacon, diced
1-1/4 cups water	2 tablespoons minced parsley
3 cups milk	

Combine potatoes, onion, celery and water. Cover and simmer 45 minutes or until done. Put vegetables through a course sieve and return to the water in which they were cooked. Add milk, salt and pepper. Reheat. Cook bacon until crisp. Just before serving, float parsley and crisp bacon pieces on soup.

SPINACH VICHYSSOISE

Serves 8   Mrs. T. W. Edwards, Jr. (Dottie)

1/4 cup butter	1 carrot, sliced
4 leeks, white part only	4 cups chicken broth
1/2 cup chopped onion	1 teaspoon salt
2 large Idaho potatoes, peeled and sliced	1 pound lightly cooked spinach
	2 cups half-and-half or milk

Melt butter; sauté leeks and onions at medium heat until yellow, not brown. Add potatoes, carrot, chicken broth and salt. Cover and simmer until potatoes and carrots are soft. Cool. Put potato mixture in blender with 1 cup of cooked spinach. Add half-and-half, correct seasonings and chill. Purée remaining spinach and season to taste. Ladle soup from a crystal pitcher into very cold punch cups with a spoonful of pureed spinach swished on top. If potato mixture becomes too dry during cooking, add more chicken stock. Variation: Omit leeks, potatoes and carrots. Add 1-1/2 tbls. flour, 1 more lb. spinach, only 1 cup cream, and 2 tbls. butter.

CUCUMBER VICHYSSOISE

Mrs. William N. Cork (Helen)

1/4	cup sliced onion	1/8	teaspoon pepper
2	cups diced unpeeled cucumbers	2	cups chicken stock
1/2	cup finely diced potatoes, raw	1/2	teaspoon salt
2	sprigs parsley and dill	1/4	teaspoon dry mustard

Put all ingredients together and boil until potatoes are barely tender. The blender will do the rest. Chill. You may sprinkle chopped chives on top when served.

POTATO VICHYSSOISE

Serves 4   Mrs. B. E. Thrailkill, Jr. (Peggy)

2	cups diced potatoes	1-1/2	teaspoon salt
1	medium onion, chopped	1/8	teaspoon pepper
3	tablespoons butter or margarine	2	cups milk
1/2	cup water	1	tablespoon parsley flakes
1/8	teaspoon minced garlic		

Cover potatoes with water, add all ingredients except milk. Cook until potatoes are done. Add milk and heat. Serve hot or put in a blender. Chill. Serve in a crystal pitcher. Ladle into demitasse cups and sprinkle with chives. Serve while guests are mingling.

BEEF VEGETABLE SOUP

Serves 10 to 12   Mrs. Robert N. McLellan (Doris)

4	pounds meaty soup bone	2	cups stewed tomatoes
1	chopped onion	1	4-ounce can tomato purée
1/2	bunch chopped celery	3	large diced potatoes
1/4	pound butter	4	teaspoons salt
2	chopped onions	1/2	teaspoon pepper
1/2	bunch chopped celery	1/4	pound frozen green peas
3	large sliced carrots	1/4	pound frozen baby lima beans
3	chopped green peppers	4	drops Tabasco sauce

Place soup bone in large pot with onion and celery. Cover with water and cook slowly for 4 hours. Skim off top of beef stock occasionally. Sauté 2 chopped onions, 1/2 bunch chopped celery, carrots and green peppers in butter. Add tomatoes, tomato purée and potatoes. Cook 30 minutes over medium heat. Add beef stock, salt and pepper. Remove meat from beef bone, chop in small pieces and add to soup. Then add peas, lima beans and Tabasco. Cook 30 minutes over low heat or until beans are done.

EASY VEGETABLE SOUP

Serves 6   Mrs. Walter Bristow, Jr. (Stewart)

1   onion   1   can water
1   pound ground chuck   1   can mixed vegetables
1   16-ounce can tomatoes   1 to 2 tablespoons Worcestershire
1   6-ounce can tomato paste   sauce
1   can beef broth   1/2 teaspoon garlic salt
                                        Salt and pepper

Brown onion in a little oil. Add and brown ground chuck, garlic salt and
Worcestershire sauce. Season to taste. Add tomatoes, tomato paste, beef
broth, water and mixed vegetables. Stir well and simmer 30 to 45 minutes.

ZUCCHINI SQUASH SOUP

Serves 6   Mrs. Nick A. Theodore (Emilie)

2   medium yellow squash   4   cups chicken stock
2   small zucchini   Salt and pepper to taste
1-1/2 cups celery leaves   Celery salt
3   tablespoons butter   2   tablespoons finely chopped
                                           parsley

Chop unpeeled squash and zucchini into small pieces. In a covered pan, cook
squash, zucchini and celery leaves with butter over very low heat until tender
(about 20 minutes). Purée mixture in blender, adding 1 cup of stock. Mix
purée with rest of stock. Correct seasoning with salt, pepper and celery salt.
Bring back to boil. Serve hot or cold, garnished with parsley or chives.

SANDWICH LOAF

Mrs. Robert N. McLellan (Doris)

A sophisticated approach to serve dip, salad or sandwiches is to buy a 10-
inch or 12-inch round loaf of bread. Cut the top off about 1-inch from the
edge of the loaf. Scoop out all the bread inside, leaving only the shell. Prepare your small sandwiches (with crusts removed) and pile into the empty
bread shell. Cover with the top, plastic wrap and refrigerate or freeze. When
you serve, put the whole loaf, served on a big round board or platter, on the
table. This method keeps the sandwiches moist. Stand the top against the
side and put it back on if there is a lull in service. If you have a lot of sandwiches, put some on platter around the loaf. You can keep the bread shell
and freeze for future use, and it is always a conversation piece. Make two —
you will need one for refills. Set a bowl in shell for serving dip or salad.

CORNED BEEF SANDWICH SPREAD

Yields: 12 to 14   Mrs. Robert C. Lake, Jr. (Carolyn)

1-1/2 cups cabbage, finely grated
1   12-ounce can corned beef, flaked with fork
3/4   cup mayonnaise or salad dressing
3/4   cup sweet pickle cubes
2   teaspoons prepared mustard
1/2   teaspoon Nature's Season Blend
Salt and pepper to taste

Mix all ingredients, stirring well. Taste. Adjust seasonings. Spread on hamburger buns or bread and toast. Also, good cut in small sandwiches and served cold.

BARBECUE CORNED BEEF

Yields: 8 to 10   Mrs. Robert N. McLellan (Doris)

1   12-ounce can corned beef
1/4   cup chopped onion
1/4   cup chopped olives
2   tablespoons Worcestershire sauce
1/2   cup catsup
1   cup cubed sharp cheese
8 or 10 hamburger buns

Mix and spread heavily between hamburger buns. Wrap separately in foil and warm at 350 degrees for 15 minutes. These can be frozen before cooking.

EGG SALAD WITH SURPRISE TOPPING

Serves 4   Mrs. Robert McLellan (Doris)

1   cup mayonnaise
2   tablespoons chili sauce
1   tablespoon chopped green onion
1   tablespoon chopped green pepper
1   egg, boiled and chopped fine
4   hard boiled eggs, chopped
1 to 1-1/2 tablespoon horseradish sauce
1   tablespoon pickle relish
1/4   teaspoon salt
Pepper to taste
Shrimp, crab meat or chicken, diced (enough for 4 sandwiches)
8   thin white slices Pepperidge Farm Sandwich Bread

Mix together the first 5 ingredients and refrigerate the sauce the day before serving. Mix together the 4 eggs, horseradish sauce and pickle relish and season to taste. Put generous amount of filling in each sandwich. Wrap and refrigerate. When you get ready to serve, place a piece of lettuce on 4 plates and top with tomato slices. Top with sandwich. Top sandwich with a generous amount of diced shrimp, crab, or chicken. (I prefer to leave the shrimp whole.) Spoon sauce over top.

CUCUMBER SANDWICH SPREAD

Mrs. Robert C. Lake, Jr. (Carolyn)

1   large cucumber (grate and drain
    on paper towel. Twist towel
    with hands to get excess
    water out)
1   8-ounce package cream cheese
1/2 cup mayonnaise

1   tablespoon fresh lemon juice
3   small onions
Tabasco sauce
Garlic salt and seasoned pepper to
    taste

Combine ingredients. Season to taste.

CREAMED HAM AND CHICKEN

Serves 6

Mrs. Robert N. McLellan (Doris)

Buttered toast triangles or tart shells
1/4 cup chopped onion
1/3 cup butter
1/4 cup flour
1/2 teaspoon salt
1/4 teaspoon white pepper
1/4 teaspoon Accent
2   teaspoons prepared mustard

1   14-1/2 ounce can evaporated milk
1   cup water
1   4-ounce can sliced mushrooms
1/3 liquid from mushrooms
1/2 cup sliced olives
1-1/2 cups cooked chicken pieces
1-1/2 cups cooked ham pieces
Pimiento strips and parsley

Sauté onion in butter until soft. Push to one side. Blend in flour, salt, pepper, Accent and mustard. Remove from heat and add milk, water, mushrooms and 1/3 cup liquid from mushrooms. Bring to boiling, stirring constantly; cook 1 to 2 minutes longer. Stir in mushrooms, olives, chicken and ham and heat. Spoon into tart shells or over buttered toast triangles. Garnish with pimiento strips and snipped parsley. Serve at a SANDWICH LUNCHEON with *chilled broccoli bisque and *baklava or *praline crepes.

GIBSON GIRL SANDWICH SPREAD

Mrs. E. S. Lake (Sarah)

Mix 2 parts grated sharp cheese with one part equal amounts of mixed raisins and chopped pecans. Mix with mayonnaise (not salad dressing) until consistency of pimento cheese. Add a dash of cayenne pepper. Use brown bread to make sandwiches.

OPEN FACED CRAB SUPREME

Serves 4   Mrs. Larry A. Martin (Susan)

8	slices toast	1	teaspoon Worcestershire sauce
Tartar sauce		1/4	teaspoon lemon juice
2	cups crab meat	1/4	cup mayonnaise
Dash Tabasco sauce		1	cup grated American cheese

Spread toast with tartar sauce. Combine crab meat, Tabasco sauce, Worcestershire sauce, lemon juice and mayonnaise. Spread bread evenly with crab mixture. Top with grated cheese. Place under broiler until cheese melts. Cut 4 slices diagonally into halves. For each serving, place 1 whole slice in center of plate with 2 halves on opposite sides. Garnish with lettuce, tomato, olives and lemon wedges.

PARTY SHRIMP SPREAD

Yields: 6 dozen party-size sandwiches   Mrs. T. Ed Garrison (Juanita)

2	3-ounce packages cream cheese, softened (optional)	4	teaspoons lemon juice
2	pounds fresh shrimp	1	teaspoon grated lemon rind
2	tablespoons grated onion	1	teaspoon salt
2	tablespoons finely chopped celery	Black pepper	
		8 to 10 drops Tabasco sauce	
2	tablespoons finely chopped green pepper	Miracle Whip or Mayonnaise	
		78	thin slices bread

Cook and peel shrimp. Put through meat grinder 2 times. Mix together cream cheese, vegetables and seasonings. Add enough Miracle Whip to spread evenly on thin slices of bread. After making sandwiches cut ends off and cut in small squares. Sandwiches may be made ahead of time, wrapped and refrigerated.

MINCEMEAT SANDWICHES

Yields 48 ribbon sandwiches   Mrs. Ed Simpson (Maureen)

1	jar mincemeat with rum or brandy	1	cup pecans, chopped
		Mayonnaise to spread	
8	ounces cream cheese		

Mix all ingredients with enough mayonnaise for spreading consistency. Spread on bread of choice.

MUSHROOM SAUCE

Mrs. Marshall B. Williams (Margaret)

1	pound fresh sliced mushrooms	1	small carton sour cream
Butter		1	teaspoon dill seed

Sauté mushrooms in butter for about eight minutes. Add sour cream and dill seed. Serve on toast points. Good over baked chicken.

PIMENTO CHEESE

Mrs. Robert C. Lake, Jr. (Carolyn)

1/2	pound cheddar cheese, grated	1	teaspoon grated peeled onion
1/2	cup chopped, drained canned		(optional)
	pimentos	1/2	cup mayonnaise

Mash all ingredients into a spreading consistency in a medium sized mixing bowl. Cover and refrigerate.

BITE PIZZAS

Mrs. W. B. Hawkins (Sarah)

1	loaf party rye	1	tablespoon onion
2	cups sharp cheese, grated	1	cup mayonnaise
1	small jar chopped black olives	Bacon bits	

Mix together cheese, olives, onion and mayonnaise. Spread on slices of rye bread. Top with bacon bits. Bake at 300 degrees for 10 to 12 minutes.

PORK AND BEAN SANDWICH

Yield: 4 sandwiches   Mrs. Jeff Richardson, Jr. (Florence)

1	14-1/2-ounce can Pork and Beans	4	slices sharp Cheddar cheese, or enough to cover bread
4	slices bread	4	slices breakfast bacon, cut in half
4	slices onion		

Toast bread lightly on both sides and place on cookie sheet or shallow pan. On each slice of toasted bread, spread 1/4 of the Pork and Beans, 1 onion slice, 1 slice cheese and 2 halves of bacon. Broil slowly until bacon is done to desired degree.

RAISIN -NUT SANDWICH SPREAD

Mrs. Robert C. Lake, Jr. (Carolyn)
Mrs. H. E. Pearce, Jr. (Jo)

1	egg	1	cup mayonnaise
1	cup sugar	1	cup raisins, chopped
Lump of butter the size of a walnut		1/2	cup nuts, chopped (or peanut butter)
Juice and grated rind of 1 lemon			

Beat egg, add sugar, butter and lemon. Stir in double boiler until mixture thickens. Remove from heat and beat in mayonnaise. Add nuts and raisins.

SLOPPY JOES

Serves 10 to 12   Mrs. Jarvis Klapman (Arlene)

1	pound ground beef	2/3	cup catsup
1	medium onion, chopped	2	tablespoons vinegar
1-1/2	tablespoons flour	1	tablespoon Worcestershire Sauce
2	tablespoons sugar	2	level teaspoons prepared mustard
1	cup water		

Brown the meat and onions in a skillet, drain. Add the remaining ingredients when the browning is completed. Stir, then cover and simmer for 30 minutes. Serve hot in hot hamburger buns.

SPINACH SANDWICHES

Yields 13   Mrs. Walter Bristow, Jr. (Stewart)
Mrs. Ramon Schwartz (Rosa)

1	10-ounce package frozen chopped spinach	1/2	cup dried parsley flakes
1	pint Hellman's mayonnaise	1	drop Tabasco sauce
1/2	cup dried minced onion flakes	1	tablespoon lemon juice

Cook and drain spinach. Cool. Add mayonnaise, onion flakes, parsley flakes, lemon juice and Tabasco. Stir well and refrigerate overnight. Spread on Roman Meal bread.

PHIL'S TOMATO SANDWICH

Serves 1   Mrs. Phil Leventis (Ev)

1 slice bread	Ripe tomato
Mayonnaise	Shredded Cheddar cheese
Mushrooms, fresh	Shredded Mozzarella cheese

Spread mayonnaise on slice bread. Add sliced tomato, top with mushrooms, sprinkle Cheddar and Mozzarella cheese on top. Place in toaster oven and remove once cheese is melted.

VEGETABLE SANDWICH SPREAD

Mrs. Robert C. Lake, Jr. (Carolyn)
Mrs. Nick Theodore (Emilie)

1/4 cup water	1/2 teaspoon paprika
1 envelope plain gelatin	1 cup grated cabbage
2 tablespoons sugar	4 carrots
2-1/4 tablespoons vinegar	1/2 cup green pepper
1/4 teaspoon black pepper	1 medium onion
2 teaspoons salt	1 large cucumber (peeled)
1/2 teaspoon Worcestershire sauce	3/4 cup mayonnaise
	2 tomatoes (optional)

Heat first 8 ingredients until gelatin dissolves. Chop all vegetables and drain well. Mix mayonnaise with vegetables. Then combine with gelatin mixture. If used as a salad, use 2 envelopes of gelatin.

VARIATION: Mrs. John M. Rucker (Harriet)

Soften 3 large packages cream cheese and add to 2 cups grated carrots, 1 tablespoon Worcestershire, 1 tablespoon grated onion and juice and season to taste. Spread on wheat bread.

In 1786, the General Assembly reluctantly agreed to move the state capitol from Charleston to the interior.

When the bill, making Columbia the new state capitol, became the law in 1786, there was no city of Columbia. The legislature agreed to purchase two plantations from Colonel Thomas Taylor that were located on the banks of the Congaree River. When the General Assembly first met in the new capitol in 1790, it was little more than a rude frontier village.

Columbia was from the very first planned as a capital city. The regular grid surveyed along the river provided for orderly development. The naming of the streets reflected the state-wide purpose of the city. Assembly Street, running east-west, and Senate Street, running north-south, were designed to be the two main arteries. The streets parallel to Assembly bore the names of Revolutionary heroes. South of Assembly they were named for officers of the Continental Line who had fought in the state; north of Assembly, they were named for South Carolina's guerilla fighters - Richardson, Marion, Bull, Pickens, Harden, and Sumter - a veritable roll call of men who helped wrest the state from Britain's grasp.

As the town grew, it took on a more permanent appearance. The opening of the South Carolina College (now USC) in 1805 was heralded across the state as a means of bringing together the sons of the upcountry and low-country so that "the political union" of the state would be advanced. The State Hospital, the Columbia City-Hall and Market, and the new sanctuaries of the Baptist, Episcopal, Methodist and Presbyterian congregations gave antebellum Columbia a more settled look.

The meeting of the Secession Convention in Columbia, December 17, 1860 was the beginning of a period of trial and economic chaos from which it took nearly a century for the city to recover. As a war-time capital, Columbia became a central supply and refugee point. The night of February 17, 1865 was one of terror for the populace. Fires, carried by extraordinarily high winds, swept through about one-third of the city. The entire business district and portions of major residential areas were levelled. A few landmarks were spared; the college buildings, Trinity Episcopal Church, and the officers' quarters of the Arsenal Academy; but many, including the first State House designed by James Hoban, were not.

Although the city eased its way out of the doldrums of the post-Civil War South, it was not until the post-World War II years that Columbia began a period of amazing growth that has continued unabated.

As Columbia approaches its bicentennial, it can look back on two centuries with pride. It has been the scene of events that shaped the course not only of the state's history, but that of the South and nation. Columbia is many things to many people - Fort Jackson to military personnel, USC to the alumni of the state's first University, a market to farmers, a distribution point and manufacturing center for industry, and a home to more than 100,000 - but above all else, for all 3 million South Carolinians it is their state capitol.

KERSHAW COUNTY

Organized in 1798, Kershaw County has seen many of the state's most important events take place within its boundaries. It is named for Joseph Kershaw, noted Revoluntionary war figure and founder of Camden. The first settlements were made around 1750 by a colony of Quakers at Pinetree just below present day Camden. They established a church and built a flour mill on Pine Creek. The small community prospered and by the end of the decade numerous other small farmers had located in the territory.

In 1760, Joseph Kershaw built his first store on a parcel of land just north of the Quaker community. As the business grew Kershaw began to expand his enterprises into land development. Lots were marked off and streets designed for a new town which Kershaw called Camden, after the British statesman Lord Camden. The new city attracted residents from throughout the area and by 1769 the city was given a charter. When Kershaw County was organized after the Revolution, Camden was designated as the county seat.

The events of the Revolutionary War almost destroyed Camden. As the most important trading center in the up-state, Camden's prosperity was dependent on the uninterrupted flow of trade from the backwoods settlements. Fourteen battles, the most important being the Battle of Camden, where the Americans under Gates were handed their worst defeat of the war, occurred in Kershaw County. Much of Camden and the surrounding countryside was destroyed during the war; prosperity did not return to the district until the early 1800s.

Today Kershaw County is best known as the home of some of the best horse racing in the south and it hosts the Carolina Cup, a premier racing event. During the colonial and antebellum periods there were numerous race tracks located in the county; plantation owners would frequently get together for challenge matches to see who had the best stables in the territory. After the Civil War the racing tradition was revived and spectators from as far away as Charleston would come to see the scheduled events.

The lively past of Kershaw County has made it one of the top tourist attractions in the state. The colonial attractiveness of Camden and the historic points of interests which abound in the county make Kershaw one of the state's prized communities.

THE ROBERT MILLS HOUSE

The Robert Mills House, built in Columbia in 1820, was designed by Robert Mills. The restored house is open to the public.

salads and dressings

BLUEBERRY SALAD

Serves 15   Mrs. Walter Bristow, Jr. (Stewart)

2 3-ounce packages blackberry-   1 8-ounce package cream cheese,
   flavored gelatin   softened
1 16-ounce can blueberries   1 8-ounce cup sour cream
1 20-ounce can crushed pine-   1/2 cup sugar
   apple with heavy syrup   1 teaspoon vanilla
                                     1 cup pecan pieces, chopped fine

Put gelatin in 2 cups boiling water and dissolve until cool. Add the blueberries and pineapple to gelatin mixture and put into a 3-quart casserole. Refrigerate until firm. Soften the cream cheese and cream in mixer. Add sugar, vanilla and sour cream. Spread on congealed salad and sprinkle nuts on top.

CHERRY CONGEALED SALAD

Serves 10 to 12   Mrs. Mona Chapman

2 3-ounce packages cherry   1 8-ounce package cream cheese,
   flavored gelatin   softened
2 cups hot water   1 8-ounce carton sour cream
1 8-ounce can crushed pineapple 1/2 cup sugar
1 21-ounce can cherry pie filling 1 teaspoon vanilla

Dissolve gelatin in hot water. Add pineapple and cherry pie filling. Mix well and pour into a 9x12-inch pan. Chill in refrigerator until congealed. Beat cream cheese and sugar together. Add vanilla and fold in sour cream. Spread over congealed salad. Refrigerate.

COCA-COLA SALAD

Serves 12   Mrs. Paul W. Derrick (Robin)

1 3-ounce package cherry gelatin   1 20-ounce can crushed pineapple
1 3-ounce package strawberry   1 8-ounce package cream cheese
   gelatin   12 ounce Coke
1 16-ounce can dark Bing   1 cup chopped pecans
   cherries, pitted

Drain cherries and pineapple, saving juice. Dissolve gelatin in hot juice. Cut cream cheese in very small chunks and add to gelatin mixture. Add cherries, pineapple, Coke and pecans. Pour into a mold and chill.

SALADS AND DRESSINGS

CONGEALED SALAD

Serves 6 to 8   Mrs. Grady Patterson, Jr. (Margie)

2   3-ounce packages apricot   1-3/4 cups buttermilk
       gelatin   8 or 9 ounces whipped topping
1   can crushed pineapple with juice (medium or large size)

Heat gelatin with pineapple and juice until bubbly. Mix together thoroughly
the buttermilk and whipped topping. Fold in the gelatin-pineapple mixture.
Pour into ring mold or dish and refrigerate. Unmold on serving platter. Fill
center and garnish outside the ring with fresh fruits in season, such as strawberries, grapes and peach slices.

MOLDED EGGS AND SHRIMP

Serves 6 to 8   Mrs. M. J. Cooper (Melba)

4-1/2 teaspoons unflavored gelatin   6   hard-cooked eggs, peeled and
       (1-1/2 envelopes)   sliced thin
1/3 cup dry white wine or cold   2   pounds cooked shrimp, sliced if
       water   large
2-1/2 cups seasoned chicken broth   Large black olives

Soften the gelatin in the wine, or cold water if you do not want the wine
flavor. Set aside. Heat the chicken broth to boiling, remove from heat and
add the softened gelatin. Cool until syrupy in texture. Pour a thin layer of
the gelatin mixture in a 1-1/2-quart fish or chicken mold and one layer of
the sliced eggs and slivers of the black olives or any other decoration you
might prefer. Refrigerate. When firm mold with alternate layers of the
shrimp and eggs, and the remaining black olives. Pour the rest of the syrupy
mixture over, cover with foil and refrigerate for several hours. Use this as a
quick method for molding seafoods, chicken and vegetables. For meats you
may prefer using beef consomme, but use the white wine for flavor.

HOLIDAY CRANBERRY SALAD

Serves 8 to 12   Mrs. Larry A. Martin (Susan)

1 6-ounce package raspberry
   gelatin
2 cups boiling water
1 tablespoon unflavored gelatin
1-1/2 cups cold water
1 16-ounce can whole cranberry
   sauce
1 8-ounce can crushed pineapple, reserve juice

1 orange, peeled and ground fine
1/2 cup celery, chopped and blanched
1/2 cup chopped nuts

DRESSING:

1/2 cup mayonnaise
1/2 cup cream or sour cream
1 banana

Dissolve gelatins with boiling water, add cold water and pineapple juice. Chill. When the gelatin is partially congealed, add the rest of the ingredients. Pour into a bundt pan lightly rubbed with mayonnaise. Chill until firm. Turn out and serve with CREAM DRESSING: 1/2 cup mayonnaise, mixed with 1/2 cup cream or sour cream and 1 finely mashed banana. This cream dressing is nice spooned over any fresh, frozen or congealed fruit salad.

CUCUMBER ASPIC

Mrs. Robert C. Lake, Jr. (Carolyn)

1 3-ounce package lime gelatin
1 teaspoon salt
1 cup boiling water
2 tablespoons vinegar
1 teaspoon onion, grated

1/2 cup mayonnaise
1 cup sour cream
2 cups cucumbers, chopped fine
   and drained
20 paper thin unpeeled cucumber
   slices

Let gelatin partially congeal; whip until fluffy. Blend in mayonnaise, sour cream, vinegar, cucumbers and onion. Pour into mold lined with thin cucumber slices. Refrigerate at least 3 hours. When ready to serve invert on platter. Fill center with cherry tomatoes and pass sour cream for topping.

CUCUMBER MOUSSE

Serves 8   Mrs. Jarvis Klapman (Arlene)
                             Mrs. Horace C. Smith (Dot)

3/4 cup boiling water
1 package lime flavored gelatin
1 cup cottage cheese
1 cup mayonnaise

2 tablespoons grated onion
3/4 cup grated cucumber with
   peeling left on
1 cup slivered almonds (optional)

Pour boiling water on gelatin, cool; add cheese, mayonnaise, grated onion, cucumber and nuts. Pour into a wet ring mold or bundt pan and refrigerate. This is a good salad to accompany any fish entree. Unmold onto a dish for a buffet and fill the center with a seafood salad.

IMPERIAL SALAD

Serves 6 to 8   Mrs. John M. Rucker (Harriet)

1/2 teaspoon salt	1 large can crushed pineapple
1 cup chopped celery	1 cup chopped nuts
1 6-ounce package lemon gelatin	1 large can pimento, sliced
1 cup boiling water	Juice of 1 lemon

Put salt on celery so it will soak in. Dissolve gelatin in boiling water. Add pineapple (juice included), nuts and pimento. Let cool. When cool, add celery and lemon juice. Pour into molds.

MANDARIN ORANGE SALAD

Serves 12 to 15   Mrs. Marion Kinon (Reba)
                                                 Senator Nell Smith

1 6-ounce package orange flavored gelatin	1 20-ounce can crushed pineapple
2 cups hot water	TOPPING:
2 11-ounce cans mandarin oranges, drained	1 envelope Dream Whip
	1 3-1/8-ounce package instant lemon pudding
1 small can frozen orange juice	1 cup milk

Dissolve gelatin in boiling water. Add remaining salad ingredients and pour into a 9x13-inch dish. Chill in refrigerator until congealed. Mix pudding and milk. Combine with Dream Whip. Spread over congealed mixture. Refrigerate two hours.

MOLDED TOMATO SOUP SALAD

Serves 6   Mrs. William Cork (Helen)

1 10-3/4-ounce can Campbell's tomato soup	1/2 cup green pepper, chopped fine
	1/2 cup onion, chopped
1 can water	2 3-ounce packages cream cheese
1/2 cup stuffed green olives, chopped	2 envelopes unflavored gelatin in 1/2 cup water
1/2 cup celery, chopped	1 cup mayonnaise

Bring tomato soup and water to a boil. Mix in dissolved gelatin. Add cream cheese and mix until smooth. Refrigerate. When partly cold add vegetables and mayonnaise. Chill at least three hours in one large oiled mold or several small molds. Serve on lettuce with mayonnaise and paprika.

VARIATION: Mrs. Robert C. Lake, Jr. (Carolyn)

For MOLDED TOMATO-TUNA SALAD, add 1 6-1/2-ounce can light tuna. Chill until firm. Turn out on salad leaves and serve with: 1/2 cup mayonnaise mixed with 1/2 cup sour cream and 1 cup finely diced celery.

SPINACH MOLD

Serves 10 to 12   Mrs. W. B. Hawkins (Sarah)

1	envelope unflavored gelatin	1/2	cup chopped celery
1/2	cup cold water	1/2	cup chopped onion
2	teaspoons sugar	1/2	cup mayonnaise
1/2	teaspoon salt	12	ounces cottage cheese
1/3	cup lemon juice and water	Dash Tabasco	
	to make 1/2 cup	1	teaspoon Worcestershire
1	10-ounce package frozen,	Bundt pan, sprayed with Pam	
	chopped spinach, cooked and drained		

Soften gelatin in water; stir over low heat until dissolved. Stir in sugar and salt. Remove from heat. Add lemon juice and water. Fold the vegetables into the gelatin mixture. In separate dish, mix together the next four ingredients. Gradually add this mixture to the other ingredients, mixing until well blended. Pour into a bundt pan or ring mold and refrigerate until ready to serve. Unmold on serving tray and garnish with pimento strips. Especially good with any ham preparation.

STRAWBERRY SALAD

Serves 20   Mrs. Mona Chapman

2-1/2 cups pretzels, coarsely		1	package Dream Whip, prepared
	broken	2	small packages strawberry gelatin
1-1/2 sticks butter, melted		2	cups water
8	ounces cream cheese, room	2	10-ounce packages frozen straw-
	temperature		berries, thawed
1	cup sugar		

Mix together and bake the first two ingredients 10 minutes at 350 degrees on cookie sheet with sides. Stir twice and cool. Spread in a 13x9x1-3/4-inch dish. Set aside. Combine cream cheese and sugar. Fold in Dream Whip and put on top of pretzel layer. Refrigerate. Dissolve gelatin in water. Add strawberries and refrigerate. After mixture begins to gel, pour over cream cheese layer. Refrigerate.

TOMATO MEDLEY ASPIC

Serves 8   Mrs. Joseph F. Anderson, Jr. (Susan)

1	1-pound can whole tomatoes, cut up and reserve juice	1/2	cup thinly sliced celery, cut on diagonal and blanched
1	3-ounce package lemon gelatin	1/4	cup thinly sliced green pepper, blanched
1	teaspoon salt		
3	tablespoons vinegar	1/4	cup green onion, sliced thin
2	teaspoons sugar	1/2	cup thinly sliced cucumber, well
1	teaspoon Worcestershire sauce		scrubbed and skin left on

Heat juice and tomatoes. Add gelatin and cool until thick. Add the next four ingredients. Cool until thickened. Blanch the celery and green peppers in boiling water for 1 minute. The color is better. Add all the vegetables to the thickened mixture. Pour into a bundt pan or ring mold. Refrigerate for several hours. Turn out onto salad greens and fill center with a salad or garnish of your choice.

UTAH'S STRAWBERRY SALAD

Serves 6   Mrs. T. Bruce Smith, III (Dot)

1	3-ounce package strawberry gelatin	1	cup cottage cheese (I usually use a carton)
1	8-ounce can crushed pineapple (use juice, too)	1/2	cup nuts, chopped
		1	small carton Cool Whip

Boil pineapple and juice two minutes. Dissolve gelatin in 1/4 cup hot water. Add to pineapple and boil three minutes. Let cool. Add nuts, Cool Whip and cottage cheese. Mix well. Pour into desired molds. Chill, serve on lettuce.

PAPER CUP FROZEN SALAD

Serves 12   Mrs. Dick Elliott (Anne)

2	cups sour cream	1	banana, diced
1	tablespoon lemon juice	4	drops red food color
1/2	cup sugar	1/4	cup chopped pecans
1/8	teaspoon salt	1	1-pound can pitted dark sweet
1	8-ounce can crushed pineapple, well drained		Bing cherries, well drained

Combine sour cream, lemon juice, sugar, salt, pineapple, banana pieces and enough red color to give a pink tint. Lightly fold in nuts and cherries. Spoon into paper muffin cups (large size) which have been placed in 3-inch muffin pans. Freeze. Cover with foil and store in freezer. Remove from freezer about 15 minutes before serving to loosen paper cups from pan. Peel off paper cup and place on lettuce or serve in dessert dish.

FROZEN FRUIT SALAD

Serves 10 to 12   Mrs. Thomas L. Hughston, Jr. (Jeanne)

1   3-ounce package cream cheese,   6   large marshmallows (cut up) or a
        softened   handful of small marsh-
1/3 cup mayonnaise   mallows
1   teaspoon lemon juice   1/4 cup mandarin oranges (1 small
2   egg whites   can)
1/3 cup sugar   1   pound can fruit cocktail, drained
1   cup Cool Whip   2   tablespoons maraschino cherries
                                   1/4 cup chopped nuts

Blend first three ingredients. Beat egg whites until foamy; add sugar and beat
until stiff. Fold egg whites and Cool Whip into cheese mixture. Add all other
ingredients. Place in a 9x12-inch pan and freeze.

COLD SPICED FRUIT

Serves 15   Mrs. Robert C. Lake, Jr. (Carolyn)

1 or 2 unpeeled oranges, sliced   1   cup sugar
1   10-ounce can pineapple chunks 1/2 cup vinegar
1   16-ounce can sliced peaches   3   sticks cinnamon
1   16-ounce can apricot halves   5   whole cloves
1   29-ounce can pears   1   3-ounce package cherry gelatin

Cut orange slices in half; place in saucepan and cover with water. Simmer until rind is tender. Drain, set aside. Drain canned fruits well, reserving all the
pineapple juice and half the peach and apricot juice. Combine reserved juice,
vinegar, cinnamon, cloves and gelatin. Simmer 30 minutes. Combine fruits in
a 9-cup container, pour hot juice mixture over fruit. Refrigerate 24 hours.

AMAZING GRACE SALAD

Serves 6 to 8   Mrs. John W. Drummond (Holly)

1   can Eagle Brand sweetened   1   large can crushed pineapple,
        condensed milk   drained
3   tablespoons lemon juice   1   cup chopped nuts
1   large Cool Whip

Mix all ingredients together for a good salad. Set in refrigerator prior to serving. Delicious!

VARIATION: Mrs. Robert C. Lake, Jr. (Carolyn)

For CHERRY-PINEAPPLE SALAD, omit lemon juice and nuts. Add 1
banana and use 1 medium can pineapple and 1 medium Cool Whip. Add 1
can cherry pie filling. Pour into a pan and freeze.

FRUIT WITH RASPBERRY CREAM DRESSING

Yields: 3 cups sauce   Mrs. Mona Chapman

1	large pineapple	RASPBERRY CREAM DRESSING:
1/4	small watermelon	1 cup whipping cream
1	small cantaloupe	1/4 teaspoon salt
3	medium bananas	1 cup mayonnaise
1-1/2 pounds plums		1/3 cup raspberry preserves
1	pound seedless green grapes	1 teaspoon grated lemon peel

Remove rind and core from pineapple, rinds and seeds from watermelon and cantaloupe, and peel from bananas. Cut fruit into bite-sized pieces. Cut plums into wedges. Discard pits. In small bowl, with mixer at medium speed, beat cream and salt until stiff peaks form. Fold in mayonnaise, raspberry preserves and lemon peel until well blended. Cover and refrigerate up to three days. Serve with cocktail picks.

LILLIE'S PINEAPPLE CHEESE MOLD

Serves 6 to 8   Mrs. Robert N. McLellan (Doris)

1	3-ounce box lime gelatin	1 8-ounce can crushed pineapple,
1	cup boiling water	well drained
1	cup evaporated milk	1/2 cup mayonnaise
1	cup cottage cheese	1/4 cup finely chopped celery
		1/4 cup finely chopped nuts

Mix all ingrediets together. Pour into a pan or into 8 small individual molds and congeal.

GEORGIA COLD STRING BEANS

Serves 6 to 8   Mrs. Herbert Kirsh (Suzanne)

1	pound string beans, fresh	1 tablespoon chopped parsley
1/4	cup minced spring onion	3 tablespoons fresh or dried dill
1	tablespoon cider vinegar	weed
2	tablespoons lemon juice	Salt to taste
2	tablespoons sugar	1/4 teaspoon fresh ground pepper
2	tablespoons Dijon mustard	1/3 cup sliced radishes
1/3 cup olive oil		1/3 cup coarsely chopped walnuts

Cook beans 5 to 7 minutes or until tender. Drain and cool under cold water to stop the cooking process. Mix all ingredients, except nuts and radishes, and pour over string beans. Refrigerate at least 2 hours (overnight best). Before serving, add the nuts and radishes and toss well.

MARINATED ASPARAGUS
Mrs. Robert C. Lake, Jr. (Carolyn)

1/3 cup vinegar	1/2 teaspoon salt
1/4 cup water	3 whole cloves
1/4 cup sugar	1 stick cinnamon
1/4 teaspoon celery seed	1 large can asparagus tips, drained

Mix thoroughly all ingredients, except asparagus. Bring the marinade to a boil and pour over about 30 asparagus tips and marinate overnight.

BUFFET BEAN BOWL

Serves 10 to 12   Mrs. Robert C. Lake, Jr. (Carolyn)

3/4 cup vinegar	1 17-ounce can French Style green beans, drained
3/4 cup sugar	1 12-ounce can shoe peg corn, drained
1 tablespoon water	1 cup finely chopped celery
1 tablespoon salt	1 cup finely chopped onions
1/4 to 1/2 teaspoon pepper	1 2-ounce jar pimento, drained
1 17-ounce can small English peas, drained	

Combine first 5 ingredients in a small sauce pan. Bring mixture to a boil; boil 1 minute. Let cool completely. Combine the remaining ingredients in a bowl and toss lightly. Pour marinade over vegetable mixture. Stir gently. Cover salad and refrigerate overnight.

VARIATION: Mrs. Robert N. McLellan (Doris)

Omit water. Add 1 16-ounce can drained carrots, 1 8-1/2-ounce can drained lima beans, 1 15-ounce can kidney beans, 1 diced bell pepper, 1/4 cup more sugar and vinegar, 1/2 cup salad oil, 1/4 teaspoon Astor brand salad herbs, 1/4 teaspoon seasoned pepper, 1 teaspoon paprika and 1/2 teaspoon seasoned salt. Marinate one day before serving. Drain and serve in a big crystal bowl.

BROCCOLI SALAD
Serves 8 to 10   Mrs. Hugh Leatherman (Jean)

3 pounds fresh broccoli	1 tablespoon monosodium glutamate
1 cup cider vinegar	1 tablespoon salt
1-1/2 cups vegetable oil	1 teaspoon pepper
1 tablespoon sugar	1 teaspoon garlic powder
1 tablespoon dill weed	

Wash and slice broccoli flowerets at an angle. Blend dressing ingredients and pour over the flowerets. Refrigerate overnight.

SUMMER SALAD

Serves 10   Mrs. John C. Land, III (Marie)

1	head cauliflower	1 to 2 cups cooked chicken, chopped
1	bunch broccoli	in bite-size pieces
2	ripe tomatoes	Romaine lettuce
1	large bottle creamy cucumber	Seasonings — salt, pepper, dill,
	salad dressing	"Mortons Nature's Seasons"

Wash cauliflower and break into small florets. Wash and skin peel from broccoli and break or cut into small florets. Do not use tough stems. Pour 1/2 bottle of dressing over the broccoli and cauliflower. Season to taste and refrigerate overnight. Before serving, line salad bowl with lettuce leaves; pour broccoli and cauliflower into middle. Mix remaining salad dressing and seasoning with chicken and put this on top. Peel and chop tomatoes and put on top of chicken. Can refrigerate for up to an hour before serving, but be sure to cover with clear wrap to keep lettuce crisp.

CARROT SALAD

Serves 6 to 8   Mrs. J. P. Gardner, Jr. (Pam)
                                                Mrs. Herbert Kirsh (Suzanne)

1	10-3/4-ounce can condensed	1/2	teaspoon Worcestershire sauce
	tomato soup		Salt and pepper to taste
1/4	cup salad oil	1-1/2	pounds cooked sliced carrots
1/2	cup sugar	1	raw bell pepper, chopped
1/4	cup vinegar	1	raw onion, sliced in rings
1/2	teaspoon prepared mustard		

Mix first six ingredients, salt and pepper, and pour over cooked carrots, bell pepper and onion. Toss lightly and refrigerate several hours or overnight.

VARIATION NO. 1   Mrs. Beattie Huff (Gladys)

Omit bell pepper. Use 1/2 lb. more carrots, 1/4 cup more oil, 1/2 cup each more sugar and vinegar and 1/2 teaspoon each more mustard and Worcestershire sauce.

VARIATION NO. 2   Mrs. Robin Tallon, Jr. (Amy)

Add 1/4 cup more oil, 1/2 cup more sugar, 1/2 cup more cider vinegar, 1/2 teaspoon more prepared mustard and Worcestershire sauce, 1/2-pound more carrots and use a purple onion.

THREE RING SALAD

Serves 4 to 5   Mrs. Robert C. Lake, Jr. (Carolyn)

3	tomatoes	1/2	cup vinegar
1	onion	1/3	cup water
1	green pepper	1/4	cup sugar
1	cucumber, if desired	2	tablespoons salad oil

Salt, freshly ground pepper, sugar

Slice the tomatoes, onion and green bell pepper into rounds and arrange in layers. Season each layer with salt, pepper and a little bit of sugar. This should be done 3-4 hours before serving. Mix remaining ingredients for dressing. Pour over salad just before serving. Recipe may be doubled.

HEARTS OF PALM SALAD

Serves 4 to 6   Mrs. Phil Leventis (Ellen)

LEVENTIS DRESSING:

1/4	cup salad oil	1/8	teaspoon dry mustard
1	tablespoon finely chopped onion	1	hard cooked egg, finely chopped
1	tablespoon snipped parsley	1	tablespoon chopped pimento
1	tablespoon vinegar	1	14-ounce can hearts of palm, chilled, drained and cut in strips
1	tablespoon lemon juice		
1/4	teaspoon salt		

In screw top jar, combine oil, onion, parsley, vinegar, lemon juice, salt and dry mustard. Cover; shake vigorously to blend. Add chopped egg and pimento. Stir well. Line salad plate with lettuce and top with hearts of palm. Pour on dressing.

LAYERED SALAD

Serves 10 to 12   Mrs. William J. McLeod (Sara)

1 head lettuce, cut in small peices	SOUR CREAM SAUCE:
1/2 cup chopped celery	1 cup Hellman's mayonnaise
1/2 cup onion, chopped	1 cup sour cream
1/2 cup bell pepper, chopped	1 teaspoon sugar
1 10-ounce package garden peas, uncooked and drained	

Salt and pepper to taste

In deep salad bowl (about 2 quart size), layer lettuce, then vegetables, then sauce. Repeat. Cover with sharp grated cheese. Place Saran Wrap over bowl and refrigerate at least 24 hours.

SALADS AND DRESSINGS

MARINATED VEGETABLE SALAD

Serves 40 to 60   Mrs. Nick A. Theodore (Emilie)

4	cups sliced zucchini	2	cups cauliflower
2	cups broccoli flowerets	1	cup halved cocktail tomatoes
1	cup sliced carrots		(add at end)
2	cups sliced squash	1	pound fresh mushrooms
1	cup sliced purple onions		

MARINADE:

1/2	cup sugar	1	tablespoon salt
1/2	cup white wine	1	teaspoon oregano
1/2	cup wine vinegar	1	teaspoon onion powder
1/2	cup lemon juice	1	teaspoon dried mustard
2	cups oil	1	teaspoon granulated garlic

Put vegetables in a large bowl. Mix marinate well and pour over vegetables. Refrigerate.

VARIATION NO. 1   Mrs. T. Bruce Smith, III (Dot)

1	onion, chopped	1	can garden peas
1	bell pepper, chopped	1	cup vinegar
1/2	cup pimento, chopped	1-1/2	cups sugar
2	stalks celery, chopped	1/2	teaspoon salt
1	can string beans, cut	1/2	cup salad oil

Mix and refrigerate overnight.

VARIATION NO. 2   Representative Ginger Crocker

2	16-ounce cans French-style green beans	1	medium onion, diced
2	17-ounce cans early green peas	1	8-ounce can water chestnuts, sliced
1	14-ounce can artichoke hearts, diced	3/4	cup sugar
1	7-ounce can pimento, chopped	1	cup red wine vinegar
1	medium green pepper, chopped	1/2	cup water
		1/2	cup oil
		1	clove garlic

Combine drained vegetables. Blend the last five ingredients and pour over the vegetables. Marinate overnight. May be prepared several days in advance. Serves 20.

CHICKEN SALAD SUPREME

Mrs. W. B. Hawkins (Sarah)

3	cups chopped chicken breasts, cooked	1/2	cup mayonnaise
1	cup celery	2	tablespoons oil
1/4	cup chopped pecans	1	tablespoon vinegar
		Salt	

Combine first 3 ingredients. Make dressing of rest of ingredients and pour over chicken. Season to taste. Toss lightly.

CURRIED CHICKEN SALAD

Serves 4 to 6   Mrs. Parker Evatt (Jane)

2	cups chicken, cooked and cut into 1/2-inch cubes	1/2	cup celery, chopped
1/4	cup water chestnuts, sliced	1/2	cup slivered almonds
1/2	pound seedless green grapes, halved	3/4	cup mayonnaise
1	8-ounce can pineapple chunks, drained	1/2	teaspoon curry powder
		2	teaspoons lemon juice

Mix mayonnaise, curry powder and lemon juice. Combine with chicken, water chestnuts, grapes, pineapple chunks, celery and almonds, and toss well. Chill for several hours. Serve on lettuce leaf.

VARIATION: Mrs. David E. Turnipseed (Cindy)

Omit almonds. Decrease mayonnaise to 1/2 cup and lemon juice to 1 teaspoon. Add 1 more cup chopped celery, 1/2 cup chopped pecans, 1 teaspoon salt, 1/4 cup sour cream and 1/2 teaspoon more curry powder.

MOCK CHICKEN SALAD

Mrs. W. B. Hawkins (Sarah)

1	cup chopped pecans	1	small grated onion
1	boiled egg, chopped	1	cup mayonnaise
1/2	cup chopped olives		

Mix together. Chill. Serve on lettuce leaf.

SALADS AND DRESSINGS

OLD FASHIONED CHICKEN SALAD

Serves 8 to 12   Mrs. Jeff R. Richardson, Jr. (Florence)

1	5-to-6 pound hen	COOKED DRESSING:
2	large or 3 medium size apples, peeled and chopped into 1/4-inch cubes	2 eggs / Salt and pepper to taste / 1/2 cup sugar
1	cup finely chopped celery	1 tablespoon flour
1	cup finely chopped nuts	1 cup sweet milk
Salt to taste		1/2 cup vinegar
		1/2 cup water

Beat eggs with salt, pepper, sugar and flour until smooth. Stir in milk and mix well. Combine vinegar and water and stir into above mixture. Cook over medium heat, stirring constantly until mixture thickens to coat the spoon (about the consistency of buttermilk). Remove from heat and cool. Dressing will keep for at least two weeks when stored in refrigerator. (This is also good on other meat and vegetable salads.) Simmer hen with water and 1 tablespoon salt until tender. Cool and remove chicken from bones. Cut into 1/2-inch cubes. Mix with apples, celery and nuts. Season to taste. Pour entire amount of COOKED DRESSING over mixture and toss well. Chill in refrigerator at least 6 hours. (One 5-pound hen will yield 1 quart cooked diced meat.)

HOT CRAB SALAD

Mrs. Jackson V. Gregory (Brenda)

2	cups crab meat	1	tablespoon mustard
1/3	cup chopped onion	1	tablespoon lemon juice
1	cup chopped celery	1	tablespoon Worcestershire sauce
2	hard cooked eggs, chopped	3/4	cup whole wheat bread crumbs
1/2	cup mayonnaise		

Combine the first 8 ingredients. Pour into buttered baking dish. Top with bread crumbs and dot with butter. Bake uncovered at 325 degrees for 30 minutes.

BEEF AND POTATO SALAD IN A PITA
OR SANDWICH LOAF

Serves 4   Mrs. Robert N. McLellan (Doris)

1	pound boiling potatoes	2	shallots, chopped
Salt		2	tablespoons chopped parsley
1	cup mayonnaise		Freshly ground pepper
1	teaspoon Dijon mustard	1	sandwich loaf (see index)
1	tablespoon vinegar	1	cup cherry tomatoes
1-1/2	pounds rare roast beef, thinly sliced		Butter
			Pita Bread

1/2 pound marinated mushrooms, (3/4 cup olive oil, 1/8 cup wine vinegar, 1/2 tsp. Dijon mustard, minced onions, garlic, parsley, salt and pepper)

Peel potatoes and cook in boiling salted water 20 minutes or until tender. Slice potatoes and dress with some of the mayonnaise mixed with mustard and vinegar while still hot. Cut roast beef into finger lengths; drain marinade from mushrooms, reserving the marinade. Toss potatoes, beef and mushrooms, together gently to keep potatoes from breaking up. Carefully mix in reserved marinade, shallots, parsley and more mayonnaise as needed. Season to taste. See index for preparing sandwich loaf shell. Butter shell generously or insert a dish, then fill with salad. Put top on and refrigerate until ready to pack picnic basket or serve. Garnish with cherry tomatoes. NOTE: Potato preparation and marinating of mushrooms may be done a day ahead, as well as roasting of beef. Salad may be packed into bread shell several hours before serving or fill pita pockets with the salad.

SEAFOOD SALAD

Senator David E. Turnipseed

1	8-ounce package elbow macaroni, cooked	2	cups diced cucumbers
		1	cup sliced pitted ripe olives
1	6-1/2-ounce can fresh or frozen crab meat	2	cups mayonnaise
		1	cup sour cream
1-1/2	cups cooked shrimp	1	tablespoon salt
4	eggs, hard cooked and diced	1	teaspoon pepper
1	large onion, chopped		Paprika
1	4-ounce can pimentos, drained		

Toss together the first 8 ingredients. Stir dressing ingredients together and pour over seafood salad. Toss. Cover and refrigerate until ready to serve.

RICE SALAD WITH SEAFOOD

Serves 8 to 10   Mrs. Robert N. McLellan (Doris)

4	cups cooked chilled rice	3	hard-cooked eggs, finely chopped
1	cup chopped crab, lobster or shrimp	2	tablespoons chopped chives
		1/3	cup chopped fresh parsley
1/2	cup slivered ham	2	tablespoons olive oil
1	cup celery, finely chopped	2	tablespoons wine vinegar
	Salt and freshly ground pepper	1/2	cup mayonnaise or half sour cream
1	tablespoon finely chopped onion		
1	10-ounce box frozen green peas, cooked and chilled		

Combine by tossing lightly the first ten ingredients. Sprinkle with oil and vinegar. Add mayonnaise or half sour cream. Let stand in refrigerator a few hours for a more tangy flavor. (Better made the day before; however, salt and pepper just before serving.) Looks nice on a buffet table if spooned into a bundt pan lightly rubbed with mayonnaise and after chilling for a few hours in the refrigerator, turn out onto a chilled serving platter. This is nice as an entree with sliced cantaloupe and honeydew. Try it at a tail-gate picnic!

ZESTY RICE SALAD

Serves 10 to 15   Mrs. Paul W. Derrick (Robin)

2	cups chilled cooked rice	1	2-ounce jar sliced pimentos, drained
1	17-ounce can chilled green peas, drained	3/4	cup mayonnaise
1/2	cup finely chopped onion	2	teaspoons salt
1	4-ounce can mushrooms, drained and sliced	1	teaspoon pepper
		2	tablespoons lemon juice
1-1/2	cups finely chopped celery	1/4	teaspoon rosemary
			Pinch garlic salt

Combine the first 6 ingredients by tossing lightly with a fork. Add the mayonnaise, salt, pepper, lemon juice, rosemary and garlic salt. Spoon into a 1-1/2-quart mold lightly rubbed with mayonnaise. Refrigerate for a few hours for a better mingling of flavors. Turn out onto a chilled serving platter or fill thin slices of ham or Swiss cheese with it and roll up like an enchilada.

ORANGE AND SPINACH SALAD

Serves 6 to 8   Mrs. Hugh Leatherman (Jean)

2   small heads Bibb lettuce, torn
     into bite size pieces
1   pound fresh spinach, torn into
     bite size pieces
2   oranges, peeled, seeded, and
     sectioned
1/2 medium onion, sliced and
     separated into rings
1/2 cup coarsely chopped walnuts
2   teaspoons butter or margarine, melted

SWEET-SOUR DRESSING:
1   teaspoon paprika
1   teaspoon dry mustard
1   teaspoon grated onion
1   cup vegetable oil
1   teaspoon celery seeds
1   teaspoon salt
1/2 cup sugar
1/2 cup vinegar

Place first four ingredients in a large bowl. Sauté walnuts in butter until lightly browned. SWEET-SOUR DRESSING: Blend all dressing ingredients together. Toss with salad just before serving.

VARIATION: Mrs. Robert N. McLellan (Doris)

Omit lettuce, onion and SWEET-SOUR DRESSING. Wash spinach and put in a closed plastic bag to crisp. (Do the day before if you wish.) Mix two tablespoons Roquefort cheese with 1/2 cup PALMETTO FRENCH DRESS-ING and toss with spinach and fruit. Add salt and cracked pepper to taste. Substitute grapefruit sometimes.

LAND'S SLAW

Serves 15 to 20   Mrs. John C. Land, III (Marie)

1   head cabbage, large-size
1   6-ounce jar salad olives
1   green pepper (optional)

1   cup Hellman's mayonnaise
1/2 package Good Seasonings Garlic
     Salad Dressing

Chop or thinly slice cabbage according to your preference. Drain salad olives reserving the juice and add olives to cabbage. Mix olive juice with dry salad mix and mayonnaise. Pour over cabbage and green pepper. Mix well, adding more mayonnaise if needed. Refrigerate until served. Best if made four hours ahead.

SALADS AND DRESSINGS

SUMMER SLAW

Serves 8 to 10   Senator Nell Smith

1	medium cabbage, grated	1	cup sugar
1	Bermuda or red onion, thinly sliced	1	cup oil
		1	teaspoon salt
1	cup diced celery	1/2	teaspoon celery seed
1	cup vinegar		

Layer the first three ingredients. Boil the next five ingredients five minutes and pour hot dressing over cabbage mixture.

TACO SALAD

Serves 6 to 8   Mrs. Nick Theodore (Emilie)

1   pound ground beef   Small amount water
Taco seasoning (1/2 to 1 packet)

Sauté meat and water in oil until meat is brown. Pour off grease and add 1/2 to 1 packet of the taco seasoning. Mix and cool. Make salad of shredded lettuce, diced tomatoes, 1 can ripe pitted olives, garbanzo beans, shredded cheese and very small diced onions. Add 1/2 package of crushed Doritos and cooled beef mixture. Toss with either Hidden Valley Ranch dressing or Green Goddess dressing. Top with Guacamole dressing or taco sauce.

VARIATION NO. 1   Mrs. Robert N. McLellan (Doris)

In a 9x13-inch dish, layer shredded lettuce, diced tomatoes, very small diced onions, a medium can Ranch Style beans, drained (use garbanzo if you can't find), grated Longhorn or Velvetta cheese and crushed Fritos. One hour before serving spread over the top 1 8-ounce bottle Wishbone Italian dressing (do not mix). This is a good picnic salad with chicken, hot dogs or hamburgers.

VARIATION NO. 2   Mrs. R. L. Altman (Nancy)

Combine a 16-ounce can refried beans with 1/4 of a 1-1/4-ounce package taco seasoning mix. Spread evenly in a 12x8x2-inch dish. Layer in order listed: 6-ounce carton avocado dip (or one avocado, mashed), 8-ounce carton sour cream, 4-1/2-ounce chopped ripe olives, 2 large diced tomatoes, 1 small finely chopped onion, 4-ounce can chopped green chilies and top with 1-1/2 cups shredded Monterey Jack cheese, with or without jalapeno peppers. Serve with large corn chips.

BOILED MUSTARD DRESSING   Senator Nell Smith

1	cup sugar	2	eggs, beaten
2	tablespoons dry mustard	1	cup milk
2	tablespoons flour	1	cup vinegar
1	teaspoon salt		

Blend the first four ingredients together. Add the next three ingredients and cook in a double boiler to consistency of custard. Great with meats and mixing meat salads.

PALMETTO FRENCH DRESSING

Makes 5 cups   Mrs. Robert N. McLellan (Doris)

1	egg	1/2	cup vinegar
1	teaspoon sugar	1/2	cup wine
2	teaspoons salt	2	cloves garlic
4	cups salad oil (half olive oil makes even better)		

Mix egg, sugar and salt together; add oil and vinegar alternately until all the oil is added, then drip the wine in slowly. Add garlic cloves, barely crushed, and store in a jar until ready to use. Toss among any collection of salad greens you may find and your salad will be a success. This dressing has a special affinity for Roquefort and bleu cheese, too.

POPPY SEED DRESSING

Yields: 3-1/2 cups   Mrs. M. J. Cooper (Melba)

1-1/2 cups sugar		3	tablespoons onion juice
2	teaspoons dry mustard	2	cups salad oil, not olive oil
2	teaspoons salt	3	tablespoons poppy seeds
2/3	cup vinegar		

Mix sugar, mustard, salt and vinegar. Add onion juice and stir in thoroughly. Slowly add oil, beating constantly, and continue to beat until thick. When you think the mixture is thick enough, beat 5 minutes longer. Add poppy seeds and beat for a few minutes. Store in a cool place or in the refrigerator, but not near the freezing coil. If the dressing separates, pour off the clear part and beat again, adding the poppy seed mixture slowly, but it will not separate unless it becomes too cold or too hot. Everyone likes this dressing on practically every kind of a fresh salad and fruit.

ROQUEFORT DRESSING

Mrs. Herbert Kirsh (Suzanne)

8	ounces Roquefort or bleu cheese, crumbled	1	small onion, grated
1	cup mayonnaise	1	tablespoon sugar
1/3	cup sour cream		Dash garlic powder
1	tablespoon cider vinegar, or a little more		Dash salt

Mix together well and refrigerate for a few hours. Can be used as a dip. If too thick, add a few drops of milk.

THEODORE'S HOUSE DRESSING

Yields: 2 cups

Mrs. Nick A. Theodore (Emilie)

2	eggs	3	tablespoons lemon juice
1	cup oil (half olive, half salad)	1	clove garlic, minced
1/2	cup grated Parmesan cheese	1	teaspoon salt
1	teaspoon Worcestershire sauce	1/2	teaspoon pepper

Put all ingredients in blender. Beat until smooth, about 45 seconds. Toss with any assorted greens or mixed vegetables. An addition of bacon bits or croutons is also good.

ST. HELENA'S EPISCOPAL CHURCH

St. Helena's Episcopal Church was built in 1724 of brick covered with cement stucco. The original steeple was removed before the civil war and replaced in 1941 in the style of St. Michael's and St. Philip's churches of Charleston.

BEAUFORT COUNTY

By 1710, when Beaufort was named for Lords Proprietor Henry, Duke of Beaufort, the flags of four nations had flown over this coastal county. Spanish explorers claimed a spot on deep water they called Santa Elena or Saint Helena's in 1521. In 1562, Jean Ribaut was struck with the wide and deep harbor he found as he brought the first Protestants to settle Charlesfort on Parris Island, that he named it Port Royal. The area that includes the present day Beaufort County was part of land claimed by England. It was William Hilton's description of the area that encouraged William Seyle's expedition to the Carolina coast. Seyle bypassed Port Royal for the more protected site where he planted the first settlement at Charles Town. A small band of Scottish coventers planted the fourth flag in 1684 at Stuart Town which lasted only a year.

This old civilization perished soon after the first shots at Fort Sumter. When the Union Army marched into the town of Beaufort virtually the entire white population had evacuated leaving 10,000 slaves behind. Northerners came South to implement what historian Willie Lee Rose has described as a "Rehearsal for Reconstruction" by cutting up once-grand plantations into small parcels and granting the promised "forty acres and a mule" to the Freedmen.

Today Beaufort profits from sharing the beauty of its beaches and tidal creeks with tourists from all over the world. The rich soil that once grew Sea Island cotton now produced profitable truck crops. Local crabs, shrimp, and oysters from the creeks support a thriving seafood industry. The site of Jean Ribaut's first settlement is now a large Marine training installation.

COLLETON COUNTY

Although Sir John Colleton, one of the Lords Proprietors, gave his name to one of the first three counties laid out in Carolina in 1682, the present county by that name dates back to 1798 when residents of Walterboro grew restive over the long trip to Charleston to conduct their legal affairs.

Most of the planters feared that the swamps surrounding their homes gave off deadly miasmas that brought on the fevers of the summer and fall. In an annual ritual, planters moved their families to Charleston during the un-

healthy season. Colleton County planters began frequenting a summer resort established by Paul and Jacob Walter in 1784; the little town's name was eventually changed to Walterboro and was designated the county seat.

Located as it was close to the colonial capital of Charleston, Colleton County played an important part in the Revolution. At the battle of Parkers' Ferry in 1781, Francis Marion's men thwarted a British and Tory advance upon the port city. That same year British troops captured Issac Hayne, captain of a militia troop, and executed him as a spy.

Colleton County citizens maintained an active interest in antebellum politics. In 1828, its court house in Walterboro that was designed by Robert Mills was the site of the first public Nullification meeting.

The Civil War ended a way of life in Colleton. The cotton market never regained its vigor; Sherman had burned many of the finest plantation homes. The famous eighteenth century racetrack that once was the center of Walterboro's social life is now quiet and survives as Live Oak Cemetary. But Colleton's people are still dedicated to a gracious way of life and enjoy the traditional pleasures of hunting and fishing. The agricultural economy is supplemented with lumber related industry as well as food and feed processing.

ALLENDALE COUNTY

Allendale, founded in 1919, is the newest of South Carolina's counties. The farming communities south of Barnwell and west of Hampton were thinly populated until the Port Royal Railroad laid tracks in this area in the 1870s. When the population increased, it became increasingly evident that it was unfair and inconvenient for the residents of this land bordering on the Savannah River to make the long trips to the county seats of Barnwell or Hampton. Thirteen local citizens and leading businessmen helped create the new county from portions of Barnwell and Hampton Counties.

Allendale County takes its name for the districts largest town and the county seat.

Although small, with only a few hundred residents at the turn of the century, Allendale must have been a lively place since it supported five bars and five livery stables. In 1901, a town hall was built that was used for many purposes including holding court, town plays, and a curb market for local women to sell the produce from the nearby truck farms. The original town grant stipulated that the streets must be 100 feet wide. Although few could have predicted it then, this was a very wise measure, since within a half century Allendale's Main Street would be incorporated into Highway 301 that carried Northern tourists to Florida. Allendale served as a major "watering place" with motels and restaurants serving the south bound trade until Interstate 95 preempted much of the traffic from the small towns.

Allendale County is going through a period of transition as the economy adjusts to the loss of the tourist trade, but is finding that its greatest resources is its people who remain loyal to the community. The county is attracting new industries and boasts large hog and peach farms. The Salke-hatchie Regional Campus of the University of South Carolina provides a cultural and educational center for the county.

HAMPTON COUNTY

On a fall day in 1878, Governor Wade Hampton stood under a large magnolia and laid the cornerstone for the court house of the new county named in his honor. As part of the ceremonies, proud members of Hamptons Red Shirts drilled in homemade uniforms of brass-buttoned red blouses trimmed with black braid.

The creation of Hampton County as a "white county" was as much a political statement as an administrative convenience. Early in the Civil War the lower portion of Beaufort District was overrun by Union troops. The slaves were freed and many homes and plantations confiscated and later sold for taxes, so many whites fled to the upper part of the district that became Hampton County, bitter over their losses. For many, the exodus did not bring safety, for Sherman's forces swept through this area too. Once a section of small farms, cotton prosperity had helped build many fine plantations that were lost to flames.

Hampton County had its first governor in 1899. Miles McSweeney had served the county in the House of Representatives and was the lieutenant-governor before his election as governor.

The County's biggest industry today is the Westinghouse Plant, but there are also other factories, especially those involved in wood byproducts. Agriculture, though, still is the backbone of the county's economy. In addition to various types of vegetables, pecans and peanuts are important crops, but watermelons are most closely associated with this area. The annual Watermelon Festival brings tourists as well as local citizens out to enjoy this traditional southern delight.

> Possum is good, tater is good,
> Ice cream and cake is mighty fine.
> But gimme, oh, gimme, I really wish you would
> Dat watermelon smiling on the vine.

Founded in 1912, Jasper County is a twentieth century creation, but its land has an ancient past. Together with Allendale and Hampton Counties, Jasper is part of the Yamassee Indian lands noted on old maps of the backcountry of the Beaufort District, and was explored by the Spanish in the sixteenth century. Its haunting beauty makes visitors forget that the Indians were driven away after the Yamassee War in 1715. William Gilmore Simm's <u>The Yamassee</u> vividly describes life in the region that remains pristine.

Remnants of the Indian culture may be found in the names of Jasper's towns. Coosawhatchie, or "Refuge of the Coosaws," was the seat of justice in the old Beaufort District for many years but lost this distinction because its location on extensive swamp proved too unhealthy. It was replaced by Gillisonville, originally founded as a summer resort, that served as the judicial center from 1840 to 1868. During Sherman's March, all the homes in Gillisonville were destroyed except that of Lt. James W. Moore of Hampton's Legion whose grandmother agreed to knit a pair of warm socks for a cold Union officer.

When Jasper County, that is named for Revolutionary War hero Sargeant William Jasper, was founded in 1912, Ridgeland was made the county seat. Founded in 1855, the settlement that had been known as Gopher Hill later changed its name to one that better described its location on a sandy ridge.

Jasper County remains scenic and unspoiled. It is still largely given over to agriculture, although wood byproducts are an important industry. Its good hunting and fishing have attracted sportsmen from all over the country. The Pineland Hunting Club founded in 1877 was the first of the plantations bought for use as hunting preserves.

Beatrice Ravenel's poem <u>The Yamassee Lands</u>, evokes a sense of the past not far removed from the present.

> "In the Yamassee Lands
> When with the blowing of wood-smoke and throbbing of
>   hidden drums
> Indian Summer fashions its spell,
> Trembling falls on the air,
> Wild things flatten themselves in the jeopardy of the shade"

THE HEPWORTH HOUSE

The Thomas Hepworth House at New and Port Republic
Streets in Beaufort was built in 1717 by the Chief Justice of the
colony. The rifle slots in the tabby foundation are so angled
that guns to repel Indians and Redcoats could fire over a wide
arc.

vegetables

VEGETABLE SALT SUBSTITUTE RECIPE

Mrs. I. S. Leevy Johnson (Doris)

1	teaspoon chili powder	3	tablespoons paprika
1	tablespoon garlic powder	1	tablespoon poultry seasoning
2	tablespoons dry mustard	2	tablespoons black pepper
6	tablespoons onion powder	1	teaspoon ground oregano

Mix all seasonings together and put in your salt shaker.

EASY HOLLANDAISE SAUCE

Yield: 6 to 8 servings   Mrs. Robert C. Lake, Jr. (Carolyn)

1/2	cup sour cream	1	teaspoon dry mustard
1/2	cup mayonnaise	2	teaspoons lemon juice

Combine all ingredients and stir over low heat until just heated through. Do not boil. Serve over broccoli or asparagus.

ASPARAGUS CASSEROLE

Mrs. Cylde Dangerfield (Betty)

1	14-1/2-ounce can cut asparagus, drained		Salt and pepper to taste
3	boiled eggs, chopped	1	small can evaporated milk
1	8-1/2-ounce can green peas, drained	1	cup grated cheese
		1/2	cup cream of chicken soup
1	small package potato chips, crumbled (1/2 ounce)		

Place ingredients, except potato chips, in 1-1/2-quart casserole alternating layers. Top with potato chip crumbs. Bake at 350 degrees for 30 minutes.

MAMO'S ASPARAGUS CASSEROLE

Serves 12   Mrs. D. H. Wilkins (Susan)

2	cans asparagus, reserve juice	1	small jar pimento
10 to 12	ounces grated sharp cheese	1/2	stick butter, melted
3	slices toasted bread, cut in cubes	3	tablespoons flour
3	hard boiled eggs, sliced	1/2	cup mayonnaise

In a saucepan; mix butter, flour and reserved liquid until thick, add mayonnaise, and a little milk if it gets too thick. In a 9x12-inch baking dish, put a layer of asparagus, bread cubes, grated cheese, dash black pepper, eggs and pimento. Pour 1/2 of the cream sauce over this. Repeat layers, and sprinkle cheese on top and a little paprika. Bake 30 minutes at 325 degrees.

BAKED BEANS

Serves 8   Representative Ed Simpson

1	quart Navy beans	3	tablespoons sugar
3/4	pound salt pork	1	tablespoon to 1 cup of molasses
1	tablespoon salt		to taste
Boiling water		1/2	teaspoon mustard, optional

Pick over beans, cover with cold water, soak overnight. Drain, cover with fresh water, heat slowly; do not boil. Cook until skins will burst (when a few are put in teaspoon, blowing on them will cause skins to burst). Drain beans. Cut through rind of pork every half inch. Put beans in pot and bury pork in them. Mix salt, molasses and sugar, add 1 cup boiling water and pour over beans. Then add enough boiling water to cover beans. Cover pot. Bake 6 to 8 hours at 250 degrees. Uncover last hour to crisp. Add water as needed. Great!

BAKED BEAN BASH

Serves 4   Mrs. Robert N. McLellan (Doris)

1	16-ounce can pork and beans	2	tablespoons catsup
2	tablespoons brown sugar	1	tablespoon molasses
1	tablespoon Dijon mustard	Dash Worcestershire sauce	
1	medium chopped onion		

Mix ingredients together and pour in a casserole. Top with bacon strips and bake at 325 degrees for 1 hour.

RANCHO BEANS

Serves 6 - 8   Mrs. Marion H. Kinon (Reba)

1 to 2 pounds hamburger		1	tablespoon mustard
1	medium onion	1	tablespoon Worcestershire sauce
1/2	teaspoon salt	1	tablespoon brown sugar
1/2	cup ketchup	2	16-ounce cans baked beans

Brown hamburger and onions. Add other ingredients. Mix and bake 30 to 45 minutes at 350 degrees.

GREEN BEAN BACON ROLL-UPS

Serves 4   Mrs. Robert N. McLellan (Doris)

1 16-ounce can Blue Lake whole   1 bottle Italian or French dressing
     green beans   4 slices bacon

Drain beans and marinate in dressing and refrigerate overnight. Pour boiling water over bacon and let blanch for 10 minutes. Drain and dry. Stretch bacon. Divide beans into 4 even stacks and roll each stack in a slice of bacon and secure with a toothpick. Place in an oblong pan and bake in a preheated 350 degree oven for 25 to 30 minutes or until bacon is crispy brown. Serve hot.

GREEN BEAN CASSEROLE

Serves 8 to 10   Mrs. Grady Patterson, Jr. (Margie)

2 16-ounce cans French style   1/2 to 3/4 package Pepperidge Farm
     green beans   Herb stuffing
2 10-3/4-ounce cans tomato soup 3/4 stick margarine, melted
1 small onion, diced fine

Arrange beans, soup, onions and bread crumbs in layers in buttered casserole dish. Drizzle melted margarine over mixture. Bake at 350 degrees until bubbly, about 30 minutes.

PENNSYLVANIA DUTCH GREEN BEANS

Serves 4 to 6   Mrs. R. M. Kenan (Sinclair)

3 strips bacon   1/4 teaspoon dry mustard
1 small onion, sliced   1 tablespoon brown sugar
2 teaspoons corn starch   1 tablespoon vinegar
1/4 teaspoon salt   1 boiled egg, sliced
1 pound can cut green beans

Fry bacon until crisp. Remove bacon and crumble. Drain off all but 1 tablespoon drippings. Add onion and brown slightly. Stir in cornstarch, salt and dry mustard. Drain beans, reserving 1/2 cup liquid. Stir reserved liquid into skillet. Cook, stirring, until mixture boils. Blend in brown sugar and vinegar. Add green beans and heat thoroughly. Turn into serving dish and garnish with egg and crumbled bacon.

MARSHA'S SWEET-SOUR GREEN BEANS

Serves 6 to 8   Mrs. D. H. Wilkins (Susan)

4	slices bacon	1/2	cup sugar
1	can mushrooms, drained	2	16-ounce cans French green
1/4	cup vinegar		beans, or use fresh
1	small onion, chopped		

Cook bacon, remove from pan. Add mushrooms and onions to bacon drippings and sauté. Add vinegar and bring to a boil. Drain beans; pour sauce over beans and cook in covered casserole for 30 minutes. Stir in crumbled bacon and serve at once.

BROCCOLI AND RICE CASSEROLE

Mrs. Robert C. Lake, Jr. (Carolyn)

1/4	pound margarine	1	10-3/4-ounce can mushroom
1	cup chopped celery		soup
1/2	cup chopped onions	1	Medium jar Cheese Whiz
2	10-ounce packages frozen	3	cups cooked rice
	chopped broccoli (thawed)		

Sauté onions and celery in margarine and add to broccoli. Combine with rest of ingredients. Pour into casserole and bake at 350 degrees for 45 minutes or until bubbly.

BROCCOLI AND CHEESE CASSEROLE

Serves 6   Mrs. Paul W. Derrick (Robin)

2	10-ounce packages frozen	8	ounces Velvetta cheese, grated
	chopped broccoli, cooked	2	stacks Ritz crackers, crushed
	and drained	1/2	stick margarine
1/2	stick margarine		

Stir margarine and cheese into hot broccoli. Pour into buttered 8x8x2-inch casserole dish. Mix together crackers and margarine and spread on top. (May double broccoli mixture without doubling topping.) Bake, uncovered, at 350 degrees until heated through.

BROCCOLI CASSEROLE

Mrs. Lewis Phillips (Ellie)

2 cups chopped broccoli
1 cup mayonnaise
1 cup shredded sharp cheddar
   cheese

1 10-1/2-ounce can cream of mushroom soup
2 eggs, beaten

Cook broccoli as directed on package. Drain and cool. Add to other ingredients. Place in buttered baking dish and add bread crumbs on top. Dot with
butter. Bake at 400 degrees for 20 minutes.

BROCCOLI-NUT CASSEROLE

Serves 6

Mrs. H. E. Pearce, Jr. (Jo)

2 10-ounce packages frozen
   chopped broccoli
1 cup sharp cheese, grated
1 10-3/4-ounce can cream of
   mushroom soup

1 cup mayonnaise
1 medium onion, chopped
2 eggs, well-beaten
3/4 cup chopped pecans
2 cups buttered breadcrumbs

Cook broccoli with salt according to directions on package. Drain. Add soup,
mayonnaise and nuts. Mix well. Add eggs and onion. Pour into greased 2-
quart casserole. Sprinkle with cheese and top with breadcrumbs. Bake at
350 degrees for 30 minutes.

CABBAGE CASSEROLE

Mrs. Michael R. Daniel (Peggy)

4 cups cabbage, shredded
1-1/2 cups corn flakes, crumbled
   with hand until fine
1 stick margarine, melted
Salt and pepper
1/2 cup mayonnaise

1 cup milk
1 10-3/4-ounce can cream of celery
   soup
1 cup shredded cheese
1 cup corn flakes, crumbled
Butter

Soak cabbage in cold water for 30 minutes. Drain. Mix together 1-1/2 cups
corn flakes and margarine. Place in bottom of baking dish and place cabbage
on top of crumbs and dot with butter. Season to taste. Mix together in a
saucepan; the mayonnaise, milk, and soup. Heat and pour over cabbage. Top
with shredded cheese and 1 cup crumbled corn flakes. Place in oven for 30
minutes at 325 degrees.

CABBAGE AND SHRIMP IN CREAM

Serves 6 to 8   Mrs. Robert N. McLellan (Doris)

1	medium cabbage, diced in bite size pieces	1	4-1/2-ounce can shrimp
		1	tablespoon caraway seeds
1/2	stick butter	1	teaspoon salt
1	cup sour cream		Freshly ground pepper

Cover cabbage with boiling water, cover and cook 10 to 15 minutes. Drain, put into a skillet with melted butter. Add sour cream and caraway seeds. Season to taste and simmer 3 minutes. Add whole shrimp and heat. You may omit the shrimp and caraway seeds and add lots of chopped parsley.

GERMAN STYLE RED CABBAGE

Mrs. William Cork (Helen)

1	small head red cabbage		Boiling water
2	tart red apples	3	tablespoons red wine vinegar
2	tablespoons bacon fat	1	teaspoon sugar
	Salt and pepper	1	tablespoon flour

After removing outer leaves from cabbage; quarter, core, and shred the head. Without peeling apples, core and slice them. Combine cabbage, apples, bacon fat, salt and pepper to taste in a heavy aluminum or stainless steel saucepan. Add just enough boiling water to cover. Cover pan and simmer until cabbage is tender, but still somewhat crisp, about 20 minutes. Drain cabbage, reserving liquid. Return cabbage to saucepan and keep hot. Mix vinegar, sugar and flour in second saucepan. Stir in reserved liquid. Cook, stirring constantly, until thickened. Stir sauce into cabbage, taste for seasoning, reheat and serve.

APRICOT GLAZED CARROTS

Serves 6 to 8   Mrs. Herbert Kirsh (Suzanne)

4	cups sliced carrots	1/4	teaspoon grated orange rind
3	tablespoons melted butter	1/4	teaspoon nutmeg
1/3	cup apricot preserves	2	teaspoons lemon juice
1/4	teaspoon salt		

Cook carrots until tender. Add enough salted water to cook, about 20 minutes, and drain. Combine remaining ingredients, stirring until well blended. Spoon over carrots, and toss well. Serve at once.

SWEET AND SOUR CARROTS

Serves 8 to 10   Mrs. Nick Theodore (Emilie)

2	cans Fingerling carrots	1/4	teaspoon pepper
3/4	tablespoon flour	1/2	cup vinegar
1/2	cup sugar	2	tablespoons butter

Bring sauce to a boil and add 2 cans Fingerling carrots. Mix and let simmer 2 to 3 minutes.

EDEN'S FLOWER

Senator Norma Russell

1	head cauliflower, separated into flowerets	1	stick butter
			Juice of 1/4 lemon
3	medium zucchini, sliced 1/2-inch thick	1	generous teaspoon basil
		1	generous teaspoon oregano
1	cup water	2	cloves garlic, pressed
1-1/2	teaspoon salt	1/2	cup grated Parmesan cheese
1/4	teaspoon coarse ground black pepper		

In skillet, poach cauliflower in water with 1/2 teaspoon salt, about 5 minutes. Pour off water, remove flowerets. Melt butter in skillet, stir in seasonings (do not forget other 1 teaspoon salt). Add zucchini first, then cauliflower. Cover. Cook on low heat for 20 minutes, stirring occasionally. Toss with 1/2 cup Parmesan cheese before serving.

COUNTRY CORN PUDDING

Serves 6 to 8   Mrs. Ralph Ellis (Eleanor)

2	16-ounce cans cream style corn	3	tablespoons self-rising flour
3	eggs, beaten	3/4	cup milk
1/2	cup sugar		Salt and pepper to taste

Mix all ingredients together and pour into buttered casserole. Dot top with butter. Bake 1-1/4 hours at 350 degrees.

VARIATION: Congressman Floyd D. Spence

Mix together 1 can cream style corn, 1 tbls. sugar, 3 tbls. flour, 3 slightly beaten eggs, 1 cup milk, 1/4 tsp. nutmeg, salt and pepper. Pour into buttered casserole and bake for 1 hour at 350 degrees. Serves 4 to 6.

EGGPLANT-CLAM CASSEROLE

Serves 4 to 6   Mrs. Ramon Schwartz (Rosa)

1	large eggplant	1	can minced clams, drained
1	stick melted butter	3/4	cup grated cheese
16	saltine crackers		Buttered bread crumbs
1	cup milk		Salt and pepper

Cook eggplant, mash and drain. Add crushed saltines and butter. Mix in remaining ingredients; milk, clams and grated cheese. Top with bread crumbs. Bake at 350 degrees for 45 minutes.

MUSHROOM CASSEROLE

Serves 6 to 8   Mrs. Michael R. Daniel (Peggy)

1	pound mushrooms, sliced	1/2	cup half-and-half
1	8-ounce can black olives, pitted	1-1/2	tablespoons butter, melted
4	ounces cheddar cheese, grated	1/2	teaspoon salt
1-1/2	tablespoons flour	1/2	teaspoon pepper

In 2-quart round casserole layer mushrooms and olives. Mix flour, half-and-half, butter, salt and pepper. Pour over mushrooms and olives. Top with cheese. If you think the casserole is too full, don't worry, it will cook down. Bake, uncovered, at 350 degrees for 30 minutes.

BUTTERED GREENS

Serves 4   Mrs. Robert N. McLellan (Doris)

2 to 2-1/2-pounds young tender kale, collards or spinach		3	slices bacon
1/2	small chopped onion	1	tablespoon butter
1	minced garlic (for spinach only)	1	teaspoon salt
		Pinch	nutmeg (for spinach only)

Strip veins and stems from greens. (I use scissors to do this.) Wash remaining leaves thoroughly, at least 3 times in water. Be sure to lift the greens out of each water so that the dirt and grit sinks to the bottom. Cook, covered, in 1/2-inch boiling water with salt (and nutmeg if spinach) for 10 to 15 minutes, or until tender. Drain and chop coarsely. Cook the bacon until crisp. Drain bacon thoroughly and crumble. Sauté onion in butter and small amount of bacon fat. (Add garlic and saute if using spinach.) Add to cooked greens with crumbled bacon. Add salt. Serve immediately.

KORN KASSEROLE

Serves 4 to 6   Mrs. Nick Theodore (Emilie)

1 16-ounce can cream style corn	1/2 cup chopped onion
1 cup milk	1/4 cup pimento
1-1/2 cups crushed saltines	2 eggs, beaten
1/4 cup chopped bell pepper	

Warm corn and milk gradually; when almost bubbly, add eggs, 1 at a time. Add pepper, pimento and 1 cup cracker crumbs. Pour in baking dish. Melt 4 tablespoons butter and mix with remainder of cracker crumbs and spoon over casserole. Bake at 350 degrees approximately 40 minutes or until brown.

EGGPLANT PARMESAN

Serves 12   Mrs. J. P. Gardner (Pam)

1 medium eggplant, peeled and cut into 1 to 1-1/2-inch cubes	1 10-3/4-ounce can tomato soup
1 large onion sliced	1 cup water
1 medium green pepper, sliced	1/4 teaspoon salt
1 clove garlic, minced	Garlic croutons
1 teaspoon oregano	Grated Parmesan cheese, fresh or canned
1/4 cup butter	

Cook eggplant in boiling salted water for 3 minutes. Drain and place in shallow baking dish. Cook onion, green pepper, garlic and oregano in butter until tender. Add soup, water and salt. Heat; pour sauce over eggplant. Bake in 350 degree oven 45 minutes. Stir often. Remove. Turn oven up to 425 degrees. Top eggplant with croutons and sprinkle with cheese. Return to oven, bake 15 minutes.

EGGPLANT CASSEROLE

Serves 6 to 8   Mrs. Walter Bristow, Jr. (Stewart)

1 eggplant peeled, cubed, cooked and drained	1 egg, beaten
1 10-3/4-ounce can mushroom soup	1/2 onion, chopped
1/3 cup milk	3/4 cup herb stuffing
	1 cup grated cheddar cheese

Mix all the above ingredients except cheese. Salt and pepper to taste. Put in 1-1/2-quart baking dish and top with grated cheese. Bake at 350 degrees for 20 minutes or until hot and bubbly.

BAKED OKRA GUMBO

Mrs. J. L. Henson (Ruby)

3/4	pound fresh okra	2	small strips bacon
1	small onion	1/2	teaspoon salt
1	16-ounce can stewed tomatoes		

Slice okra about 1/2-inch thick and place in a 1-quart casserole. Cover with diced onion, and then stewed tomatoes. Place bacon strips over the top and bake covered for about 40 minutes at 350 degrees.

ONION PIE

Serves 6 to 8   Mrs. Robert N. McLellan (Doris)

1	cup saltine crackers, crushed in blender	1	cup milk
		1	teaspoon salt
1/3	cup melted butter	1/2	teaspoon pepper, freshly ground
4	large sweet onions	4	eggs, slightly beaten
1/4	pound butter	3/4	cup grated sharp cheese

Mix saltines and butter and press into bottom and sides of a 10-inch pie pan. Slice onions thin and sauté in butter until transparent. Pour cooked onions and butter into crust. Combine milk, salt, pepper and eggs. Pour over onions. Sprinkle top generously with grated cheese and bake in a 350 degree oven for 30 minutes. (A good substitute for potatoes served with beef fondue or steak.)

POTATOES AND ONIONS CHANTILLY

Serves 10   Mrs. John Land (Marie)

4	cups potatoes, boiled and mashed	1	3-1/2-ounce can French fried onions
1/4	cup butter	1	cup unsweetened whipped cream
1-1/2	teaspoon salt	2/3	cup grated sharp cheddar cheese
1/2	teaspoon pepper	1-1/2	teaspoon parsley flakes or fresh chopped parsley

Butter a 1-1/2-quart casserole dish. Combine potatoes, butter, 1 teaspoon salt and pepper and whip with a fork until fluffy. Stir in all but 1/2 cup of French fried onions. Spoon into the buttered casserole. (Do not push potatoes down as you want them light and fluffy.) Combine 1/3 cup cheese, whipped cream and 1/2 teaspoon salt. Spread lightly over the potato mixture. Sprinkle with remaining cheese and onions. Bake at 325 degrees for 25 to 30 minutes or until the top is delicately browned. Let this casserole stand for 3 or 4 minutes before serving so that the cream can settle.

HASH BROWN AU GRATIN

Serves 4 to 6   Mrs. Alex S. Macaulay (Maria)

1	12-ounce package frozen hash brown potatoes, defrosted	2	tablespoons butter
1/2	cup milk	1/2	teaspoon white pepper
1	12-ounce carton sour cream with chives	1	teaspoon seasoned salt
		2	cups cheddar cheese, grated

Gently mix together potatoes, milk, sour cream, butter, white pepper, salt and 1-1/2 cups cheddar cheese. Heat over medium heat until cheese melts. Pour into a greased 9x9-inch baking dish and top with remaining 1/2 cup cheddar cheese. Bake at 350 degrees for 30 minutes. (A nice breakfast or brunch dish.)

CURRIED POTATOES

Serves 6 to 8   Mrs. P. P. Leventis (Ellen)

5	cups cooked diced potatoes	5	tablespoons flour
1/2	cup chopped onion	2	teaspoons curry powder
2	tablespoons tomato paste	1/4	teaspoon chili powder
2-1/2	cups chicken bouillon	1	teaspoon salt
4	tablespoons butter or margarine	1	teaspoon pepper

Put potatoes into buttered casserole. Sauté onion in butter until tender. To onions add curry, flour, chili, salt and pepper. Mix well. Add bouillon gradually, stirring constantly. Cook and stir over medium heat until mixture boils. Stir in tomato paste. Pour mixture over potatoes. Bake 30 minutes at 375 degrees.

PARTY POTATOES

Mrs. W. B. Hawkins (Sarah)

8 to 10	potatoes, boiled and peeled	4	tablespoons butter
1	8-ounce package cream cheese	1/3	cup chopped chives
1	carton sour cream		Paprika, salt and pepper

Beat potatoes and add rest of ingredients. Pour into greased casserole. Dot with butter. Sprinkle with paprika. Bake at 350 degrees for 25 minutes.

PARMESAN FRITTATAS

Serves 4   Mrs. I. S. Leevy Johnson (Doris)

2   tablespoons margarine or butter
6   eggs, slightly beaten
1   cup cooked, chopped potatoes
1/2   cup grated Parmesan cheese
Dash pepper

6   slices bacon, fried crisp and crumbled
1/4   cup green onion slices
1/4   cup milk

Melt butter in a 10-inch oven proof skillet or omelet pan over low heat. Combine remaining ingredients, pour into skillet. Bake 350 degrees for 20 minutes. Sprinkle with additional cheese, if desired.

PATIO POTATOES

Serves 8 to 10   Mrs. William J. McLeod (Sara)

6   medium Idaho potatoes
1   cup cottage cheese
1   cup sour cream
2   tablespoons chopped green onions

2   tablespoons butter
1/4   cup parmesan cheese (or 1/2 cup sharp grated cheese)
Garlic salt, optional

Cook potatoes. Mash and season to taste. Add cottage cheese, sour cream and onions. Place in lightly buttered casserole dish. Dot with butter and bake at 350 degrees until thoroughly heated, 30 to 45 minutes. Add cheese last 10 minutes. This may be prepared ahead, and it freezes nicely. (Bake after freezing.)

VARIATION: Mrs. T. L. Hughston (Jeanne)

Add 2 12-ounce cartons cottage cheese and 1 cup sharp cheese. Instead of mashed potatoes, use cooled and diced potatoes. Mix all ingredients together and sprinkle top with parsley and paprika.

ROAST POTATOES

Mrs. Robert N. McLellan (Doris)

1-1/2 pounds potatoes, new or old   1/4   cup fat, clarified dripping or shortening

I think nothing is more delicious than new potatoes, washed, dried then roasted in their skins. If roasting old potatoes, peel and divide large potatoes into convenient-sized pieces. Keep in cold water until ready to cook. Dry thoroughly. Make sure the fat around the meat or in a separate roasting pan is really hot. There is no need to use more than 1/4 cup fat for this amount of potatoes. Roll the potatoes in the hot fat and roast in a hot oven, 425 degrees. Allow 45 to 55 minutes for medium-sized potatoes. Turn the potatoes once during cooking. Slow roasting is not suitable for roast potatoes. These are the favorite accompaniment with most roast joints.

SOUTH CAROLINA SWEET POTATO SURPRISE

Serves 8 to 10   Mrs. Robert N. McLellan (Doris)

6   large South Carolina sweet   1/4 teaspoon salt
    potatoes, cooked and halved 1/8 teaspoon cinnamon
    lengthwise (or 1-pound can   1   teaspoon shredded orange peel
    sweet potatoes)   Orange juice
1-1/4 cups brown sugar   1   1-pound can apricot halves
1-1/2 tablespoons cornstarch   2   tablespoons butter
                               1/4 cup pecan halves

Place sweet potatoes in greased 10x6x1-1/2-inch baking dish. In saucepan combine next 5 ingredients. Drain apricots and reserve syrup. Add orange juice to make 1 cup. Stir 1 cup apricot syrup into cornstarch mixture. Cook and stir over medium heat until boiling. Boil 2 minutes. Add apricots, butter and pecan halves. Pour over sweet potatoes. Bake, uncovered, in a 375 degree oven for 25 minutes. NOTE: If possible don't omit orange peel! It adds flavor. If less than 1 cup apricot syrup, round out with orange juice.

RATATOUILLE

Serves 8   Mrs. Larry A. Martin (Susan)

3   medium-sized zucchini   1   cup thin sliced onion
1   medium-sized eggplant, peeled 1/4 cup salad oil
4   tomatoes, peeled   1   clove garlic, finely minced
2   green peppers   Salt and pepper

Slice zucchini and eggplant into 1/4-inch slices. Cut tomatoes in medium dice. Seed the peppers, slice thin and blanch. Sauté the onion in the oil until soft; do not brown. Add tomatoes, cook 1 minute. Mix the rest of the ingredients, cover and bring to boiling point. Cook 5 minutes. Remove cover and cook at simmer heat until all liquid has evaporated. Correct seasonings; sprinkle with chopped parsley. This is the most versatile of all vegetable dishes. You may use it hot or cold, as an hors d' oeuvre, salad, main dish or in crepes; keep it covered in your refrigerator for several days.

SPINACH AND ARTICHOKE CASSEROLE

Serves 12   Mrs. J. Verne Smith (Jean)

2   15-ounce cans artichoke hearts,   1   can water chestnuts, sliced
      drained   1/2   pound butter
2   8-ounce packages cream cheese   Onion flakes
1   clove crushed fresh garlic   Seasoned bread crumbs
7 or 8 10-ounce packages frozen   Salt and pepper to taste
      chopped spinach, cooked and well drained

Place artichoke halves in buttered 9x13-inch casserole. Add water chestnuts. Mix cream cheese and butter together in double boiler. After it is soft mix with spinach. Add garlic, onion flakes, salt and pepper to taste. Pour over artichokes and chestnuts. Bake at 350 degrees for 30 minutes. Sprinkle with seasoned bread crumbs and bake another 10 minutes.

SPINACH CASSEROLE

Serves 8   Mrs. Horace C. Smith (Dot)

1/2   pound sliced bacon   1   teaspoon salt
2   packages frozen chopped   2/3   cup soft bread crumbs
      spinach   1-1/2 cups shredded Provalone cheese
2   eggs   Paprika
2   cups milk

Dice bacon and pan broil until crisp. Drain on absorbent paper. Cook spinach according to directions. Drain thoroughly. Beat eggs slightly. Add milk and salt. Stir in the spinach, bread crumbs, bacon and half the cheese. Pour mixture into a 1-1/2-quart baking dish. Sprinkle remaining cheese around outside edge. Sprinkle with paprika. Cook in a 375 degree oven 30 to 35 minutes.

SQUASH PARMESAN

Serves 6   Mrs. Ramon Schwartz (Rosa)

12 to 14 small squash, sliced   1   8-ounce carton sour cream
2 or 3 grated carrots   1   cup Pepperidge Farm herb-
2 or 3 cut up onions   seasoned dressing
1   stick butter   Grated Parmesan cheese

Melt butter. Sauté squash, carrots, onions, salt and pepper. Add sour cream and Pepperidge Farm dressing. Mix well and put in greased casserole dish. Top with grated Parmesan cheese. (May add a few mushrooms.) Cook at 350 degrees for 30 minutes.

SQUASH CASSEROLE

Serves 8 to 10   Mrs. L. Edward Bennett (Peggy)

6	large yellow squash (3-pounds)	Salt and pepper to taste	
1	large onion, chopped	1	rounded teaspoon sugar
1	green pepper, minced	Dash of Accent	
2	tablespoons butter	Bread or cracker crumbs	
1	egg	3 or 4 slices bacon	

Slice squash and boil in small amount of salted water for 10 minutes or until tender. Drain. Sauté green pepper and onion in melted butter until tender but not brown. Beat egg in large mixing bowl. Add squash, green pepper, onion, butter, sugar, Accent, salt and pepper. Mix well. Put in baking dish 2-inches deep. Sprinkle with cracker crumbs and lay strips of bacon across top. Bake in oven at 350 degrees for 30 to 40 minutes, turning bacon once to crisp. Freezes well; however, omit crumbs and bacon until ready to cook.

VARIATION NO. 1:   Mrs. David E. Turnipseed (Cindy)

Add 1/2 cup cracker crumbs and top with 1-1/2 cups buttered bread crumbs. Omit green pepper, sugar and bacon. Add 1 10-3/4-ounce can cream of chicken soup. Use 2 cups cooked and drained squash, 1/2 onion and 1/4 cup margarine. Bake at 275 degrees for 35 to 40 minutes.

VARIATION NO. 2:   Senator Norma Russell

Omit bacon, green pepper and sugar. Increase eggs to 2 and butter to 1/2 stick. Add 4 cups cooked squash, drained and 1 cup medium sharp cheese, grated. Use 1-1/4 cups milk.

STUFFED SQUASH-LEBANESE
Representative Bob Sheheen

10 to 12 medium yellow squash		1	8-ounce can tomato sauce
1	pound ground chuck	Salt and pepper	
1/2	cup rice	Dash of cinnamon	
1	large can tomatoes	1/4	cup butter

Wash and cut necks off squash. Save the core of the squash and discard insides. Make mixture of chuck, rice and tomatoes. Season with salt, pepper and a dash of cinnamon. Chop butter into small pieces with paring knife and mix into stuffing mixture. Stuff squash with mixture and arrange in pot with open ends up. Use necks to fill in spaces between squash to prevent tipping over. Pour in tomato sauce and enough water to reach the top of squash. Cover and bring to a boil. Simmer for 20 to 40 minutes until a fork indicates necks are tender. Serve with its' own sauce.

SQUASH SOUFFLE

Serves 8   Mrs. Walter Bristow, Jr. (Stewart)

1	quart cooked squash, drained	2	tablespoons melted butter
1	medium onion, chopped fine	1	teaspoon baking powder
1/2	cup grated sharp cheese	1-1/2	tablespoons flour
3	tablespoons milk	1/8	teaspoon pepper
2	eggs		Salt to taste

Add onion, cheese and milk to cooked squash. Then whip together eggs, butter, baking powder and flour. Add to squash. Add salt and pepper. Pour into greased 2 or 2-1/2-quart round baking dish and bake at 325 degrees for 45 minutes.

SPINACH CHEESE PIE

Serves 6 to 8   Mrs. John Spratt (Jane)

Combine 2 cups seasoned crushed croutons and 1/4 cup butter. Mix well, press into pie pan. Combine 4 tbls. grated Parmesan cheese, 1 box drained and thawed chopped spinach, 1 cup small curd cottage cheese, 4 ounces cubed Jack cheese, 3 beaten eggs, 1/4 cup chopped onion, 2 tbls. sour cream, 1 clove garlic and 1/2 tsp. salt. Pour into pie pan. Sprinkle with 2 tbls. Parmesan cheese. Bake 35 minutes at 350 degrees. Let stand 5 minutes before serving.

ARTICHOKE AND SPINACH AU GRATIN

Serves 4 to 6   Mrs. Nick Theodore (Emilie)

Sauté 1 15-oz. can artichoke hearts, drained and halved, in 1 tbls. butter. When cool add 3 pkgs. frozen chopped spinach, cooked and drained; 1 8-oz. softened cream cheese; 1 tsp. salt; 1/2 tsp. pepper; and 1 cup chopped onion. Mix well and pour into a baking dish. Top with 1 cup grated Swiss cheese and paprika. Bake at 350 degrees for 30 minutes.

VEGETABLES

HERBED TOMATOES
Serves 3 to 4   Mrs. Michael R. Daniel (Peggy)

1	28-ounce can whole tomatoes, drain and save juice	1-1/2 teaspoons sugar
1-1/4	cups chicken and herb flavored stuffing mix	1 teaspoon salt
1	small onion, chopped fine	1/4 teaspoon dried whole oregano
		1/4 teaspoon whole rosemary
		1 tablespoon butter

Divide stuffing in half. Cut tomatoes and combine with tomato juice, onion, sugar, salt, oregano, rosemary and 1 cup stuffing. Pour in greased 1-quart casserole. Sprinkle with remaining stuffing. Dot with butter. Bake at 375 degrees for 45 minutes.

TOMATO SIDE DISH
Serves 6   Mrs. William Cork (Helen)

2 16-ounce cans solid pack tomatoes
8 whole cloves
8 whole peppercorns
1 bay leaf
Salt
1/2 yellow onion, chopped
1/4 cup brown sugar
3 or 4 slices white bread pulled into dime-sized pieces
2 tablespoons butter

Put cloves, peppercorns and bay leaf in cheesecloth bag. Cook tomatoes, undrained, cheesecloth bag and a dash of salt on top of stove very slowly for 30 minutes. Stir occasionally. Remove cheesecloth bag. Add onion, sugar, bread, and butter. Place in greased baking dish, and bake at 400 degrees for 1 hour. This may be made ahead, refrigerated, and baked later.

SCALLOPED TOMATOES
Serves 6 to 8   Mrs. William J. McLeod (Sara)

1/2 cup chopped celery
1 28-ounce can tomatoes, undrained
1/2 cup chopped onions
1 teaspoon salt
2 tablespoons margarine
1 tablespoon sugar
2 tablespoon flour
2 cups bread cubes

Cook onions and celery in margarine until tender. Add other ingredients, reserving 1 cup bread cubes for topping. Bake at 350 degrees until cubes are brown, about 20 to 30 minutes.

CHEESY-NUT VEGETABLE PIE

Mrs. R. L. Altman (Nancy)

1	10-ounce package frozen cut broccoli	1	cup milk
1	small onion	1	cup Swiss cheese
1	8-ounce can whole kernel corn	2	eggs, beaten
2	tablespoons margarine	1/2	cup peanuts
2	tablespoons flour	1	10-inch pie crust

Cook broccoli; then cook onion in margarine. Add flour and milk, stir until blended. Add cheese, stirring until melted. Add vegetables and nuts. Put in pie shell and bake for 35 minutes in a 350 degree oven. Optional: Make crust strip from additional pie crust to lay on top of pie before baking.

ZUCCHINI PARMIGIANA

Serves 4   Mrs. Robert N. McLellan (Doris)

3   medium zucchini squash, sliced
Flour
1/2 cup salad oil
1   8-ounce package Mozzarella cheese, cut into small pieces
1   8-ounce can tomato sauce
1/2 teaspoon onion salt
1/2 teaspoon garlic salt
1/2 teaspoon oregano, ground in palm of hand
Fresh Parmesan cheese, grated
White pepper, to taste

Sprinkle zucchini with salt and allow to set 1 hour. Rinse all salt and squeeze liquid from it. Dip sliced zucchini in flour and fry in salad oil until lightly browned. Later in a lightly greased 1-1/2-quart casserole dish as follows: zucchini, cheese, and tomato sauce. Season each layer with onion salt, garlic salt, oregano and white pepper to taste. Top with Parmesan cheese. Bake, uncovered, in a 350 degree oven for 35 to 45 minutes. Serve immediately. Delicious when reheated in a moderate oven or microwave.

VEG-ALL CASSEROLE

Serves 8   Cookbook Committee Selection

Mix together and pour into an oven-proof casserole: 2 16-oz. cans drained Veg-All; 1 cup each chopped celery; chopped onions; sliced water chestnuts; grated cheese; and mayonnaise. Cover with Ritz cracker crumbs and grated cheese. Dot with butter and bake 30 minutes at 350 degrees.

The first recorded white settler into the territory now known as Fairfield County was Thomas Nightingale. This adventurer established a farm and trading post on Little Cedar Creek in the late 1730s. By 1750 the country side was dotted with numerous small farms. Groups of Scotch-Irish, German, Swiss, and Welsh immigrants searching for land and religious freedom located in the county, establishing communities at Beaver Creek and Peay's Ferry. Robert Mills reported in his Statistics of South Carolina that numerous rattlesnakes of "extraordinary size" infested the forest of Fairfield. According to an account a snake large enough to have eaten a fawn was killed near Fort Waggoner around the time of the Cherokee war.

General Richard Winn, founder of Winnsboro, served at Fort Moultrie and distinguished himself at the battle of Hanging Rock in Lancaster County. Although no major battles were fought in the county, Cornwallis used the district as the winter headquarters for his army in 1780. Legend has it that Cornwallis found the surrounding countryside so pleasant that he referred to it as Fair Fields. The title stuck and in 1791 when the territory was organized as a county, Fairfield became its official name.

Winnsboro was designated as the county seat and a court house was built on the town square. The present County Court House was built in 1823 from a design by Robert Mills. Nearby stands the old Town Clock, built in France and assembled in the town square in 1833. This time piece is said to be the oldest continuously running clock in the United States.

Modern Fairfield County retains all of the beauty and charm that first attracted settlers to the area in the 1700s. Although some industrialization has come in recent years, ponds, pines and pastures continue as the mainstays of Fairfield's economy.

CHESTER COUNTY

Immigrants from Pennsylvania and Virginia established settlements in Chester County as early as 1750. Prior to the arrival of these small farmers the area had been principally inhabited by the Catawba Indians. The numerous navigable streams located in and around Chester made the territory an attractive sight for settlements. The Broad and Catawba rivers which flow the length of the county connected the early residents with markets in the midlands. Chesterville situated between the waters of these two major rivers became the center of commerce in the county. During the colonial period the town prospered and after the Revolution the city was designated as the county seat of Chester County.

The county is named for Chester, Pennsylvania, where the majority of Scotch-Irish who settled the county had originally made their homes.

In the town square of Chester stands an interesting monument to one of the city's early visitors. In 1802 Aaron Burr was brought through the city on his way to stand trial in Richmond for treason. When the escort reached the town square Burr broke away, jumped up on a large rock and began begging the local residents for help. The soldiers quickly subdued their prisoner and spirited him away to Lewis Tavern where Burr was locked in a room for the night.

The Landsford Canal is another important landmark. This two mile stretch of canal was originally designed as part of a planned system linking Charleston with the Mississippi. The canal's three stone locks were carved from granite quarried in the county. Although the entire network of waterways was never completed, the Landsford Canal operated as an important link in South Carolina's early inland transportation system.

The county's economy began changing toward the end of the 19th century. Cotton mills located there and other industry soon followed. The Great Falls were harnessed by hydroelectric generators in the early 20th century. The abundant supply of electricity produced by local power plants made the county an attractive sight for industrial expansion and relocation.

LANCASTER COUNTY

Lancaster is the only county in the state that can claim a U.S. President as a native son. In 1767 at the Waxhaw settlement near the North Carolina border, Andrew Jackson, the country's seventh president, was born. The Jackson homestead is now encompassed within the boundaries of the Andrew Jackson State Park.

The county is named for Lancaster, Pennsylvania, first home of the Scotch-Irish colonists who relocated to South Carolina during the 1750s.

Numerous skirmishes occurred in the county during the war. The area around Lancaster was filled with backcountry partisans who rallied to the American cause after a detachment of British cavalry under the command of Bannister Tarleton massacred an American force in the county. It was at what is now known as Buford's Battlefield that Tarleton, after defeating the Americans in a fierce battle, ordered his men to take no prisoners. The American defeat at Buford's Battlefield was avenged in 1780 when an American force under the command of General Sumter captured and destroyed a British garrison at the Battle of Hanging Rock.

After burning Columbia, Sherman's army headed north stopping in Lan-

145

caster before crossing over into North Carolina. A detachment of soldiers entered the city of Lancaster and proceeded to set fire to the court house and jail. The town residents quickly assembled in the square, organized a bucket brigade and promptly extinguished the fires. Both buildings were saved preserving for later generations two fine examples of Robert Mills' handiwork.

In the modern era Lancaster County has developed as one of the major textile centers in the state. The Springs family began their manufacturing businesses in the county. Today Springs Mills produces some of the best textile products in the country. Gold was also once a major export from the county. The Haile Gold Mine produced ore until the early 1940s. Today Lancaster County is one of the upcountry's most thriving communities. Its comfortable climate and hospitable communities make it one of the hallmark counties in the state.

After the Revolution George Washington visited the county during his tour of the southern states. The country's first president spent the night at the Ingram House which in 1865 was used by General Sherman as a staff headquarters.

THE McCREIGHT HOUSE

The McCreight House in Winnsboro was built in 1774 by Colonel William McCreight. It is said to be the first frame house built in Fairfield County. The three storied building is being renovated.

eggs, cheese and grains

HAM AND CHICKEN CASSEROLE

Serves 15   Mrs. Robert C. Lake, Jr. (Carolyn)

1/2	pound spaghetti (broken in 1-inch pieces and cooked until just tender)	2	10-3/4-ounce cans cream of chicken soup
2 to 3	cups diced chicken	1	cup chicken broth
1	cup diced ham	1/4	teaspoon celery salt
1/2	cup chopped pimento	1/4	teaspoon pepper
1/2	cup green pepper, chopped	1	large grated onion
		2	cups grated cheese

Mix all together and pour into 3 quart casserole. Add 1 extra cup of grated cheese to top of casserole. Bake at 350 degrees for 1 hour.

"PASTITSIO", GREEK MACARONI SQUARES

Yield: 24 to 30   Mrs. Nick A. Theodore (Emilie)

2	onions, grated	1	teaspoon cinnamon
1-1/2	sticks butter	1	12-ounce package macaroni
2	pounds ground beef		Salt and pepper to taste
1	small can tomato sauce	4	eggs
1	cup water	1	quart milk
1	cup grated Romano cheese	2/3	cup flour

Sauté onions in 1/4 stick butter. Add ground meat, tomato sauce and 1 cup water. Cook 1 hour. In the last half hour, add 4 tablespoons grated cheese and cinnamon. Boil macaroni. Drain. Add 1/2 stick melted butter. Add grated cheese, salt, pepper, 2 whole eggs and 2 egg whites that have been well beaten. Set aside. Melt 1/2 stick butter. Add flour and mix well. Add slowly 1-quart lukewarm milk, stirring constantly. Cook slowly until mixture thickens. Add salt and 2 egg yolks. Line 11x14-inch pan with butter and sprinkle with bread crumbs. Spread a thick layer of macaroni in pan. Add meat sauce and spread evenly over macaroni. Add remaining macaroni, spreading over meat sauce layer. Pour cream sauce over all. Bake at 350 degrees for 1 hour. Cut into squares.

BAKED SPAGHETTI

Mrs. W. B. Hawkins (Sarah)

5	large onions, chopped	1	28-ounce can tomatoes
1-1/2	pounds lean ground meat	1	stick margarine
5	whole cloves	1	pound grated sharp cheese
4	bay leaves, crumbled	Spaghetti, cooked	

Cook onions and spices in margarine for 5 minutes. Add meat and brown. Place grated cheese and tomatoes in bowl. Pour over hot spaghetti. Add rest of cooked ingredients. Let stand for several hours. Bake at 350 degrees for 1 hour stirring several times.

MACARONI MOUSSE

Serves 8 to 10   Mrs. Frank McGill (Peggy)

1	cup macaroni	MUSHROOM SAUCE:	
1	cup soft bread crumbs	1-1/2 cups milk	
1	small jar chopped pimiento	1	tablespoon butter
1	tablespoon chopped onion	4	tablespoon flour
3/8	teaspoon salt	1/4	teaspoon salt
Dash paprika		Dash paprika	
1-1/2	cups scalding milk	1/2	cup mushroom liquor, drained
1/4	cup melted butter		from mushrooms
1	tablespoon chopped parsley	1	6-ounce can mushrooms
1-1/2	cups grated cheese	1/8	teaspoon pepper
1/8	teaspoon pepper		
3	eggs		

Cook macaroni in boiling salted water, blanch in cold water and drain. Pour scalded milk over bread crumbs; add remaining ingredients except eggs. Add well-beaten eggs. Place macaroni in a thickly buttered 3-quart dish and pour milk and cheese mixture over it. Bake about 50 minutes at 325 degrees, or until loaf is firm and will hold its shape when turned out onto a platter. Serve with MUSHROOM SAUCE: Combine all ingredients except mushrooms. Thicken over low heat. Add mushrooms and pour over macaroni loaf. Excellent for holiday dinners; especially with poultry or game dishes. Garnish platter with parsley.

NOODLES

Mrs. Jarvis R. Klapman (Arlene)

3	cups plain flour	1-1/2	teaspoons salt
1-1/2	teaspoons baking powder	1	egg
2	tablespoons melted fat	1/3	cup half water and half milk

Sift dry ingredients together. Beat egg, add melted fat and 1/3 cup of the water-milk mixture. Beat together. Add this mix to the dry ingredients and mix to make a very stiff dough (if necessary, add more water-milk mix or flour). Roll out between sheets of waxed paper. Cut into desired widths. Drop into boiling stewed chicken, beef stock or soup. Cook until done, about 8 to 15 minutes.

NOODLES AND BEEF CASSEROLE

Serves 8   Mrs. Beattie E. Huff (Gladys)

1 to 1-1/2 pounds ground beef
1   big jar Ragu thick and zesty
       sauce
8   ounces egg noodles, cooked
       and drained
1   small chopped onion

1/2 cup freshly grated Parmesan
       cheese
8   ounces sour cream
1   small container small curd
       cottage cheese
Salt to taste

Sauté meat and drain. Add sauce and simmer 1 hour. Mix together the noodles, onion, sour cream and cottage cheese. Season to taste. Layer noodle mixture and meat sauce mixture twice into a buttered 3 quart casserole. Cover with Parmesan cheese and bake at 350 degrees for 30 minutes or until hot and bubbly.

GREEN NOODLES

Serves 6   Mrs. Larry A. Martin (Susan)

1   8-ounce package green noodles
1   teaspoon salt

1   cup sour cream
Cracked pepper

Cook noodles in boiling water (with a little olive oil added to keep the noodles from boiling over) until tender. Drain, but do not wash. Add sour cream and toss with seasonings until well blended.

HAMBURGER CASSEROLE

Serves 6   Mrs. Ben F. Hornsby (Esther)

1	pound ground beef	1	cup Cheddar cheese, grated
2	cups egg noodles	1	bell pepper, chopped
1	onion, diced	1	16-ounce can tomato soup
1	10-3/4-ounce can mushroom soup		

Sauté onions and peppers; add to browned ground beef in 9-inch skillet. Stir in tomato soup; season to taste. Let simmer 10 minutes. Take off heat and stir in grated cheese. Pour over cooked noodles in casserole dish. Top with mushroom soup. Bake at 350 degrees for 30 minutes.

VERMICELLI AND VEGETABLE STROGANOFF

Serves 6   Mrs. Dill Blackwell (Margaret)

2	cups chopped cauliflower	2	tablespoons flour
2	cups chopped broccoli	2	cups milk
1-1/2	cups thinly sliced carrots	1/2	teaspoon chicken bouillon
3	cups sliced mushrooms		granules
1	small onion, chopped	1/3	cup sliced black olives
1	clove garlic, minced	1	cup Ricotto or cottage cheese
3	tablespoons butter	1/2	cup Parmesan cheese
12	ounces vermicelli or other pasta	3/4	cup sour cream

Cook cauliflower, broccoli and carrots in boiling salted water 5 minutes. Drain well and set aside. Cook mushrooms, onions and garlic in butter until tender. Stir in flour; add milk and chicken bouillon and cook and stir until thick and bubbly. Stir in vegetables and olives. In separate bowl; combine cottage cheese, sour cream, and half of the Parmesan cheese. Gradually stir in 1 cup of the vegetable mixture, a little at a time, so that sour cream mixture does not become hot too quickly. Return this mixture to vegetable mixture. Heat thoroughly over low heat. Do not let boil. Salt to taste. Cook pasta and drain well. Toss hot pasta with vegetable mixture. Sprinkle with Parmesan cheese before serving.

MACARONI AND CHEESE

Serves 8   Cookbook Committee Selection

Cook 1-1/2 cups macaroni. Drain and put in large bowl with 1 stick margarine and 1/2 to 1 lb. grated cheese. Mix well. Add 2 cups milk, 3 beaten eggs and 1/2 tsp. salt. Mix and pour into a 2 qt. dish. Top with grated cheese. Bake at 350 degrees for 45 to 60 minutes.

PASTA ITALIAN TOMATO SAUCE

Serves 8 to 10   Mrs. James Craven (Beverly)

2	pounds bulk sausage	2	16-ounce cans tomatoes, crushed
2	12-ounce cans tomato paste	2	12-ounce cans tomato sauce
2	cloves of garlic, chopped	1	can water for each can tomato
2	tablespoons sweet basil		product
2	tablespoons fennel seeds	2	tablespoons oregano

In large saucepan; add tomato products, water and garlic. Bring to boil. Add sausage meat, which has been cooked and drained, (microwave is great for cooking sausage) and seasoning. Salt and pepper to taste. Lower heat and cook two or three hours. Great sauce for spaghetti, lasagna, manicotti, etc.

RICE AND MUSHROOM CASSEROLE

Serves 8 to 10   Mrs. H. E. Pearce, Jr. (Jo)

5 to 6	cups cooked rice	1	small can pimento, chopped
1	large onion, chopped	1	small package slivered almonds
1	large green pepper, chopped	1	teaspoon garlic salt
1/2	stick butter or margarine	1	small can sliced mushrooms
1/4	cup Soy sauce		

Saute onion and pepper in butter. Add other ingredients, mix well and heat, uncovered, in moderate oven 20 to 30 minutes. Excellent with baked ham or poultry.

RICE PAPRIKA

Serves 4 to 6   Mrs. Herbert Kirsh (Suzanne)

3	tablespoons cooking oil	3 cups cooked rice
1	large onion, chopped	Garlic powder
1/2	large green pepper, chopped	Paprika
1/2	pound fresh mushrooms, sliced	Salt and pepper

In skillet saute onion in oil. Cook just before browning stage. Add green pepper and fresh mushrooms and cook about 20 minutes. Add cooked rice. Stir together. Season to taste. Turn heat to low. Sprinkle generously with paprika to give it a red color, stirring constantly so it will not stick.

BAKED BEEF HASH RICE

Serves 8 to 10   Mrs. Clyde M. Dangerfield (Betty)

2 pounds ground beef	1/2 cups each bell pepper and
1 quart tomatoes	onions, chopped
1 teaspoon chili powder	1 cup uncooked rice

Brown beef; add onions, bell pepper, tomatoes and chili powder. Combine this mixture with 1 cup uncooked rice. Bake in covered casserole at 350 degrees for 1 hour.

OVEN BAKED ORANGE RICE

Serves 4   Mrs. Robert C. Lake, Jr. (Carolyn)

3/4 cup regular long grain rice	1 tablespoon orange peel, grated
2/3 cup celery, chopped	1 teaspoon salt
2 tablespoons onion, chopped	3/4 cup orange juice
2 tablespoons melted butter	1-1/4 cups water

Preheat oven to 350 degrees. Mix rice, celery, onion, butter, orange peel and salt together and pour into a buttered 1-quart casserole. Heat orange juice and water together in a saucepan to boiling. Add orange juice mixture to casserole and stir. Cover and bake about 45 minutes or until rice is fluffy and tender. Toss with a fork and sprinkle with chopped parsley or slivered almonds.

BEEF-A-RICE

Serves 6   Mrs. Coleman G. Poag (Genie)

1 pound ground beef	1 cup rice, uncooked
1 16-ounce can tomato sauce	4 to 6 slices American cheese
1 small onion, chopped	

While rice is cooking in separate pan; saute onion and brown ground beef. Add tomato sauce and simmer. When rice is done, add it to beef sauce. Simmer until most of liquid is absorbed. Top with grated cheese. Cover. Heat until cheese is melted.

BROWN RICE CASSEROLE

Serves 8   Mrs. Mona Chapman

1	cup converted rice	2	10-3/4-ounce cans beef bouillon
1	small onion, chopped	1	stick margarine

Melt butter. Sauté onions and add to rice and bouillon. Put in a 9x12-inch casserole. Bake, covered, at 350 degrees for 1 hour.

VARIATION: Mrs. Robert N. McLellan (Doris)

Add 1 4-ounce can mushrooms, drained, to above ingredients. Omit onion, substitute 1 10-3/4-ounce can onion soup in place of 1 can beef bouillon.

SHRIMP FRIED RICE

Serves 8 to 10   Mrs. Rembert C. Dennis (Natalie)

2	cups raw rice		3 or 4 cups boiled shrimp
1	cup chopped onions	1	cup chopped bell pepper
1	cup chopped celery	1	can water chestnuts, sliced
1	can Chinese vegetables		Mushrooms
Soy sauce			

Cook rice. Sauté onions, bell pepper and celery. Add water chestnuts, vegetables, shrimp and rice. Season with plenty soy sauce.

RED RICE

Serves 6 to 8   Mrs. Thomas F. Hartnett (Bonnie)

1	can tomato paste	3	teaspoons sugar
1-1/2 - 2 cans water		4	strips bacon, cooked
2	onions, finely chopped	8	tablespoons bacon grease
3	teaspoons salt		Good dash pepper
2	cups raw rice		

Fry bacon, remove from pan. Sauté onion in grease; add tomato paste, water, salt, sugar and pepper. Cook uncovered, slowly, about 10 minutes until mixture measures 2 cups; then add it to rice in top section of steamer. Add the 1/2 cup additional grease. Steam for 1/2 hour, then add crumbled bacon, and stir with a fork. Cook 30 to 45 minutes longer.

BROWN RICE PILAF

Serves 8 to 10   Mrs. Edward Simpson (Maureen)

4	slices bacon	1/2	cup chopped onion
1/2	cup chopped celery	3	cups beef broth
1	cup brown rice	1/2	cup dry white wine
1/4	cup toasted slivered almonds	1/2	teaspoon salt

Cook bacon until crisp; drain, reserving 2 teaspoons drippings. Crumble bacon and set aside. Cook onions and celery in reserved drippings until tender but not brown. Stir in broth, uncooked rice, wine, almonds, salt and bacon; heat to boiling. Bake, covered, in a 325 degree oven for one hour.

PAPOU'S RICE PILAF

Serves 4   Mrs. Nick Theodore (Emilie)

1	10-3/4-ounce can chicken broth	1/2	can water
1	cup long grain rice (Uncle Ben's)		Salt to taste

Bring liquid to boil. Add rice, stir and reduce heat (do not cover). Let water boil down without stirring. If rice is still not tender, add about 1/4 cup water and cook until rice is tender. Melt 1/2 stick butter until brown, pour over rice and stir; cover for about 5 minutes.

WILD RICE AU VIN

Serves 8   Representative Irene K. Rudnick

1	cup Reese wild rice		Salt and pepper to taste
1	cup grated Cheddar cheese	1/2	cup finely chopped onions
1	cup chopped ripe olives	1/4	pound butter, melted
1	16-ounce can tomatoes	1	cup Claret wine
1	cup mushrooms, fresh or canned		

Wash rice and soak it overnight. When ready to prepare the casserole, drain rice in a colander. (Or save yourself all the bother and use Reese instant wild rice.) Reserve half the cheese for topping. Combine one half of the cheese with all other ingredients, including the prepared wild rice. Place mixture into a 2-1/2-quart casserole and top with remaining cheese. Bake at 350 degrees for 1 hour.

WILD RICE AND SAUSAGE

Serves 8   Mrs. Robert N. McLellan (Doris)

1	pound hot sausage	1/2	cup evaporated milk
1	large can chopped mushrooms, drained	2-1/2	cups chicken broth
1	6-ounce box Uncle Ben's wild rice	1	teaspoon Accent
		1	tablespoon salt
1/4	cup flour	1/8	teaspoon pepper
1/2	pound slivered almonds		Pinch each ground oregano, thyme, marjoram

Sauté sausage meat and drain. Cook wild rice as directed on box. Combine flour and milk in a saucepan and mix until smooth. Add chicken broth and cook until thick on low heat. Season with herbs, salt and pepper. Combine with cooked wild rice, sausage, and mushrooms. Pour into a casserole dish and sprinkle with almonds. Cook, uncovered at 350 degrees for 30 minutes, or until bubbly and brown. You may substitute grapes, toasted almonds, cooked peas, sautéed apples, add more mushrooms, anything your heart and stomach desire for the sausage. The apple combination is especially good with duck. The grape combination is especially good with beef.

FRIED RICE

Serves 4   Representative John P. Gardner

4	strips bacon	4	cups cooked rice, cold
2	eggs	1	cup shredded meat (pork, ham, beef, shrimp, chicken or a combination)
1	cup vegetables (combine 2 of these; mushrooms, water chestnuts, bamboo shoots, bean sprouts, or snow pea pods)		
		1/2	cup diced green onions
		2	tablespoons soy sauce
		1/2	teaspoon sugar

For best results, start with well chilled cooked rice or this dish will be gummy. This is a super way to use leftovers. Fry bacon until crisp. Remove and save bacon. Fry rice in grease on medium heat for 5 minutes, fork stirring constantly. In separate pan pour beaten eggs and cook in thin sheet, then shred and add to rice mixture. Add bacon and other shredded meat. Add vegetables and onions. Season with soy sauce and sugar.

RICE ALMOND SAUSAGE CASSEROLE

Serves 8   Mrs. D. Les Tindal (May)

1-1/2 pounds pork sausage
1   small chopped green pepper
1   cup chopped onion
1   cup chopped celery
1/2   pound slivered almonds

1/2   soup can water
2   cups cooked rice
1   large can mushrooms, drained
2   10-3/4-ounce cans cream of
      mushroom soup
1   can drained water chestnuts

Saute sausage, pour off fat. Add green pepper, onions, celery, almonds and rice. Cook together 5 minutes. Add remaining ingredients. Pour into a 9x13-inch pan. Bake at 350 degrees for 30 minutes.

BAKED CHEESE

Serves 4   Mrs. Rex L. Carter (Floride)

3   eggs, beaten
1   cup bread crumbs
1   pint milk

2   tablespoons melted margarine
3/4   cup grated cheese
Salt and pepper to taste

Soak the bread crumbs in the milk for 20 minutes. Then stir in the eggs, margarine, salt, pepper and grated cheese. Put into buttered baking dish and bake 350 degrees for 30 minutes. During the last few minutes of baking, sprinkle a little more grated cheese on top of mixture.

CHEESE GRITS

Serves 8 to 10   Mrs. Don H. Holland (Betty)

1   cup grits
4   cups water
1   stick margarine
Salt to taste

1/2   cup cheddar cheese, grated
1   6-ounce roll garlic cheese
2   tablespoons Worcestershire sauce
2   egg whites, beaten stiff

Add salt to boiling water and cook grits covered on low heat until done (about 25 minutes). Stir in the margarine, grated cheese, garlic cheese, cut into small pieces, and Worcestershire sauce. Fold in the stiffly beaten egg whites. Pour into a buttered casserole dish and bake at 350 degrees for 30 minutes.

QUICK CHEESE GRITS

Serves 12   Mrs. Nick A Theodore (Emilie)

1	cup grits (quick)	6	beaten eggs
4 to 6 cups water		2	cups milk
1	teaspoon salt	1-1/2	teaspoon salt
2	cups sharp grated cheese		

Add salt to boiling water and cook quick grits about 6 minutes. While hot add cheese. Let cool and stir in eggs, milk and salt. Put in a buttered baking dish. Bake at 375 degrees for 45 minutes.

NASSAU GRITS

Serves 8   Representative Gene Dukes

8	slices bacon	1/4	teaspoon sugar
1	medium onion, chopped	6	cups water
2	small green peppers, finely chopped	1	teaspoon salt
		1-1/2	cups uncooked regular grits
1	16-ounce can tomatoes, undrained and chopped		

Cook bacon in skillet until crisp. Drain bacon, crumble and set aside. Pour off all but 2 tablespoons drippings. Sauté onion and green pepper in skillet, stir in tomatoes and sugar. Bring to a boil, reduce heat and simmer 30 minutes, stirring occasionally. Bring water to a boil. Add grits and salt. Cook 20 minutes, stirring frequently until grits have thickened. Remove from heat and stir in tomato mixture. Sprinkle bacon on top. May add ham, sausage and mushrooms.

CHEESE PUDDING

Serves 6 to 8   Mrs. J. F. Anderson, Jr. (Susan)
                                           Mrs. M. Judson Busbee (Nancy)
                                               Mrs. John Gardner (Pam)

8 to 10 slices white bread		1	pound semisharp cheese, shredded
6	eggs, beaten		
Salt and pepper to taste		2	cups milk
1	teaspoon grated onion (optional)	1	teaspoon dry mustard

Remove crusts from bread. Spread half of the cheese in the bottom of a greased 7-1/2x12-inch baking dish. Cover cheese with slices of bread; cut to fit so that the entire cheese layer is covered. Sprinkle remainder of cheese over bread. Beat eggs. Add milk, salt, pepper and mustard; pour over cheese and bread mixture. Cover and refrigerate overnight. (Best to refrigerate 2 days.) Take out 2 hours before baking. Set in a pan of hot water and bake 1 hour at 275 degrees to 300 degrees.

158

CLASSIC CHEESE SOUFFLÉ

Serves 6 to 8   Mrs. Jeff Richardson, Jr. (Florence)

3	tablespoons butter	6	eggs, separated
2	tablespoons flour	1	cup sweet milk
1	teaspoon salt	2	cups grated extra sharp
Pepper to taste			Cheddar cheese

Pre-heat oven to 400 degrees. Separate eggs, placing whites in large mixing bowl and set aside. Sprinkle pepper on yolks and beat well. Melt butter in a saucepan over low heat. Add salt and flour, and stir until smooth. Slowly add milk and stirring constantly, increase heat to medium and cook until mixture thickens and coats spoon (as for "white" or "cream" sauce). Reduce heat and add cheese, stirring until melted. Add well beaten egg yolks and mix thoroughly. Remove from heat and let cool. When cheese mixture has cooled to luke-warm, or cooler, beat egg whites until stiff and fold in cheese mixture slowly until well mixed. Pour into souffle pan(s) or deep casserole dish and bake in moderate oven, 400 degrees, for 30 to 35 minutes. Serve at once. Baking in individual dishes cuts baking time by about 10 minutes.

MI-MI'S LAYERED CHEESE SOUFFLÉ

Serves 6 to 8   Mrs. T. W. Edwards, Jr. (Dottie)

10	strips French bread, cut	1-1/3	teaspoon salt
	lengthwise and crust removed	4	eggs, beaten
2	cups sharp Cheddar cheese,	3	cups milk
	grated		

Butter one side of each strip of bread; cut each strip into 8 slices. Line a buttered long casserole dish with slices. Add 1/3 of the cheese to casserole, add another layer of bread slices and top with 1/3 of the cheese. Beat milk, eggs and salt, and pour over cheese. Sprinkle top with the rest of cheese. Let stand overnight in refrigerator. Take out 1 hour before baking and bake 20 minutes, or until puffy, at 350 degrees. Serve immediately.

CHEESE TOMATO PIE

Serves 6   Mrs. Robert C. Lake, Jr. (Carolyn)

1	pie shell	Sweet basil	
Tomatoes		1	cup grated New York State
Salt and pepper			cheese
3	spring onions	1	cup mayonnaise

Bake pie shell almost done. Slice peeled tomatoes thick and completely cover bottom of pie shell. Add salt and pepper. Chop spring onions and cover tomatoes. Sprinkle with sweet basil. Mix cheese with mayonnaise and spread over pie. Bake until hot and bubbly.

BRUNCH EGG CASSEROLE

Serves 12 to 15   Mrs. Nick A. Theodore (Emilie)

1	pound sharp cheese	4	cups sour cream
2	pounds sausage, cooked and drained	10	eggs, beaten

Salt, pepper and paprika, to taste

In a 9x13-inch pyrex dish, layer 1/2 cheese, 1/2 sour cream and sausage. Then add other 1/2 cheese and other 1/2 sour cream. Add salt, pepper and paprika to eggs and pour on top. Bake at 350 degrees for 30 minutes.

SAUSAGE AND EGG CASSEROLE

Serves 8   Mrs. Robert C. Lake, Jr. (Carolyn)

1	pound hot sausage cooked, drained and crumbled		Beat together:
3	slices thick bread, buttered and cubed in bottom of casserole	6	eggs
		2	cups milk
		1	teaspoon dry mustard
		1/2	teaspoon salt

Put sausage over bread cubes in 2-quart casserole. Pour egg and milk mixture over this and then one cup grated cheese. Refrigerate overnight. Bake 30 minutes at 350 degrees.

SAUSAGE BAKE

Serves 6 to 8   Mrs. R. L. Altman (Nancy)

2	pounds sausage (1 hot and 1 mild)	1	cup raw grits
1-1/2 cups grated cheese			Salt and pepper
1-1/2 cups milk		5	eggs
		2	tablespoons butter

Cook and drain sausage. Cook grits and cool, adding butter to grits. Put sausage into bottom of a 13x9-inch pyrex dish. Combine all other ingredients and pour over sausage. Bake for 1 hour at 350 degrees. Can be made ahead and reheated.

ROBERT'S OF CHARLESTON CHEESE ROULADE
WITH SPINACH AND MUSHROOMS

Serves 8   Mrs. Robert N. McLellan (Doris)

Prepare this in the early morning or afternoon and let set on the kitchen counter. DO NOT REFRIGERATE. When ready to serve, reheat.

3	cups milk	1/4	teaspoon nutmeg
1-1/2	teaspoons salt	4	shakes Tabasco sauce
1/4	teaspoon white pepper	1	teaspoon Worcestershire sauce

Grease bottom and sides of 15x10x1-inch jellyroll pan with vegetable oil. Line with parchment or waxed paper, allowing paper to extend beyond ends of pan; grease waxed paper with vegetable oil. Warm milk with all the seasonings in a saucepan.

1/4	pound butter	2/3	cup flour, all purpose

In another saucepan prepare a roux. Melt butter. Add flour over low heat until a paste is formed. Stir for 2 minutes, over low heat. Whip 1/2 of this into above milk and cook for 5 minutes over medium heat. (Save out 1/2 to go in spinach.)

8	egg yolks	1/4	teaspoon cream of tartar
8	egg whites		

Stir egg yolks into above mixture. Whip egg whites and cream of tartar until stiff. Fold into above in a large bowl.

1/4   pound grated Swiss cheese

Take all and fold gently into above. Bake 10 minutes in parchment lined pan in a 400 degree oven.

1	10-ounce package frozen spinach	3/4	pound mushrooms, chopped fine in food processor
1/4	cup olive oil	1	tablespoon freeze-dried shallots
2	teaspoons chopped garlic	1	teaspoon lemon juice
2	teaspoons Robert's Special Seasonings		

(I use 1/2 teaspoon each of salt and thyme, 1/4 teaspoon each of white pepper, ground nutmeg, tarragon and dry mustard.)

Defrost spinach and squeeze out all moisture. Chop mushrooms. Using 2 separate sauté pans, cook spinach with olive oil and seasonings on medium heat until cooked throughout but keeping the spinach a bright green color. Cook mushrooms on medium heat, with nothing else in the skillet, until all water has evaporated and they are somewhat dry and pasty. Stir into spinach and mix well. Remove from heat and check for salt and pepper. Let cool a few minutes. Take the remaining 1/2 of cream sauce and 1 teaspoon lemon juice and add to spinach.

Spread evenly over the surface of the roulade and roll up similar to rolling a jelly roll cake. Roll onto heat proof serving platter with the open edge down. Brush with melted butter and reheat for 10 to 15 minutes in a 400 degree oven and slice with a serrated knife while warm.

GRANOLA

Mrs. William Cork (Helen)

5	cups rolled oats	1	cup chopped nuts
2	cups wheat germ	1	cup safflower oil, or other
1	cup coconut, shredded and sweetened	1	tablespoon vanilla mixed with 1 tablespoon water
1	cup sesame seed	3/4	cup brown sugar
1	cup chopped dried fruit or raisins	1	cup sunflower seed

Preheat oven to 350 degrees. Put all ingredients, except fruit, in a large shallow pan. Mix well and spread out evenly. Bake 1 hour, stirring every 15 minutes to prevent burning. If using fruit, add only during the last 2 minutes of cooking. Cool thoroughly and store in air-tight containers.

ITALIAN MEAL IN A DISH

Serves 8   Mrs. Jackson V. Gregory (Brenda)

1	onion, chopped	2	cups cottage cheese
1	clove garlic, minced	1	egg, beaten
1	pound ground beef	1	10-ounce package frozen chopped spinach, thawed and drained
2	8-ounce cans tomato sauce		
1	6-ounce can tomato paste		
1	teaspoon salt	1	8-ounce package flat noodles
1/2	teaspoon oregano	1/2	pound sliced Mozarella cheese
1/4	teaspoon basil	1/2	cup Parmesan cheese

Brown onion, garlic and meat. Drain. Add tomato sauce, tomato paste, salt, oregano and basil. Simmer 15 minutes. Drain. Combine cottage cheese, egg and spinach. Cook and drain noodles. Butter a 9x13-inch dish. Cover with a layer of 1/3 meat mixture, noodles, sliced cheese, cottage cheese mixture; then 2/3 meat mixture, ending with Parmesan cheese. Bake at 350 degrees for 30 minutes.

LASAGNA

Serves 8   Mrs. Marion H. Kinon (Reba)

2	pounds hamburger	1	onion chopped
Garlic powder to taste		1	tablespoon basil
1	pound can tomatoes	2	6-ounce cans tomato paste
Salt and pepper		Big container cottage cheese	
1/2	cup Parmesan cheese	2	tablespoons parsley flakes
2	beaten eggs	1	teaspoon salt
1/2	teaspoon pepper	1/2	pound Mozarella cheese slices
10	ounces lasagna noodles		

Simmer hamburger, onion, garlic, basil, tomatoes and tomato paste together, uncovered, for 30 minutes. Season to taste. Mix cottage cheese with the Parmesan cheese, parsley flakes and eggs. Season to taste. Cook noodles as directed on package. Layer in a 2-quart casserole half of each: lasagna noodles, cottage cheese mixture, meat sauce, Mozarella cheese and Parmesan cheese. Repeat layers until all ingredients are used. Top with Parmesan cheese. Bake at 350 degrees until heated through.

NEW STYLE LASAGNA

Serves 4 to 6   Mrs. William J. McLeod (Sara)

2	16-ounce cans Chef Boy-ar-Dee	1	pound cottage cheese
	Spaghetti Sauce with Meat	8	ounces Swiss cheese
9	Lasagna noodles	1/4 to 1 cup Parmesan cheese	

Boil noodles; heat sauce. Layer noodles, cheese and sauce in 11-3/4x7-1/2-inch baking dish. Bake at 350 degrees for 35 to 40 minutes or until thoroughly heated.

VARIATION: Mrs. Robert C. Lake, Jr. (Carolyn)

Omit spaghetti sauce with meat. Add 1 pound ground meat cooked and drained and seasoned with 1 teaspoon salt and 1/4 teaspoon pepper. Use 3-1/2 cups of spaghetti sauce. Place a layer of uncooked lasagna noodles in a 13-1/2x9x2-inch casserole. Cover with a layer of 1 cup spaghetti sauce, then a layer of cooked beef, then a layer of cottage cheese, then Swiss cheese slices. Continue layering in the same order, ending with spaghetti sauce on top. Cover tightly. Bake in a 350 degree oven for 1 to 1-1/2 hours, depending on the number of layers. Top with 1/4 cup Parmesan cheese while hot. Serves 8.

MANICOTTI OR LASAGÑA

Serves 8 to 12   Mrs. Robert N. McLellan (Doris)

8   ounces Manicotti, cooked and   Worcestershire sauce to taste
      drained or 12 wide lasagna   1   teaspoon salt
      noodles, cooked   3   cups Ricotta or creamy cottage
1-1/2 pounds ground beef   cheese
1   large onion, chopped   1/2   cup grated Parmesan cheese
1   bell pepper, chopped   1   pound freshly grated Mozzarella
1/4   cup celery, chopped   cheese
2   cloves garlic, minced   2   tablespoons parsley flakes
1   teaspoon oregano   2   beaten eggs
2   teaspoons basil   2   teaspoons salt
1   8-ounce can tomato paste   1/2   teaspoon pepper
1   10-3/4-ounce can tomato soup   2   cups freshly grated Parmesan
1   10-3/4 ounce cream of mush-   cheese
      room soup

Brown ground beef, garlic, celery, onion and bell pepper. Drain. Add the
next 7 ingredients and simmer for about 1-1/2 hours. Mix together the last 7
ingredients and spoon the cheese mixture into Manicotti. Arrange in a single
layer in a 13-1/2x8-3/4x1-3/4-inch baking dish. Pour the sauce mixture over
Manicotti and top with any left over cheese mixture and sprinkle with Parmesan cheese. Cover with aluminum foil and bake at 350 degrees for 20 minutes. Uncover and bake 10 to 20 minutes more. Use the same recipe to make
LASAGNA: Slice Mozzarella cheese and do not mix with cheese mixture.
Preheat oven to 350 degrees. Butter a 9x13x2-inch baking dish, and put 4
lasagna noodles on the bottom, overlapping slightly. Cover with 1/2 of the
meat sauce, 2/3 cup cottage cheese mixture, 2/3's of the sliced Mozzarella
and 2/3 cup grated Parmesan. Repeat with the noodles, sauce, cheese mixture and Mozzarella, twice, finishing with the Parmesan cheese. Bake uncovered at 350 degrees for about 20 minutes. Let stand 10 minutes before
cutting into 12 squares. Both manicotti and lasagna may be prepared ahead
and refrigerated before baking.

YORK COUNTY

For most of the state's early history York County was referred to as the "New Acquisition." During the middle 1700s both the North Carolina and South Carolina colonial governments claimed York as part of their territories. Throughout most of this period the area of the present county was administered by courts operating out of Mecklenberg, North Carolina. The boundary dispute was settled in 1772 when York was officially acquired by South Carolina.

White settlers first moved to the area in the 1750s. Devout Scotch-Irish Presbyterians and their hard working families moved to the county from York, Pennsylvania naming their new home in honor of their original one. A small settlement called Yorkville took hold and by 1760 the area was a flourshing agricultural community. One of the most crucial battles of the Revolution was fought in the county. King's Mountain Battlefield, located in the northern tip of York commemorates the 1780 defeat of a British Tory force under the command of Major Patrick Ferguson by a rag tag band of backwoods militia.

The abundant water resources of the county began attracting industry to York in the 1880s. Textiles have since become a major industry in the county. Fort Mill is home of Springs Mills and various other textile companies operate plants in the area. For a brief period cars were manufactured in the county. In 1916 John G. Anderson converted the facilities of the Rock Hill Buggy Company into an auto assembly plant. The business peaked in 1920 but declining sales forced Anderson to close in 1924.

York is the only county in the state that has an Indian reservation within its boundaries. Prior to the white man's entry the county had been inhabited by Indians of the Catawba Nation. The heritage and culture of these early Carolinians still exerts a strong influence on the county. The York County Museum exhibits artifacts found in the county and numerous unexplored Indian mounds still dot the countryside.

Formed in 1785 from a portion of the Old Ninety-Six District, Union county occupies a central location in the Piedmont plateau. For over a century its shape was basically triangular but the upper section of the point was relinquished in 1897 with the formation of Cherokee County.

The county was located strategically along nineteenth century transportation routes, both water and land. A seven-lock canal built at Lockhart's shoals on the Broad River increased cotton farmers' access to markets in Columbia in the early 1800s. On land, the old State Road which ran from Charleston to North Carolina traversed the southern end of the county, linking it with other sections of the state.

Many of the county's place names conjure up a mental picture of the environment in the early days. Native animals were recalled with the naming of the Tyger River and the town of Buffalo. "Fair forest" describes well the verdant region through which a yet un-named creek meandered. Indian nomenclature has been retained with the Enoree and Pacolet rivers. A well known antebellum plantation - now a state park - is called "Rose Hill" for its once prolific rose garden and for the rose-colored brick from which it was constructed by Gov. William Henry Gist. The vision of ecumenical unity is perpetuated in the very name of the county itself, so-named for "Union Church," built in 1765 and attended jointly by Episcopalians and Presbyterians.

The county seat, originally known as Unionville, once sported a handsome Mills-designed stone court house built of native granite. It no longer remains, but a similar structure, the county jail (completed in 1823), was placed on the National Register of Historic Places in 1974. Union, the largest town in the county, is also home of a regional campus of the University of South Carolina and host of a recently organized Kudzu Festival.

BRATTONSVILLE REVOLUTIONARY HOUSE

Brattonsville Revolutionary House, located on the York-Chester Road, is Brattonsville's oldest building. It was built in 1823 and is Federalist in style. One quarter mile behind the house in 1780 the Patriots defeated the Tories in the first British defeat after the fall of Charleston.

meats

BEEF MARINADE

Mrs. D. H. Wilkins (Susan)

3/4 cup olive oil
1 teaspoon parsley
1/4 cup wine vinegar
1/4 cup lemon juice
1/2 cup soy sauce

1 teaspoon pepper
1 teaspoon salt
Dash Worcestershire sauce
2 cloves garlic, minced

Keeps 2 to 3 weeks. Delicious on all cuts of beef.

CLAIRE'S BARBECUE SAUCE

Mrs. William Cork (Helen)

3/4 cup sugar
4 14-ounce bottles catsup
4 catsup bottles filled with
    white vinegar (56 ounces)
1/4 to 1/2 small can black pepper,
    to taste
1/8 cup Tabasco Sauce

1 stick margarine
Juice of 2 lemons
1 small bottle Worcestershire sauce
1 small jar prepared mustard
Salt - measured in pepper can about
    1/4 to 1/2 full, to taste

Bring all ingredients to a boil; reduce heat to medium and simmer for 30 minutes. Cool slightly. Sterilize the catsup bottles and vinegar bottle and seal Barbecue Sauce in them. Bottle while warm. May be kept on pantry shelf until opened.

SWEET AND SOUR BAR-B-Q SAUCE

Senator "Liz" Patterson

1/3 cup catsup
1/3 cup cider vinegar
1 cup dark brown sugar
1 teaspoon mustard
1 tablespoon lemon juice

1/3 cup chili sauce
1/3 stick butter or margarine
3 large cloves garlic, grated
1-1/2 teaspoons Tabasco
1/8 teaspoon salt

Mix all ingredients in a 1-quart saucepan. Heat mixture for 5 minutes. It will keep for 2 weeks in the refrigerator. (Best if doubled or tripled.)

TARRAGON BUTTER FOR GRILLED STEAK

Serves 6   Mrs. H. E. Pearce, Jr. (Jo)

2	medium shallots	1/2	teaspoon fresh ground pepper
2	tablespoons parsley, chopped	1	stick butter, softened
4-1/2	teaspoons wine vinegar	6	steaks for grilling
3/4	teaspoon tarragon, crumbled		

Mix, roll in waxed paper and freeze. Slice into rounds for grilled steaks.

STEAK DIANE

Serves 2   Mrs. Nick Theodore (Emilie)

1/2	pound fresh mushrooms	1	teaspoon Worcestershire
2	tablespoons butter	1	teaspoon A-1 Steak Sauce
1	tablespoon oil	1	teaspoon chives
1	tablespoon shallots or green onions, minced	1	teaspoon parsley
		2	1/2-inch filets

French's Mustard

Sauté mushrooms in butter and oil for a few minutes. Add green onions. Add Worcestershire, steak sauce, chives and parsley. Heat mixture through. Add filets (pushing mixture to side of skillet). Salt and pepper steaks. Spread a little French's Mustard on each side while cooking. When steak reaches desired doneness, place mushroom mixture on top. Can be doubled for 4.

MANDARIN BEEF AND VEGETABLES

Serves 4 to 6   Mrs. James B. Stephen (Ginger)

1	pound tender boneless beef, cut in thin 3-inch strips	1/2	pound sliced mushrooms
4	tablespoons corn oil	1	carrot, cut in 2-inch julienne strips
2	cloves garlic, minced	2	tablespoons cornstarch
2	cups broccoli flowerets and sliced stems	1-1/4	cups water
2	onions, cut in thin wedges	1/3	cup soy sauce
1/4	teaspoon red pepper	1/3	cup corn syrup

In a bowl mix cornstarch and water until smooth. Stir in soy sauce, corn syrup and red pepper. Set aside. In a large skillet or wok, heat 2 tablespoons corn oil over medium high heat. Add beef and garlic; stir fry 5 minutes or until tender. Remove from skillet. Heat 2 tablespoons oil; add broccoli, onions and carrot. Stir fry 2 minutes. Add mushrooms and stir fry 1 minute or until tender crisp. Return beef to skillet and add sauce. Stirring constantly, bring to a boil and boil 2 minutes. Serve over rice. (1 pound chicken or 1 pound pork may be substituted for beef.)

MARINATED FLANK STEAK

2 or 3 flank steaks   Mrs. Grady Patterson, Jr. (Margie)

1/2 cup soy sauce
1   cup water
3   tablespoons vinegar

3   tablespoons lemon juice
Lemon pepper

In a plastic bag marinate flank steaks in soy sauce, water and vinegar in re-frigerator for 12 hours. Remove 1 hour before cooking and sprinkle both sides generously with lemon pepper. Grill and let set 5 minutes before slic-ing thin against the grain of the meat.

FRESH MUSHROOMS FOR STEAK

Mrs. W. B. Hawkins (Sarah)

1   pound sliced mushrooms
2   medium onions, chopped
1   stick melted margarine

1/2 cup soy sauce
1   cup dry sherry

Sauté mushrooms and onions in margarine. Add soy sauce. Add wine before serving over steak.

CHINESE PEPPER STEAK

Serves 4   Representative Larry A. Martin

1/4 cup vegetable oil
1   clove garlic, crushed
1-1/2 to 2 pounds sirloin steak, cut
     in small thin strips
1   teaspoon ground ginger
Salt to taste
1/2 teaspoon pepper
1/2 cup beef bouillon
3   large green peppers, sliced

2   large onions, sliced
4   green onions, chopped
1/4 cup soy sauce
1/2 teaspoon sugar
1/2 cup cold water
1   tablespoon cornstarch
1   8-ounce can water chestnuts,
     sliced
Cooked rice

Heat pan; add oil and garlic. When garlic browns, remove. Add beef and fry a few minutes. Season with ginger, salt and pepper. Add bouillon and continue to cook, adding green peppers and onions. Add soy sauce, sugar, water and cornstarch mixed together. Cook until mixture thickens, stirring slowly. Fold in water chestnuts. Serve over cooked rice.

BEEF ORIENTAL

Serves 8   Representative Thomas L. Hughston, Jr.

1 pound boneless round steak (3/4-inch thick)	1/2 cup each diagonally sliced carrot, celery and green onions
1/4 teaspoon ground ginger	1 10-3/4-ounce can Beefy Mushroom Soup
2 tablespoons butter or margarine	
1-1/2 cups water	1 tablespoon each cornstarch and soy sauce
1 16-ounce can Chinese vegetables, drained	1/2 teaspoon salt
1 teaspoon brown sugar	

Slice meat in thin strips. In skillet, cook carrot, celery and onions with ginger in butter until just tender; push to one side. Add meat; cook until color just changes (about 3 to 4 minutes). Add remaining ingredients. Cook, stirring until thickened. Serve over rice. May be prepared ahead. Good served with broccoli spears and baked apples.

ROUND STEAK CREOLE

Serves 4 to 6   Representative Jarvis Klapman

1-1/2 pounds round steak	2 tablespoons vegetable oil
1 10-3/4-ounce can Old Fashioned Tomato and Rice Soup	1 medium onion
	1/2 bell pepper
1/3 cup water	1 teaspoon Worcestershire sauce
Flour	Salt and pepper to taste

Sprinkle the steak with salt, pepper and flour. Pound these into the steak. Brown the steak in a hot skillet (350 degrees if an electric skillet) to which the oil has been added. Pour off the excess fat and pour tomato and rice soup over the steak. Slice the onion and cut the pepper in lengthwise strips and place these on top of the steak. Add Worcestershire sauce to water and pour into skillet. Cover and simmer until tender, about forty minutes. Additional rice may be cooked and the gravy used on it.

BARBECUE BEEF ON BUNS

Cocktail Buffet Dish - Serves 25   Mrs. J. Verne Smith (Jean)

1/4	cup vinegar	1	thick slice lemon
1/2	cup water	1	onion, chopped
2	tablespoons sugar	1	clove garlic, minced (optional)
1	tablespoon prepared mustard	1/4	cup butter
1/2	teaspoon pepper	1/2	cup catsup
1-1/2	teaspoons salt	2	tablespoons Worcestershire sauce
Chafing dish		3 to 4	pound chuck beef roast (stew beef will not work)

Rub meat with about 4 teaspoons salt. In a small amount of water, simmer until tender. This will take about 4 hours or until the meat can be pulled apart. Trim off the fat and shred finely. Mix first 10 ingredients; simmer for 20 minutes and add catsup, Worcestershire sauce and 1 cup broth from cooked meat, if needed. Stir well and add meat. Cover and simmer 1/2 hour. Add more broth if it seems too thick. Serve in chafing dish with small buns. Will keep in refrigerator for 1 week or may be frozen. This is good served over rice or to take to the beach for a quick meal.

BRAISED BEEF

Serves 6 to 8   Representative Robert N. McLellan

2 to 3 pound lean boneless beef (stew beef, chuck or sirloin tip)		2	tablespoons butter
		1/4	cup water
1	carrot, thinly sliced	1	onion, chopped
1	clove garlic, crushed	1/2	cup celery, diced
1	cup canned or fresh tomatoes	1	tablespoon chopped parsley
1/4	teaspoon pepper	1	teaspoon salt
		1/4	teaspoon paprika

Leave whole or cut the meat into cubes; brown in hot frying pan with drippings. Stir the meat so it will cook quickly and not lose its juices. Remove the pieces to a closely covered roaster that can be used either on top of the stove or in the oven. Rinse the pan with a quarter cup of boiling water to save all browned bits, and pour this over the meat. Cover tightly and simmer gently on top of the stove or in a 275 degree oven for 2 hours. For the Sauce melt butter and brown the onion, carrot and garlic in a hot frying pan. Add parsley, celery and tomatoes. Heat thoroughly. Add seasonings. Pour the sauce over the meat and continue cooking for another hour. This is nicer fixed a day ahead.

BUFFET BAKED BARBECUE BRISKET

Cocktail Buffet Dish — Serves 12 to 15   Mrs. Robert N. McLellan (Doris)

1	7-pound choice fresh boneless corned beef brisket	14	ounces catsup
2	tablespoons Hickory liquid smoke flavoring	1/4	cup water
		1	tablespoon liquid smoke
Garlic salt		2	tablespoons Worcestershire sauce

BARBECUE SAUCE:
1-1/2 tablespoons brown sugar
3   tablespoons butter

1-1/2 teaspoons dry mustard
1   teaspoon celery seed
Salt and pepper to taste

Rub Hickory liquid smoke flavoring on brisket. Lightly salt with garlic salt. Wrap brisket well in double thickness of heavy foil and refrigerate overnight. The next day put the brisket, wrapped in foil, in a deep pan and bake in a 325 degree oven for 5 hours. Drain, do not unwrap, and cool. Refrigerate overnight. The day you are ready to serve, unwrap and cut excess fat from brisket. Slice meat into very thin slices. THIS IS DELICIOUS WITHOUT THE BARBECUE SAUCE. Serve on platter with assorted sandwich breads and crocks of mayonnaise and mustard. BARBECUE SAUCE: Combine all the barbecue sauce ingredients and bring to a boil. Lower the heat and simmer, uncovered, 30 minutes, stirring occasionally. (The sauce may be frozen.) Spoon between the slices and bake 30 minutes at 325 degrees. Watch that it doesn't burn. Serve in chafing dish with assorted small sandwich rolls.

EYE OF THE ROUND ROAST

Senator Nick Theodore

1/2	cup soy sauce	Instant marinade	
1/2	cup cooking Sherry	2	teaspoons garlic powder
Juice of 2 lemons		4 to 5 tablespoons parsley flakes	
Bacon slice		Eye of the round roast, any size	

Mix together all ingredients except roast. Set aside. Rinse roast and pat dry. Put into baking bag, pour marinade on top, tie bag. Leave out (not in refrigerator) overnight or at least 4 hours. Twenty minutes before baking, add 2 teaspoons instant marinade. Pre-heat oven to 400 degrees, remove roast from bag and put into roasting pan. Place slice of bacon on top of roast. Bake, uncovered, for 10 minutes at 400 degrees, reduce to 300 degrees and cook 1 hour. Turn off oven and leave until completely cool.

MEATS

OLD ENGLISH BEEF ROAST
Mrs. Heyward E. McDonald (Sylvia)

Beef roast (prime rib, sirloin tip, rump)
Pepper

Rock salt
1 cup water
Worcestershire sauce

Preheat oven to 500 degrees. Rub pepper and Worcestershire sauce all over meat. Put layer of rock salt in bottom of roasting pan. Sprinkle 1/2 cup water over salt. Place roast on top of salt. Then pour more rock salt over top of roast until roast disappears. Sprinkle another 1/2 cup water over salt. Place in oven and cook 13 minutes per pound for a rare roast. Cook longer per pound if you want it medium or well done. You can use a hammer to break the salt away from the roast.

MARINATED ROAST TENDERLOIN
Cocktail Buffet — Serves 30 to 40   Representative Ginger Crocker

1 5- to 8-pound tenderloin roast or eye of round roast
Garlic powder (not salt)
Coarse black pepper
1-1/2 to 2 cups soy sauce

Powdered horseradish (if available)
Bacon or salt pork
1 onion
1 bell pepper
1/2 to 3/4 cup bourbon

Wipe surface of meat and sprinkle liberally with garlic powder and pepper. Combine soy sauce, bourbon and horseradish and pour over meat. Marinate for at least 2 hours at room temperature or overnight in the refrigerator. Let roast stand at room temperature for at least 1 hour. If the roast is very lean you may want to have it larded or place bacon or salt pork over it while it bakes. Preheat oven to 450 degrees. Put meat on rack in an open roasting pan. Pour marinade on roast and put onion and bell pepper in the pan. Reduce heat to 400 degrees and cook 35 to 50 minutes for a rare roast, or until desired doneness. Refrigerate 2 hours, or overnight and slice thin. Serve with an assortment of breads and small rolls.

NICK'S "NO-PEEK" OVEN BEEF STEW
Serves 4   Senator Nick Theodore

1-1/2 pounds stewing beef, cut in cubes
5 potatoes, peeled and cubed
1 tablespoon sugar
2 cups water

5 carrots, peeled and cubed
2 cups celery diced
4 tablespoons Minute Tapioca
1-1/2 cups tomato juice (or 1 can tomato soup)

Combine all ingredients in a roasting pan with lid. Bake at 275 degrees for 3-1/2 hours. DO NOT OPEN OVEN DOOR!

ROBBER ROAST

Serves 8   Senator Norma Russell

5	pound beef roast	Orange wine
1/2	cup flour	Salt

Brown roast in own fat in Dutch oven. Add orange wine to cover halfway, then coat each side with salt. Cook on stove top about 2 hours, or until tender. Midway in cooking, stir 2 cups of pot gravy into flour. Return to roast and blend well to thicken. Serve with rice or noodles.

SAUCE FOR ROLLED RIB ROAST ON ROTISSERIE

Speaker of the House Ramon Schwartz

1	cup brown sugar	1	cup cherry (not Sherry) wine
3	generous dashes of	1	cup dark port wine
	Worcestershire sauce	3	generous dashes soy sauce
2	tablespoons favorite meat sauce	Rolled rib roast	

Rub salt, pepper and crushed garlic into roast before cooking. Bring sauce to a boil and baste roast while it cooks on rotisserie. Baste frequently during early stage, but none during the last 30 minutes, so that roast can form a crust on the outside.

BEEF STEW IN TOMATO-CHEESE SAUCE

Serves 6   Mrs. Robert N. McLellan (Doris)

2	pounds lean stewing beef, cut in bite size pieces	2	8-ounce cans tomato sauce with cheese
12	small onions	1	cup water
1	cup chopped celery	1-1/2	teaspoons salt
2	large potatoes, cut into eights	1/8	teaspoon pepper
6	carrots cut in 6-inch pieces	Dill seed	
1	slice white bread, cubed	Parmesan cheese	

Combine all ingredients in casserole; top with Parmesan cheese, cover, and bake at 250 degrees for 4-1/2 to 5 hours. Do not open oven door.

BEEF BRISKET WITH ITALIAN SEASONING

Serves 10   Mrs. Ramon Schwartz (Rosa)

5 to 6 pound brisket		1	teaspoon instant coffee
1 or 2 garlic cloves		1	beef bouillon cube
1	cup water	2	onions
Salt and pepper		Italian Seasoning	

Brown brisket in frying pan. Place in heavy pot. On one side only, season with salt, pepper, coffee, Italian Seasoning, chips of garlic and slices of onion. Put water and bouillon cube in bottom of pan. Cover and cook at 325 degrees for 3 hours. Slice thin. Cut across the grain. Serve hot or cold.

SHORTRIBS OF BEEF

Serves 8   Mrs. Robert N. McLellan (Doris)

8	pounds shortribs	1	cup diced celery
1	cup flour	3	garlic cloves, minced
1	tablespoon salt	3	tablespoons brandy
1/2	teaspoon white pepper	4	cups red wine
1/2	cup butter or shortening	1	bay leaf
2	cups diced onion	1/2	cup chopped parsley
1	cup diced carrots	1/8	teaspoon thyme

Cut the ribs into serving pieces; dredge in flour, salt and pepper. Place in an oiled roasting pan and roast uncovered at 450 degrees for 25 minutes. Drain off excess fat. Saute the vegetables in the butter until yellow. Add to the shortribs. Ignite the brandy and add with the wine and seasonings. Cover and bake at 350 degrees for about 2 hours or until tender. You can do ahead of time as shortribs freeze well. VARIATION: Brown 8 pounds ribs in shortening. Drain skillet, leaving ribs. Slice 4 onions on ribs. Mix together a sauce: 4 cups beef bouillon (made from cubes), 8 teaspoons sugar, 8 tablespoons vinegar, 8 tablespoons catsup, 4 tablespoons Dijon mustard, salt and pepper. Pour over ribs and onions and simmer, covered, for 2 hours.

BEEF AND TATER TOTS

Mrs. Clyde M. Dangerfield (Betty)

2	pounds ground chuck	1	envelope Lipton Onion Soup
2	10-3/4-ounce cans Cream of	1	cup milk
	Chicken Soup	1	bag frozen tater tots

Put meat in oblong casserole dish. Mix other ingredients together. Pour over meat; add tater tots on top. Cook at 325 degrees for 1-1/2 hours.

BEEF CASSEROLE

Serves 4   Mrs. Horace C. Smith (Dot)

1-1/2 cups diced leftover roast beef   1/2 green pepper, cut into strips
2   tablespoons vegetable oil   1   small can sliced mushrooms
2 or 3 small tomatoes, quartered   1-1/2 cups thin brown gravy
Pepper to taste   2   ounces noodles
3/4   cup thinly sliced onions   Grated Parmesan cheese

Sauté beef, onions and green pepper in oil until brown. Add mushrooms
and tomatoes. Simmer for a few minutes. Add gravy and simmer for 10 minutes. Cook noodles in boiling salted water until tender. Drain and combine
with beef mixture. Add pepper to taste. Place in casserole and sprinkle with
Parmesan cheese. Bake at 350 degrees for 30 minutes.

TERIYAKI

Serves 6   Mrs. William N. Cork (Helen)

2   pounds sirloin or filet of beef   Dash of bourbon, optional
      (or uncooked peeled shrimp)   1   cup soy sauce
2   tablespoons sugar   1   tablespoon finely chopped ginger
2   cloves garlic, minced

Slice the meat into thin slices or strips. Combine all remaining ingredients,
pour over meat, and allow to marinate no less than 2 hours. Thread the meat
onto long skewers and broil quickly over charcoal, turning once. Serve with
wild rice and Ceasar's salad.

CHILI CON CARNE

Serves 6   Mrs. William J. McLeod (Sara)

1-1/2 pounds ground beef   1   medium onion, chopped
1   28-ounce can whole tomatoes   1   6-ounce can tomato paste
1   cup water   1   beef bouillon cube
1   16-ounce can red kidney beans, 2   tablespoons diced green pepper
      drained   2   cloves garlic, minced (optional)
2   teaspoons salt   2   teaspoons oregano
2   teaspoons chili powder   Red pepper or Tabasco to taste
1   bay leaf

Combine meat, onions and peppers in Dutch oven. Brown meat and drain off
fat. Add other ingredients. Cover and simmer 1-1/2 hours, stirring occasionally. Remove bay leaf before serving.

CHOW MEIN

Mrs. Michael R. Daniel (Peggy)

1	pound ground beef	1	medium diced onion
1	10-3/4-ounce can mushroom soup	1	cup diced celery
		1	thinly diced potato
1	14-ounce can bean sprouts	2	thinly diced carrots
1	medium diced bell pepper		LaSoy sauce to taste

Brown meat in skillet with a little oil or bacon fat until all red is gone. Add soup, bell pepper, onion and celery, stirring well. Add bean sprouts (water and all). Fold in potatoes and carrots. Add LaSoy sauce until you have a strong flavor. You may add black pepper, but will not need salt as LaSoy sauce is salty. Simmer for 30 to 45 minutes and serve over rice and top with Chinese noodles, if desired.

MOCK FILET MIGNON

Serves 4   Mrs. Robert N. McLellan (Doris)

1	pound ground meat	1	teaspoon garlic salt
1	tablespoon Worcestershire sauce		Salt and pepper to taste
1	teaspoon dried minced onion	4	slices bacon
1/4	cup catsup		

Pour boiling water over bacon and let stand 5 minutes; drain and dry. Stretch the bacon as long as you can to go around patty. Set aside. Mix meat, Worcestershire, onion, catsup and garlic salt. Season to taste. Divide mixture into 4 equal parts and shape into patties. Wrap a slice of bacon around each patty, secure with toothpicks. Broil until brown, approximately 7 minutes on each side.

MEAT LOAF

Mrs. B. E. Thrailkill (Peggy)

	1-1/2 to 2 pounds ground beef	1	cup catsup
	Salt and pepper to taste	1/2	cup water
2/3	package Ritz crackers, crumbled	2	tablespoons Worcestershire sauce
		2	tablespoons vinegar
1	egg	2	tablespoons sugar
1	medium onion, chopped	6	tablespoons onion, chopped
1/4	cup milk		

Mix first 6 ingredients together and shape and place in loaf pan. Mix sauce ingredients together and pour over meat loaf. Bake at 325 degrees for 1 hour or until done.

BEEF BURGUNDY ROLL-UPS

Serves 8   Representative Parker Evatt

8   thin slices sirloin (approximately 5-ounces each)
1/4   cup chopped parsley
1   tablespoon chopped chives
Salt and pepper to taste
Olive oil
2   tablespoons tomato paste
1   cup sliced mushrooms

1   pound pork sausage
2   cloves garlic, finely chopped
1/2   cup chopped green onions
1   cup raisins
Flour
3   cups Burgundy wine
1   10-3/4-ounce can beef consommé
1/2   cup sliced olives

Combine uncooked sausage, garlic, parsley, onions, chives and raisins. Divide mixture evenly and spread on each steak. Roll jelly roll fashion and tie ends with string. Sprinkle with salt and pepper and coat well with flour. Cover bottom of heavy skillet with olive oil, and brown rolls. Add wine, consommé and tomato paste. Cover and simmer 1 hour. During last 15 minutes thicken sauce, if necessary; add mushrooms and olives. Serve beef rolls and sauce over fine noodles, buttered and sprinkled with poppyseeds. Melted butter will keep noodles from sticking to each other.

MARINATED BEEF SHISH KABOBS

Serves 4   Mrs. David E. Turnipseed (Cindy)

2   pounds sirloin or tenderloin, cut into 1-1/2-inch cubes
1/2   cup olive oil
1/4   cup lemon juice
1   teaspoon salt
1   teaspoon marjoram
1   teaspoon oregano
1/2   teaspoon pepper

1   clove garlic, minced or 1/4 teaspoon granulated
1-1/2 cups onion chunks
1/4   cup parsley, chopped or 1 tablespoon flakes
1   8-ounce can large button mushrooms, drained
Cherry tomatoes
2   green peppers, cut into 1-inch squares

Trim fat off meat, combine remaining items, except last 3. Marinate meat in mixture for 6 hours, turn often. Add mushrooms and peppers to marinade sauce and marinate 2 more hours. Alternate sirloin, mushrooms, green peppers, tomatoes and onion chunks on skewers. Broil at least 20 minutes. Try using fresh whole brussel sprouts.

BEEF STROGANOFF

Serves 4   Mrs. Nick Theodore (Emilie)

2	pounds round steak, cut into 1/2-inch cubes	1	large onion, minced
1	10-3/4-ounce can mushroom soup	1	tablespoon garlic salt
		1	8-ounce carton sour cream
Salt to taste		8	drops Tabasco sauce
		2	tablespoons Worcestershire sauce

Flour the steak cubes and brown with minced onion in Crisco oil and 1 table-spoon garlic salt. After lightly browned, drain off excess grease. Mix 1 can soup, 2 soup cans water, sour cream, Tabasco and Worcestershire. Cover the pan and simmer the meat, stirring often, for 45 minutes until meat is tender. Serve over rice or noodles.

VARIATION NO. 1   Mrs. J. P. Gardner, Jr. (Pam)

Omit mushroom soup and add beef broth with 2-1/2 tablespoons flour and 1 pint chopped mushrooms.

VARIATION NO. 2   Mrs. David E. Turnipseed (Cindy)

Omit mushroom soup. Decrease meat to 1-1/2 pounds (cut in strips) and Worcestershire to 1 teaspoon. Add 1 garlic clove, 1 can mushrooms, 2 cups chopped onions, 2 beef bouillon cubes dissolved in 1 cup boiling water. After meat and vegetables have cooked 5 minutes, add beef bouillon and cook on low about 40 minutes. Stir in sour cream before serving.

MEAT LOAF SUPREME

Mrs. I. S. Leevy Johnson (Doris)

2	pounds ground beef, chuck or round	2	tablespoons minced onion
1	egg, slightly beaten	1/4	teaspoon granulated garlic
2	teaspoons salt, 1/2 tsp. pepper	1	8-ounce can tomato sauce
1	cup bread or cracker crumbs	1/2	cup sour cream
		1/2	cup shredded sharp cheese

Combine ground meat with salt, crumbs and all ingredients except grated cheese. Divide mixture in half. Place half in baking dish, shaping into loaf. Make a well in center from end to end. Sprinkle on cheese. Top with remaining meat mixture and seal. Bake at 350 degrees for 45 minutes. If you prefer, you may use 1 pound ground beef and 1 pound mixture of ground pork and veal.

MARINARA SAUCE

Mrs. I. S. Leevy Johnson (Doris)

2 to 3 cloves garlic, mashed
1/4 cup olive oil
1 32-ounce can Italian tomatoes

1 teaspoon oregano
Salt and pepper to taste

In medium pan sauté garlic in oil. Add tomatoes and oregano. Season to taste. Cook 25 to 30 minutes until thickened. Good over meat loaf or as a sauce for pizza.

MOM'S MEAT LOAF

Mrs. James E. Lockemy (Ellen)

4 pounds ground beef
2 cups bread crumbs
4 eggs
1 cup evaporated milk
1/2 cup chopped parsley
1/2 cup celery, chopped

1/2 cup green peppers, chopped
2-1/2 tablespoons grated onions
1/2 teaspoon garlic powder
2-1/2 teaspoons salt
1 teaspoon pepper

Mix ground beef with bread crumbs, eggs, evaporated milk, chopped parsley, celery, green pepper, onion, garlic powder, salt and pepper. Shape into loaf. Cover with bacon and bake in flat pan lined with foil for 2-1/2 hours at 325 degrees. Recipe may be cut in half and cooked at 350 degrees for 1 hour. VARIATION: Omit bacon and cover with Marinara Sauce before baking.

COWBOY CASSEROLE

Serves 10

Mrs. L. Edward Bennett (Peggy)

1 pound hamburger
2 16-ounce cans pork and beans, undrained
1 tablespoon Worcestershire sauce
2 tablespoons brown sugar

2 cups chopped onions
1 16-ounce can kidney beans, drained
1 tablespoon prepared mustard

Brown hamburger in large frying pan until white. Drain. Mix together with all other ingredients and bake in 2-quart casserole at 350 degrees for 30 to 40 minutes. This is a favorite of children, young and old. May be prepared ahead.

MEATS

BURGHER PIE

Mrs. Nick A. Theodore (Emilie)

1 pound hamburger	1-1/2 cups onion, chopped
1-1/2 cups celery, chopped	1/2 cup green pepper
1 16-ounce can tomatoes	2 tablespoons mustard
1/4 cup catsup	Salt and pepper to taste
1/2 cup grated cheese	2 unbaked pie shells

Sauté celery, onion and green pepper until tender. Add meat, salt and pepper and brown. Add other ingredients and cook on low 45 minutes. Pre-bake pie shell about 5 minutes. Add 1/2 cup grated cheese to pie crust. Pour mixture into pie crust. Add top crust. Bake at 400 degrees for 45 minutes.

ORIENTAL CASSEROLE

Serves 6 to 8   Mrs. Nick A. Theodore (Emilie)

1 to 2-pounds ground beef	2 cups chopped celery
1 cup chopped onion	1 10-3/4-ounce can chicken and rice soup
1 10-3/4-ounce can cream of mushroom soup	1 10-3/4-ounce can vegetable soup
1 can chow mein noodles	

Brown beef, celery and onion. Add soups and noodles. Mix and pour into a 13x9-inch greased casserole dish. Bake at 325 degrees for 1 hour.

BAR-B-Q HAMBURGERS

Serves 6   Mrs. Walter Bristow, Jr. (Stewart)

1-1/2 pounds ground beef	1 tablespoon white sugar
1 onion, chopped	1 tablespoon vinegar
1 tablespoon Worcestershire sauce	1 cup catsup
1 tablespoon mustard	

Brown meat and onion. Drain. Add other ingredients and simmer 10 minutes Serve on hamburger buns. VARIATION: Mix together 1 cup bread crumbs and 1/2 cup milk with meat. Add salt and pepper. Mix together 4 tablespoons Worcestershire sauce, 2 tablespoons vinegar, 2 tablespoons sugar, 1 cup catsup and 1 chopped onion. Pour over hamburgers and bake at 300 degrees for 1-1/2 hours.

182

MAN-SIZE "CARTERBURGERS"

Allen R. Carter, Sr.

1	pound chopped sirloin (ground beef)	1	medium size onion, chopped
1	egg, beaten	1	slice bread, softened with water
1	teaspoon prepared mustard	1	tablespoon catsup
1	teaspoon salt	1	teaspoon Worcestershire sauce
		1/4	teaspoon black pepper

Mix all ingredients well. Form into five or six mounds. Roll into flour. Fry in skillet with bacon grease or shortening until done. May be broiled, leaving off flour.

HOT DOG CHILI

Mrs. Robert N. McLellan (Doris)

1	pound ground beef	1	tablespoon water
1	onion, chopped fine	4	tablespoons Dijon mustard
1/4	cup catsup	1/4	teaspoon salt

Cook meat and onion together, stirring constantly, until meat changes color. Drain. Add rest of ingredients, cover and simmer about 30 minutes. If it gets too dry, add a little water.

CABBAGE AND HAMBURGER CASSEROLE

Serves 4 to 6   Mrs. Jarvis Klapman (Arlene)

1	pound hamburger meat	1/3 cup raw rice
Salt and pepper to taste		Small head of cabbage
1	10-3/4-ounce can tomato soup	1/2 can water

Brown the hamburger with the rice. Season with salt and pepper. Cut a small head of cabbage into coarse pieces and place on bottom of a casserole. Spread the meat-rice mixture on top and pour the tomato soup, mixed with the water, over the top. Cover and bake for 1 hour in a 350 degree oven.

GLAZED HAM

Serves 12   Mrs. T. Ed Garrison (Juanita)

10 to 12-pound country ham, or a good-quality canned ham	3/4 cup Dijon mustard
	3/4 cup dark brown sugar

Preheat oven to 350 degrees. Follow directions for preparing COUNTRY HAM. If using a good-quality canned ham, no preliminary cooking is required. Combine mustard and sugar. Score the fat of the ham, and spread the glaze generously over the surface of the ham. Bake at 350 degrees for 30 to 45 minutes, until the glaze is brown and crusty.

CORN LASAGNA

Serves 6   Mrs. Nick Theodore (Emilie)

1	17-ounce can whole kernel corn, drained	1-1/2	pounds ground beef
1	8-ounce can tomato sauce	1	tablespoon all-purpose flour
1/4	teaspoon ground cinnamon	1/2	teaspoon garlic salt
1-1/2	cups cream-style cottage cheese with chives, drained	2	slightly beaten eggs
		1/4	cup grated Parmesan cheese
Slivered almonds (optional)		1	4-ounce package (1 cup) Mozzarella cheese

Spread corn in an ungreased shallow 1-1/2 quart casserole or a 10x6x2-inch baking dish. In medium skillet brown ground beef, drain off excess fat. Add flour, cook and stir for 1 minute. Stir in tomato sauce, garlic salt and cinnamon; pour over corn in dish. Bake in 350 degree oven for 15 minutes. Meanwhile, combine eggs and cottage cheese, spread over meat mixture. Top with Parmesan and Mozzarella. Sprinkle nuts over, if desired. Bake 10 to 15 minutes more.

"EMILIE'S" MOUSSAKA

Serves 6 to 8   Mrs. Nick Theodore (Emilie)

2	pounds eggplant	1	large tomato, sliced (optional)
1/2	cup chopped onions	1/2	cup yogurt or sour cream
1	pound ground beef	Nutmeg	
1	8-ounce can tomato sauce	5	tablespoons chopped parsley
1/2	cup cooking Sherry	Garlic salt	

Slightly pare eggplant, cut into 3/8-inch slices and soak in salt water for 15 minutes. Flour eggplant and brown in butter or oil. Drain slices well. Set aside. Sauté onions with ground beef, cook for 5 minutes. Add parsley, garlic salt, salt and pepper, tomato sauce and cooking Sherry. Let simmer 20 to 25 minutes or until liquid is gone. The drier the better. Alternate 1/3 of the fried eggplant slices and 1/2 meat sauce in layers, beginning and ending with eggplant. Top with slices of tomato overlapping in a circle. In bowl beat 2 eggs with 1 tablespoon flour until smooth, blend in 1/2 teaspoon salt and 1/2 cup yogurt or sour cream and add a dash of nutmeg. Pour over eggplant. Top with Parmesan cheese. Bake at 375 degrees for 40 minutes or until brown. NOTE: The eggplant slices may be broiled instead of fried. This can be done by arranging the slices side by side on a cookie sheet and brushing each side with oil. Broil until brown, turn, bursh reverse side and broil.

COUNTRY HAM

Serves 16   Mrs. T. Ed Garrison (Juanita)

14 pound Smithfield ham,   1/2 gallon domestic red wine
    pepper-coated   Brown sugar (optional)

Scrub the ham thoroughly with a stiff brush, and soak 24 to 36 hours in cool water to cover, changing the water several times. Soaking removes the strong saltiness. In a pan large enough to hold the ham, put red wine, the ham, and cool water to cover. Cover and simmer the ham over low heat for about 20 minutes per pound, or 4-1/2 hours. Remove the ham to a large platter. When cool enough to handle, carefully cut away the skin on the fat side of the ham. Preheat oven to 350 degrees. Score the fat with a sharp knife, cutting diagonally across the surface one way, and then the opposite way to form diamond shapes. At this point, the ham may be glazed (see GLAZED HAM) if desired. It is served unadorned, since it is accompanied by the pungent MUSTARD SAUCE. Bake 350 degrees for about 1/2 hour, until nicely browned. FRIED COUNTY HAM: Cut slices 1/4-inch thick (very important). Fry on each side and remove from pan immediately. To hot grease, add 1/4 teaspoon sugar and 4 tablespoons coffee or water. Cover pan and simmer a few more minutes to make RED-EYE GRAVY. Add paprika to make redder.

GLAZED HAM LOAF

Serves 10   Mrs. J. M. Cooper (Melba)

2   pounds ground smoked ham   SAUCE:
2   pounds ground lean pork   1/2 cup mayonnaise
1-1/2 cups cracker crumbs   1/2 cup sour cream
1/3   cup onion, finely chopped   1/4 cup prepared mustard
4   eggs, well beaten   1   tablespoon minced olives
2   cups milk   2   tablespoons horseradish
2   tablespoons chopped parsley   Salt
                                    Lemon juice
GLAZE
1   cup brown sugar, packed
1/2   cup cider vinegar
1-1/2 tablespoons dry mustard

Mix well the first ingredients and shape in bundt pan or angel food pan. Bake at 350 degrees for 30 minutes. Pour off fat. While this is baking, prepare GLAZE by mixing sugar, vinegar and mustard and boiling 1 minute. Pour over ham loaf and bake 1 hour longer. Turn out and serve with SAUCE prepared by mixing well the sauce ingredients.

185

MEATS

PUNGENT MUSTARD SAUCE

Makes 2 to 3 cups   Mrs. T. Ed Garrison (Juanita)

1	2-ounce can dry mustard	3	eggs
1	cup cider vinegar	1	cup granulated sugar

Combine mustard and vinegar in a bowl and allow to stand overnight. Break eggs into a heavy saucepan and blend in sugar. Stir over low heat until smooth. Add the mustard and vinegar mixture. Cook slowly, stirring constantly, over medium heat until thick. Cool and store in jar in refrigerator. Keeps well indefinitely and makes nice gifts in small crocks.

JACK McGILL'S BARBECUE PIG

Serves 35 adults   Mrs. Frank H. McGill (Peggy)

80	pound pig, dressed	1	ounce red pepper
1/4	pound butter	2	cups salt
3	ounces black pepper	1-1/2	gallons Heinz vinegar

Mix together the red and black pepper, salt and vinegar, and heat for the sauce. Place the pig on a pit on its stomach. Cook for 8 hours at good, even heat. Then clean skin with paper towels. Mop skin with butter. Turn pig on back. Have sauce hot, but not boiling. For first application, put 2 quarts sauce in pig and let boil real good for 20 minutes. Remove sauce from pig and discard. For second application, put another 2 quarts of sauce in pig and let boil for 20 minutes. Remove sauce and save for gravy. For third application, put final 2 quarts of sauce in pig and let boil 20 minutes. Remove sauce and save for gravy also. PIG IS DONE! When applying sauce, use small mop. When sauce boils in pig, keep mopping through all 3 applications.

CHINESE SPARERIBS

Mrs. Marion H. Kinon (Reba)

1	cup chicken stock	1/3	cup catsup
1/3	cup honey	1/3	cup soy sauce
	Garlic salt		Spareribs

Mix together and pour over spareribs. Marinate in refrigerator overnight. Cook, uncovered, 400 degrees for 10 minutes; then 350 degrees for 1-1/2 hours or until tender. Baste with the leftover marinade.

BARBECUE PORK CHOPS

Serves 4 to 6   Mrs. J. M. Cooper (Melba)

6 pork chops, or number of your choice	1 soup can water
Salt and pepper	1/4 cup vinegar
1 large onion, diced	1/2 tablespoon sugar
1/4 cup catsup	Dash pepper
1/2 cup Worcestershire sauce	1-1/4 teaspoon salt
1 10-3/4-ounce can condensed tomato soup	1 clove garlic, minced
	1/2 tablespoon margarine

Mix all ingredients together and put into a deep big Dutch oven. Salt and pepper pork chops and drop into sauce. Cover and cook at 325 degrees for 2 hours. You do not have to turn meat or open oven door. You can add a cut up chicken or spare ribs on top of the pork chops with same amount of sauce and you have two meals in one.

SWEET AND SOUR PORK

Serves 8   Mrs. T. Ed Garrison (Juanita)

2 pounds boneless pork loin	3/4 cup sugar
2 tablespoons sherry	1/2 cup soy sauce
4 tablespoons soy sauce	2 tablespoons sherry
4 tablespoons flour	4 tablespoons vinegar
2 tablespoons corn starch	4 tablespoons tomato puree
Peanut oil	4 tablespoons catsup

Cut pork in 1-inch cubes. Flatten with palm of hand. Mix with sherry and soy sauce. Roll in the flour mixed with cornstarch. Fry in peanut oil at 375 degrees until brown and crisp, about 5 minutes. Set aside. Bring to a boil the last 6 ingredients. Add 2 tablespoons cornstarch, stirred in 1-1/2 cups water, and cook until clear. Set aside. Heat 4 tablespoons oil in a large skillet or wok. Add 4 slices canned pineapple, quartered and 2 green peppers, cut into chunks. Cook at high heat for 2 minutes, stirring constantly. Add the pork and the sauce, cover, and cook at medium heat for 2 or 3 minutes. Serve with white rice.

CROWN ROAST OF LAMB FILLED WITH MUSHROOM SOUFFLÉ

Serves 8   Mrs. Larry A. Martin (Susan)

1 crown roast of lamb, consisting of 16 well-tied chops	MUSHROOM SOUFFLÉ:
Salt, pepper	1-1/2 pounds fresh mushrooms
1 clove garlic, slivered	1/4 cup finely diced onion
	1 teaspoon salt
	Pinch thyme
	6 tablespoons butter
	4 tablespoons flour
	1-1/2 cups hot milk
	8 egg yolks, beaten
	8 egg whites, beaten stiff
	2 tablespoons grated Parmesan cheese

Sprinkle lamb inside and out with salt and pepper. Trim all fat. Insert garlic here and there. Place an empty can in center to make a smooth well to hold the MUSHROOM SOUFFLÉ. Cover the chop ends with foil. Roast at 400 degrees for 20 minutes. Remove from oven. Remove can. Pour off all fat. Cut out a circle of foil to cover bottom of roast and place the roast on it. Fill the center with MUSHROOM SOUFFLÉ. Wash, dry and chop the mushrooms fine. Sauté with the onion, salt and thyme in the butter until onions are soft. Add flour and cook until foamy. Cook 1 minute more. Add hot milk and cook until thickened, stirring constantly, for about 5 minutes. Cool slightly and add the beaten egg yolks. Cool and stir in 1/3 of the beaten egg whites. Fold in the rest, and pour into the lamb roast cavity. Sprinkle with Parmesan cheese. (Fold remaining soufflé in a buttered souffle dish and bake along with the lamb.) Return to oven and bake at 350 degrees for 40 minutes. Remove to a heated platter, remove foil and strings. Carve 1 double chop for each guest, including some of the soufflé; and pass the following sauce: Add 1 cup beef consommé to roasting pan, and cook for 5 minutes. Add 1 tablespoon currant jelly, 1 tablespoon red wine vinegar, cook until jelly is melted or pass hot pepper jelly.

POTTED LAMB CHOPS

Serves 4   Mrs. Herbert Kirsh (Suzanne)

4	large lamb shoulder or large rib chops-trim off fat		Parsley
1	onion - large		Salt, pepper
1/2	green pepper	1	can tomato sauce
2	large peeled potatoes	1	can small green peas

Cut up onion in rings and 1/2 green pepper in pan. Lay out lamb chops; sprinkle with salt, pepper, parsley. Slice potatoes and lay around chops. Add can of tomato sauce and 1 can of water. Cover pan and bake for 1 hour at 325 degrees. Lift cover and add canned peas. Brown for 10 minutes uncovered.

ITALIAN SAUSAGE AND ZUCCHINI

Serves 4   Senator John C. Land, III

8	sausage links (Italian if available; hot or sweet)	4	white potatoes, sliced in circles
2	onions, cut in strips	1	medium zucchini, unpeeled and sliced in circles
1	large bell pepper, sliced in strips	4	ripe tomatoes, peeled, and chopped (or 1 can tomatoes, undrained)
1	clove garlic or garlic salt		
1	small eggplant, peeled and chopped (optional)	1	teaspoon sugar

Oregano, basil, parsley, Hot red   Salt and pepper to taste
pepper (all depending on personal taste; and if using Italian sausage, use less of each)

In a large, deep frying pan cover sausage with water and simmer with lid for 10 minutes. Remove sausage from pan and begin slowly browning the sausage in another pan. To the sausage broth add all vegetables, spices and sugar. Simmer until potatoes are firm but done, add the browned sausage. Simmer together another 10 minutes and then serve. This is even better reheated the next day. The quantity of vegetables can vary by your family's taste. Serve with hot crusty bread and salad.

CHATEAUBRIAND

Cookbook Committee Selection

Sprinkle both sides of a 3 to 4 inch steak, weighing 13-ounces, with salt and white pepper and spread with softened butter. Broil 6 to 8 minutes on each side. Allow to rest in hot oven for approximately 10 minutes for easier carving. If the chateaubriand is very thick, you may wish to start it in a 375 degree oven and then finish under the broiler. This steak recipe was created in 1812 by Champeaux Restaurant in the Place de la Bourse in Paris. The dish honors François René de Chateaubriand after the publication of his book, *Itieraire de Paris à Jerusalem.*

MARINATED PORK LOIN ROAST

Serves 10   Mrs. William N. Cork (Helen)

1/2	cup soy sauce	1/2	cup dry sherry
2	cloves garlic, minced	1	tablespoon dry mustard
1	teaspoon ginger	1	teaspoon thyme, crushed
1	4 to 5-pound boned, rolled and tied pork loin roast		

Combine soy sauce, sherry, garlic, mustard, ginger and thyme. Place roast in large clear plastic bag; set in deep bowl to steady roast. Pour in marinade and close bag tightly. Let stand 2 to 3 hours at room temperature or overnight in refrigerator. Occasionally press bag against meat in several places to distribute marinade evenly. Remove meat from marinade. Place roast on rack in shallow roasting pan. Roast, uncovered, in slow oven, 325 degrees 2-1/2 to 3 hours until meat thermometer registers 175 degrees, basting occassionally with marinade during last hour of roasting time.

SAUCY RIBS

Representative James E. Lockemy

1/4	cup lightly packed dark brown sugar	2	cups water
2	teaspoons dry mustard	6	tablespoons lemon juice
2	tablespoons seasoned salt	6	tablespoons Worcestershire sauce
1/2	teaspoon pepper	1/4	cup cider vinegar
2	teaspoons prepared horseradish	1/2	cup instant minced onion
6	pounds spareribs	6	drops Tabasco sauce

In saucepan, blend sugar, mustard, salt and pepper. Stir in remaining ingredients to make sauce. Bring to boil, cover and simmer 10 minutes. In conventional oven, brown ribs in roasting pan at 350 degrees. Pour off fat. Spoon sauce over ribs; cover tightly with foil and cook about 1 hour. You may also brown ribs on both sides in Dutch oven, heavy skillet, or saucepan. Pour off fat. Pour sauce over ribs. Bring to boil. Cover and simmer and steam for 1 to 1-1/2 hours. Baste and turn ribs often.

STUFFED PORK CHOPS FOR COMPANY

Serves 4   Mrs. Lloyd Hendricks (Sue)

4	loin pork chops, 1-inch thick, and slit to make a pocket	4	slices Swiss cheese, diced
1/2	cup fresh mushrooms, chopped	1/4	cup fresh parsley, snipped
1	egg, slightly beaten	1/2	teaspoon salt
3	tablespoons oil		Dry bread crumbs
		1/2	cup Chablis

Mix cheese, parsley, mushrooms and salt. Fill pockets in pork chops. Dip each chop in egg and then bread crumbs. In hot oil in skillet, brown chops well on both sides. Add Chablis; simmer, covered, 45 minutes or until tender.

BAKED HAM A LA FRUIT GLAZE

Mrs. Larry E. Gentry (Barbara)

1	16-ounce can fruit cocktail	1	teaspoon curry powder
1/3	cup honey	1/4	teaspoon nutmeg
1	tablespoon lemon juice	2	bananas, cut in 1-inch diagonal slices
1	tablespoon cornstarch	1	baked ham

Drain fruit cocktail, reserving 2/3 cup syrup. In saucepan, mix syrup with next five ingredients. Cook, stirring until thickened. Add fruit cocktail and heat. Arrange ham on platter and surround with banana chunks and pour on hot sauce.

VEAL PICCATA

Mrs. Robert C. Lake, Jr. (Carolyn)

1	pound veal scallops, flattened to 1/4-inch thick	1/4	cup olive oil
	Flour for dredging	3	tablespoons white wine or vermouth
	Salt and pepper	3	tablespoons lemon juice
1/4	cup butter	1/4	cup chopped parsley
		1/2	cup lemon, thinly sliced

Place veal between two pieces of foil and beat with mallet until very thin, but not torn. Dredge in the flour with salt and pepper; shake off excess flour. Sauté veal in very hot oil and butter on medium heat until golden brown, about 4 to 6 minutes turning only once. (Don't overcook.) Transfer meat to warm platter. Pour off all but 2 tablespoons of fat. Add wine and lemon juice. Scrape all pan drippings to loosen cooking residue. Pour sauce over veal. Garnish with parsley and lemon slices. Serve immediately.

VEAL MARSALA

Serves 4 to 6   Judge James B. Stephen

2   pounds veal top round steak,   1/2 cup butter or margarine
    thinly sliced and cut in   1   4-ounce can sliced mushrooms,
    2-inch strips   drained or fresh
Marsala wine or sherry   Salt and pepper
Flour   Lemon wedges

Pound flour into veal strips; brown meat quickly in heated butter. Cover
with mushrooms; add wine to cover. Simmer, covered, 10 to 15 minutes or
until tender. Season with salt and pepper, garnish with lemon wedges. Serve
with rice pilaf, a vegetable, green salad and hot rolls.

VEAL PARMIGIANA

Serves 4   Mrs. Robert N. McLellan (Doris)

1   pound veal cutlets   1/4 cup water
1   egg, slightly beaten   1   clove garlic, crushed
1/2 cup fine dry bread crumbs   1/8 teaspoon thyme
2   tablespoons salad oil   8   mushrooms, sliced
1   10-3/4-ounce can tomato soup   4   ounces Mozzarella cheese, grated
2   tablespoons freshly grated   1/4 cup minced onion
     Parmesan cheese

Dip veal in egg, then in bread crumbs, and fry in salad oil until brown on
each side. Place veal in a shallow baking dish, 12x7-1/2x2-inch. Blend soup,
water, onion, garlic and thyme. Pour over meat. Top with mushroom slices,
Mozzarella cheese and sprinkle with Parmesan cheese. Bake in a 350 degree
oven, about 30 minutes or until hot and bubbling.

NOTES

LAURENS COUNTY

Laurens County, which lies midway between Greenville and Columbia, might serve as a stepping stone for a giant who was tip-toeing diagonally across the state, Cherokee inhabitants on the path gave way to white settlers in mid-eighteenth century as Scotch-Irish families immigrated into the attractive Piedmont farm area.

In 1785 the county was carved from the Old Ninety-Six District with the Enoree and Saluda rivers serving as its major liquid boundaries. The county is named for Henry Laurens, popular statesman of the Revolution and President of the Continental Congress. Laurens himself never lived in the region but another future-President made his home in Laurensville in the early 1800s. Andrew Johnson, 17th President of the U.S., operated a tailor shop with his brother William.

From the earliest days there was a strong bent toward literature and education in the county. One William Jacobs, a Presbyterian minister who arrived in the lively railroad town of Clinton in 1865, made gigantic strides in improving the goals of the town. From a strong library society grew a high school which later became Presbyterian College (1900) and from an interest in homeless children came the establishment of Thornwell Orphanage in 1875. Another dynamic leader, Miss Wil Lou Gray, began her well known assistance to the underprivileged in Laurens County.

The most profitable nineteenth century crop was cotton which laid the groundwork for a successful textile industry. The sand and silicates in the area were found appropriate for glass making. A profitable glass works, one of the few in the South, makes an assortment of bottles and other containers. Past and present, nature and industry have melded well in Laurens, making it a county in which its namesake would take great pride.

194

Abbeville County was once considered rough and tumble back-country yet it produced some of the state's most polished and erudite leaders. Aristocrats and farmers, French immigrants and Indians have left their imprint on the area which was first settled in the mid-1750's.

Fertile farm lands nestled between the Savannah and Saluda rivers attracted eighteenth century Scotch-Irish settlers led by Patrick Calhoun, father of John C. Calhoun. In their footsteps came a group of Huguenot exiles, guided by the Rev. Mr. Jean Louis Gibert, who adopted the name "Abbeville" in honor of a recently abandoned French town.

Near the present town of Due West (then known as De Witt's Corner) a treaty was signed on May 20, 1777 whereby the Cherokee Indians relinquished extensive land claims in South Carolina. With the removal of the Indian threat and the end of the Revolutionary war, life became more stable in the back-country. The Associate Reformed Presbyterian Church established Erskine College in Due West (1839), the state's first four-year church-related college. This institution perpetuated the county's early lead in educational initiative and achievement.

Abbeville produced ante-bellum leaders who spanned the political spectrum. Orator and firey secessionist John C. Calhoun was a native son as was James L. Petigru, Charleston's lone Unionist in 1860. Ironically, both had been educated by Moses Waddell at the Willington Academy, a rude but respected school then located in Abbeville District (now McCormick County).

Both the opening and closing days of the Civil War could be viewed from the hilly court house town, causing some to label Abbeville "the cradle and the grave of the Confederacy." On November 20, 1860 a meeting was held on Magazine Hill which hosted the first secession document and began the full fledged southern movement. Five war-torn years later the Confederate Cabinet, in retreat after Lee's surrender, held its final meeting at the Burt Mansion in May 1865.

Around the turn of the century Abbeville's Opera House was well known in the entertainment world, drawing such "greats" as Fanny Brice, Jimmy Durante and Groucho Marx. When the days of traveling road shows faded, so did the Opera House. But in recent years it has been restored and rejuvinated by live local theater and musical productions, one example of a vibrant community combining its rich past with twentieth century ingenuity.

Greenwood lies strategically on a ridge above the Saluda and Savannah rivers, once at a fork in the Cherokee Path, later an important railroad junction. In 1897 the present county was carved from portions of Abbeville and Edgefield counties, which were descended from the former Ninety-Six District.

Greenwood boasts a colorful colonial history. At the frontier village of Ninety-Six was the first white settlement and the first court house in the Piedmont area as well as the state's first battle in the Revolutionary War (November 19, 1775). Its star-shaped fort was militarily significant, a key outpost protecting the capital in Charles Town against Indian and British attack. Remaining ruins and historical restoration bring the region alive for visitors today.

Legends abound on the origin of the unusual name of "Ninety-Six." According to the most popular one an Indian maiden ("Cateechee" in Cherokee language, or "Isaqueena" in Choctaw) rode a distance of 96 miles to warn her white lover of an impending Indian raid. On her journey she made rest stops at One Mile Creek, Six Mile Branch and Twelve Mile Creek, upcountry names which have persisted through the years. However, others insist that traders bestowed the names to indicate the approximate mileage from the Cherokee town of Keowee.

The nineteenth century saw the establishment of Woodville - later Greenwood - as the county seat and the advent of the railroad. The depot was placed uncompromisingly in the center of town, making the main street unusually wide to accomodate the tracks. The county's dependable fertile soils produced excellent crops, particularly cotton, laying the groundwork for a flourishing textile industry in the early 20th century. By the 1920s large mills were producing cloth in Ware Shoals, Ninety-Six and Greenwood.

Lake Greenwood and its adjacent Greenwood State Park form the northeastern boundary of the county. Water sports and recreation are easily accessible in this hilly, green county which is also the home of one of the nation's largest seed supply companies. Greenhouses and test gardens are appropriate complements to the natural flora of the area.

A strong agricultural-Germanic-Lutheran heritage permeates Newberry County, which lies in the upper reaches of the pie-shaped fork between the Saluda and Broad rivers. In the early days the region was noted for vast forests, lush grape and muscadine vines and even a bald eagle or two. The setting attracted one settler, John Duncan, in 1752 who was followed closely by groups of Germans and Quakers filtering in from Pennsylvania.

Bounded by two navigable rivers and peopled increasingly by Swiss and German families, the rich farm area came to be known as "Dutch Fork," a term which has persisted. As might be expected, the Germans brought with them an affection for the Luthern Church which generated numerous rural congregations.

Slicing a portion of territory from the Old Ninety-Six District, state officials created Newberry County in 1785, making it one of the state's earliest counties. The county seat was located in Newberry Village which has had a series of handsome Court Houses for the accomodation of county business.

Historically observers have commented on the narrow streets and eclectic but pleasing architecture of Newberry. Writing in the 1820s Robert Mills mentioned the narrowness of the town's streets and suggested widening them; more than a century later another historian attributed the crowded feeling of the business district to the narrow streets. Spacious homes and utilitarian buildings are in close proximity.

Scattered through the rural county are a number of small towns whose raison d'etre can be ascribed to cotton mills, railroad junctions or agricultural centers. The face of the countyside may have changed but not its spirit. Windmills have given way to Interstate exit signs and log cabins to week-end lake cottages, but the serenity of this central Midlands county remains. It is quiet and stable, a good place to live.

BELFAST

Belfast, built by John Simpson in 1786 of brick made in Ireland, is one of the most interesting and best preserved historic spots in Laurens County. This Georgian, two and a half storied manor house is constructed of brick made in Ireland.

poultry

CORN BREAD DRESSING

Mrs. Larry A. Martin (Susan)

1-1/2 cups white corn meal
1-1/2 cups plain flour
1 teaspoon baking powder
1/2 teaspoon salt
4 eggs
1-1/2 cups milk
1-1/2 cups white bread crumbs
1/2 cup grated onion

1/2 cup finely diced celery
3 cups strong chicken broth
1/2 tablespoon pepper
1/2 teaspoon sage
1/2 teaspoon thyme
4 tablespoons butter
1 pint raw oysters, simmered until edges curl (optional)

Mix the corn meal, flour, baking powder, salt, eggs and milk and bake in a greased pan at 425 degrees for 20 minutes. Crumble while hot and add the hot chicken stock, onion, celery, bread crumbs, herbs, pepper and oysters, if desired. Bake in a buttered 7-1/4x11-1/4x3/8-inch pan at 350 degrees for about 35 to 45 minutes or until done.

TURKEY LOAF

Serves 8 to 10

Mrs. J. M. Cooper (Melba)

2 pounds raw turkey or chicken meat, ground (no skins)
4 eggs
1 cup undiluted canned cream of mushroom soup
1-1/2 teaspoon salt
2 tablespoons chopped pimento

2 tablespoons chopped green pepper, blanched
1 cup white bread crumbs
1/4 teaspoon white pepper
1/4 teaspoon Worcestershire sauce
American cheese, sliced

Mix all the ingredients except the cheese. Put half in a buttered bundt pan or angel food pan, then a layer of American cheese. Fill pan with rest of mixture. Cover and bake in a 350 degree oven for about 1 hour. Turn out and serve with MUSHROOM FONDUE or any sauce of your choice. Leftover turkey loaf makes a good sandwich the following day, and any sauce reheated and poured over makes it doubly so. MUSHROOM FONDUE, page 200.

MUSHROOM FONDUE

Yields: 3 cups

1/2	pound fresh mushrooms	2	cups half-and-half
1/4	cup butter	1	pound Gruyere cheese, diced
1/4	cup flour	1/4	cup dry sauterne or sherry

Wash and dry the mushrooms and cut in fourths, leaving the stems on. Sauté in the butter for 5 minutes, stirring constantly. Add the flour, cook until bubbly. Add the half-and-half and cook over low heat, stirring rapidly. No lumps. Add cheese and wine. Keep warm and serve.

CHICKEN OR TURKEY CASSEROLE

Serves 8   Mrs. D. Les Tindal (May)

1	16-ounce can French cut green beans, drained		2 or 3 cups chopped, cooked chicken or turkey
1	16-ounce can Chinese mixed vegetables, drained	1	10-3/4-ounce can cream of mushroom soup with 1/2 soup can sweet milk
1	14-ounce can mushrooms, drained	1	2-1/2-ounce can French fried onions
1	small chopped onion		
1/2	pound grated sharp cheese		Salt to taste

Alternate layers of vegetables, meat and cheese in a casserole dish. Pour soup mixture over this and bake at 350 degrees for 40 minutes. Remove and put crushed French fried onions on top and cook 20 minutes more.

DEVILED ROCK CORNISH HENS

Serves 8   Mrs. Larry A. Martin (Susan)

8	10 to 12-ounce Rock Cornish hens	3	tablespoons minced shallots
	Salt and white pepper	1/2	cup butter
1/2	cup Dijon mustard		White wine
2/3	cup white bread crumbs	8	squares of foil

Rub each bird with salt, pepper and 1 tablespoon of the mustard. Sprinkle with bread crumbs. Place each in a square of foil and fold to center. Add 1 teaspoon shallots, 1 tablespoon butter and 3 tablespoons white wine to each package. Fold over the foil tightly and bake at 400 degrees about 50 minutes or until Cornish hens are done. Serve hot or cold.

BREAST OF CHICKEN IN ASPIC

Serves 8   Mrs. Larry A. Martin (Susan)

8	6-ounce boned whole chicken breasts or half breasts		(Lucul, gelatin Swiss granulated, in gourmet shops)
4	cups canned chicken consomme		Pâté de fois gras
2	tablespoons unflavored gelatin	1/2	cup white wine
			Truffles or hard-cooked eggs

Poach the chicken breasts in the consomme until tender, about 20 minutes. Remove skin and fat. Use 2 cups of consomme, pour in 1/2 cup white wine, heat, and add softened gelatin. Pour a thin layer of the consomme in a shallow pan; refrigerate to set. Place the breasts on top and pour over a thin layer of gelatin mixture. Refrigerate. Spread a tablespoon of pate on top of each breast and again pour over a thin layer of gelatin. Refrigerate until set. Decorate with truffles, sliced hard-cooked egg or both. Repeat with the gelatin mixture. When remaining gelatin becomes syrupy, pour over and chill thoroughly. Remove chicken to a chilled tray, chop the extra aspic and surround the chicken.

COUNTRY CAPTAIN

Serves 10   Mrs. Robert N. McLellan (Doris)

10	chicken breasts, fried	2	tablespoons dry sherry (not cooking sherry)
1	cup brown rice, cooked		
2	tablespoons butter	1/2	teaspoon thyme
1	large onion, chopped	1/2	teaspoon mace
2	green peppers, chopped	1	teaspoon Worcestershire sauce
1	clove garlic, chopped	1/3	cup raisins
1	tablespoon curry powder	1/3	cup toasted almonds
1	1-pound 14-ounce can tomato purée	1	teaspoon salt
		1/2	teaspoon pepper

Combine butter, onion, pepper, garlic and curry powder in a saucepan and cook 1 minute. Add tomato purée, sherry, thyme, mace, Worcestershire sauce, raisins, salt and pepper and simmer 10 minutes. Put cooked rice in bottom of 9x13-inch casserole dish, cover with fried chicken breasts and ladle sauce over chicken. Cover with foil. You can leave in refrigerator a couple of days. Cook 25 minutes in a 350 degree oven. If taken out of refrigerator, cook 45 minutes at 350 degrees. Garnish with toasted almonds and sprigs of parsley. Good with Spinach salad and baked peach half filled with chutney.

HOT CHICKEN SALAD SOUFFLE

Serves 6   Mrs. Nick A. Theodore (Emilie)

6 slices white bread	3/4 teaspoon salt
2 cups diced cooked turkey	Dash pepper
or chicken	1-1/2 cups milk
1/2 cup chopped onion	2 beaten eggs
1/2 cup chopped green pepper	1 10-3/4-ounce can mushroom
1/2 cup finely chopped celery	soup
1/2 cup mayonnaise	1/2 cup shredded sharp cheese

Cube 2 slices bread, place in bottom of 8x8x2-inch greased baking dish. Combine turkey, vegetables, mayonnaise and seasonings and spoon over bread cubes. Trim crusts from remaining bread, arrange slices on top of turkey mixture. Combine eggs and milk; pour over all. Cover and chill 1 hour or overnight. Spoon soup over top. Bake at 350 degrees about 1 hour or until set. Sprinkle cheese over top during last few minutes of baking.

JULIENNE BREAST OF CHICKEN AND ASPARAGUS

Serves 4 to 6   Mrs. Dick Elliott (Anne)

2 to 4 cooked chicken breasts,	2 10-3/4-ounce cans cream of
boned and cut in strips and	chicken soup
skin removed	1 cup mayonnaise
2 16-ounce cans asparagus,	1 tablespoon lemon juice
drained	1 cup sharp grated cheese
	1 cup bread crumbs

Poach the chicken breasts in chicken broth or water about 20 minutes. Cut in strips. Grease a 9x13-inch casserole dish with butter. Place asparagus in bottom of casserole. Put julienne chicken in a layer over asparagus. Mix soup, lemon juice and mayonnaise. Pour over chicken. Place grated cheese over soup mixture. Sprinkle with bread crumbs. Bake at 350 degrees for 30 to 40 minutes.

BREAST OF CHICKEN GRUYÈRE

Serves 6   Mrs. Butler Derrick (Martha)

Season 3 chicken breasts (split, boned and skin on) and cook in 2 tbls. butter at med. heat, 10 minutes, turning once. Arrange side by side in dish just big enough to hold them. Cook a large handful of plain breadcrumbs in chickens' cooking butter, stirring until crisp. Set aside. Deglaze pan with 1/3 cup white wine, reducing by 1/2. Whisk together 3/4 cup heavy cream, 3 egg yolks, 3 ounces grated Gruyere cheese, salt and pepper. Then add juice of ½ lemon and deglazing liquid to mixture. Pour evenly over chicken. Sprinkle top with a few breadcrumbs. Bake at 400 degrees for 20 to 25 minutes. The surface will be deep gold in color when done.

CHICKEN AND ARTICHOKE HEARTS IN WINE SAUCE

Serves 4   Mrs. Edward Simpson (Maureen)

4	whole chicken breasts, boned and skin left on	1/2	cup chopped shallots
			Few slivers of fresh garlic
1/4	cup clarified butter	1	cup dry white wine
16	small canned artichoke hearts	1	tablespoon arrowroot or flour
2	cups sliced mushrooms		

Cut the chicken breasts, with skin, into bite-sized pieces. Saute these pieces in clarified butter, skin side down, turning carefully until they are brown on all sides. Place them on a heated platter to one side. In the same pan, saute artichoke hearts until they are brown. Remove them to the same heated platter. In the same pan, add sliced mushrooms and sauté until tender, while at the same time adding chopped shallots with garlic. When the mushrooms are tender and the shallots transparent, transfer chicken and artichoke hearts to pan. Add white wine; simmer until the chicken is tender. Remove everything from the juices and thicken with arrowroot or flour and pour over chicken mixture.

PARTY CHICKEN BREASTS

Serves 12   Mrs. Robert N. McLellan (Doris)

12	chicken breast halves, skinned and boned	4	cloves garlic, crushed
		4	teaspoons salt
2	cups sour cream	1/2	teaspoon freshly ground pepper
1/4	cup lemon juice	3	cups fine club cracker crumbs
4	teaspoons Worcestershire sauce		(Keebler brand)
4	teaspoons celery salt	1/2	cup butter
2	teaspoons paprika	1/2	cup salad corn oil

In large bowl, combine sour cream with the next seven ingredients. Mix well. Add chicken breasts to mixture, coating each piece well. Let stand, covered, in refrigerator overnight. Next day, preheat oven to 350 degrees. Remove chicken from mixture, roll in cracker crumbs, coating evenly and arrange in single layer in large, shallow baking pan. Melt butter and mix with corn oil in small saucepan and spoon half over chicken. Bake chicken, uncovered, 45 minutes. Spoon rest of butter/oil mixture over chicken and bake 10 to ·15 minutes longer or until chicken is tender and nicely browned.

BREAST OF CHICKEN PIQUANTE

Serves 4   Mrs. B. L. Hendricks, Jr. (Carolyn)

2	whole chicken breasts, halved and skin removed	4	tablespoons water
1-1/2 cups Rosé wine		2	teaspoons ground ginger
1/2	cup soy sauce	2	tablespoons brown sugar
1/2	cup cooking oil	1/2	teaspoon ground oregano
		1/4	teaspoon garlic salt

Remove bone from chicken or buy boneless. In baking pan, place chicken with meaty side up. In bowl, mix together wine, soy sauce, oil, water, brown sugar, ginger, oregano and garlic salt; pour over chicken. Bake, uncovered, in a 375 degree oven for 1 hour. Serve with rice.

CHICKEN AND BACON ROLLS WITH CREAM

Serves 4 to 8   Mrs. John M. Rucker (Harriet)

1	2-1/2-ounce jar dried beef	1	carton sour cream
8	chicken breasts, boned	1	10-3/4-ounce chicken soup
8	slices bacon	1	10-3/4-ounce cream celery soup

Shred dried beef on bottom of casserole dish. Roll each breast in a piece of bacon, and place on top of dried beef. Mix soup and sour cream and spread over chicken. Bake covered for 2-1/2 hours at 275 degrees. Uncover and bake 30 minutes more.

VARIATION

Omit chicken soup. Season chicken. Place 1 slice dried beef under each breast. Wrap a bacon strip around each piece of chicken. Mix sour cream with 1 10-3/4-ounce can cream of mushroom soup and pour over chicken. Bake covered at 325 degrees for 1-1/2 hours. Uncover, sprinkle with paprika and finish baking at 350 degrees for 30 minutes. Garnish with slivered almonds. This dish can be frozen after assembly but prior to cooking.

CHICKEN CASSEROLE

Serves 15 to 18   Mrs. Gene Dukes (Gerry)

2	3-pound fryers, cooked and chopped	1	small can sliced water chestnuts
2	heaping cups cooked rice	2	cans cream of chicken soup
2	cups celery, chopped	1-1/2 cups mayonnaise	
2	medium onions, chopped	1	small jar pimento, chopped
		Cheese crackers, crushed, buttered	

Mix all ingredients well and pour into a greased 9x13-inch pan. Top with cheese crackers that have been crushed and buttered. Bake at 350 degrees for 1 hour or until bubbly, and crackers begin to brown. Freezes well.

CHICKEN DIVAN

Serves 6   Mrs. Robin Tallon, Jr. (Amy)

3 whole chicken breasts (or 1 small turkey breast)	1 cup grated sharp cheese
3 packages frozen broccoli	1 tablespoon lemon juice
2 cans cream of chicken soup	1 teaspoon (or less to taste) curry
1 cup mayonnaise	Salt and pepper to taste
1 carton sour cream	Parmesan cheese
	Paprika

Cook chicken breasts (simmer water with onion, celery, carrot, bay leaf, pepper corn, salt, etc.). Cook broccoli. Mix soup, sour cream, mayonnaise, grated cheese and seasoning. Drain broccoli and arrange in bottom of flat greased casserole (3 quart). Sprinkle generously with Parmesan cheese. Remove skin from chicken and take chicken from bone, pulling apart into pieces, and spread over broccoli. Sprinkle again with Parmesan cheese. Pour sauce over all. Sprinkle with Parmesan cheese and paprika. Dot with butter. Cook 30 to 40 minutes at 350 degrees or until hot and bubbly.

CHICKEN KIEV

Serves 6   Mrs. Frank H. McGill (Peggy)

6 chicken breasts, boned and skin removed	Juice of 1 lemon
Salt to taste	1/2 cup softened butter or margarine
Pepper to taste	1 cup flour
3 tablespoons chopped spring onions	1/2 teaspoon sage
	2 eggs, beaten with 2 tablespoons water
3 tablespoons finely chopped fresh parsley	1 cup bread crumbs

Pound each chicken breast with a meat mallet until about 3/8 to 1/4-inch thin. Sprinkle with salt and pepper to taste. Add 1/2 to 1 teaspoon lemon juice. Add 1/2 tablespoon each of spring onions and chopped parsley. Roll the chicken breast tightly, securing with wooden toothpicks. Combine flour and sage. Dredge each chicken roll in flour mixture. Then dip into egg mixture. Finally, coat with bread crumbs. Refrigerate for about 30 minutes. Fry in hot oil until golden brown. To make ahead, prepare as directed, freeze and reheat in 350 degree oven prior to serving. Can be frozen without prior cooking, if desired. Separate each roll with wax paper. Recipe doubles well. Good served with CRAB MEAT SAUCE (see Index) ladled over each portion.

POULTRY

CHICKEN CHOW MEIN NOODLE CASSEROLE

Yields: 2 large casseroles — Mrs. Michael R. Daniel (Peggy)

4	chicken breasts, cooked and cut up	2	tablespoons corn starch
1	10-3/4-ounce can chicken soup	1	4-ounce can mushrooms
1	10-3/4-ounce can mushroom soup	1	can chow mein noodles
1	13-ounce can Pet milk	1	cup celery, diced
1	can water chestnuts	1/2	cup bell pepper, diced
1	small can Parmesan cheese	1/2	cup onion, diced
		2	sticks margarine

Saute bell pepper, celery and onion in margarine and thicken with corn starch. Mix all but noodles and cheese. Alternate layers with mixture, noodles and cheese. Bake at 350 degrees for 40 minutes. Can be frozen.

CHICKEN SALTIMBOCCA

Serves 6 — Mrs. William Cork (Helen)

3	large chicken breasts, skinned, boned and halved lenghtwise	1/2	teaspoon dried sage, crushed
6	thin slices boiled ham	1/3	cup fine dry bread crumbs
3	slices Mozzarella cheese halves	2	tablespoons grated Parmesan cheese
1	medium tomato, seeded and chopped	2	tablespoons snipped parsley
		4	tablespoons butter, melted

Place chicken, boned side up, on cutting board. Place a piece of clear plastic wrap over. Working from the center out, pound lightly with meat mallet to 5x5-inches. Remove wrap. Place a ham slice and half slice of cheese on each cutlet, cutting to fit. Top with some tomato and a dash of sage. Tuck in sides; roll up jelly-roll style, pressing to seal well. Combine bread crumbs, Parmesan, and parsley. Dip chicken in butter, then roll in crumbs. Place in shallow baking pan. Bake in 350 degree oven 40 to 50 minutes.

HERB CHICKEN BAKE

Serves 6 — Mrs. Grady L. Patterson, Jr. (Margie)

6 to 8	half chicken breasts	1/2	cup margarine, melted
2	cups Pepperidge Farm Herb Stuffing	1	teaspoon salt
		1/2	teaspoon pepper

Salt and pepper chicken breasts. Dip chicken into melted margarine, then roll in crushed Pepperidge Farm Herb Stuffing crumbs. Pour rest of margarine over and bake at 350 degrees for 1 hour. If chicken begins to brown too quickly, cover loosely with foil.

HERBED CHICKEN

Serves 4   Mrs. Thomas L. Hughston, Jr. (Jeanne)

4	chicken breasts	1/2	teaspoon thyme
Salt and pepper to taste		1	tablespoon melted butter
1	10-3/4-ounce can cream of chicken soup	1	can water chestnuts, sliced thin
		1	can mushrooms
3/4	cup white wine	2	tablespoons chopped green pepper

Salt and pepper chicken. Place in casserole and pour over it the sauce made from the soup, wine, thyme and butter. Cover and cook at 350 degrees for 1 hour or until tender. Before serving add water chestnuts, mushrooms and green peppers. Cook again only until the last ingredients are heated thoroughly.

CHICKEN CHOW MEIN

Serves 4   Mrs. B. E. Thrailkill, Jr. (Peggy)

1/4	cup margarine	2	cups cooked chicken, cut in thin strips
1	medium onion, chopped		
2	cups diced celery	2	tablespoons cold water
1	teaspoon salt	2	tablespoons cornstarch
1-1/2 cups hot water		1	tablespoon soy sauce
1	can Chinese vegetables, drained	1	teaspoon sugar
			Chow mein noodles

Melt butter in skillet. Add onion and cook 3 minutes. Add celery, salt and hot water. Cover and cook 5 minutes. Add vegetables and chicken. Mix well and cook 5 minutes. Combine thickening ingredients; add to chicken mixture and cook 1 minute. Serve hot over chow mein noodles.

BAKED PARMESAN CHICKEN

Serves 6   Mrs. Thomas L. Hughston (Jeanne)

1	cup dry bread crumbs	Salt to taste	
1/3	cup grated Parmesan cheese	1	clove garlic
1/4	teaspoon ground oregano	3/4	cup melted butter
1/4	teaspoon pepper	1	chicken, cut up, ur use deboned breasts

Combine bread crumbs, cheese, oregano, pepper and salt. Set aside. Lightly sauté garlic in 2 tablespoons butter. Dip chicken in butter and roll in bread crumb mixture. Place in a 13x9x2-inch pan. Sprinkle with remaining butter over crumbs. Bake at 350 degrees for 55 minutes.

CHICKEN PIE

Serves 8 to 10   Mrs. Robert C. Lake, Jr. (Carolyn)

2	pie crusts	2	boiled eggs, chopped
1	3-pound broiler, cooked and cut into pieces, reserve 1 can stock	1	17-ounce can English peas, drained
2	10-3/4-ounce cans cream of chicken soup	1	16-ounce can carrots, drained (optional)

Boil chicken in water to cover with salt, onions, celery and carrot until tender, about 1 hour. Remove chicken from bones and cut in large chunks. Cook 1 pie crust and set aside. Combine chicken, soup, stock and eggs. Put one-half mixture in 2 quart casserole. Pour half the peas and carrots over the mixture. Break cooked pie crust in bite size pieces and layer over chicken. Add remaining chicken and vegetables. Cut second pie crust into strips to top pie. Cook at 350 degrees for about 30 minutes or until brown.

VARIATION NO. 1   Mrs. Timothy A. Brett (Reta)

Instead of the pie shells, pour a crust mixture of 1 cup self-rising flour, 1 stick melted margarine and 1 cup milk mixed together over the top of chicken, soup mixture, eggs and vegetables. Bake at 350 degrees for 45 minutes or until crust is brown.

VARIATION NO. 2   Mrs. Nick A. Theodore (Emilie)

Substitute 1 10-1/2-ounce can celery soup and 1-1/2 cups chicken broth in place of 2 cans cream of chicken soup. Mix 1 cup + 2 tablespoons plain flour, 2 teaspoons baking powder, 1/4 teaspoon salt, 1/4 teaspoon pepper. Add 1 stick softened margarine until crumbly. Add 1 cup milk. Mixture will be soupy. Spoon over chicken broth mixture. Bake at 425 degrees, uncovered, for 30 minutes.

COCK-A-CHEESY

Serves 4   Mrs. Robert N. McLellan (Doris)

2 to 3	pounds chicken parts	1/4	cup water
3	tablespoons butter, melted	1/4	cup white wine
1	10-3/4-ounce can cheddar cheese soup	1	clove minced garlic
			Salt and pepper

Preheat oven to 400 degrees. Move oven rack to top part of oven. Season the chicken parts. Put the chicken, skin side down, in a 12-3/4x9-inch pan. Pour melted butter over the chicken and bake in the top part of the oven for 20 minutes. Turn skin side up and bake 400 degrees for 20 more minutes. Mix together the rest of ingredients and pour over the top of chicken and bake 400 degrees for 20 minutes more.

CHICKEN PICCATA

Serves 4 to 8   Mrs. William Cork (Helen)

4 whole chicken breasts, skinned, boned and halved	1 tablespoon olive oil
1/2 cup flour	2 to 4 tablespoons dry Madeira or water
1-1/2 teaspoons salt	3 tablespoons fresh lemon juice
1/4 teaspoon freshly ground pepper	Lemon slices
Paprika	3 to 4 tablespoons capers
1/4 cup clarified butter	1/4 cup minced fresh parsley

Place chicken breasts between 2 sheets of waxed paper and pound them until thin (about 1/4-inch). Combine flour, salt, pepper and paprika in a bag. Add breasts and coat well; shake off excess. Heat butter and olive oil in large skillet until bubbling. Sauté chicken breasts, a few at a time, 2 to 3 minutes on each side. Do not overcook. Drain on paper towels and keep warm. Drain off all but 2 tablespoons of butter and oil. Stir Madeira or water into drippings, scraping bottom of skillet to loosen any browned bits. Add lemon juice and heat briefly. Return chicken to skillet, interspersing with lemon slices, and heat until sauce thickens. Add capers, sprinkle with minced parsley. Good with pasta, a green salad and toasted garlic bread.

BUTTERMILK BAKED CHICKEN

Serves 4 to 6   Mrs. J. I. Rogers, III (Carolyn)

1 3-pound frying chicken, cut in parts	1/4 teaspoon pepper
2 cups buttermilk	1/4 cup margarine
3/4 cup flour	1 10-3/4-ounce can cream of chicken soup
1-1/2 teaspoon salt	

Mix flour, salt and pepper. Dip chicken pieces in 1/2 cup buttermilk and roll in the seasoned flour. Put margarine in a 13x9x2-inch baking pan and melt in a 425 degree oven. Put chicken in pan, skin side down, and bake 30 minutes. Turn and bake 15 minutes. Mix remaining buttermilk with the soup and pour around chicken. Bake 15 minutes longer or until tender. Makes a delicious gravy served with rice.

CHICKEN AND SAUSAGE CASSEROLE

Serves 8   Mrs. James B. Stephen (Ginger)

1   cooked chicken, diced
1   6-ounce package Uncle Ben's
    Wild Rice Mix
1   pound sausage, browned and
    crumbled
Sliced water chestnuts (optional)

2   medium onions, chopped
2   10-3/4-ounce cream of mush-
    room soup
Buttered bread crumbs
Mushrooms (optional)
Chopped pecans (optional)

Cook rice according to directions on box, using the chicken stock in place of water. Sauté onions in sausage drippings. Combine onions, sausage, soup, boned chicken and rice. Pour into a 9x13-inch pan. Top with buttered bread crumbs. Bake, uncovered, at 350 degrees for 30 minutes. This may be frozen before cooking in oven. Good for a large crowd.

GLAZED CHICKEN

Mrs. Herbert Kirsh (Suzanne)

1   frying chicken, cut in parts
1   8-ounce bottle creamy French
    Dressing

8   ounces apricot preserves
1   1-1/2-ounce envelope onion soup
    mix

Place chicken pieces in a big bowl. Combine dressing, preserves, and soup mix and coat chicken well with mixture. Place on a foil lined cookie sheet and bake, uncovered, for 1 to 1-1/2 hours at 325 degrees.

VARIATION: Mrs. Clyde M. Dangerfield (Betty)

Omit apricot preserves and onion soup mix. Mix 3/4 cup French Dressing and 1/4 cup vinegar together and pour mixture over chicken parts. Cover with foil and bake 1 hour at 350 degrees.

CHICKEN TETRAZZINI

Serves 8 to 10   Mrs. Nick A. Theodore (Emilie)

1   3-pound hen or large fryer
1/2   pound spaghetti
1/4   pound bacon
2   large onions, chopped
1   cup grated cheddar cheese

1   16-ounce can tomatoes
1   8-ounce can mushrooms
1   small bottle stuffed salad olives
Few drops Tabasco sauce

Stew hen or chicken in a good bit of water for about 45 minutes to 1 hour. Save stock. Cook spaghetti in stock according to directions on package. Drain and set aside. In large skillet fry bacon. Take out bacon and saute onions; add tomatoes, mushrooms and olives with juice. Add crumbled bacon, cut up chicken, salt to taste and Tabasco. In casserole put layer of spaghetti, cover with sauce. Repeat. Cover with cheese and bake, covered, until bubbly in 350 degree oven.

CHICKEN TETRAZZINI A LA CARO

Serves 12   Mrs. T. Eston Marchant (Caro)

1	8-ounce package spaghetti	3	cups cooked chicken or turkey, cut into strips
1	cup onion, chopped	1	8-ounce can mushrooms
1	cup celery, chopped	2	10-3/4-ounce cans cream of mushroom soup
1/2	cup green pepper, chopped		
1/2	pound sharp cheese, grated		Sherry (optional)
1	cup chicken broth		

Sauté onions, celery and pepper until soft. Cook spaghetti in chicken broth as directed on package. Mix all ingredients and put into a 9x13-inch casserole dish. Sprinkle grated cheese on top. Cook, covered, 30 minutes at 375 degrees. Then cook uncovered until cheese is melted. A wonderful make-ahead recipe and it freezes well before baking.

CHICKEN AND WILD RICE

Serves 12   Mrs. Horace C. Smith (Dot)

3	whole cooked chicken breasts or 1 whole cooked chicken, diced	2	10-3/4-ounce cans cream of mushroom soup
1	6-ounce box Uncle Ben's Wild Rice (quick)	1	13-ounce can evaporated milk
		1-1/2	sticks margarine, melted
1	large can mushrooms, drained	1	small bag Pepperidge Farm regular stuffing mix

Cook rice as directed on box. Add chicken to rice. Add mushrooms, soup and milk to chicken and rice. Pour into casserole dish. Mix the margarine and stuffing mix together and put on top of casserole. Place foil on top of casserole and bake for 30 minutes at 375 degrees. Remove foil and cook 15 minutes longer.

COMPANY CHICKEN

Mrs. I. S. Leevy Johnson (Doris)

1	2-1/2 to 3-pound fryer, cut into 6 to 8 pieces	1	10-3/4-ounce can cream of mushroom soup
1	10-3/4-ounce can cream of chicken soup	1/2	cup dry white wine
1	10-3/4-ounce can cream of celery soup	1/2	cup slivered almonds
		1/4	cup grated Parmesan cheese

Wash, dry, salt and pepper chicken pieces. Put chicken pieces in greased casserole. Pour remaining ingredients over chicken in the order given. Bake at 350 degrees 1 to 1−1/2 hours, depending on oven. Good served over rice or noodles. May add curry for a change and serve dish with raisins, coconut, chutney and other appropriate condiments.

211

POULTRY

EASY CHICKEN CASSEROLE

Serves 8 to 10   Mrs. R. M. Kenan (Sinclair)
                                   Mrs. William J. McLeod (Sara)

1	3-pound fryer plus 1 chicken breast	1	pint sour cream
1	teaspoon peppercorns	1	stick butter
1	teaspoon rosemary	1	8-ounce package Pepperidge Farm Herb Stuffing
2	10-3/4-ounce cans cream of chicken soup		

Cook together first three ingredients until tender and debone chicken. (Use thighs instead of breast if you prefer dark meat.) Mix chicken with chicken soup and sour cream. Melt butter and mix with Pepperidge Farm Herb Stuffing. Reserve 1/2 cup. Mix all together and put in a 9x13-inch casserole. Top with rest of stuffing. Decorate with chopped almonds, if desired. Bake at 350 degrees for 30 minutes. An excellent luncheon main dish. Freezes well before baking.

VARIATION: Mrs. Walter Bristow, Jr. (Stewart)

Omit sour cream and butter and add 1/2 cup mayonnaise, 1 cup diced celery and 2 tablespoons grated onion.

HAWAIIAN CHICKEN

Serves 6   Mrs. Herbert Kirsh (Suzanne)

2	3-pound broiler-fryer chicken parts, or your favorite parts	14	ounces water
3	tablespoons oil	2	tablespoons white vinegar
1	large onion, chopped	1/2	cup brown sugar
14	ounces tomato ketchup	2	tablespoons soy sauce
		1	20-ounce can pineapple chunks, drained

Sauté onion in hot oil until golden brown. Add ketchup, water, vinegar and brown sugar. Heat until sugar dissolves. Put chicken pieces in a greased casserole and pour sauce over it. Sprinkle with soy sauce. Bake, uncovered, at 325 degrees for 1 hour and 15 minutes. Baste every 10 minutes. Add pineapple chunks and bake 15 minutes longer.

ITALIAN CHICKEN

Serves 4   Mrs. Robert N. McLellan (Doris)

1	broiler-fryer chicken, cut in parts	3	garlic cloves, minced
1	pound mild cheddar cheese, grated	1	cup or more milk
1	loaf unsliced French bread		Salt and pepper
		1/2	stick butter, or more
			Garlic powder

The night before serving put French bread in a 200 degree oven for 1 hour. Leave unrefrigerated and unwrapped overnight. Next day put through a blender on grate. Mix together the grated cheese, bread, garlic, salt and pepper. Dip chicken in milk and roll in bread crumb mixture. Lay in a 9x13-inch baking dish. Pour remaining crumb mixture over chicken. Add garlic powder and dot with butter. Cover with foil and bake 350 degrees to 400 degrees for 2 hours. Take cover off the last 15 minutes to brown.

MARINATED CHICKEN FOR THE GRILL

Serves 8   Representative Robert L. Helmly

2	fryers, cut up or quartered	1	cup lemon juice
1	large bottle Kraft's Italian Dressing (pour off some of the oil)	1/4	cup sherry or other wine, (optional)
1/2	cup vinegar		Dash Worcestershire sauce
			Salt and pepper to taste

Salt and pepper chicken. Combine all other ingredients and pour over chicken in large plastic container. Cover with foil and marinate for 12 to 24 hours. Cook over charcoal, basting frequently. Great with baked beans, slaw and rolls.

SWEET 'N' SMOKY OVEN BARBECUED CHICKEN

Serves 4   Representative Larry E. Gentry

1	broiler-fryer chicken, quartered	1/2	cup catsup
1	large onion, sliced	1/2	cup corn oil
1	teaspoon hickory-smoked salt	1/2	cup maple syrup
1/4	teaspoon pepper	1/4	cup vinegar
1	teaspoon Accent flavor enhancer	2	tablespoons prepared mustard

Place chicken, skin side up, in a shallow baking pan. Tuck onion slices in and around the chicken. Sprinkle hickory smoked salt, pepper and flavor enhancer on chicken. Bake uncovered in 375 degree oven for 30 minutes. Make barbecue sauce by mixing together the last 5 ingredients. Pour sauce over chicken and bake 30 minutes longer, or until fork can be inserted with ease

GEORGETOWN COUNTY

Georgetown is the third oldest settlement in the state. It was laid out in 1735 on a tract donated by the Reverend William Screven and named for the Prince of Wales who later became George II. Before the English secured their claim in this area, the Spanish had explored around Winyah Bay, and Indians lived in the bay area.

The incredibly rich land of this county produced the staple crops of indigo and rice with such success that the planters of the area became quite wealthy. Out of this rice culture emerged a lowcountry aristocracy that became an important political force in the state. By 1740, prosperous rice plantations were already lining the narrow strip called Waccamaw Neck. Many famous visitors have enjoyed the "perpetual breezes and saline vapours" of this pleasant part of the county including Lafayette in 1777, George Washington in 1791, James Monroe in 1819, Churchill in 1932, and Franklin Roosevelt in 1944. Pawleys Island was a summer resort for planters escaping malaria during the dangerous season from May to November. The earliest houses were destroyed in the hurricane of 1822, but buildings from the 1850s, including the summer academy and the rectory of All Saints Episcopal Church, still remain.

By the Civil War the prosperity of the rice culture was already on the wane. Mr. and Mrs. Archer Huntington combined the lands of four plantations to create Brookgreen Gardens in 1932 "for the preservation of the flora and fauna of the Southeast and to exhibit objects of art."

The county's economy has stabilized with the new and important industries that have been attracted there. As a port, Georgetown ranks second to Charleston. The biggest industry is tourism and development of the beautiful natural beaches of Litchfield, Garden City, Murrell's Inlet and Pawley's.

Some of the prominent men of Georgetown County include Francis Marion; Thomas Lynch, signer of the Declaration of Independence; William Allston, father of Washington Allston — "the American Titian"; Joshua John Ward of Brookgreen, the "king of the rice planters."

   Geography has played the most significant role in shaping the history of Horry County. Inland swamps and thin soil combined with the lack of a good harbor and the distance from Charleston markets to prevent Horry from following the pattern of development of other coastal counties with their large plantations. Scotch-Irish settlers who braved the hardships of this beautiful, but isolated area, tenaciously wrested a living from small family farms. Their fierce pride and solitary, spartan existence, so different from the lifestyle of their neighbors to the south, won the district the sobriquet of the "Independent Republic of Horry."

   Originally laid out in 1732 as part of Governor Robert Johnson's scheme to protect the coastal towns from invasion and encourage expansion into the backcountry, Kingston Township on the Waccamaw River served as the northeastern anchor of this buffer zone. Kingston was eventually incorporated into All Saints Parish and later Georgetown District. In 1801, this area became a county in its own right. In response to a petition from local residents, the state legislature discarded the old colonial name of Kingston and named the new county after Peter Horry, a Revolutionary war hero.

   When the rails were extended to the beach in 1900, Conway, formerly Conwayborough, gained fame as the "Gateway to the Grand Strand." It soon boasted not only a Robert Mills-era courthouse and sidewalks, but also fourteen general stores, two good hotels, a telephone exchange, and "an up-to-date Chinese laundry."

   Few could imagine that as the little steam engine, the Black Maria, fired its engines for the first excursion to the shore, it would mark the beginning of an annual migration that would, eighty years later, attract over 36 million tourists a year and generate over $700 million in one summer season. Or, that the Seaside Hotel which offered three meals and a room for $2 in 1901 would spawn a vast system that could accomodate over 200,000 people at one time.

THE HERIOT-TARBOX HOUSE

The Heriot-Tarbox House was built in 1740 at number 15
Cannon Street in Georgetown. This charming house is on the
river across from the Tarbox Red Store Warehouse and Wharf.

fish and shellfish

BEER BATTER FOR SEAFOOD, CHICKEN OR VEGETABLES

Makes 1/2 cup   Mrs. William Cork (Helen)

1/4 cup cornstarch	1/4 cup all purpose flour
1/4 cup beer, room temperature	3 tablespoons butter, melted
1 egg, separated	1 small garlic clove, minced
Salt and freshly ground pepper	Oil for frying vegetables, chicken or fish

Combine cornstarch and flour and mix well. Blend in beer, butter, egg yolk and garlic. Beat egg white until stiff. Fold into batter with salt and pepper to taste. Heat oil to between 375 and 395 degrees. Dip vegetables, chicken or fish in batter; allow excess to run off. Fry in batches until golden. Excellent for vegetables, onion rings, chicken or fish. If using batter for fruit fritters, omit pepper and garlic and add 1 teaspoon sugar.

FISH STEW

Representative H. E. Pearce, Jr.

2-1/2 pounds flounder or mackerel fillets	1/2 bottle catsup
2 pounds onion, chopped	3 teaspoons Heinz 57 sauce
1 large can tomato juice	1/3 stick butter or margarine
2 cans tomato soup	2 teaspoons hot sauce
	Salt and pepper to taste

Cook onions slowly until brown. Add other ingredients; except fish, and let stand overnight. Add fish and cook 15 to 20 minutes until fish flakes. Serve over rice in bowls. This freezes well.

RED CATFISH STEW

Serves 20   Representative Lloyd I. Hendricks

10 pounds fish, cooked in broth	1/3 to 1/2 bottle catsup
5 pounds potatoes, chopped	Hot sauce to taste
5 pounds onions, chopped	Salt and pepper to taste
1/4 pound side meat, bacon or streak of lean	1/3 small bottle Worcestershire sauce
1/2 pound of butter or margarine	2 10-3/4-ounce cans tomato soup
	1 46-ounce can tomato juice

Start potatoes and onions in pot. Have the fish boned and save some of the fish broth. Add fish after potatoes and onions have cooked down some. Add fish broth (1-quart plus) and other ingredients. Season to taste.

SOUTH CAROLINA CATFISH STEW

Serves 24   Senator Rembert C. Dennis

10	pounds catfish	1	stick butter
3	pounds white potatoes,chopped	1	can tomato paste
2	pounds onions, chopped	1/2	bottle Worcestershire sauce
1	pound streak of lean meat	1/2	bottle hot sauce
1	can tomatoes		Black pepper
1	bottle catsup		Salt
1	can tomato sauce		Garlic

Red pepper

Dice streak of lean meat and cook until slightly brown. Remove from pan, leave grease. Cook potatoes and onions separately in grease until slightly brown. Cook catfish in pot until soft enough to remove from bones; place fillet of catfish, streak of lean meat, onions and potatoes in pot with hot water; add tomatoes, catsup, tomato sauce, tomato paste, butter, hot sauce, Worcestershire sauce, pepper, salt and garlic to taste. Cook and simmer approximately one hour, gauging water to produce desired consistency.

BASS FILLETS

Serves 4   Senator Norma Russell

4	bass fillets	1	tablespoon minced onion
1	10-3/4-ounce can shrimp soup	2	teaspoons Worcestershire sauce
1/4	cup grated cheese and bread crumbs		

Bake fillets, plain, in 350 degree oven for 7 to 8 minutes in glass baking dish. Cover with sauce, sprinkle with cheese and bread crumbs. Broil 2 or 3 minutes until crumbs brown.

FISH SCALLOPINI

Serves 6 to 8   Representative H. E. Pearce, Jr.

3 to 4 pounds King Mackerel, boned and skinned	2	tablespoons parsley, chopped
		Peanut oil and olive oil
1	egg	1-1/2 sticks butter
1/2	cup milk	1	cup dry white wine

Sauce and gravy flour

Melt butter in frying pan, add wine and heat slowly. Meanwhile, heat a 1-inch mixture of olive oil and peanut oil in another frying pan. Salt fish lightly and roll in flour. Dip floured fish in mixture of beaten egg, parsley and milk. Brown in oil, drain and simmer in wine mixture for 5 to 10 minutes.

BAKED FISH WITH CRAB SAUCE

Serves 4   Representative H. E. Pearce, Jr.

2	pounds fish fillets (flounder, mackerel, pompano)	1/2	cup white crab meat
12	fresh mushrooms, sliced	1/2	cup dry white wine
1	cup medium white sauce	Salt	
		Paprika	

Add crab meat and 1/4 cup wine to white sauce and season to taste. Cover flat pan with a large sheet of heavy foil. Place fillets, mushrooms and 1/4 cup wine on foil. Spread sauce evenly over fish and seal foil. Bake at 400 degrees for 15 to 20 minutes. (Check for doneness.) Open foil, sprinkle with paprika and put under broiler for 5 minutes.

CORNBREAD STUFFED FLOUNDER

Serves 8 to 10   Representative H. E. Pearce, Jr.

1	large fish (flounder or King Mackerel)	Salt, pepper	
3/4	cup grits, cooked	3	cans tomato soup
2	cups Pepperidge Farm Cornbread, crumbled	4 to 6	strips bacon
		1	small onion, chopped

Mix cornbread, grits and onion with water until moist, but firm. Season to taste with salt and pepper. Split fish and put in large, foil lined baking pan. Sprinkle inside with salt and pepper. Stuff with cornbread mixture and sew or close fish. Add 2 cups water to pan. Cover with bacon strips and bake at 350 degrees for 1 hour or until fish flakes. Pour soup over fish and return to oven for 10 minutes.

HERB STUFFED FISH

Serves 4   Mrs. Michael R. Daniel (Peggy)

1	pound white fish fillets	1	cup herbed seasoned stuffing mix
1	10-3/4-ounce can New England Clam Chowder	2	tablespoons butter or margarine
1/2	cup milk	1	cup loosely packed grated cheddar cheese, or 4 slices sharp process cheese, cut in half diagonally

In shallow baking dish arrange fish. Combine soup and milk; pour over fish. Sprinkle generously with black pepper. Top with stuffing mix; dot with butter and bake at 350 degrees for 25 minutes or until done. Top with cheese and bake until cheese melts.

PALMETTO MARSHLANDS DEVILED CRAB

Yield: 4 crab shells   Mrs. Marion H. Kinon (Reba)

1	pound or 3/4 cup crab meat	2	dashes Tabasco
1/2	cup mayonnaise	1/2	teaspoon salt
1-1/2	teaspoons lemon juice	1	egg
1	teaspoon Worcestershire sauce	1/2	cup grated cheese
1	teaspoon mustard	1/2	stick melted butter
1	teaspoon parsley flakes	4	crab shells sprayed with Pam

Italian bread crumbs

Mix all together and pile into crab shells. Sprinkle Italian bread crumbs and grated cheese over top and bake at 350 degrees for 25 minutes or until brown.

CRAB MEAT CASSEROLE

Serves 8   Mrs. Donald H. Holland (Betty)

1	pound crab meat	1	cup milk
1	stick margarine	1	package Pepperidge Farm dressing mix
2	tablespoons parsley		
1	cup mayonnaise	2	tablespoons onion, chopped
3	eggs, beaten	1	10-3/4-ounce can celery or mushroom soup
1	small jar pimento		
1/2	chopped medium bell pepper		Salt and pepper to taste
			Accent to taste

Saute crumbs and parsley in butter until lightly browned. Leave about 1/4 cup crumbs for topping and mix the rest with all other ingredients. Place in greased casserole and bake at 350 degrees just until bubbly all through and golden brown. Do not over cook.

CRAB MEAT CASSEROLE IN WINE SAUCE

Serves 10 to 12   Mrs. Rembert C. Dennis (Natalie)

2	pounds crab meat, picked	2	tablespoons capers
6	tablespoons butter	1	can sliced water chestnuts
6	tablespoons flour	3	tablespoons sherry wine
3	cups milk		Salt and pepper
1/2	cup chopped pimento		

Make a cream sauce with the butter, flour and milk. Remove from heat and add crab meat and other ingredients. Top with bread crumbs or cover with pastry. Bake in casserole for 30 minutes at 350 degrees.

CRAB MEAT AU GRATIN

Serves 4   Representative William N. Cork
                                                    Mrs. Marion H. Kinon (Reba)

2 tablespoons butter	Dash freshly ground nutmeg
2 tablespoons flour	1/2 pound crab meat
1 cup half-and-half	1/3 cup breadcrumbs, buttered
1/4 teaspoon salt	1/4 cup grated cheese, medium
White pepper	cheddar

Blend butter and flour together over low heat. Slowly add half-and-half; cook and stir over low heat until smooth and thickened. Season with salt, pepper and nutmeg. Add crab meat. Put in a shallow baking dish or in ramekins. Cover with 1/3 cup buttered breadcrumbs mixed with grated cheese. Bake at 350 degrees until the crumbs are a delicate brown.

BAKED CRAB MEAT A LA IRIS

Serves 8   Mrs. Carroll A. Campbell, Jr. (Iris)

1 pound crab meat	1/2 teaspoon salt
1 cup mayonnaise	1 tablespoon Worcestershire
1/2 cup chopped green peppers	1/2 can chicken broth
1/4 cup minced onions	2 cups crushed potato chips
1/2 cup chopped celery	

Mix all ingredients together in a bowl; except the potato chips. Place mixture in a large baking dish and cover with the crushed potato chips. Bake in 325 to 350 degree oven for about 40 minutes.

SOUTH CAROLINA "LOW COUNTRY" STUFFED CRAB

Serves 6   Mrs. James Craven (Beverly)

1 pound crabmeat	3 tablespoons catsup
1-1/2 cups bread crumbs	1-1/2 tablespoons mustard
1 medium onion	Hot pepper sauce to taste
1 medium green pepper	4 saltine crackers, crushed
3 slices bacon	1 tablespoon butter

Finely chop onion, green pepper and bacon and saute until tender. Add crab meat, bread crumbs, catsup, mustard and hot sauce. Mix well. Stuff into crab shells or a buttered casserole dish. Sprinkle with cracker crumbs and dot with butter. Bake at 400 degrees for 20 to 25 minutes.

DEVILED SOUTH CAROLINA CRAB

Yields: 6 crab shells

Mrs. Clyde M. Dangerfield (Betty)
Mrs. Thomas F. Hartnett (Bonnie)

4	tablespoons butter	Dash celery salt	
2	tablespoons flour	1	pound fresh crab meat
1	cup milk	2	tablespoons chopped onion, optional
1	teaspoon prepared mustard		
2	tablespoons lemon juice	2	tablespoons minced bell pepper, optional
1/2	cup bread or cracker crumbs		
1	beaten egg	1	tablespoon chopped parsley, optional
1	tablespoon Worcestershire sauce		

Mix egg, lemon juice and seasoning. Make a cream sauce with butter, flour and milk. Add onion and cook until thick. Mix with egg mixture. Add chunks of crab meat last. Pile into shells and top with cracker crumbs. In center of each shell place a touch of butter. If not to be used immediately, wrap for freezer. When ready to use, thaw and bake in 400 degree oven for 30 minutes.

JAMBALAYA

Serves 4

Mrs. James Craven (Beverly)

1/2	cup chopped green onion	2	dozen raw oysters (or 1 cup cubed cooked ham)
1/2	cup chopped white onion		
1	large green pepper, chopped	1	pound can tomatoes, mashed
1/2	cup chopped celery	1	cup chicken broth
1	garlic clove, minced	1/2	teaspoon salt
1/3	cup butter	1/4	teaspoon cayenne pepper
1/2 to 1 pound raw shrimp, peeled and cleaned		1	cup raw rice

In a large pan, saute onion, green pepper, celery and garlic in butter until tender but not browned. Add shrimp and oysters and cook 5 minutes. (If ham is used add it when you add the rice.) Add tomatoes, chicken broth, salt, cayenne pepper and rice. Stir and cover. Cook 25 to 30 minutes over low heat or until rice is done. If mixture becomes too dry, add tomato juice. Taste for seasoning. FOR A SEAFOOD GUMBO: Omit oysters and use ham. Cook 1/4 pound bacon with vegetables. Add 2 cups sliced okra with the tomatoes and cook 5 minutes. Add the shrimp and 3 cups crab meat or fish (you may vary this by using ham or chicken or both in place of the crab meat or use all three) and cook an additional 5 to 10 minutes or until seafood is done; do not overcook. Gumbo file may be added to taste just before serving. Do not boil the gumbo after the file is added or it will become stringy. Serve the gumbo over white rice with a green salad and hot rolls.

SAUTÉED OYSTERS

Mrs. William N. Cork (Helen)

Butter   Oysters
Chopped onion   Salt and pepper

Melt butter in skillet and sauté onions until tender. Add oysters and their liquid. Sauté until edges curl. Salt and pepper to taste. Increase ingredients according to the amount of oysters you use.

SCALLOPED SOUTH CAROLINA OYSTERS

Serves 4   Mrs. Larry A. Martin (Susan)

1   pint oysters, drained (reserve   1/4   teaspoon Worcestershire sauce
      1/4 cup liquor)   2   tablespoons sherry
2   cups saltine cracker crumbs   1/2   teaspoon salt
3/4 cup half-and-half   Freshly ground pepper
1/2 cup butter, melted

Drain oysters and add to 1/4 cup liquor, the half-and-half, Worcestershire sauce, sherry and salt. Set aside. Combine butter and cracker crumbs. Spread 1/3 of the crumbs in a 8x8x2-inch baking dish, cover with 1/2 of the oysters and sprinkle with pepper. Spread a second layer with 1/3 of the crumbs and remaining oysters. Sprinkle with pepper. Pour liquor and half-and-half mixture over oysters. Top with remaining crumbs. Bake at 325 to 350 degrees for 40 minutes or until done. Serve immediately.

SAUTÉED SHRIMP

Mrs. William N. Cork (Helen)

Butter   Shrimp, peeled and deveined
1   garlic clove, chopped   Salt and pepper
Chopped parsley

Melt butter in skillet; add garlic and parsley and sauté a few minutes. Add uncooked shrimp and sauté, tossing lightly until done. Salt to taste. Increase ingredients according to amount of shrimp used.

STEAMED OYSTERS AND SCALLOPS

Serves 4 as main dish, 8 as appetizer   Mrs. I. S. Leevy Johnson (Doris)

2	tablespoons butter	2 or 3 dashes garlic powder	
1/4	teaspoon lemon and pepper seasonings	1/8	teaspoon tarragon
		1	pint oysters
1/4	teaspoon salt	1	pint scallops
1/8	teaspoon parsley flakes		

Melt butter in skillet; add oysters and scallops with slotted spoon. Sprinkle with spices and seasonings. Allow oysters to simmer until edges begin to curl; the scallops will be done within the alloted time of 3 to 5 minutes. Do not overcook.

QUICK AND EASY SALMON PATTIES

Serves 4 to 6   Mrs. D. Les Tindal (May)

1	16-ounce can pink salmon	1/2	cup flour
1	egg	1-1/2	teaspoons baking powder
1/3	cup minced onion	1-1/2	cups Crisco

Drain salmon and reserve 2 tablespoons of the juice. In a medium mixing bowl, mix salmon, egg and onion until sticky. Stir in flour. Add baking powder to salmon juice, stir into salmon mixture. Form into small patties and fry until brown (about 5 minutes) in hot Crisco. Serve with Ceasar Salad dressing or TARTAR SAUCE: Combine 1 cup mayonnaise with 1/2 medium chopped onion, 2 large pimento-stuffed chopped olives, 1 medium sweet or sour chopped pickle, 1 tablespoon chopped parsley and 1 tablespoon capers.

SOUTH CAROLINA SEAFOOD CASSEROLE

Serves 12   Mrs. Robert C. Lake, Jr. (Carolyn)

1	pound shrimp	1/2	cup sherry
1	pound scallops	1	teaspoon dry mustard
1	pound crab meat	2	tablespoons mayonnaise
2	tablespoons lemon juice	1/2	cup grated cheese
1	small onion, grated	1	small jar sliced mushrooms
4	eggs	1	stick butter, melted
1/2	cup milk	8 to 10 saltines, crumbled	

Mix all together. Put in 3 quart greased casserole and crumble crackers and melted butter on top. Bake 30 minutes at 350 degrees.

SEAFOOD FANCY CASSEROLE

Serves 10 - 12   Mrs. Gene Dukes (Gerry)

2	pounds fresh shrimp, cleaned and deveined	3/4	cup hot water
3	cups Pepperidge Farm stuffing	1	pound crab meat, cleaned
1	cup celery, minced fine	1	cup chopped onion
2	teaspoons dry mustard	1	cup mayonnaise
2	tablespoons Worcestershire	1/2	teaspoon curry powder
		2	tablespoons capers, optional
			Ritz crackers

Saute vegetables in butter. Mix all ingredients. Refrigerate several hours or overnight. Place in a greased 3-quart casserole. Sprinkle with crushed Ritz crackers, but add more hot water beforehand if casserole dried out overnight. Bake at 350 degrees for 30 to 45 minutes until brown.

CORRIE GAY'S SEAFOOD CASSEROLE

Serves 12   Honorable Solomon Blatt

2	6-ounce cans crab meat	1	tablespoon prepared mustard
2	6-ounce cans lobster	1	cup heavy sweet cream
3	cups cleaned and deveined shrimp	1	cup shredded sharp Cheddar cheese
2	tablespoons butter	1	tablespoon Worcestershire sauce
1	cup chopped celery	1	teaspoon finely cut chives
1	cup finely chopped onion	2	teaspoons minced parsley
1	medium diced bell pepper	3	eggs, well beaten
2	cups grated bread crumbs		Salt and pepper to taste
1	cup mayonnaise	1/3	cup sherry

Put cleaned shrimp, crab meat and lobster in bowl. Mix well with juice of one lemon. Let stand while you saute the onions, celery and bell pepper in the butter. When tender, remove from stove and add all other ingredients, but only 1/2 cup bread crumbs, reserving the rest of crumbs for casserole topping. After mixing everything thoroughly, add shrimp, lobster and crab meat and mix well. Put in 13-1/2x8-1/2-inch oblong casserole and top with remaining bread crumbs. Bake at 350 degrees for about 45 minutes, until crumbs are brown and casserole is hot through.

EASY SEAFOOD CASSEROLE

Serves 8 to 10   Mrs. John M. Spratt, Jr. (Jane)

1	4-1/2 to 6-ounce can crab meat	Vermouth, if desired
1	4-1/2 to 6-ounce can shrimp	1/2 stick melted butter
1	4-1/2 to 6-ounce can lobster	1 cup bread crumbs
1	can mushroom soup	1 cup grated Cheddar cheese
1	tablespoon mayonnaise	

Rinse and break crab meat, shrimp and lobster into pieces. Mix together mushroom soup and mayonnaise. Add a little Vermouth if desired. Butter bottom of casserole and line with 1/2 mixture of bread crumbs and grated cheese. Add seafood mixture, top with remaining bread crumbs. Sprinkle with grated cheese. Bake at 350 degrees for 35 minutes.

SEAFOOD RAGOUT

Serves 8 to 10   Mrs. Rembert C. Dennis (Natalie)

2	cups cooked shrimp	1/2 cup bell pepper, chopped
1	cup scallops	1 small onion, chopped
2	tablespoons butter	Mushrooms, sliced
2	tablespoons flour	Salt
2	cups milk	Pepper
1	cup cheese, grated	2 tablespoons sherry
1	cup celery, chopped	1 tablespoon parsley

Make sauce of butter, flour and milk. Add cheese; sauté chopped onion, bell pepper and celery, and add to cream sauce. Add seasonings, shrimp, scallops and mushrooms. Serve hot over rice. For a quick dish, an undiluted can of celery or mushroom soup may be used instead of the cream sauce. This is delicious with crab, too.

CATHERINE'S SHRIMP CASSEROLE

Serves 8   Mrs. Donald H. Holland (Betty)

1	small bell pepper, chopped	2 cups cooked shrimp
1	medium onion, chopped	1 can cream of mushroom soup
2	ribs celery, chopped	1/2 cup grated cheddar cheese
2	cups cooked rice	4 tablespoons milk

Sauté pepper, onion and celery in butter. Add rest of ingredients and bake in casserole dish for 30 minutes at 350 degrees.

SHRIMP-CRAB CASSEROLE

Serves 12   Mrs. William W. Doar, Jr. (Terry)

2	pounds shrimp, peeled but not cooked	1	cup V-8 juice
3-1/2	cups cooked rice (drop 2 chicken bouillon cubes in water while cooking)	1	large can mushrooms
		1	tablespoon Worcestershire sauce
		1	tablespoon fresh chopped parsley
			Salt and pepper to taste
1	cup mayonnaise		Few sprinkles Tabasco sauce
1	cup finely chopped celery	1	tablespoon lemon juice
1/2	cup finely chopped onion		Lightly toasted slivered almonds
1	pound claw crab meat (check for shells)		
1/2	cup chopped green pepper		

Mix all ingredients together and bake in a large rectangular casserole dish about 30 minutes at 325 degrees or until heated through. Put almonds on top and cook for 15 minutes more.

SHRIMP CREOLE SAUCE

Mrs. Dick Elliott (Anne)

2	large bell peppers	1	8-ounce can tomato paste
2	onions	2	tablespoons Worcestershire sauce
1	clove garlic, minced	1	teaspoon or less Tabasco sauce
1	cup diced celery	1	teaspoon Soy sauce
2 to 3	tablespoons bacon drippings		Pinch ginger
1	16-ounce can tomatoes	1	teaspoon dry mustard
2	cans mushrooms	1	teaspoon Accent
1	bay leaf		Salt to taste
	Pinch thyme		Pepper to taste

Sauté bell peppers, onions, garlic and celery in bacon drippings. Add undrained canned tomatoes, mushrooms, tomato paste, Worcestershire, Tabasco, Soy sauce, ginger, dry mustard, Accent salt and pepper. Add bay leaf and thyme. Bring to a boil. Turn off and add cooked shrimp (as much as you wish). Serve over hot rice.

BAKED SHRIMP CREOLE

Serves 8 to 10   Mrs. D. Les Tindal (May)
                                                  Mrs. Clyde M. Dangerfield (Betty)

3	pounds raw shrimp	1	can sliced mushrooms
1	cup cooked rice	1	pound grated sharp cheddar
1	cup celery and bell pepper, mixed		cheese
1	small onion, chopped	1	tablespoon Worcestershire sauce
1	10-3/4-ounce can tomato soup		

Saute celery, onion, and bell pepper in butter until clear. Add other ingredients. Cook shrimp and rice and add to other ingredients. Reserve 1/3 of the cheese and sprinkle on top. Bake in a casserole dish at 350 degrees for 30 to 40 minutes or until cheese is melted. Freezes well for a short time.

SOUTH CAROLINA SHRIMP CREOLE

Serves 10   Mrs. J. F. Anderson, Jr. (Susan)

1	pound fat back, sliced	2	10-3/4-ounce cans tomato soup
5	pounds onions	2	cans water
3 or 4	bell peppers	1-1/2	small bottles catsup
5	pounds shrimp		Salt to taste
1	bunch celery		Pepper
1	No. 2 can tomatoes, or		Worcestershire sauce to taste
	larger, if you prefer		

Fry the fat back and remove from the pan. Chop onions, bell pepper and celery; and saute in the grease. Add all other ingredients except shrimp. Simmer 1-1/2 hours, covered, in an electric fry pan (or the equivalent). Boil and clean shrimp; add to mixture and simmer 15 minutes before serving. You can make the sauce ahead and freeze. When ready to use, thaw, heat and add the shrimp. Serve over hot rice.

SHRIMP MARINARA

Serves 4   Mrs. James B. Stephen (Ginger)

1	pound raw peeled shrimp		Pepper to taste
2	tablespoons olive oil	1	teaspoon dried basil
2	cloves garlic, minced	1/4	teaspoon oregano
1	6-ounce can tomato paste	1/2	cup finely minced green onions
1	teaspoon salt	1	cup chicken broth

Cook garlic briefly in oil. Stir in remaining ingredients except shrimp and simmer for 5 minutes. Add shrimp and simmer 3 to 5 minutes. Serve over hot vermicelli, thin spaghetti noodles, or rice.

ELEGANTÉ SHRIMP

Serves 4 to 6   Mrs. Nick A. Theodore (Emilie)

3	tablespoons butter or margarine	1/4	teaspoon dry mustard
1	pound shelled shrimp		Dash cayenne pepper
1/2	pound fresh mushrooms,sliced	2	cups light cream
1/4	cup butter	3	teaspoons cooking sherry
1/4	cup all purpose flour	1/4	cup Parmesan cheese

Melt 3 tablespoons butter in skillet, add shrimp and mushrooms and cook over medium heat 5 minutes, stirring frequently, until mushrooms are tender and shrimp are pink. Remove from skillet. Add 1/4 cup butter to skillet, blend flour and seasonings. Stir in cream all at once and cook, stirring constantly, until mixture thickens and boils. Add shrimp and mushrooms to sauce, heat through 2 to 3 minutes. Stir in cooking sherry, Parmesan cheese and salt to taste. Serve over rice with parsley and butter.

SHRIMP ETOUFFEÉ

Serves 4   Mrs. Marion Kinon (Reba)

1	pound peeled shrimp	2	cloves garlic, minced
1/2	cup butter	1/2	cup water
1/2	cup onion, coarsely chopped	1	tablespoon flour
1/2	cup celery, coarsely chopped	1/3	cup dry sherry wine
1	cup bell pepper, coarsely chopped		Juice of 1/2 lemon
2	cups sliced mushrooms	1/4	teaspoon salt
2	tablespoons chopped parsley	1/4	teaspoon white pepper
		1	cup green onions,coarsely chopped

Melt butter and quickly stir-fry all vegetables. Cook over medium heat for 5 minutes, stirring constantly. Gradually add the water, flour and wine, stirring constantly. Add shrimp. lemon juice, salt and pepper. Stir, cover, and simmer 8 to 10 minutes. Serve over hot rice.

EASY SHRIMP CURRY

Serves 4   Mrs. Marshall B. Williams (Margaret)

1	10-3/4-ounce can cream of mushroom soup	1	small carton sour cream
1	10-3/4-ounce can cream of shrimp soup	2	teaspoons curry powder
		1	pound cooked shrimp
			White wine or sherry

Heat together all the ingredients. Thin with white wine or sherry. Serve over rice or baked fish.

FISH AND SHELLFISH

SHRIMP PIE

Serves 6   Mrs. W. B. Hawkins (Sarah)

1/2	green pepper, chopped	1	cup Miracle Whip
1	small onion, chopped	1	cup fresh buttered bread crumbs
1	cup chopped celery	1	teaspoon Worcestershire sauce
1	pound fresh shrimp, cooked	1/2	teaspoon salt
	and deveined	1/4	teaspoon pepper

Mix all ingredients together except crumbs. Top with crumbs. Bake at 350 degrees for 30 minutes.

SHRIMP SCAMPI

Serves 6   Mrs. Marion H. Kinon (Reba)

36	shrimp, large	3/4	cup olive oil
6	cloves garlic, minced	1/4	cup minced parsley
2	teaspoons salt	2	tablespoons lemon juice
3/4	cup butter, melted		Ground black pepper

Pour ingredients over shrimp in broiler pan. Broil about 7 minutes. Baste. Serve shrimp and sauce over rice or in individual ramekins.

CAPER SAUCE FOR FISH

Serves 6   Mrs. William N. Cork (Helen)

4	tablespoons sweet butter		Lemon juice
6	scallions, minced	1	4-1/2-ounce can medium shrimp
1	cup heavy cream		10 to 12 sprigs fresh parsley, minced
1	bottle (3-1/4-ounces) capers well drained		

Heat butter in heavy skillet. When hot, add the scallions and 1/2 cup water. Cook over medium heat until the water has boiled away and the scallions are soft. If necessary, add a little more water. Stir in the heavy cream and bring to a boil. Boil for a couple of minutes or until sauce has thickened slightly. Add the capers and juice of half a lemon. Taste. It may need salt or more lemon juice. Can be made in advance to this point. If so, seal with plastic wrap to prevent a skin from forming. Add the shrimp and the parsley and bring to a boil only. Good over all baked fish.

CRAB MEAT SAUCE

Yields: 6 cups   Mrs. Alex S. Macaulay (Maria)

2	cups white crab meat	4	tablespoons butter
1/4	cup dry vermouth	4	tablespoons flour
1	cup sliced mushrooms	2	cups sour cream
1	tablespoon chopped chives	2	cups milk

Marinate crab meat in vermouth. Sauté mushrooms in butter until tender. Stir in flour and cook several minutes; then add sour cream and milk and cook, stirring until thickened. Fold in chives and the crab meat.

LEMON BARBECUE SAUCE FOR FISH

Mrs. John Drummond (Holly)

1/2	cup lemon juice	2	tablespoons grated onion
1/2	teaspoon salt	1	teaspoon dry mustard
1/4	cup salad oil or margarine	2	tablespoons brown sugar
1/2	teaspoon pepper	1	cup Kraft Italian dressing
		1	pound fish fillets

Mix ingredients well, stirring until sugar is dissolved. Place 1-pound fish fillets in a shallow pan and pour sauce over. Heat broiler about 3 minutes. With pan about 2 inches from heat, broil fish on both sides until brown and tender, basting with sauce. Serve immediately. This recipe can be used on charcoal grill also.

Located in the lower pine belt, Williamsburg County enjoys a reputation as one of the fishing and hunting paradises in the nation.

Years before any white settlement, an unknown explorer spotted a tall white pine similar to those growing in the New England hills. He marked this oddity with his ax and reported to British officials in Charleston his discovery of the King's Tree, the species reserved for the towering spars of the Royal Navy's sailing vessels. Throughout the colonial period, "Kingstree" served as a reference point for backcountry travelers. In 1732, when "poor Calvinists" settled in Williamsburg Township, they so-named their village which eventually became the county seat, Kingstree.

County leaders have long understood the need for Williamsburg to diversify its economy. In the 1870s Williamsburg planter Dr. Robert T. Maurice won a contest sponsored by the Charleston News and Courier to encourage tobacco production in the area. It took the boll weevil to convince many farmers to realize that cotton was no longer king in the South. Now seeking new job opportunities for Williamsburg residents, the Williamsburg Regional Manpower Training Center is working to supply skilled laborers for potential industries to locate in this beautiful county.

CLARENDON COUNTY

Clarendon is a familiar name in South Carolina, a legacy from Edward, Earl of Clarendon, once a Lord High Chancellor and one of the colonial Lords Proprietors. The present day Clarendon County was organized in 1855 from a portion of the Sumter District.

Manning, a lovely town on the old Charleston-Camden trading road, is the county seat. The road through the town is broad because when General Cornwallis was menacing the area he ordered his troops to cut a wide swath through the settlement so that he might more easily move his heavy artillery. Manning also suffered during the Civil War when Sherman burned the county courthouse out of revenge for the killing of one of his officers by a Manning resident.

In addition to producing cotton, lumber, and naval stores, Clarendon has a well deserved¹ reputation for producing state leaders, and has produced five governors. These gubernatorial families were not only connected by residence in the same county, but also by blood. Richard I. Manning's wife, Elizabeth Peyer Richardson Manning, holds the record for any woman being related to governors. She was simultaneously the mother of a governor, the aunt and foster mother of a governor, the sister of a governor, the niece of a governor, and the wife of a governor.

The Santee River has played an important part in the history of Clarendon County. At Fort Watson on the banks of the river, the British built a stockade on an old Indian mound that overlooked both the Santee and the road to Charleston. It was one of the first forts retaken by the Patriots in 1781. During the antebellum period, a century before the Santee-Cooper Dam, there was active navigation on the river.

Today, the residents of this prosperous county that ranks among the top six counties in agricultural revenues enjoy fishing and other water sports on Lake Marion.

SUMTER COUNTY

The earliest known settlement in Sumter occurred in 1750 when Samuel and James Bradley established a small farm in the eastern portion of the county. Prior to this time the county had been used by wandering cattle farmers as range land. The county was chiefly settled by relocated Virginians during the 1750s and 60s.

One of these Virginians, Thomas Sumter, became one of the state's and the county's most important residents. Arriving in the state in 1762, Sumter set off to develop a fortune in land. The events of the Revolution forced Sumter to take up arms against the British. His home was burned by a detachment of British soldiers, forcing him to retire to the backwoods of the state where he began to recruit an army of upcountry partisans. He was eventually made General of the state militia, a position which he executed with great military ability. Known as the "Fighting Gamecock" Sumter was present at most of the major military engagements fought in the state. After the war the General returned to his land in the county. In 1783 he founded the city of Stateburg which he attempted to have named as the site for the new state capital. When the county was formed in 1800 it was named in honor of the General. The county seat also bears Sumter's name.

The availability of good timber gave rise to an important local industry. Furniture making became a profitable enterprise in Sumter and today the area is still known as the furniture capital of the state. Tobacco was introduced into the economy in the 1880s and its success as a cash crop displaced cotton as the staple of the region in the 20th century.

Sumter County was spared most of the destructiveness of the Civil War years. The economy of the region suffered along with the rest of the state but by the turn of the century the county had regained its momentum. Railroads built into the county provided area merchants and farmers with new outlets for their products. And the Sumter Brick works began marketing its distinctive product to builders along the east coast. The location of Shaw Air Force Base in the county added a major employer to the region. Today Sumter County enjoys the prosperity of its various enterprises.

LEE COUNTY

Organized in 1902, Lee County was one of the last six counties created by the state legislature. Named in honor of General Robert E. Lee, the county was created from parts of Darlington, Sumter and Kershaw counties. The early history of Lee is completely intertwined with the events and personalities that helped shape its parent counties. Like the surrounding counties, Lee was settled in the 1750s by displaced immigrants from the northern colonies. The soil in the county was adaptable to numerous crops and by 1760 grains produced in the territory were being traded at markets in Camden.

Agriculture and raising livestock were the principle activities of the early residents. The pace of life revolved, as it still does today, around the demands of planting and harvesting. Events of the Revolutionary War played an important part in the county. The swamps and forests of the area were the favorite hiding places for Francis Marion and his band of raiders. It was at places like "Scape Ore Swamp" that the famed "Swamp Fox" attacked and defeated numerous British forces throughout the war.

Cotton flourished in the area throughout the antebellum period; numerous plantations harvested the crop in large commercial ventures. During the depressed conditions of the Reconstruction period many of these large estates were broken up and sold for taxes.

One of the last duels fought in South Carolina occurred in Lee County immediately following the years of Reconstruction. At Shannon Mill on July 5, 1880, Col. E.C.B. Cash mortally wounded Col. William Shannon. Publicity over the duel forced a public outcry in the state prompting the legislature to pass a law prohibiting the practice of dueling.

Lee County also claims a number of important South Carolinians as natives. Among them are Mary McLeod Bethune, one of this country's most important Black educators, and "Cotton" Ed Smith, the flamboyant U.S. Senator who represented the state during the first quarter of this century. Senator Smith's home at Tanglewood Plantation continues today as one of the few remaining totally self-sufficient plantations in the South.

THORNTREE

Thorntree was built by James Witherspoon in 1749. Relocated in Kingstree, the house has been restored and furnished. Its outstanding features are original "memory work," and a history that includes a visit from Tarleton in the Revolutionary War.

game

DOVE BREASTS STROGANOFF

Serves 4 or 5   Mrs. William Cork (Helen)

16 Dove breasts
1 medium onion, chopped
2 tablespoons melted butter
1 10-3/4-ounce can cream of
   celery soup
1 4-ounce can mushrooms
1/2 teaspoon oregano

1/2 teaspoon rosemary
Salt and pepper to taste
1 teaspoon bottled Brown Bouquet
   Sauce
1 cup commercial sour cream
Cooked wild rice

Place doves in a 2-quart casserole with lid. Saute onion in frying pan with butter. Add remaining ingredients to pan; except sour cream and wild rice. Heat. Pour mixture over doves. Cover casserole and place in preheated 350 degree oven for 1 hour. Remove casserole, add sour cream and stir. Return to oven and bake 30 more minutes. Serve over hot rice.

DRUMMOND'S DOVE DINNER

Mrs. John Drummond (Holly)

Doves
1 stick butter
4 cups water
Salt and pepper to taste
4 tablespoons sherry
1 medium onion, chopped

Paprika
3 tablespoon flour
1 pint water
Stock from doves
2 cans mushrooms, cut up

Salt and pepper doves. Brown in butter in Dutch oven. Add more butter if needed. Remove as they brown. To drippings, add about 4 cups water and the sherry wine. Add onion. Sprinkle doves generously with paprika and return to pot. Simmer, covered, for about 2 hours. (They should almost fall apart.) Place doves in covered casserole with enough of the stock to keep from sticking. Reheat in 400 degree oven just before serving. Make gravy by shaking flour and 1-pint water together in a jar. Stir into the stock in Dutch oven until thick. Add salt, pepper, and mushrooms. Serve with hominy grits, tossed salad, and hot biscuits.

SMOTHERED DOVES
Senator Peden McLeod

Salt and pepper doves; dredge with flour, and brown in hot fat. Make a gravy by using same frying pan (with enough fat to take up 2 tablespoons flour). Add water or milk for a creamy gravy. (About 1-1/2 cups liquid should be enough.) Put doves back in pan with gravy; cover, and let simmer until tender.

BRAISED SOUTH CAROLINA QUAIL
Representative H. E. Pearce, Jr.

6   quail, cleaned   Flour, salt and pepper mixed together
1/4 cup butter or bacon fat

Heat fat in Dutch oven. Roll quail in seasoned flour and brown over medium heat. Remove quail and add flour and liquid to make gravy. Return quail to pot and simmer 1 to 1-1/2 hours, until tender. Serve on toast with gravy.

QUAIL WITH WHITE WINE
Serves 8   Congressman Floyd D. Spence

8   quail   1   cup dry white wine
1/2 cup butter or margarine   2   tablespoons lemon juice
2   cups sliced mushrooms   Salt
1/2 cup chopped green onion   Freshly ground black pepper

Brown the quail in butter; remove and set aside. Saute mushrooms and onion in butter. Place quail, mushrooms and onion in a shallow pan and cover with heavy-duty aluminum foil. Bake at 350 degrees for 1 hour. Combine wine, lemon juice, salt and pepper; baste quail often. The last 15 minutes of cooking time, remove foil. Serve with wild rice.

CORRIE GAY'S QUAIL ON HAM
Honorable Solomon Blatt

Rub cleaned and dressed quail with Accent, salt and pepper. Brown slowly in butter or margarine. After browning on all sides, place quail on rack in pressure pot. Add 2 or 3 cups water to drippings in fry pan and stir well. Pour this liquid over quail in pressure pot. Seal lid on pot, after pressure builds up, reduce heat to medium high and cook for 10 minutes. Remove from stove and let cool. After the pressure is out of the pot, remove quail. Mix 2 or 3 tablespoons cornstarch with cold water. Let liquid come to a boil in pot, add cornstarch. Season to taste. Boil a few minutes to desired consistency. Spoon gravy over quail and serve on a slice of thinly cut Country Ham.

GAME

WILD DUCK A L'ORANGE

Serves 10   Mrs. Robert C. Lake, Jr. (Carolyn)

5	ducks	2	apples
2	oranges	5	strips bacon
Salt and pepper to taste		3	tablespoons powdered sugar
2	onions	3	tablespoons concentrated orange juice

Clean ducks. Salt and pepper well on outside and in the cavity, too. Stuff with apple, orange and onion plugs. Place stuffed ducks in Dutch oven. Place bacon strips over ducks. Cover and cook at 325 degrees for 2 hours and 45 minutes. Turn ducks over and cook 30 minutes uncovered. Turn back over and brown under broiler. Mix and stir the orange juice and sugar together; add 4 tablespoons duck drippings, and mix well. Brush the sliced duck with the orange sauce and serve at once.

VARIATION: Representative H. E. Pearce, Jr.

Stuff 2 large or 5 small cleaned wild ducks with celery stalk, apple, orange wedges and whole small onions. Cook as above for 3 hours. Slice meat from bones and serve with ORANGE SAUCE: Strain pan juices into saucepan and add orange juice to make 2 cups. Add 2 tablespoons cognac, 1 tablespoon and 1 teaspoon brown sugar. Bring to a boil, simmer until ready to serve.

MALLARD DUCK

Serves 12   Mrs. J. C. Land, III (Marie)

6	ducks	1	cup chopped onion
6	apples, diced	1	cup chopped celery
Salt and pepper to taste		1/2	cup flour
24	strips bacon	1/2	cup cream
1	stick butter	1	cup water

Place ducks in a large roasting pan with one diced apple inside of each duck cavity. Sprinkle generously with salt and pepper. Place four strips of bacon on each duck. Bake for 2-1/2 hours, with lid on, at 300 degrees. Sauté onion and celery in butter; add flour, and mix until blended. Remove ducks from roasting pan, and add to the drippings in the pan the cream, flour, water, butter, onion and celery mixture. Stir until smooth. Place ducks back into the gravy and bake 30 minutes at 300 degrees. Serve with wild rice.

FRIED QUAIL

Mrs. Rex L. Carter (Floride)

1 or 2 whole quail per person   Salt
Flour   Pepper

Salt and pepper birds; roll in flour. Then drop into a preheated heavy skillet of hot cooking oil. When quail are brown on all sides, pour off most of oil and add a small amount of water (1/4 cup) to drippings left in skillet. Cover tightly and simmer until tender.

BAKED VENISON AND GRAVY

Serves 8   Mr. Hicks Harwell

1 4-pound venison roast, marinated overnight or 2 or 3 hours before baking in 2 cups dry red wine and 1 cup apple cider. Salt marinated roast lightly and place in 3-quart covered casserole, or cover deep glass baking dish with foil. Bake approximately 2-1/2 hours at 325 degrees. Serve with SOUR CREAM GRAVY:

SOUR CREAM GRAVY

1/2 cup sour cream   1/2 cup dry red wine
1   cup drippings from roast   2   tablespoons flour

Stir together drippings and flour. Add wine and cook over medium heat until thickened, stirring constantly. Reduce heat to simmer. Stir in sour cream. Keep warm until ready to serve either over venison or rice.

SOUTH CAROLINA VENISON STEAK OR ROAST

Mrs. T. N. Rhoad (Chessie)

Venison meat   1   10-3/4-ounce can cream of mush-
Flour   room soup
Salt and pepper   1   10-3/4-ounce can onion soup
Cooking oil

Flour, salt and pepper meat. Brown in a little oil in frying pan. Place meat in roasting pan. Pour cream of mushroom soup and onion soup over meat, cover tightly and bake at 400 degrees for about 1-1/2 hours.

VENISON ROAST

Serves 12   Mrs. Rex L. Carter (Floride)

6	pounds venison	1	cup ketchup
2	cups chopped celery	2	teaspoons Worcestershire
2	cups chopped onion	1	cup water
1/2	cup vinegar	Hot sauce to taste	
1/2	cup sugar	3	medium pieces of salt pork

In skillet, fry the salt pork and then brown the roast on all sides in the rendered fat. Place meat in covered roaster or into a deep electric frying pan and salt. To the frying fat, add all the remaining ingredients. Cover meat with mixture and cook at 350 degrees, basting occasionally for about 4 hours. The gravy is excellent served on rice.

Exquisite mountain beauty and natural wonders grace the northwestern corner of South Carolina embraced by Oconee County lines. Touching on two other states, Georgia and North Carolina, Oconee contains most of the state's portion of the Blue Ridge Mountains. Magnificent waterfalls, rivers and lakes, once revered by Indian nations, continue to draw appreciative outdoorsmen and nature lovers.

Agriculture has always been the mainstay of the area's economy. Apple growing is especially profitable. The town of Westminster celebrates its fall fruits with an Apple Festival and enjoys the blossoms in the spring. The nation's first Soil Conservation District Plan was initiated on a farm near Seneca in 1938.

Indian legends and appellations resound through centuries of romantic lore. Chattooga. Tugaloo. Keowee. Seneca. Chauga. Jocassee. Isaqueena. "Oconee" itself is said to be the name of a mountain in the Cherokee nation. But mid-eighteenth century found the white man opposing the Cherokees from a series of forts and guard houses. The last remaining one is Oconee Station, built of native fieldstone, which stands a lonely sentinel today, subject for artists and photographers and reminder of a frontier past.

The present county was created in 1868 when a 650 square mile area was cut off from the western portion of Pickens County. The Court House was transferred from Pickens to Walhalla, the picturesque town settled in 1850 by Gen. John A. Wagener and others from the German Colonization Society of Charleston. The enthusiastic settlers brought their Germanic roots with them, naming the beautiful spot for Walhalla, "Garden of the Gods," and establishing a small, austere Luthern Church called St. John's.

Two dramatic waterways are on the must-see list, Whitewater Falls and the treacherous Chattooga River which separates South Carolina from Georgia for over 40 miles. Lake Jocassee, Keowee and Hartwell may be less spectacular but are equally beautiful.

Tamassee, another Indian word meaning "Sunlight of God," is the name of the DAR Industrial School for underprivileged children which was established in 1914. It was built near the site of General Andrew Pickens' plantation which bore the same name. One of two such schools in the U. S., it has been widely acclaimed for the Christian and educational training it provides.

241

Water and water generated power have highlighted the history of Anderson County. Hydro-electric power produced at Portman Shoals in the 1890s caused the county seat to be nicknamed the "Electric City" as it became the first town in the South to have an unlimited supply of hydro-electric power. This achievement spurred the development of industry, particularly textiles, along the rivers which had once been quietly plied by Indian traders.

The Seneca, Savannah and Saluda rivers figured prominently in colonial trade and travel. The latter two were used as boundary lines when the present borders for this Piedmont county were laid out in 1826. The damming of the Savannah and its tributaries to form Hartwell Lake and Reservoir created a twentieth century mecca for those seeking water related activities.

Although it was inland, Pendleton played an early and dramatic role in the development of culture and enterprise. One of the nation's oldest Farmer's Societies is housed in the graceful Farmers Hall (completed in 1828) whose massive columns still dominate the village green.

In the peaceful days which followed the American Revolution, many patriot soldiers were paid by a gift of land, portions of the State's recent acquisition from the Cherokee Indians. One of those early settlers was Gen. Robert Anderson, for whom the later county was named.

Once rural, Anderson has shifted to the urban and industrial column. Anderson Cotton Mills, said to be the first U.S. textile mill powered by electricity transmitted over long distance power lines, began the County's industrialization. It continues today with Interstate highway connections to other industrial centers and Tri-County Technical College which provides appropriate training for Pickens and Oconee counties as well as Anderson. The County rests proudly on a rich past, but, more importantly, it looks expectantly into the future.

Pendleton, which was the seat of a predecessor county by the same name, was the site of fine carriage and cabinet makers who rivaled those in Charleston and Europe. Mercifully preserved, largely through the efforts of the Pendleton Historical and Recreational Commission, the entire town of Pendleton was placed on the National Register of Historic Places in 1970.

OCONEE STATION

Oconee Station was one of three outposts erected by Colonel Montgomery in 1756 for protection of settlers from the Indians. This is an unusual building with one foot thick field stone walls.

desserts, cookies and candy

APPLE CRISP

Mrs. Mona Chapman

1	20-ounce can apple pie filling	1	cup chopped pecans
3/4	cup light brown sugar	3/4	cup margarine
1/2	cup plain flour	4-1/2	cups confectioner's sugar
1/2	cup Quick Oatmeal, uncooked	3	teaspoons vanilla
3/4	teaspoon cinnamon	4	tablespoons milk
1/3	cup margarine, cut up		

Spread pie filling in 8x8-inch pyrex dish. Mix the next 6 ingredients together and sprinkle over pie filling. Bake at 375 degrees for 30 minutes. Cool 10 minutes. Mix together the next 4 ingredients and spread on top.

QUICK APPLE CRISP

Mrs. Rembert C. Dennis (Natalie)

2	20-ounce cans sliced apples, unsweetened	1	cup plain flour
1	cup packed brown sugar	1	stick oleo
			Cinnamon

Mix together oleo, sugar and flour. Put apples into 12x6-inch baking dish and sprinkle with cinnamon. Pour mixture over apples and press down. Bake at 350 degrees for 30 minutes or until brown. Delicious topped with ice cream. Blueberries, peaches or pears may be used.

SUPER APPLESAUCE

Mrs. J. L. Henson (Ruby)

6	medium sized cooking apples		Dash cinnamon
3/4	cup sugar	1/4	cup dry sherry

Pare and quarter apples. Place in a large saucepan and add other ingredients. Cook over medium heat until boiling; reduce heat and cook for 10 or 15 minutes until apples are soft. Serve warm or cold as an accompaniment with meats or with whipped cream as a light dessert.

BAKLAVA

Yield: 48   Mrs. Nick A. Theodore (Emilie)

3 pounds pecans, chopped	SYRUP:
3 teaspoons cinnamon	4 cups sugar
1 teaspoon cloves	3 cups water
1 cup sugar	1/2 lemon
1 pound butter, unsalted, melted	1 stick cinnamon
1 pound fila	1 jigger brandy
	4 tablespoons honey

Combine pecans, cinnamon, cloves, sugar and mix well. Grease a 17-1/2x 12-1/2x2-inch pan with melted butter. Place 8 fila in pan, brushing each fila with melted butter. Sprinkle top fila with layer of nut mixture. Cover with 3 fila, brushing between each with butter and sprinkling top fila with nut mixture. Continue the 3 fila procedure until all nut mixture is used. Finish with 6 fila on top brushing each with butter. With an electric knife, or a sharp pointed knife, cut into small squares or diamond shapes. Bake in preheated oven for 1-1/2 hours at 300 degrees. Remove from oven, cool and pour hot SYRUP over baklava. SYRUP: Mix ingredients together, bring to a boil and boil to a medium consistency, about 10 minutes.

"EASY" CHERRIES JUBILEE

Serves 6 to 8   Mrs. Nick Theodore (Emilie)

1 20-ounce can dark pitted cherries	1 teaspoon cornstarch
1 teaspoon sugar	2 teaspoons brandy or rum
	Dash cinnamon

Drain cherries and set aside. Combine sugar and cornstarch in small saucepan. Add cherry syrup and cinnamon. Heat, stirring constantly, until clear and thickened. Add cherries and brandy or rum. Blaze and spoon flaming cherries over ice cream.

BOILED CUSTARD

Senator Nell Smith

3/4 cup sugar	4 eggs
2 level tablespoons cornstarch	1 quart milk

Sift the first 2 ingredients together. Break the eggs into mixture and beat. Scald milk in double boiler. When a skim forms on milk, pour slowly over egg-sugar mixture. Return to double boiler and cook until the spoon is coated. Stir all the time. Pour through a sieve and cool. An old Virginia family recipe. I use this as a base for homemade ice cream.

BANANAS FOSTER

Serves 4   Mrs. William Cork (Helen)

1/2 cup butter	4 slightly under-ripe bananas,
3/4 cup firmly packed light	peeled and halved lengthwise
brown sugar	1/3 cup brandy or light rum
2 tablespoons lemon juice	

Melt butter in a chafing dish, flame-proof casserole, or pan, over moderately low heat; mix in sugar and lemon juice and heat, stirring until sugar dissolves. Add bananas and simmer, uncovered, about 10 minutes, turning gently now and then with a slotted spatula to glaze evenly. Warm brandy in a small saucepan, pour over bananas, blaze and spoon over bananas until flames die. Serve at once with vanilla ice cream.

MONA'S DESSERT

Mrs. Mona Chapman

1-1/2 cups flour	2 3-ounce packages instant
1-1/2 sticks margarine	pistachio or chocolate pudding
1 cup nuts, chopped	3 cups milk
12 ounces cream cheese, softened	1 large carton Cool Whip
1-1/2 cups powdered sugar	

Mix flour, margarine and nuts. Press into a 13x9-inch pan. Bake at 350 degrees about 20 minutes. Cool. Cream cheese and sugar. Spread on cooled crust. Whip pudding and milk with mixer until thick, about 2 minutes. Fold in 1/2 carton Cool Whip. Spread on top of cream cheese layer. Spread other half Cool Whip on top, if desired.

HOT FRUIT COMPOTE

Serves 10 to 12   Mrs. D. H. Holland (Betty)
                                              Mrs. Dick Elliott (Anne)

1 small bottle cherries	1 teaspoon curry powder(optional)
1 29-ounce can sliced peaches	1/4 cup margarine
1 29-ounce can Barkley pears	1 cup sugar
1 20-ounce can chunks pineapple	4 tablespoons flour
1 17-ounce can apricots	2 cups sherry
1 jar apple rings	Maraschino cherries

Drain fruit and place in a 10x6x1-1/2-inch casserole. In double boiler heat margarine, sugar, flour and sherry until like cream; pour over fruit. Let stand overnight. Bake at 350 degrees for 30 minutes. Garnish with maraschino cherries.

STRAWBERRY AND RASPBERRY COMPOTE

Serves 8   Mrs. Larry A. Martin (Susan)

3   pints strawberries, washed   Juice of 1 to 2 limes
    and hulled   1/4   cup Cointreau
3   pints raspberries, washed   1/4   cup Barbados rum
    and hulled

Combine the strawberries with the raspberries in a pretty crystal bowl and add the lime juice, Cointreau and rum. Mix gently. Refrigerate several hours before serving to allow flavors to blend. Remove from refrigerator 1/2 hour before serving.

CHOCOLATE ECLAIR CAKE

Yields: 15 squares   Mrs. J. L. Henson (Ruby)

Whole graham crackers   2   3-ounce packages French vanilla
3   cups milk   instant pudding
1   can Supreme Fudge frosting 1   8-ounce container Cool Whip

Butter a 13x9-inch dish. Arrange a layer of graham crackers in bottom of dish. Mix pudding and milk. Chill a short time and fold in Cool Whip. Pour half of pudding on graham crackers, then add another layer of crackers. Spread on remainder of pudding. Top with another layer of crackers. Spread canned frosting on top. Refrigerate at least 24 hours before serving.

VARIATION: Mrs. Heyward McDonald (Sylvia)

Omit fudge frosting. Make CHOCOLATE FROSTING by melting 1 stick margarine, 2 1-ounce squares chocolate; add 2 cups powdered sugar and 1 egg. Mix well and spread over top of cake.

DATE LOAF

Senator Nell Smith

1   small can evaporated milk   30   marshmallows, chopped
1   cup nuts, broken up   1/2   pound Graham crackers, crushed
1   pound dates, chopped

Mix all together, saving some cracker crumbs to sprinkle over the roll. Serve with whipped cream. Using a food processor, this is easily and quickly prepared and very good!

DESSERTS, COOKIES AND CANDY

HAZEL'S FRUIT DELIGHT
Mrs. Robert C. Lake, Jr. (Carolyn)

3 cups unpeeled apples, chopped
2 cups cranberries
1 cup sugar
1/2 cup margarine, melted
1/2 cup brown sugar
1/2 cup oatmeal
1/2 cup nuts

Combine apples, cranberries and sugar. Pour into casserole. Mix last 4 ingredients and put on top. Bake at 350 degrees for 45 minutes.

SOUR CREAM DRESSING
Mrs. Robert C. Lake, Jr. (Carolyn)

1 8-ounce carton sour cream
1/4 cup firmly packed brown sugar
1/2 teaspoon Morton Natures Seasons Blend

Combine all ingredients. Store in refrigerator. Keeps well 3 to 4 days. Use to accompany fruit platter.

"GYPSY"
Mrs. M. E. McDonald (Anne)

1 quart sweet milk
1/2 cup sugar
4 large egg yolks (5 or 6, if small)
12 large marshmallows
2 jiggers sherry wine (or 2 teaspoons vanilla)
2 boxes plain Lady Fingers
1 8-ounce container Cool Whip

Beat egg yolks and sugar together while milk is heating in double boiler. When milk has heated some, stir egg mixture into milk very slowly, stirring constantly. Add marshmallows. When marshmallows have melted, and it has thickened, remove from heat and add wine or vanilla. Split Lady Fingers. Place layer of Lady Fingers in dish, then a layer of custard, and a layer of Cool Whip. Repeat layers. This is better to make ahead and refrigerate overnight.

FROZEN LEMON CUSTARD
Serves 6 to 8
T. Eston Marchant, Adjutant General

3 eggs, separated
1/2 cup sugar
4 tablespoons lemon juice
1/2 pint whipping cream

Cook egg yolks and sugar in saucepan over medium heat, stirring constantly, until thick. Remove from heat, add lemon juice. Add beaten egg whites and whipped cream. Line 9-inch pie pan with vanilla wafer crumbs. Pour in the lemon custard. Freeze. Serve frozen.

CHOCOLATE MOUSSE

Serves 6 to 8   Representative Harriet H. Keyserling

1   6-ounce package semi-sweet   4   eggs, separated
      chocolate bits   1   tablespoon rum
1/2   pint whipping cream

Scald the cream. Put the bits into blender and pour scalded cream over; blend until smooth. Add egg yolks and rum, blend. Beat the 4 egg whites until almost stiff. Fold into the chocolate mixture. Chill in refrigerator, preferably overnight for best taste and texture. Takes 10 minutes to prepare.

VARIATION: Mrs. Walter Bristow, Jr. (Stewart)

Omit rum. Blend together 3 minutes 1/2 cup more scalded milk, 1 more package chocolate chips, 1/4 cup Cointreau, 1/3 cup brewed coffee and 2 teaspoons vanilla. Pour into 12 dessert cups and chill.

FROZEN CHOCOLATE MOUSSE

Serves 6 to 8   Mrs. Beattie Huff (Gladys)

2   eggs   2   ounces cold water
3   yolks   1   package gelatin
1/2   cup sugar   Zest and juice of 1 orange
1   tablespoon Grand Marnier   1   cup whipping cream,
6   ounces semi-sweet Baker's   half whipped
      chocolate (no other)

Have all ingredients at room temperature. Beat eggs, yolks and sugar until it becomes very thick and forms a ribbon (like whipped cream). Add Grand Marnier or orange liqueur. Melt chocolate in the water in the top of a double boiler. Add orange rind. Put juice in a small pan. Sprinkle gelatin over juice and let stand for 2 minutes. Melt gelatin over low heat. Add to eggs and sugar mixture. Fold in chocolate. Fold in lightly whipped cream. Chill for 4 hours. May be frozen several weeks ahead. Before serving, garnish top with sweetened, whipped cream and chocolate shaving. TIP: frozen egg whites may be reserved for souffles or roulades.

LEMON MOUSSE

Serves 8   Mrs. Ben F. Hornsby (Esther)

1	8-ounce can evaporated milk		Juice and rind of 4 lemons
1	cup sugar	1	box vanilla wafers, finely crumbled

Add evaporated milk to a bowl and chill until icy crystals form around edge of bowl. Beat milk until it peaks. Add sugar, lemon juice and grated rind. If you want more of a lemon taste add a few drops of ReaLemon. Butter a ring mold and make a crust of vanilla wafers. Pour lemon mixture into mold, spreading evenly. Sprinkle top generously with vanilla wafer crumbs. Freeze. Unmold and decorate with fresh fruit. Freezes well.

ORANGE SHELL GLACE

Serves 8   Mrs. Larry A. Martin (Susan)

8	large navel oranges	1/2	cup slivered preserved or candied
1	quart vanilla ice cream		ginger
1	tablespoon grated orange peel		Freshly grated coconut
Slivered almonds			

Cut the blossom end of the orange 1/4-inch deep in wide scallops. Put the point of a sharp paring knife about halfway through the orange, then cut in a zigzag scallop or notch until you meet the point where you started. Pull the top and bottom of the orange apart. Cut along the inside of the orange with a sharp knife to loosen the pulp and lift out the fruit with a dessert spoon. Mix the ice cream with orange peel and ginger and pack into the empty shells. Wrap in clear plastic and deep freeze. When ready to serve, allow time at room temperature to soften, cover with the coconut and almonds.

PEACH HALVES WITH CHUTNEY

Serves 10   Mrs. J. M. Cooper (Melba)

10	peach halves	Curry powder (optional)
10	tablespoons peach chutney (see Index)	

Preheat oven 350 degrees. Put peach halves in a casserole dish and put 1 tablespoon peach chutney in each. Sprinkle lightly with curry powder, if desired. Bake for 20 minutes or until heated through. Serve immediately.

FROZEN FRUIT SHERBET

Yield: 12 parfaits   Mrs. Dick Elliott (Anne)

1	12-ounce can frozen orange juice	1	large can crushed pineapple
3	juice cans water	1	9-1/2-ounce jar sliced cherries
1	cup sugar	4	bananas, diced

Mix first 3 ingredients and freeze. After mixture is frozen, make into a slush and add the next 3 ingredients. Fold into orange slush and scoop into parfait glasses and freeze. Leave at room temperature a few minutes before serving.

IRISH COFFEE PARFAIT

Serves 6   Senator Norma Russell

1-1/2 cups strong black coffee   4   tablespoons Irish Whiskey
1   envelope plain gelatin   1   cup whipped cream with 2
3   tablespoons sugar   tablespoons sugar and 2
Water: 1/2 cup cold and 1/2 cup boiling   tablespoons sour cream

Soften gelatin in cold water; dissolve in boiling water. Take off heat; add coffee and sugar. Cool. Add Irish Whiskey and pour into parfait glasses. When parfait has begun to set in refrigerator, spoon whipped cream mixture on top.

PIOUS ANGEL PARFAIT

Mrs. J. L. Henson (Ruby)

1   envelope unflavored gelatin   3   tablespoons creme de menthe
1/2 cup hot water   3   tablespoons brandy
3   eggs, separated   1   envelope Dream Whip, prepared as
1/4 cup sugar   directed on box

Dissolve gelatin in hot water and set aside. Add sugar to egg yolks, stirring constantly; add creme de menthe, brandy and gelatin. Beat egg whites until stiff. Fold in green mixture and whipped topping. Spoon into parfait glasses and chill until firm. Garnish with whipped topping and green cherries, if desired.

PINEAPPLE CASSEROLE

Mrs. W. B. Hawkins (Sarah)

2	15-1/2-ounce cans pineapple chunks, drained	1-1/2	cups grated sharp cheese
5	tablespoons plain flour	1	roll Ritz crackers, crushed
3/4	cup sugar	1	stick melted margarine

Place pineapple in a casserole dish. Cover with a layer of flour, then sugar, then a layer of grated cheese, then crushed crackers, ending with melted margarine. Bake at 350 degrees for 30 minutes.

VERY CHOCOLATE PUDDING BAKE

Serves 6 to 8   Mrs. Jeff Richardson (Florence)

2	cups sugar	2	eggs, slightly beaten
6 to 8	tablespoons cocoa	2	cups sweet milk
4	tablespoons flour	1	teaspoon vanilla
Pinch of salt		2	tablespoons butter

Mix the dry ingredients well in a 2-quart baking dish. Add eggs and mix to a thick paste. Slowly stir in milk and mix thoroughly; add vanilla and stir well. Cut butter into small pieces and spread it evenly over the top of mixture. Bake in a 400 to 425 degree oven for 40 to 45 minutes. Can be served warm or cold and topped with whipped cream or vanilla ice cream. Mixture can be baked in two 8-inch uncooked pastry shells for 30 to 35 minutes.

FRUIT PUDDING

Mrs. John C. Land, III (Marie)

1	6-ounce package vanilla instant pudding	1	16-ounce can regular fruit cocktail
1	16-ounce can pineapple chunks	2	bananas, sliced
1	16-ounce can peaches, chopped	1	red apple, chopped with peel on
1	16-ounce can chunk style fruit cocktail	3	heaping tablespoons Tang
			Orange juice

Drain all canned fruit; pour fruit into large bowl and reserve the juice. This should make three cups liquid; if not, add enough orange juice to make three cups. Mix fruit juice and dry pudding mix with a wire wisk until well blended. Add Tang and pour over fruit. Just before serving, add sliced banana and apple to mixture. Very pretty served in clear crystal bowl with a small silver ladle allowing guests to serve themselves. Do not prepare sooner than the day being served. This is especially good as a topping for a pound cake.

LEMON SPONGE PUDDING

Serves 8 to 10   Mrs. Rembert C. Dennis (Natalie)

2	tablespoons shortening	1/4	cup plain flour
1	cup sugar	5	tablespoons lemon juice
3	eggs	1-1/2	cups milk

Cream shortening, add sugar, stir in egg yolks, flour, lemon juice and grated rind of one lemon. Add 1/2 cup milk and mix well. Add rest of milk and fold in stiffly beaten egg whites. Pour into buttered baking dish. Set in pan of warm water. Bake in a 300 degree oven about 45 minutes. I use a 10x 6-1/2-inch dish. Cool and serve with whipped cream. Delicious!

MOLASSES PUDDING

Mrs. James E. Lockemy (Ellen)

1	quart milk	1/4	teaspoon ginger
3/4	cup molasses	1/4	teaspoon nutmeg
1	cup cornmeal	1/4	teaspoon cinnamon
1/4	cup butter	2	beaten eggs
2	tablespoons sugar	1	teaspoon vegetable shortening

Heat milk in saucepan. Add molasses and cornmeal. Stir until mixed and bring to boil. Remove pan from heat. Add butter, ginger, nutmeg, cinnamon and sugar. Cool ten minutes. Stir in beaten eggs. Grease baking dish with shortening. Pour in pudding and bake at 325 degrees for about 1 hour or until tester comes out clean. This is my great-great-grandmother's recipe.

BRIGHAM'S CHOCOLATE SAUCE

Mrs. Robert C. Lake, Jr. (Carolyn)

1	stick butter	1	tall can evaporated milk
5	squares semi-sweet chocolate	4	tablespoons white Karo syrup
1	box confectioners sugar		

Melt butter and add chocolate. Stir until melted together. Add evaporated milk and syrup. Beat in confectioners sugar. Simmer 8 minutes. Use for sauce over ice cream, fruit or cake.

FIG SAUCE

Yields: 3-1/2 cups   Mrs. William Cork (Helen)

12 to 15 fresh ripe figs, peeled	1 tablespoon butter
1/2 cup sugar	1 tablespoon cornstarch
1 cup water	3 tablespoons lemon juice

Combine figs, sugar, water and butter in a saucepan; bring to a boil. Simmer 5 to 8 minutes or until figs are tender. Combine cornstarch and lemon juice, mixing until smooth. Stir into fig mixture. Cook over low heat, stirring constantly, until thickened and bubbly. Serve warm over vanilla ice cream.

APPLE SOUFFLE

Serves 8   Mrs. L. Edward Bennett (Peggy)

2 cups applesauce	24 vanilla wafers, crushed
1 cup sugar	Dash cinnamon
1/4 pound butter	2/3 cup milk
2 eggs	Marshmallows

Melt butter. Beat eggs and add crushed vanilla wafers, applesauce, milk, sugar, melted butter and cinnamon. Put in greased casserole dish and bake at 350 degrees until slightly brown, 30 to 40 minutes. Remove from oven and cover top with marshmallows. Brown slightly.

ORANGE SOUFFLE

Serves 6 to 8   Mrs. E. Crosby Lewis (Cleo)

8 eggs	1/2 cup fresh orange juice
1 cup sugar	2 tablespoons grated orange rind
2 packages unflavored gelatin, dissolved in the heated juice of 1 orange	2 cups heavy cream, whipped to soft peaks with 2 tablespoons powdered sugar added
1/4 cup cointreau	Orange slices to decorate

Beat the eggs and sugar in a mixer bowl over hot water for about 10 minutes. Cool the dissolved gelatin and add, very slowly, to the egg mixture. Pour in the cointreau, orange juice and rind. Put oiled wax paper collar around outside of souffle dish. Fold the whipped cream into the egg and juice mixture and pour into prepared souffle dish. Put in freezer for 2 hours. Turn out onto serving dish. Remove paper collar and decorate with whipped cream put through a pastry tube and garnish with orange slices.

SAVANNAH TRIFLE

Serves 12 to 14   Mrs. William Cork (Helen)

6 cups milk	1/2 cup cream sherry
1-1/2 cups sugar	1-1/2 pounds sliced pound cake
2 tablespoons cornstarch	2 cups whipping cream, whipped
6 eggs	Maraschino cherries

Scald milk in top of double boiler. Combine sugar and cornstarch, stirring well. Add eggs to sugar mixture; beat with an electric mixer until well blended. Stir some of hot milk into egg mixture; add to remaining hot milk in double boiler, stirring constantly. Cook, stirring constantly, until custard thickens and coats a metal spoon. Cool completely. Stir sherry into custard. Place half of pound cake evenly in a 5-quart serving bowl. Pour half of custard over pound cake. Spread half of whipped cream over custard. Repeat layers. Garnish top of trifle with cherries.

FRESH STRAWBERRY TRIFLE

Serves 20   Mrs. John C. Land, III (Marie)

Jelly	1 6-ounce package instant vanilla
1 sponge cake (recipe p. 290)	pudding
2 pints strawberries, sliced in	1/2 pint whipping cream
half (wash and dry)	3/4 cup sherry

Make a jelly roll pan size sponge cake. Cool and spread currant, wild plum or apple jelly on top. Cut cake down middle and put two jelly sides together like a sandwich. Cut cake into small bite size squares and drop into a large glass trifle bowl or punch bowl. Pour sherry over this. Prepare instant pudding and pour over the top of the cake; cover and refrigerate overnight. Make a layer of strawberries on top of the pudding, a layer of whipping cream and top with remaining strawberries. This needs to be served within a few hours of the final preparation.

YAM YUMS

Serves 6 to 8   Mrs. Robert C. Lake (Carolyn)

2 apples, sliced	2 17-ounce cans yams, drained
1/3 cup chopped pecans	1/4 cup margarine
1/2 cup brown sugar	2 cups miniature marshmallows
1/2 teaspoon cinnamon	

Toss apples and nuts with combined sugar and cinnamon. Alternate layers of apples and yams in a 1-1/2-quart casserole. Dot with margarine. Cover. Bake at 350 degrees for 35 to 40 minutes. Sprinkle marshmallows over yams and apples. Broil until browned.

MICROWAVE YOGURT

Mrs. Nick A. Theodore (Emilie)

In a glass loaf pan add 1 quart milk. (Milk should come almost to top of pan.) Microwave 15 minutes on high. Take out and let cool until thermometer registers between 125 and 130 degrees. Then add 2 to 2-1/2 tablespoons of a yogurt starter (Dannon's Plain Yogurt will do) to 1/2 cup of the milk. Mix well, then pour back into pan and stir very well. Cover with plastic wrap and wrap two dish towels around pan. Leave out on counter 8 hours, then refrigerate.

BOURBON BALLS

Yield: 4 dozen   Mrs. William Cork (Helen)

1	cup vanilla wafer crumbs	1/4	cup bourbon
1	cup finely chopped pecans	1-1/2	tablespoons light corn syrup
1	cup powdered sugar		Powdered sugar for rolling
2	tablespoons cocoa		

Combine crumbs, pecans, sugar and cocoa. Blend bourbon and syrup. Mix all ingredients. Shape into 1-inch balls. Roll in powdered sugar. Refrigerate.

BROWNIES

Yield: 12   Mrs. M. H. Kinon (Reba)

2	sticks butter	2	cups sugar
4	1-ounce squares semi-sweet	1	teaspoon vanilla
	chocolate (3-1/2 tablespoons	4	eggs
	cocoa plus 1/2 tablespoon	1	cup self-rising flour
	butter equals 1 chocolate	2	tablespoons milk
	square)	1	cup nuts

Melt butter and chocolate together; cool 5 minutes. Beat eggs, 1 at a time. Add sugar, flour, milk, chocolate mixture, vanilla and pecans. Pour into 2 greased and floured 7x7-inch pans. Bake at 350 degrees for 25 minutes. Do not let brownies get too done; they should be moist. VARIATION: Reduce butter to 3/4 cup. Use 2/3 cup cocoa instead of chocolate squares. Increase flour by 1/2 cup and add 1/2 teaspoon salt. Pour into a greased 9x13-inch pan and bake at 350 degrees for 30 minutes. As soon as brownies are taken from oven, cover with a large bag of miniature marshmallows. Return pan to oven until marshmallows are slightly melted. Mix together 1/3 cup cocoa, 1 box powdered sugar, 1/2 cup evaporated milk and 1/4 teaspoon salt and spread over marshmallows for HEAVENLY BROWNIES. If you wish to keep brownies and similar cookies a longer time, cut and wrap individually in foil or clear plastic before storing.

MAMA'S BLONDIES

Mrs. T. Bruce Smith, II (Dot)

1	stick margarine	1	egg
1/2	cup granulated sugar	1	teaspoon baking powder
1/2	cup brown sugar	1	cup chopped nuts
1	cup plain flour		

Mix the first 3 ingredients in a pot; melt on very low heat. Add the next four ingredients and pour into a 9x11-inch greased pan. Bake at 300 degrees for 35 minutes.

CHEESE BROWNIES

Mrs. David E. Turnipseed (Cindy)

2	8-ounce packages cream cheese	1	tablespoon lemon juice
2/3	cup sugar	1	box brownie mix OR
1	egg	1	mixed recipe for brownies
1	teaspoon vanilla		

Use food processor, blender, wooden spoon or 1 finger. Combine brownie mix with the first 5 ingredients. Mix well. Pour into a 9x13-inch pan lined with foil and bake at 350 degrees for 40 minutes.

BUTTERSCOTCH COOKIES

Mrs. Larry A. Martin (Susan)

2	cups dark brown sugar	1/4	teaspoon salt
1/2	cup butter	1	teaspoon vanilla
2	eggs, well beaten	1	cup nuts
2	cups plain flour	2	teaspoons baking powder

Cream the sugar and butter together until butter is slightly melted. Add eggs and beat well. Add dry ingredients except baking powder, and mix thoroughly. Add baking powder and mix in well. Add vanilla and nuts. Grease and flour an 8x8-inch pan and bake in a 300 degree oven for 30 minutes. Cut in strips. Roll in powdered sugar, if desired.

CHOCOLATE COCONUT SQUARES

Yield: 3 dozen   Mrs. Robert N. McLellan (Doris)

2 cups flour	1 cup water
2 cups sugar	2 eggs, beaten
1/2 teaspoon salt	1/2 cup buttermilk
1 cup butter or margarine	1 teaspoon soda
3 tablespoons powdered cocoa	1 teaspoon vanilla

Sift together flour, sugar and salt. Set aside. Mix butter, cocoa and water. Bring to a boil, pour over flour mixture. Add well-beaten eggs, buttermilk, soda and vanilla. Pour into 2 buttered shallow 9x9-inch cake pans. Bake at 375 degrees for 30 minutes. Spread with Chocolate Coconut Topping:

CHOCOLATE COCONUT TOPPING

1/2 cup butter	1/2 teaspoon vanilla
6 tablespoons half-and-half	1 cup shredded coconut
3 tablespoons cocoa	1 cup chopped nuts
2 cups powdered sugar	

Mix and bring to a boil butter, half-and-half and cocoa. Add mixture to powdered sugar, vanilla, coconut and nuts. Mix and spread over cookies as they come from oven. Cut in squares. A good picnic cookie and a nice change from brownies.

CHOCOLATE STICKS

Yields: 48   Mrs. Robert C. Lake, Jr. (Carolyn)

1 can Eagle Brand condensed milk	2 cups nut meats
4 squares Baker's Chocolate	1 teaspoon vanilla
2 cups crushed vanilla wafers	1/8 teaspoon salt

Combine wafers and nuts. Toss as you would a salad. Melt chocolate in milk until it coats a spoon. Pour this over nuts and vanilla wafers. Place in buttered pan about 1/2-inch thick and chill. Cut in fingers as you would fudge. Roll in powdered sugar. Will keep well for two weeks.

SCOTTISH SHORTBREAD

Yields: 2 Dozen squares   Mrs. I. S. Leevy Johnson (Doris)

Let 1 C. sweet butter soften. Combine 1/2 C. sugar and 2 cups sifted all-purpose flour with hands until a ball forms. Place in baking pan 9x13 or 2 pie tins. Pat down. Score with a fork. Bake in 325 degree oven 45-50 minutes.

CHOCOLATE YUMMIES

Yield: 4 dozen   Mrs. Lloyd Hendricks (Sue)

1/2 cup milk	2 cups granulated sugar
1/2 cup cocoa	1/2 cup coconut, shredded
1/2 cup butter	3 cups quick oats
1 teaspoon vanilla, optional	

Combine milk, cocoa, butter, vanilla and sugar in saucepan. Cook 2 minutes. Cut heat off and add coconut and oatmeal. Mix well and drop on waxed paper with spoon. Chill and serve.

VARIATION: Mrs. Mona Chapman

Reduce amount of oatmeal to 2 cups, and add 1/2 cup peanut butter and 1/2 cup pecans.

ARGENT'S CHRISTMAS BALLS

Mrs. T. Bruce Smith, II (Dot)

1 cup Crisco	1 teaspoon cinnamon
1-1/2 cups brown sugar	1 teaspoon rum flavoring
2-1/2 cups Swans Down cake flour	4 slices candied pineapple, cut in
1 teaspoons soda	small bits
1 teaspoon vanilla	1/2 pound candied cherries, chopped
1/2 teaspoon salt	in small bits
1/2 pound dates, chopped	2 cups nuts, chopped

Cream Crisco and sugar and blend well. Add the rest of the ingredients. Form into 1-inch balls. Bake at 300 degrees for 15 minutes (no longer) on greased baking sheet.

ALMOND CHRISTMAS COOKIES

Yield: 4 dozen   Mrs. John C. Land, III (Marie)

1 cup butter, softened	1 teaspoon vanilla
1/2 cup confectioners sugar	1 16-ounce container candied
2 cups sifted plain flour	cherries (red or green, or both)
1/2 teaspoon salt	1 cup ground almonds

Cream butter in mixing bowl. Add sugar and blend until light and fluffy. Add flour, salt, almonds and vanilla. Take one teaspoon of the dough, put a cherry in middle, and roll dough around it to form a ball. Flour your hands or chill dough if it is too sticky to work with. Bake on a greased cookie sheet at 325 degrees for 30 minutes. Remove from oven and roll in confectioners sugar.

SOUTH CAROLINA MERRY CHRISTMAS COOKIES

Yield: 10 dozen   Mrs. Alex S. Macaulay (Maria)

1	cup butter or margarine	1	teaspoon vanilla
1	cup dark brown sugar	1	teaspoon soda
3	eggs, well beaten	6	slices green crystalized pineapple
1/2	cup milk	2	cups red crystalized cherries
3	cups plain flour	2	cups dates
1	teaspoon cinnamon	9	ounce box seedless raisins
1/2	teaspoon salt	7	cups pecans, chopped

In a big container; cut into small pieces all the fruit and mix with chopped pecans. In a big container cream butter and sugar; add well beaten eggs and mix together the milk, flour, cinnamon, salt, flavoring and soda. Add fruits and chopped nuts and stir until well mixed. Drop by teaspoon onto greased cookie sheet. Bake at 250 degrees for about 25 minutes. Should be completely cold before wrapping for storage. These can be frozen. Delicious!

COCONUT MACAROONS

Yield: 1 dozen   Mrs. J. M. Cooper (Melba)

1	egg white	1/2	teaspoon vanilla
1/2	cup sugar	1/2	cup shredded coconut
1/4	teaspoon salt	1	cup cornflakes

Beat egg whites until stiff, but not dry. Add salt and sugar slowly. Beat well. Fold in corn flakes and coconut. Mix carefully. Drop by teaspoonful onto a well greased baking sheet. Bake in a 350 degree oven for 20 minutes. Remove immediately from pan.

DATE BARS

Mrs. T. Ed Garrison (Juanita)

3	eggs, separated	1	cup chopped dates
1	cup sugar	2	teaspoons baking powder
1	cup plain flour	1/4	teaspoon salt
1	cup chopped nuts	1	teaspoon vanilla

Mix sugar and yolks, add nuts and dates. Add vanilla, flour and other ingredients with well beaten egg whites into the mixture. Bake in a well greased 8x8-inch pan, in a 350 degree oven for 30 minutes. Cool, cut in bars and roll in powdered sugar.

SOUTH CAROLINA FINGER CHEWS

Yield: 48   Mrs. Larry A. Martin (Susan)

1 cup light brown sugar	1 teaspoon salt
1 cup butter	1/2 teaspoon vanilla
2 cups plain flour	
4 eggs, lightly beaten	ORANGE GLAZE:
1/4 cup flour	1 cup powdered sugar
3 cups dark brown sugar	1 tablespoon orange juice
1 cup Angel Flake coconut	1/2 teaspoon orange rind
2 cups coarsely chopped pecans	

Mix together the first 3 ingredients and spread evenly over an 8x12-inch pan. Bake at 350 degrees for 15 minutes. Remove from oven and cool. Mix together the rest of the ingredients and spread on baked and cooled layer. Bake at 325 degrees for 35 to 40 minutes or until cookie is firm. For ORANGE GLAZE: Mix together 1 cup powdered sugar mixed with 1 tablespoon orange juice and 1/2 teaspoon orange rind. Dribble ORANGE GLAZE over top while cookie is warm. When cold, cut in fingers.

FRUIT NUT BARS

Mrs. Robert N. McLellan (Doris)

2 cups plain flour	2 more cups chopped dates
2 teaspoons baking powder	
1/2 teaspoon salt	ORNAMENTAL ICING:
4 eggs	1 box confectioners sugar
2 cups packed brown sugar	1/3 cup Crisco shortening
2 teaspoons vanilla	1/4 cup water
2 cups chopped nuts	1 teaspoon vanilla
2 cups chopped dates	1/2 teaspoon cream of tartar
2 cups chopped fruits, OR	Pinch salt

Beat eggs to lemon color, add sugar and vanilla. Add dry ingredients which have been sifted together. Add nuts, dates and fruit (or more dates). Pour into a 9x13x2-inch pan lined with wax paper and greased. Bake at 325 degrees for 25 minutes. Mix together the ORNAMENTAL ICING ingredients and beat 5 minutes. Spread on Fruit Nut Bars while warm. Cut in preferred shapes and remove from pan while warm. Keep covered with a damp cloth.

DESSERTS, COOKIES AND CANDY

FORTYNINERS

Mrs. John Drummond (Holly)

1	box light brown sugar	2	cups roasted pecans
2	cups Bisquick	1-1/2	teaspoon vanilla
4	eggs		

Combine all ingredients and bake cookies at 350 degrees for 30 minutes.

ICEBOX COOKIES

Yield: 72 cookies   Mrs. J. L. Henson (Ruby)

1	cup butter	1	teaspoon vanilla
2	cups light brown sugar	2-1/2	cups self-rising flour
1/2	cup white sugar	1	cup chopped pecans
2	eggs		

Cream butter; add sugar and cream well. Add beaten eggs, vanilla, flour and nuts. Mix and form into rolls about 1-1/2 to 2-inches in diameter, using wax paper. Leave dough wrapped and keep in refrigerator overnight or for as long as 2 weeks. Slice thin and bake on greased cookie sheet at 400 degrees for 10 minutes. Children love this!

LEMON BARS

Yield: 3 dozen   Mrs. Thomas L. Hughston, Jr. (Jeanne)

2	cups all-purpose flour	1/4	cup all-purpose flour
1/2	cup powdered sugar	1/2	teaspoon baking powder
1	cup butter	1/3	cup lemon juice
4	eggs		Confectioners sugar
2	cups granulated sugar		

Cream butter and powdered sugar. Add flour. Press in ungreased cookie sheet pan. Bake at 350 degrees for 20 minutes. Let cool. Mix the next 5 ingredients and pour over cooled crust. Bake 25 minutes more at 350 degrees. Take out and sprinkle with confectioners sugar. Cool before cutting into squares.

BANANA OATMEAL COOKIES

Yield: 6 dozen   Mrs. William Cork (Helen)

3/4 cup shortening	1-1/2 cups all-purpose flour
1 cup sugar	1/2 teaspoon soda
1 egg	1/2 teaspoon baking powder
1 cup mashed bananas	1/4 teaspoon salt
1 cup quick-cooking oats,	3/4 teaspoon ground cinnamon
uncooked	1/4 teaspoon ground nutmeg

Combine shortening and sugar in large mixing bowl; cream until light and fluffy. Beat in egg; then stir in bananas and oats. Combine remaining ingredients and stir into creamed mixture. Drop by teaspoonfuls onto greased cookie sheets. Bake at 400 degrees for 13 minutes.

FIVE-MINUTE QUICK OATMEAL COOKIES

Mrs. John Drummond (Holly)

2 cups sugar	2 cups oatmeal
1/3 cup cocoa	1/2 cup crunchy peanut butter
1/2 cup milk	Pecans, optional
1 stick margarine or butter	

Cook first 4 ingredients for five minutes; stirring constantly. Add oatmeal and peanut butter. Add a few pecans. Beat a little and drop from tablespoon onto wax paper. Let cool.

PEANUT BUTTER CUP TARTS

Yield: 36 cookies   Mrs. Mona Chapman

36 Reese's miniature milk	1 15-ounce roll refrigerated peanut
chocolate peanut butter cups	cookie dough

Refrigerate candies so paper will peel off easily. Unwrap each. Slice cookies as directed, quartering each slice. Place each piece in greased miniature muffin cup. Place in preheated 350 degree oven 6 to 8 minutes or just until cookie puffs up and is barely done. Remove from oven and immediately push a candy cup into each cookie-filled muffin cup. The cookie will deflate and form a tart shell around the peanut butter cup. The heat of the cookie will melt the chocolate topping. Let pan cool; then refrigerate until the shine leaves the chocolate. Remove from refrigerator and gently lift each tart from the cup with the tip of a knife.

BOILED OATMEAL RAISIN COOKIES

Yield: 96   Mrs. James E. Lockemy (Ellen)

2	cups water	1	teaspoon salt
1	15-ounce package raisins	4	cups oatmeal
1-1/4	cups cooking oil	2	cups nuts
1-3/4	cups sugar	2	teaspoons baking soda
3	beaten eggs	1	teaspoon each cinnamon,
4	cups sifted flour		nutmeg, cloves and ginger
2	teaspoons baking powder	1	small package chocolate chips (optional)

Boil raisins in water, covered for 20 minutes. Add oil and sugar. Cool and add rest of ingredients. Bake at 350 degrees for 12 to 15 minutes.

REFRIGERATOR COOKIES

Mrs. Allen R. Carter (Helen)

1-1/2	cups Crisco or margarine	1	teaspoon salt
1	cup brown sugar, well packed	1	teaspoon cinnamon
1	cup granulated sugar	1	teaspoon nutmeg
3	eggs, well beaten	1	cup pecans
5	cups plain flour	1	teaspoon vanilla
2	teaspoons soda		

Cream shortening; add sugar and eggs. Sift flour and dry ingredients together. Combine well. Add nuts and vanilla. Divide dough into 6 or 7 parts; roll each into long roll, about the size of a half dollar, in waxed paper. Place in refrigerator or freezer overnight. Cut into thin slices, about 1/4-inch. Bake on cookie sheet about 12 to 15 minutes in a 350 degree oven. Store in airtight container. Will keep fresh for months.

CRUNCHY SNOBALLS

Yield: 2 to 3 dozen   Mrs. John I. Rogers, III (Carolyn)

1	pound white chocolate	3	cups Rice Krispies
3	cups miniature marshmallows	2 to 3	tablespoons peanut butter

Melt chocolate in a 200 degree oven for 20 minutes. Add other ingredients and stir gently. Drop by spoonfuls onto wax paper. Let cool at room temperature. These are an easy-to-fix Christmas treat!

DA-TEE'S TASSIES

Yields: 4 dozen   Mrs. T. W. Edwards, Jr. (Dottie)

3	ounce package cream cheese	PECAN FILLING:
1/2	cup butter	1 egg
1	cup sifted flour	3/4 cup brown sugar
		1 tablespoon soft butter
		1 teaspoon vanilla
		Dash salt
		2/3 cup coarsely chopped pecans

Blend cream cheese and butter together and stir in flour. Chill 1 hour or overnight. Press marble size rounds of dough in bottom and sides of ungreased tiny muffin tins. Beat together the filling ingredients. When smooth, stir in pecans. Put 1 teaspoon filling on top of uncooked dough and bake at 325 degrees for 20 to 25 minutes until filling is set. Remove from tins and place on towels to cool.

TOLL HOUSE COOKIES WITH OATMEAL

Yield: 100   Mrs. Thomas L. Hughston, Jr. (Jeanne)

1-1/2	cups sifted flour	2	eggs, unbeaten	
1	teaspoon soda	1	teaspoon hot water	
1	teaspoon salt	1	cup nuts, optional	
1	cup shortening	1	12-ounce package toll house	
3/4	cup brown sugar		morsels	
3/4	cup granulated sugar	2	cups oatmeal	
		1	teaspoon vanilla	

Sift flour once before measuring, then sift with soda and salt. Cream shortening until soft; add sugar, creaming until light and fluffy. Add eggs, 1 at a time. Add hot water, then dry ingredients. Add nuts, oatmeal and chocolate morsels. Mix well. Add vanilla. Drop 1/2 teaspoonful on greased cookie sheet. Bake at 375 degrees for 8 minutes.

CHRISTMAS CANDY

Senator "Liz" Patterson

2	pounds white chocolate	2	cups spanish peanuts
2	cups Rice Crispies	2	cups colored miniature marsh-
2	cups Life cereal		mallows

Melt white chocolate. Stir into other ingredients (which are already measured in large bowl). Do this FAST; chocolate will harden quickly. Place on waxed paper in bite-sized servings. Allow 5 minutes to harden.

DESSERTS, COOKIES AND CANDY

ALMOND ROCA

Mrs. Horace C. Smith (Dot)

1   cup butter
1   1-pound Hershey almond bar
1   cup sugar

1   cup almonds, finely chopped and
    divided

Cook butter and sugar over medium heat, stirring until a light caramel color. Pour onto aluminum foil which has been covered with 1/3 cup finely chopped almonds. Break Hershey bar into squares and place on top of warm sugar mixture. When soft spread over mixture and sprinkle with remaining almonds. Refrigerate. When candy hardens break with knife handle. Store in tight container and keep in cool place.

BUTTERSCOTCH BITES

Mrs. Horace C. Smith (Dot)

2   small packages butterscotch
    morsels
1   small can peanuts

1   large can Chinese noodles
1/2 cup crunchy peanut butter

Melt butterscotch in top of double boiler, adding peanuts and peanut butter. Stir until smooth and add noodles. Remove from heat and stir until noodles are coated. Drop onto wax paper in mounds and refrigerate until candy sets up.

FIVE MINUTE FUDGE

Mrs. Horace C. Smith (Dot)

1-2/3 cups sugar
2   tablespoons butter
1/2 teaspoon salt
1   teaspoon vanilla
16 marshmallows, diced

1   6-ounce package semi-sweet
    chocolate bits
1/2 cup chopped nuts, or more
2/3 cup undiluted evaporated milk

Combine sugar, butter, salt and milk in saucepan. Bring to a boil over medium high heat and cook for 5 minutes. Remove from heat. Add chocolate bits, marshmallows and nuts to milk and sugar mixture. Beat vigorously for one minute or until chocolate and marshmallows are melted. Add vanilla. Pour fudge into a buttered 8-inch pan.

"ANGEL'S" FUDGE BARS

Mrs. Nick A. Theodore (Emilie)

1	stick margarine	1/2	cup flour
4	1-ounce squares unsweetened chocolate	4	eggs
2	cups sugar	1	teaspoon vanilla

Melt margarine and chocolate together. Beat eggs; add sugar, flour, margarine, chocolate and vanilla. Pour into a greased and floured 9x13-inch pan. Bake at 350 degrees for 25 to 30 minutes. Cut into squares while warm.

PEANUT BRITTLE

Yield: 3 pounds   Mrs. J. M. Cooper (Melba)

2	cups shelled, raw peanuts	1	teaspoon salt
3	cups sugar	1/6	stick butter or margarine
1	cup white Karo syrup	2	teaspoons soda
1/2	cup water		

Combine sugar and Karo in heavy saucepan. Cook until sugar is dissolved and boil until it spins a thread. Add peanuts and cook until a golden brown. Remove from heat and carefully blend in salt and butter. Add soda last and let foam, stirring hard about 3 minutes. Pour on aluminum foil in cookie pan. When cool, break into pieces. Store in airtight container. Will keep up to a month.

TEXAS PRALINES

Senator Nell Smith

3	cups sugar	2	tablespoons butter
2	cups broken pecans	1	tablespoon vanilla
1	cup buttermilk		

Mix sugar, pecans and butter in deep saucepan and bring to boil. Stir occasionally and reduce heat as mixture begins to boil. Cook until soft ball stage occurs. Remove from heat, add butter and vanilla. Beat with wooden spoon until mixture loses gloss. Do not overbeat or it will crystalize. Drop spoonfuls onto wax paper and allow to cool. Do not double recipe. These are really great and different from pralines made in our area.

PRALINES

Mrs. William J. McLeod (Sara)

1	cup dark brown sugar	2	sticks margarine
1	cup chopped nuts	22	Graham cracker halves

Heat thoroughly the brown sugar, nuts, and margarine, about 2 minutes. Pour over Graham cracker halves. Bake 10 to 12 minutes at 325 to 350 degrees. Cool thoroughly before cutting into squares.

CHOCOLATE BUTTONS

Yields: 54 cookies   Mrs. Hugh K. Leatherman (Jean)

1-1/2 cups sugar
1/4 cup margarine, softened
3 1-ounce squares unsweetened
   chocolate, melted
1 teaspoon vanilla
3 eggs
2 cups plain flour

2 teaspoons baking powder
1/2 teaspoon salt
Powdered sugar
1 package chocolate stars, kisses,
   or non-pariels topped
   chocolate wafers

Blend sugar, margarine, chocolate and vanilla. Beat in eggs. Stir in flour, baking powder and salt. (Note: Can add an extra tablespoon flour to make dough easier to handle.) Chill dough for several hours. Shape dough into 1-inch balls. Roll in powdered sugar. Place on ungreased cookie sheet. Bake at 350 degrees for 12 to 15 minutes. Press chocolate candy in center of cookie. Cool.

CHOCOLATE BALLS

Mrs. Gene Dukes (Gerry)

1	cup margarine or butter	1/4	cup cocoa
1/2	cup sugar	1-3/4	cups plain flour
2	teaspoons vanilla	1/2	teaspoon salt
2	teaspoons instant coffee	2	cups finely chopped pecans

Mix all ingredients together, shape into small balls. Bake at 325 degrees for 15 minutes. Sprinkle with powdered sugar. Freezes well.

Midway along the western edge of the state lies Edgefield County whose placid appearance belies its stormy past. In antebellum days it maintained a reputation for fiery upheavals and riots. A long list of local sons went out as "diamonds in the rough" to shine on both the state and national level. One chronicler has observed that the county had "more dashing, brilliant, romantic figures, statesmen, orators, adventurers and dare-devils than any other county in South Carolina, if not any rural county in America."

The county was formed in 1785, the child of an earlier and larger Edgefield District. Well known families inhabited the area but life was rugged and rough.

Farm lands began to wear out and restless sons moved on. A large emigration to states further west (especially Georgia, Alabama and Mississippi) caused a temporary decrease in the county's population in the early 1800s. But all was not lost for many stable families remained, making tremendous contributions to the political and military development of South Carolina. A total of ten Palmetto State Governors and five Lt. Governors have called Edgefield home.

Beautiful old homes remain in the quiet town of Edgefield; in fact, some forty sites within one square mile have been placed on the National Register of Historic Places.

In 1826 the Furman Academy and Theological Institution was established in the village. This Baptist school became the forerunner of both Furman University in Greenville and Southern Baptist Theological Seminary in Louisville, Ky. The soil and heritage of Edgefield are rich, producing ideas, traditions and leaders to mold the state.

Preston Brooks, Benjamin R. Tillman, Butler Derrick, Jr., and Strom Thurmond are among the county's most passionate patriots.

Like most of its surrounding counties, Lexington was first settled by small farmers of Swiss, German and English stock. Small numbers of these groups entered the area in the 1730s and homesteaded lands in Dutch Fork and Cayce. By the 1750s displaced Virginians and Scotch-Irish Presbyterians from Pennsylvania began moving into the county. The Congaree River provided these early settlers with a good route to Charleston and by the 1760s the area had become a flourishing trading center.

Its proximity to the upstate and strategic command of the Congaree and Saluda rivers made the Lexington area an important military target during the state's early history.

After the Revolution, industry and trade increased in the county. In 1785 the county was officially organized and named Lexington, in honor of the first battle of the Revolution. Prior to this time the territory had been administered as part of the Orangeburg District. The first county seat was located in Granby although it was moved to the town of Lexington in 1818.

The county suffered badly during the Civil War. One quarter of the male population of Lexington was lost fighting for the Confederate cause. Sherman camped the bulk of his army near the county seat during the seige of Columbia. The Court House in Lexington was burned by the army and much of the surrounding farmland was torched.

After the war economic recovery was slow in the county. In the 1890s two railroad lines were built through the county, providing area farmers and manufacturers with easy access to distant state markets. By the turn of the century textile mills had opened in Batesburg, Lexington, Red Bank, and West Columbia. The building of airport facilities and the construction of Interstates 20 and 26 has in recent years added to Lexington County's economic prospects. Today the county has one of the fastest growing populations and strongest industrial bases in the entire state.

Created in 1916, McCormick is a late-comer in the family of South Carolina counties. Yet its roots are richly diverse, encompassing territory carved from portions of historic Edgefield, Greenwood and Abbeville counties. Today it maintains its rural identity along the western border of the state serving as a hunting and fishing paradise.

Rivers and lakes provide the life blood of this county which covers 379 square miles. The Savannah River separates the county - and the entire state of South Carolina - from Georgia. Little River and Long Cane, Steven, and Cuffytown creeks meander nearby. Clark Hill Reservoir, with its 600 miles of shoreline, provides a focal point for three state parks and all types of sportsmen.

McCormick takes its name from Cyrus W. McCormick, inventor of the reaper, who donated large portions of land where the town of McCormick is located. Another well known name in the area persists in the John De La Howe School, which has provided industrial training for boys and girls since 1797. It is named for the emigre judge and Huguenot counselor who bequeathed his estate "Lethe," near Bordeaux, to be used as a school for orphans in the county. The school, now under state control, is believed to be one of the first schools of its type in the nation.

Another educational institution made headlines in the early nineteenth century. Dr. Moses Waddell, was master of a rural academy for boys in Willington which commanded a national reputation. His self-paced program of log cabin classics and strict discipline molded any lad with promise, rich or poor. The then-Abbeville District academy drew young men from far away coastal towns and even from Georgia. Among its noted graduates were John C. Calhoun, George McDuffie, James L. Petigru, Augustus Longstreet and Hugh Legare.

Though now depleted, there was once a gold mine on Persimmon Branch which yielded ore worth more than one million dollars. W.B. "Billy" Dorn and his hound dog stumbled onto the precious vein while running a fox in 1852. For the next nine years Dorn expanded his coffers and his slave holdings as he blasted through his find.

Legends and lore about the Dorn Mine no doubt gave rise to the modern Gold Rush Day summer celebration. Community festivals and family recreation are characteristic of McCormick County with its golden past and peaceful present.

The town of Saluda sits squarely in the center of its county with state highways radiating in all directions. Much like the hub of a wheel the county seat is joined by equidistant spokes to Columbia, on the east, and the Savannah River, on the west. Perhaps its large traffic circle, familiar to Carolina travelers, is symbolic of the county's strategic location which straddles the Piedmont Plateau and the Coastal Plain.

Since early days the area has appeared in transportation records. On his trip northward through South Carolina in May 1791 George Washington spent the night on the 21st at the Jacob Odom house, between Ridge Spring and Monetta. The visit was noted in the President's diary. By the mid-1800s there was a regular Stagecoach stop and inn at the Lake House for those who were traveling the Edgefield-Columbia-Camden-Cheraw route. No commercial boon came from navigation of the Saluda River, however, despite Robert Mills' 1826 prediction that water travel "promises great facilities of intercourse with Columbia."

An indelible agricultural and rural print is on the face of Saluda County. Its low, rounded, sloping hills and abundant water supply are ideal for cultivation. The very name "Saluda" comes from the Cherokee word for "corn" and "Corn River" had been known as such long before the coming of the white man.

However, selection of the county's official appellation gave rise to a political battle in 1895 when the 435 square mile area was severed from Edgefield County. The open feud between brothers, George and Benjamin Tillman, clearly illustrates the class and family struggles of the period. At the state constitutional convention George proposed naming the county "Butler" for a prominent family in the region. But influential Benjamin, then-U.S. Senator, and his powerful forces, opposed the aristocratic name and succeeded with the adoption of "Saluda."

Peaceful daily life and continuity of traditions prevail in Saluda. Nature and its preservation are important to citizens of Saluda County. Lake Murray on the northeastern boundary and Sumter National Forest in the southwestern corner provide recreation and beauty, essentials for the good life.

HORN'S CREEK BAPTIST CHURCH

Horn's Creek Baptist Church was built in 1790, six miles south of Edgefield on U. S. 133. The basic structure has remained unchanged. It contains some of the original heart pine benches and a unique ceiling decoration, painted and stenciled in egg tempera. Both British and Patriot troops worshipped here.

cakes and pies

APPLE CAKE

Serves 10 to 12   Mrs. Theo W. Mitchell (Greta)

CAKE: BROWN SUGAR ICING:
2/3 cup Crisco   1   stick margarine, melted
2   cups sugar   8   tablespoons brown sugar
2   eggs   4   tablespoons self-rising flour
2   teaspoons vanilla   3/4 cup pecans, chopped
4   cups sliced apples, peeled
3   cups plain flour
2   teaspoons soda
1   teaspoon salt

Cream Crisco, sugar, eggs and vanilla until well blended. Mix dry ingredients and add gradually. Add apples. Pour into a greased and floured 10-inch tube or bundt pan. Bake 350 degrees about 45 to 60 minutes or until cake tester inserted in center of cake comes out clean. Let stand 15 minutes and turn out. Mix the margarine, sugar and flour over low heat and stir constantly until syrupy. Pour over cake. Cover with chopped pecans.

VARIATION: Mrs. Woody M. McKay (Nancy)

Increase ingredients to 3 eggs, substitute 1-1/4 cups Wesson Oil for Crisco, 3 cups diced apples, add 1 cup raisins, 1 cup chopped nuts, 1/2 teaspoon almond flavoring, 1/4 teaspoon rum flavoring and 1 teaspoon vanilla. Bake at 350 degrees for 1 hour and 20 minutes. Boil together 1 cup brown sugar, 1 stick butter and 1/4 cup milk for 2 minutes; pour over hot cake.

HOMESPUN APPLESAUCE CAKE

Serves 8 to 9   Mrs. James E. Lockemy (Ellen)

2   cups sifted cake flour   1/2 teaspoon salt
1   teaspoon baking soda   1/2 cup butter
1   teaspoon baking powder   1   cup sugar
1/2 cup raisins   1   well beaten egg
1   grated lemon rind   1-1/2 cups thick applesauce
1   teaspoon cinnamon   1/2 cup nuts

Mix flour, baking powder and salt. Sift and set aside. Cream butter, sugar, cinnamon and lemon rind until soft and smooth. Add egg and beat until fluffy. Add applesauce, baking soda, raisins and nuts. Stir in dry ingredients. Mix well. Turn into well greased and floured 8-inch square cake pan. Bake at 350 degrees for 1 hour. (Omit 2 tablespoons flour if using standard flour.)

JEWISH APPLE CAKE

Serves 10 to 12   Mrs. Herbert Kirsh (Suzanne)

3	cups sifted flour	1/2	teaspoon salt
2-1/4	cups sugar	1/3	cup orange juice
1	cup oil	2-1/2	teaspoons vanilla
4	unbeaten eggs	3	teaspoons baking powder
6	apples, peeled and sliced	2	teaspoons cinnamon
3	tablespoons sugar		

Cream oil and sugar until well blended. Add the eggs, one at a time, beating after each addition. Mix dry ingredients and add alternately with the orange juice; add vanilla. In another bowl mix together the apples, cinnamon and sugar. In a greased and floured 10-inch tube or bundt pan alternate layers of plain batter and apples, ending with apples. Bake at 350 degrees for 60 minutes or until a cake tester inserted in center of cake comes out clean. Let stand 15 minutes and turn out. Serve plain or with ORANGE OR LEMON GLAZE or SHERRY GLAZE.

ORANGE OR LEMON GLAZE

1	cup sugar	1/4	cup orange or lemon juice

Bring to a boil.

SHERRY GLAZE

1-1/2 cups sugar	1/2 cup sherry

Mix and stir over low heat constantly until syrupy. Pour over cake.

CHEESECAKE

Serves 8 to 10   Mrs. Woody M. McKay (Nancy)

3	8-ounce packages cream cheese, softened	1	teaspoon vanilla
			Graham cracker crumbs
1	cup sugar	1	cup sour cream
4	egg whites	3	tablespoons sugar
Dash salt		1/2	teaspoon vanilla

Beat together until stiff the egg whites. In a separate bowl, with same beaters, cream together cream cheese, sugar and vanilla. Fold in egg whites and pour into large buttered spring form pan which has been sprinkled with graham cracker crumbs. Cook 25 minutes at 350 degrees. Mix together the sour cream, sugar and vanilla. Remove cake from oven and pour on sour cream mixture. Cook five minutes at 400 degrees. Remove and let cool. Refrigerate for 24 hours.

275

CARAMEL CAKE

Mrs. Robert N. McLellan (Doris)

1	cup butter
2	cups sugar
3	cups plain flour
4	eggs
1	cup milk
1	teaspoon vanilla
1/4	teaspoon salt
2	teaspoons baking powder

QUICK CARAMEL ICING:

1/2	cup butter
1	cup brown sugar
1/4	teaspoon salt
1/4	cup milk
1	box powdered sugar
1	teaspoon vanilla

Remove butter and eggs from refrigerator at least one hour before mixing. Sift flour and measure. Add baking powder and salt, and sift together. Set aside. Cream butter and sugar until very soft and fluffy. Beat in eggs, one at a time, beating thoroughly after each is added. Add flour mixture alternately with milk and vanilla. Pour into 2 greased and floured 9-inch cake pans. Bake in a 350 degree oven 25 to 30 minutes or until cake tester comes out clean. Cool and remove from pans. Spread layers and sides of cooled cakes with QUICK CARAMEL ICING: Mix butter and sugar together in heavy pot and place on low heat, stirring until completely dissolved, about 2 minutes. Add milk and cook to boiling stage. Cool. Add powdered sugar, salt and flavoring slowly, beating well. Chopped nuts may be added for an extra touch. Icing is sufficient for 1 9x12-inch sheet cake, as well as a 9-inch 2 layer cake.

CARROT CAKE

Serves 10 to 12   Mrs. William N. Cork (Helen)

2	cups all-purpose flour
2	cups sugar
2	teaspoons baking soda
1	teaspoon salt
2	teaspoons cinnamon
4	eggs
1	cup cooking oil
4	cups grated raw carrots
1/2	cup pecans, chopped

CREAM CHEESE-MAPLE ICING:

4	tablespoons butter, softened
2	3-ounce packages cream cheese, softened
4-1/3	cups powdered sugar, sifted
1	teaspoon vanilla
1	teaspoon maple flavoring

Sift flour, sugar, soda, salt and cinnamon. Beat eggs until frothy; slowly beat in oil. Add flour mixture and beat until well blended. Beat in carrots and nuts. Pour into 3 greased and floured 8-inch round cake pans. Bake in 350 degree oven for 25 to 30 minutes or until cake tester comes out clean. When done, leave in pan for 10 minutes. Remove and cool thoroughly before icing. CREAM CHEESE-MAPLE ICING: Cream the cheese and butter. Add sugar, vanilla and maple flavoring. Add a little milk, if necessary, to aid in spreading.

CHOCOLATE CHEESECAKE

Serves 16 to 20   Mrs. Beattie E. Huff (Gladys)

18	Famous chocolate wafers	1	teaspoon vanilla
1/4	cup melted butter	2	cups sour cream
1/4	teaspoon cinnamon	1	cup sugar
1	8-ounce package Baker's semi-sweet chocolate (no other kind)	3	eggs
		2	teaspoons cocoa, sifted
		3/4	cup sweetened whipped cream
1-1/2 pounds cream cheese, softened		Chocolate shavings	

All ingredients must be at room temperature. Crush or process crumbs. Mix with butter and cinnamon. Grease bottom and sides of an 8-inch spring form pan. Press crumbs onto bottom and sides of pan. Chill. Melt chocolate in top of double boiler. Beat cream cheese until fluffy and smooth. Beat in sugar. Add eggs, one at a time, beating after each addition. Be sure that there are no lumps, as they will show in the chocolate cake. Beat in melted chocolate, cocoa and vanilla. Beat in sour cream. Pour into spring form pan. Bake at 325 degrees to 350 degrees for 1 hour. Open oven door and leave in oven 5 to 10 minutes more to keep from cracking. Cool at room temperature. Chill in refrigerator for at least 5 hours. Let stand at room temperature for several hours before serving. Garnish with 3/4 cup sweetened whipped cream. Make lattice lines on top and garnish with chocolate shavings. Freezes well, but put whipped cream on after thawing.

MINIATURE CHEESECAKES

Yield: 12 to 16   Mrs. Herbert Kirsh (Suzanne)

2	8-ounce packages cream cheese	1	teaspoon vanilla
3/4	cup sugar	12 to 16 vanilla wafers	
2	eggs	1	20-ounce can cherry pie filling
1	tablespoon lemon juice		

Line muffin tins with paper cupcake liners. Place 1 vanilla wafer in bottom of each liner. Combine remaining ingredients, except pie filling, and mix well. Spoon mixture over vanilla wafer. Bake for 20 minutes at 350 degrees. Cool thoroughly and place a small amount of cherry pie filling on top of miniature cheesecake.

VARIATION: Mrs. Marion H. Kinon (Reba)

Use foil cupcake liners, decrease sugar to 1/2 cup. Omit lemon juice, and bake at 350 degrees for 10 to 12 minutes.

GRAND MARNIER CHEESECAKE

Serves 15   Mrs. Frank McGill (Peggy)

1-1/4 cups graham cracker crumbs	Grated rind of 1 lemon
1/4 cup sugar	Grated rind of 1/2 orange
1/4 cup margarine	5 large eggs, room temperature
5 8-ounce packages cream cheese, softened	2 egg yolks
	1/4 cup heavy cream
1-3/4 cups sugar	1/3 to 1/2 cup Grand Marnier Liqueur
7 tablespoons flour	

Melt margarine, add crumbs and sugar. Mix thoroughly. Line sides and bottom of 10-inch spring form pan. Preheat oven to 500 degrees. Beat cheese until creamy, using electric mixer. Mix sugar, flour and grated rinds and gradually add to cheese. Add eggs and egg yolks, one at a time, beating thoroughly after each addition. Stir in cream and liqueur and mix thoroughly. Pour into prepared crumb mold and bake in preheated oven at 500 degrees for 10 minutes without opening oven door. Reduce heat to 200 degrees and bake 1-1/4 to 1-1/2 hours or until cake is firm. Remove and cool at room temperature away from drafts. Refrigerate for at least 5 hours.

VARIATION: Mrs. Hugh K. Leatherman (Jean)

Spread 1 20-ounce can cherry pie filling on top of cheesecake before serving.

GRETA'S ORIGINAL CHEESECAKE

Serves 6 to 8   Mrs. T. Bruce Smith, II (Dot)

1 cup milk	1 6-ounce package cream cheese
1/2 cup sugar	3 teaspoons lemon juice
1 envelope plain gelatin	1 9-ounce carton Cool Whip
1/2 cup sugar	Graham cracker crust

Heat the first 3 ingredients on low heat until they are melted. Set aside. Beat together the sugar and cream cheese and fold into the gelatin mixture. Add lemon juice. Fold Cool Whip into mixture and pour into graham cracker crust. Refrigerate for 6 hours.

CHOCOLATE CAKE

Serves 12 to 16   Mrs. J. F. Anderson, Jr. (Susan)
                                                      Mrs. Horace C. Smith (Dot)

1	cup self-rising flour	CHOCOLATE CHIP ICING:
1	stick soft margarine	1-1/2 cups sugar
1	16-ounce can Hersheys syrup	1/2 cup evaporated milk
1	cup sugar	3/4 cup chocolate chips
4	eggs	3/4 stick soft margarine
1	teaspoon vanilla	

Put all ingredients in a bowl and mix until smooth. Pour into a greased and floured 9x13-inch pan. Bake at 350 degrees for 30 minutes. Cool and spread with CHOCOLATE CHIP ICING: Cook sugar, margarine and milk for 2 minutes, stirring constantly. Add chocolate chips and beat by hand until chips have melted and icing is thick enough to spread on cake. Serve with ice cream, if desired.

CHOCOLATE CHIP-PECAN CAKE

Representative Bob Sheheen

1	cup butter	1	teaspoon salt
2	cups sugar	1	teaspoon baking soda
5	eggs	2	teaspoons vanilla
1	cup sour milk (1 cup milk	1/2	cup chopped pecans
	plus 3 tablespoons vinegar)	1	large package chocolate chips
2-1/2 cups plain flour			

Preheat oven to 350 degrees. Combine flour, salt and baking soda. Set aside. Cream butter and sugar, add vanilla. Add eggs, one at a time. Add flour mixture alternately with sour milk. Stir in pecans. Grease and flour 3 9-inch cake pans and fill with cake mixture. Sprinkle chocolate chips on top of batter. Bake 20 to 25 minutes at 350 degrees. Remove from pans immediately and cool on racks. Ice layers, with bottoms facing up, with RUM ICING.

RUM ICING

3	tablespoons cold milk	1/2	teaspoon salt
1	cup soft Parkay	1/2	teaspoon rum flavoring
1	box powdered sugar		

Whip soft Parkay with milk until fluffy. Add salt and rum flavoring. Add sugar by large spoonfuls until each is whipped into mixture. Spread between layers and over outside of cake.

DR. PEPPER CHOCOLATE CAKE

Yields: 2 tube pans or 72 cupcakes   Mrs. John C. Land, III (Marie)

4	cups plain flour	DR. PEPPER ICING:	
8	tablespoons cocoa	1/2	cup butter
3	teaspoons cinnamon	1/2	cup Dr. Pepper
1	teaspoon salt	6	tablespoons cocoa
2	teaspoons soda	1	cup chopped pecans
4	cups sugar	2	teaspoons vanilla
1	pound butter	2	boxes powdered sugar
4	eggs		
1	cup buttermilk		
4	teaspoons vanilla		
2	cups Dr. Pepper		

Sift together all dry ingredients. Set aside. Heat butter and Dr. Pepper until butter melts. Add eggs, vanilla and buttermilk and mix well. Add liquids to dry ingredients and beat until smooth. Batter will be very thin. Pour into greased and floured 11x17-inch pan and bake at 350 degrees for 30 minutes. Will fill 2 tube pans or 72 paper-lined cupcake tins. Bake tube cakes 60 minutes and cupcakes, 15 minutes. This cake must be iced while warm. DR. PEPPER ICING: Heat butter and Dr. Pepper. Do not boil. Add the next 4 ingredients and mix well.

$1,000,000 CHOCOLATE CAKE

Serves 12 to 16   Mrs. Nick A. Theodore (Emilie)

2	cups sugar	COCOA ICING:	
2	cups plain flour	6	tablespoons milk
1	cup water	4	tablespoons cocoa
1	cup oil	1	stick margarine
1	stick margarine	1	tablespoon vanilla
4	tablespoons cocoa	1	box powdered sugar
1/2	cup buttermilk		
2	eggs		
1	teaspoon soda		
Dash salt			

In a large bowl mix the sugar and flour. In a saucepan bring the next 4 ingredients to a boil and cook 1 minute, stirring constantly. Pour over sugar and flour. Beat well. Add the next 4 ingredients and pour into a greased and floured 9x13-inch pan. Bake at 350 degrees for 40 minutes. COCOA ICING: Combine first 4 ingredients; bring to a boil. Remove from stove and cool slightly. Add powdered sugar, beating well, and pour over hot cake.

CHOCOLATE ROLL

Serves 10   Mrs. Robert M. McLellan (Doris)

1/2 cup cake flour	FILLING:
1/2 teaspoon baking powder	1/2 pint whipping cream
1/4 teaspoon salt	2 teaspoons sugar
2 to 3 1-ounce squares Baker's un-	1 teaspoon vanilla
sweetened chocolate, melted	
4 eggs, separated	CHOCOLATE ICING:
3/4 cup sugar	1 ounce square Baker's
2 tablespoons sugar	unsweetened chocolate
1/4 teaspoon soda	1 tablespoon butter
3 tablespoons cold water	2 tablespoons melted Crisco
1 teaspoon vanilla	shortening
	1 teaspoon vanilla
	1 16-ounce box powdered sugar

Mix the flour, baking powder and salt. Beat the egg whites until stiff and beat in 1/4 cup sugar. Beat the yolks until thick and beat in the vanilla. Melt chocolate and add immediately 2 tablespoons sugar and cold water. Stir until thick and light and beat into the yolks with 1/2 cup sugar and soda. Fold into the egg whites, then fold in the flour mixture. With heavy wax paper, line the bottom of a 15x10-inch shallow pan. Butter the paper and pour in the mixture. Spread evenly. Bake in a 370 to 375 degree oven for 15 to 20 minutes or until done. Turn out on a towel or foil sprinkled with confectioners sugar. Pull off paper quickly. Cut edges off so cake will roll evenly. Roll in the towel and let cool for 30 minutes. Beat together the whipping cream, sugar and vanilla. Unroll and spread with the FILLING. Roll cake up like a jelly roll and wrap in wax paper and refrigerate. When cool, spread top and sides with CHOCOLATE ICING: Melt the chocolate, add butter and melted Crisco shortening. Add a little milk and vanilla. Mix with confectioners sugar. Will ice tops and sides of 2 chocolate rolls. Wrap in wax paper and refrigerate or freeze until ready to serve.

CAKES AND PIES

COCONUT CAKE

Serves 12 to 16   Mrs. Nick Theodore (Emilie)

1	18-1/2-ounce box Duncan Hines Deluxe II Yellow Cake Mix	1	cup milk
		1	9-ounce package frozen coconut
2	cups sugar	1	3-ounce package coconut
		1	9-ounce container Cool Whip

Prepare cake as directed on box and pour into a 13x9x2-inch pan and bake according to directions on box. Bring to a boil the sugar, milk and 9-ounce package of coconut. When cake comes from oven, spoon mixture over cake. Insert knife in about 6 places to allow mixture to penetrate. Cover with foil and cool. Spread thawed Cool Whip over cake and sprinkle with 3-ounces coconut. Replace foil and leave in refrigerator 2 to 3 days before serving.

DUMP CAKE

Congressman Floyd D. Spence

1	can cherry pie filling	1	can coconut
1	large can crushed pineapple	1	stick margarine
1	box Duncan Hines butter recipe cake mix	1/2	cup chopped nuts

Pour cherry pie filling, pineapple, cake mix and coconut in a 9x13-inch pan. Melt margarine and pour over all the ingredients. Over this sprinkle the chopped nuts. Bake at 350 degrees for 1 hour.

FAT LADIES

Yields 30 to 60 squares   Mrs. David E. Turnipseed (Cindy)

1	box German Chocolate Cake Mix	1	cup chopped pecans
1-1/2	sticks margarine, melted	40	caramels
1/3	cup evaporated milk	1/2	cup evaporated milk
12	ounce package semi-sweet chocolate chips		

In heavy saucepan, combine caramels and 1/2 cup milk. Cook over low heat, stirring constantly until caramels are melted (or melt in microwave). Set aside. Combine cake mix, margarine and 1/3 cup milk. Stir by hand until dough holds together. Press 1/2 of dough into a 9x13-inch pan which has been greased and floured. Bake at 350 degrees for 6 minutes. Remove from oven and sprinkle chocolate chips over baked layer. Then sprinkle pecans over the chips and then spread the caramel mix over the pecan layer. Crumb remaining cake mixture over top of caramel layer. Bake 18 to 30 minutes longer. It may appear not to be thoroughly cooked, but once it cools it will be soft and chewy. Cool before cutting into small squares. A very rich brownie-type square.

BITE SIZE FRUIT CAKES

Yields: 7 dozen   Mrs. Herbert Kirsh (Suzanne)

2	sticks butter	2	8-ounce boxes mixed candied
1	cup sugar		fruits
5	eggs	2	cups white raisins
2	cups plain flour	2	cups pecans, chopped
1-1/2	teaspoons baking powder	1	teaspoon almond flavoring
1	teaspoon salt	2	cups frozen coconut, thawed
1/2	cup orange juice	1/2	cup candied cherries

Cream butter and sugar. Add eggs, 1 at a time. Add flour, baking powder, salt and orange juice. Stir in nuts and fruit. Bake in small tart shell papers in a 300 degree oven for 25 to 30 minutes.

FUDGE CAKE

Serves 16   Mrs. R. M. Kenan (Sinclair)

2	cups self-rising flour	COCOA NUT FROSTING:	
2	cups sugar	1	cup nuts, chopped
1/2	cup sour cream	1	box confectioners sugar
2	eggs	1	stick margarine
2	sticks margarine	6	tablespoons milk
1	cup water	3-1/2	tablespoons cocoa
3-1/2	tablespoons cocoa		

Mix first 4 ingredients until well blended. Cook to boiling point the margarine, water and cocoa. Add cooked mixture to the blended batter. Pour into greased and floured 9x13-inch pan. Bake for 25 minutes at 350 degrees or until cake tester comes out clean. Spread with COCOA NUT FROSTING while hot. COCOA NUT FROSTING: Cook margarine, milk and cocoa over low heat. Stir well; do not boil. Remove from heat. Add confectioners sugar. Blend and add vanilla and chopped nuts. Pour over hot cake. Cut into squares.

HOT MILK CAKE

Serves 12   Mrs. B. L. Hendricks, Jr. (Carolyn)

4	eggs		Pinch salt
2	cups sugar	1	teaspoon vanilla
2	cups flour	1	cup milk
1	tablespoon baking powder	1/4	pound butter or margarine

Beat eggs until creamy; add sugar and beat well. Mix flour, baking powder and salt. Add to sugar mixture and beat well. Add vanilla. Have milk and butter hot, but not boiling. Add milk to cake mixture. Pour into a greased 13x9x2-inch pan and bake at 375 degrees for about 15 or 20 minutes. Makes an excellent shortcake. Put crushed strawberries or peaches on top, cover top and sides with whipped cream. Add whole strawberry or peach slice on middle of each serving. Serve individual squares on 12-inch crystal plates. This is also good with a COCONUT FILLING: Mix together 1/4 cup margarine, 3/4 cup brown sugar, 3 tablespoons thin cream and 1 cup coconut and cook about 5 minutes or until thick, add 1/2 cup chopped nuts. Spread on cake and return to oven to brown slightly. Let cool in pan and cut in squares.

ITALIAN CREAM CAKE

Serves 12   Mrs. Hugh K. Leatherman (Jean)

1	stick margarine	1	cup chopped nuts
1/2	cup vegetable shortening	5	egg whites, stiffly beaten
2	cups sugar		
5	egg yolks		CREAM CHEESE FROSTING:
2	cups all-purpose flour	1	8-ounce package cream cheese,
1	teaspoon soda		softened
1	cup buttermilk	1/2	stick margarine
1	teaspoon vanilla	1	box powdered sugar
1	small can angel flake coconut	1	teaspoon vanilla
			Chopped pecans

Cream margarine and shortening. Add sugar and beat until mixture is smooth. Add egg yolks and beat well. Combine flour and soda and add to creamed mixture alternately with buttermilk. Stir in vanilla. Add coconut and chopped nuts. Fold in stiffly beaten egg whites. Pour batter into 3 greased and floured 8-inch cake pans. Bake at 350 degrees for 25 minutes or until cake tester comes out clean. Cool. Frost with CREAM CHEESE FROSTING: Beat cream cheese and margarine until smooth. Add sugar and mix well. Add vanilla and beat until smooth. Spread between layers, on top and sides of cake. Sprinkle top with pecans.

MANDARIN ORANGE CAKE

Serves 16 to 20   Mrs. Parker Evatt (Jane)

1   18-1/2-ounce box yellow   PINEAPPLE FILLING:
    cake mix   1   9-ounce carton Cool Whip
3/4 cup vegetable oil   1   3-1/2 -ounce box vanilla instant
4   eggs   pudding mix
1   11-ounce can mandarin oranges   1   20-ounce can crushed unsweeten-
    (with juice)   ed pineapple, slightly drained

Combine first 4 ingredients together and beat with mixer according to package directions. Pour into 3 foil-lined and greased 9-inch cake pans and bake 15 to 20 minutes at 350 degrees or until cake tester comes out clean. Cool thoroughly. Combine pudding mix with crushed pineapple and some juice. Fold in thawed Cool Whip. Spread between layers, on top and sides of cake. Refrigerate overnight. Keeps for days in refrigerator.

PINEAPPLE ICE BOX CAKE

Serves 12   Mrs. Edward Simpson (Maureen)

1   cup crushed vanilla wafers   1/4 pound butter
1   3-ounce box lemon gelatin   1   13-ounce can crushed pineapple
3/4 cup boiling water   1   cup pecans, chopped
3/4 cup sugar   3   egg whites, stiffly beaten
3   egg yolks

Dissolve gelatin in boiling water. Cream sugar, butter and egg yolks for 15 minutes. Add crushed pineapple, chopped pecans and crushed vanilla wafers. Add gelatin and stiffly beaten egg whites. Line pan with wafers. Pour in mixture. Cover with crushed wafers. Place in refrigerator for 12 hours. Serve with whipped cream. This was my grandmother's recipe. She insisted the egg yolks be beaten 15 minutes.

CREAM CHEESE POUND CAKE

Serves 10 to 12   Mrs. Woody M. McKay (Nancy)

3   sticks margarine or butter   3   cups sifted cake flour
1   8-ounce package cream cheese   1-1/2 teaspoons vanilla
3   cups sugar   Dash salt
6   large eggs

For best results have all ingredients at room temperature. Cream margarine, cream cheese and sugar until light and fluffy. Add eggs, one at a time, until well blended. Stir in flour. Spoon mixture into large greased and floured tube pan and bake at 300 degrees for 1 hour and 20 minutes. For small tube pan, cook 50 minutes or until a cake tester comes out clean.

BLACK WALNUT POUND CAKE

Serves 10 to 12   Mrs. Timothy A. Brett (Reta)

CAKE:

2	cups sugar
3	eggs
1	cup oil
1	7-3/4-ounce jar junior prunes
1	tablespoon allspice
2	cups self-rising flour
1	cup walnuts, chopped

CREAM CHEESE ICING:

1	box powdered sugar
1	8-ounce package cream cheese, softened
1/2	stick butter
1	teaspoon vanilla

Cream sugar and eggs. Beat in the prunes and allspice; add the flour. Stir in the walnuts. Pour into a greased and floured tube pan and bake at 350 degrees for 1-1/2 hours. Do not preheat oven. Remove from pan and ice with CREAM CHEESE ICING: Cream the cheese and butter. Add sugar and vanilla. Add a little milk, if necessary, to aid in spreading.

GERMAN CHOCOLATE POUND CAKE

Serves 10 to 12   Mrs. Hugh K. Leatherman (Jean)

1	4-ounce bar German sweet chocolate
2	sticks margarine
3	cups sugar
1/2	cup shortening
5	eggs
3	cups flour
1	teaspoon baking powder
1/2	teaspoon salt
1	cup milk

| 1 | teaspoon almond extract |
| 1 | teaspoon vanilla |

COCOA-MOCHA FROSTING:

6	tablespoons coffee
1	teaspoon vanilla
1	box powdered sugar
1	cup sifted cocoa
1/2	teaspoon salt
6	tablespoons butter or margarine

Melt chocolate and margarine together. Cream sugar and shortening and add to chocolate mixture. Add the eggs and mix well. Sift flour, baking powder and salt, and add alternately with milk. Add almond and vanilla, and mix well. Bake in a greased tube pan at 350 degrees for 1-1/4 to 1-1/2 hours. When cool, mix together COCOA-MOCHA FROSTING and spread on cake. COCOA-MOCHA FROSTING: Combine medium strength cold coffee and vanilla in mixing bowl. Sift sugar and all dry ingredients together and add to liquids in three parts, beating until smooth after each addition. Gradually beat in soft butter or margarine, 1 tablespoon at a time. Beat until smooth and creamy. Frosting is enough to spread on a 2-layer 9-inch cake. (I prefer to use half of this recipe for a cake in a tube pan.)

SOUR CREAM POUND CAKE

Serves 10 to 12   Mrs. Robert L. Helmly (Vera)

3	cups sugar	1/4	teaspoon salt
3	cups cake flour	1/2	teaspoon soda
8	eggs	1/2	pound butter
1-1/2	cups sour cream	1	teaspoon vanilla, optional

Sift flour, soda and salt together. Set aside. Cream butter and sugar; mix thoroughly. Add eggs, 1 at a time, and beat mixture until light. Stir the flour mixture into the egg mixture alternately with the sour cream. Add the vanilla and pour into a well greased and lightly floured tube pan. Put into cold oven. Turn oven to 300 degrees for one hour. Increase heat to 325 degrees for 30 minutes. Turn out, and while cake is warm, pour over the top a lemon juice and sugar glaze. Freezes well.

VARIATION: Mrs. Herbert Kirsh (Suzanne)

To make a SOUR CREAM MARBLE POUND CAKE, melt 2 1-ounce squares unsweetened chocolate. Add 2 tablespoons sugar, 2 tablespoons boiled water and 1/4 teaspoon baking soda and mix well. Add to half of batter. Alternate the chocolate batter with the plain part of batter as you pour into a tube pan. Lightly stir them together for 15 seconds.

CAROLINA POUND CAKE

Serves 10 to 12   Senator "Liz" Patterson

2	sticks butter or margarine	2	teaspoons vanilla
1/2	cup shortening	1	teaspoon lemon extract
3	cups sugar		
5	eggs		LEMON ICING:
1	cup milk	1	box powdered sugar
3-1/4	cups plain flour	1	tablespoon shortening
1/2	teaspoon baking powder		Juice and rind of 1 lemon
1/2	teaspoon salt		Canned milk (as needed)

Cream butter and shortening. Add sugar gradually. Add one egg at a time and beat until fluffy. Add dry ingredients alternately with milk and mix well. Add flavoring. Bake in tube pan at 325 degrees approximately 1-1/2 hours or until cake tester comes out clean. Cool thoroughly before removing from pan.

VARIATION: Mrs. James E. Lockemy (Ellen)

Vary flavoring using 1 teaspoon almond or black walnut. May add fruit or nuts.

CAKES AND PIES

WHITE POUND CAKE

Serves 10 to 12   Mrs. Herbert Kirsh (Suzanne)

2 sticks margarine
1/2 cup Crisco
3 cups sugar
4 cups plain flour, sifted
1/2 teaspoon baking powder
1 cup whole milk
5 eggs
Dash salt
1 teaspoon each almond, vanilla and lemon extract

WHITE BIRTHDAY ICING:
1 egg white
1/4 cup milk
1 box powdered sugar
1/4 to 1 cup Crisco
1 teaspoon vanilla
1/2 teaspoon almond extract, optional
Pinch salt, optional

Have all ingredients at room temperature. Sift together flour, baking powder and salt. Set aside. Cream sugar, margarine and Crisco until very soft and fluffy. Beat in eggs, 1 at a time, beating thoroughly after each is added. Add flour mixture alternately with milk and almond, vanilla and lemon extract. Beat for 2 minutes. Pour batter into a greased 9-inch tube pan. Put in cold oven. Turn oven to 300 degrees and bake 1 hour and 30 minutes or until cake tester comes out clean. Cool. Sprinkle with confectioners sugar, or spread with WHITE BIRTHDAY ICING, FRUIT PUDDING, CHOCOLATE FUDGE ICING or an icing of your choice. WHITE BIRTHDAY ICING: Beat egg white until stiff, add Crisco and sugar. Beat in milk and flavoring. Add salt and cream until icing is smooth.

CHOCOLATE FUDGE ICING

Mrs. Ralph Ellis (Eleanor)

1-1/2 cups white sugar
1/4 cup cocoa (Hershey's)
2 tablespoons white Karo syrup
1/4 cup hot milk
1 stick butter or margarine
1 teaspoon vanilla

Mix ingredients in a heavy saucepan on lowest heat. Do not stir while cooking. Bring to a rolling boil. Cool. Beat until consistency to spread. Icing is enough to spread on a 3-layer cake or 1 tube cake.

For a CHOCOLATE POUND CAKE follow recipe above for WHITE POUND CAKE, but omit almond and lemon extract and add 1/2 cup cocoa. Use only 3 cups plain flour and use 1 tsp. baking powder. Let cool in pan. For a CHOCOLATE BIRTHDAY ICING follow recipe for WHITE BIRTHDAY ICING, but omit almond extract. Add 1 to 2 squares Bakers unsweetened chocolate

PRUNE CAKE

Serves 12 to 16   Mrs. Robert N. McLellan (Doris)

1 cup salad corn oil	BUTTERMILK ICING:
1-1/2 cups sugar	1 cup granulated sugar
3 eggs	1/2 cup buttermilk
2 cups plain flour	1 tablespoon dark corn syrup
1/2 cup buttermilk	1/2 teaspoon soda
1 cup cooked pitted prunes,	1 stick butter
cut into small pieces	1 teaspoon vanilla
1 cup pecans, chopped fine	1/4 teaspoon salt
1 teaspoon each cinnamon, allspice,	
salt, vanilla, nutmeg and soda	

Sift together flour, cinnamon, allspice, nutmeg, salt and soda. Set aside. Blend sugar and cooking oil, add eggs and blend. Add buttermilk and sifted dry ingredients alternately. Add vanilla, nuts and prunes. Mix well and pour into a greased 13x9x2-inch baking pan. Cook at 300 degrees for 1 hour. BUTTERMILK ICING: Start icing 15 minutes after cake has been put in oven and boil until it is honey colored. Do not beat. Pour over cake when you take it from the oven and let set in pan. Freezes well.

RUM NUT CAKE

Serves 10 to 12   Mrs. Donald H. Holland (Betty)

1 18-1/2-ounce box Duncan	1 cup pecans, chopped
Hines golden cake mix	
1-3/4-ounce box vanilla instant	RUM GLAZE:
pudding mix	1 stick margarine
1-1/2 cups light rum	1 cup sugar
1/2 cup water	1/4 cup rum
1/2 cup vegetable oil	1/4 cup water
4 eggs	

Put pecans in bottom of a bundt pan. Set aside. In a large bowl mix the cake and pudding mix. Add eggs, rum, oil and water. Beat for 2 minutes and pour carefully into a bundt pan over the pecans. Bake 50 to 60 minutes at 350 degrees. Leave in pan and carefully place knife around sides and center of cake. Boil the RUM GLAZE for 3 minutes and pour the hot glaze over cake at once. Allow to cool for 30 minutes before removing from pan.

SPONGE CAKE

Serves 12 to 18   Mrs. John C. Land, III (Marie)

4 eggs	1/2 teaspoon salt
3/4 cup sugar	1 teaspoon baking powder
3/4 cup all-purpose flour	1/2 teaspoon almond or vanilla extract

Preheat oven to 350 degrees. Grease a 15-1/2x10-1/2-inch pan. Line with wax paper and grease wax paper. In a large bowl, with mixer on high speed, beat eggs until foamy. Gradually sprinkle in sugar; beating until fluffy and very pale yellow, about 7 minutes. At low speed beat in flour, baking powder, salt and extract. Spread evenly in prepared greased 15-1/2x10-1/2-inch pan (or 2 8-inch round pans). Bake 20 minutes or until cake springs back when lightly touched in a 350 degree oven. Cool about 10 minutes in pan on rack. Invert from pan onto cooking rack and remove paper; cool thoroughly.

TIPSY SQUIRE

Serves 8 to 10   Mrs. Robert N. McLellan (Doris)

A 15-1/2x10-1/2-inch Spongecake (recipe above) cut into squares and split horizontally or 12 split ladyfingers	3 tablespoons sugar
	1/4 teaspoon salt
	4 egg yolks
	1 cup heavy cream, whipped
1/3 cup seedless black raspberry jam	1 tablespoon sugar
1/2 cup wine	1 teaspoon vanilla
1-1/2 cups milk	1/4 cup toasted slivered almonds

Spread spongecake with jam, cover with a top layer, and put in a 15-1/2x 10-1/2-inch glass dish. Pour wine over the top and refrigerate about 4 hours. Cook the milk, sugar, salt and yolks over low heat, stirring constantly, until thickened. Do not allow to come near the boiling point. Whip cream, sugar and vanilla until stiff. Add the custard to the spongecake in the dish and top with whipped cream and toasted almonds just before serving. A true Irish version of the classic trifle.

WHISKEY CAKE

Serves 10 to 12   Mrs. Alex S. Macaulay (Maria)

1/2 cup butter	1 9-inch freshly baked single-layer white or yellow cake, cooled
1 cup sugar	
1 cup bourbon, cognac or rum	3/4 cup confectioners sugar

Heat butter and sugar until bubbling. Stir in liquor. Punch large holes with a 2-prong fork in the top of cake. Pour topping over sides and top of cake. Just before serving, sieve confectioners sugar generously over the cake.

SOUR CREAM COFFEE CAKE

Serves 8 to 10   Senator "Liz" Patterson

1	18-ounce box Duncan Hines White Cake Mix	4	eggs
1	cup sour cream	4	tablespoons brown sugar
1/2	cup sugar	2	teaspoons cinnamon
3/4	cup Wesson Oil	1	cup chopped nuts

Mix first five ingredients together and beat until smooth. Put in pan in layers: a layer of batter, cinnamon, sugar and nuts; another layer of batter; cinnamon, sugar and nuts; and top with layer of batter. Bake at 325 degrees for 1 hour.

PIE PASTRY

Yield: 2 crusts   Mrs. Larry A. Martin (Susan)

2	cups all-purpose, unbleached flour	4 to 7 tablespoons ice water
1/2	teaspoon salt	1 cup cold fat (butter, shortening, margarine or a combination

Sift flour and salt together. Cut shortening into flour mixture until mixture is the consistency of coarse meal. Add water. Never let it form a ball. Shape the pastry into the form it will take when rolled out, a circle or a rectangle. If the dough is crumbly, it may be sprinkled with water before being wrapped tightly in plastic wrap or foil. Refrigerate at least 1 hour or overnight. May be frozen for 1 to 2 months. Defrost overnight in refrigerator or 1 to 2 hours at room temperature. Remove dough from refrigerator 1/2 hour before rolling it out, if hard. Roll between 2 sheets of wax paper or on lightly floured pastry cloth or board. Lift to pie plate. Trim and crimp edges of pastry. Crumple enough wax paper to fill entire shell and extend over edge; place in shell. Fill with dry beans, rice, or commercial pie weights. Place in refrigerator 10 to 20 minutes for dough to relax before baking. Bake at 375 degrees for 15 to 20 minutes. Remove beans or rice and paper, reserving beans or rice for future pastries. Fill as desired and bake if necessary. This "blind baking" results in a firm, nicely textured crust with no sogginess. Baked crusts may be kept in an airtight bag or frozen. If you like a brown pie crust, sprinkle a little granulated sugar on the top or brush lightly with egg beaten with a little water.

CAKES AND PIES

COCONUT CRUMB CRUST

Yield: 1 9-inch crust   Mrs. Larry A. Martin (Susan)

1-1/2 cups tender-thin flaked   1/4 cup finely crushed graham
      coconut   crackers, ginger snaps, vanilla
2   tablespoons butter, melted   wafers, or chocolate wafers
2   tablespoons sugar   Pinch of cinnamon

Combine coconut and butter and mix well. Add sugar, cinnamon and cookie
crumbs, mixing thoroughly. Press firmly on bottom and sides of pie pan.
Bake in a 355 degree oven for 10 to 12 minutes or until lightly browned.
Cool. Fill crust with coffee ice cream or ice cream of your choice. Serve
immediately, or deep freeze to serve later, or fill with chiffon or cream pie
filling and chill until firm.

COOKIE CRUMB CRUST

Yield: 1 9-inch crust   Mrs. Larry A. Martin (Susan)

1-1/2 cups chocolate wafer, graham   Melted butter (6 tablespoons with
      cracker, ginger snap or vanilla   graham cracker crumbs; 1/4
      wafer crumbs   cup with other crumbs)
1/4 cup powdered sugar

Cookies may be crushed with rolling pin, in blender or in food processor.
Mix sugar and melted butter with cookie crumbs. Press mixture on sides and
bottom of pie pan. Bake at 350 degrees for 10 to 15 minutes. Cookie selection depends on choice of filling. Chopped nuts or 1/2 teaspoon cinnamon
may be added to crust mixture before baking.

ANGEL PIE

Yield: 1 9-inch pie   Mrs. William Cork (Helen)

3   egg whites   1   cup chopped pecans
1   teaspoon vanilla   1   teaspoon baking powder
1   cup sugar   1/2   cup whipping cream
1   cup graham cracker crumbs

Beat egg whites and vanilla until soft peaks form; gradually add sugar, beating until stiff peaks form. Combine graham cracker crumbs, pecans and baking powder; fold into meringue mixture. Spread evenly in greased and floured 9-inch pie plate. Bake in a 325 degree oven for 20 to 25 minutes. Cool
completely. Cut pie in wedges and serve with a dollop of whipped cream on
top.

OCONEE APPLE PIE

Makes 1 9-inch pie   Mrs. Robert N. McLellan (Doris)

Pastry for 2-crust (9-inch) pie   1 or 2 tablespoons flour, if apples are
6   apples
1/2 to 2/3 cup sugar   juicy
1/4   teaspoon salt   2   tablespoons butter
1/2   teaspoon cinnamon   1/4   teaspoon nutmeg

Pare and slice apples. Sift dry ingredients together and mix with apples. Line a 9-inch pie pan with pastry, fill with apple mixture, dot with butter and cover with top crust. Bake in a very hot 450 degree oven for 15 minutes; reduce temperature to moderate 350 degrees and bake 45 minutes longer.

JEAN'S ORIGINAL APPLESAUCE PIE

Yield: 1 8 or 9-inch pie   Mrs. J. Verne Smith (Jean)

2   16-1/2-ounce cans applesauce   3   tablespoons fresh lemon juice
1/2   cup sugar   6   tablespoons melted butter
1-1/2 teaspoons cinnamon   2   8-inch or 9-inch frozen pie shells,
1/2   teaspoon nutmeg   thawed

Cook the bottom pie crust at 400 degrees for 5 minutes. Blend together the first 6 ingredients and pour into the baked pie crust. Cover the applesauce mixture with the other pie crust, pressing loosely on the sides of the pie pan. Bake in preheated 350 degree oven for 30 minutes or until brown. It is delicious served hot and topped with ice cream.

GRANDMA'S CHESS PIE

Mrs. James E. Lockemy (Ellen)

1/2   cup pure white butter   1   teaspoon vanilla
1-1/2 cups sugar   1   teaspoon vinegar
3   eggs   1   teaspoon cornmeal

Mix butter with sugar. Beat eggs and add to butter and sugar. Beat vanilla, cornmeal and vinegar and add to eggs, butter and sugar. Pour into pie plate. Bake at 350 degrees for 30 minutes until done.

CHOCOLATE CHESS PIE

Mrs. Marion Kinon (Reba)

1	stick margarine	2	eggs
1	1-ounce square unsweetened chocolate	1	teaspoon vanilla
1	cup granulated sugar	1	unbaked pie shell

Beat sugar and eggs until fluffy. Melt margarine and chocolate squares over low heat. Cool. Stir in sugar and egg mixture. Mix well. Add vanilla. Put into unbaked pie shell and bake at 325 degrees for 35 minutes.

CHOCOLATE CHIP PIE

Mrs. Grady L. Patterson, Jr. (Margie)

1/2	cup flour	1	cup pecans, chopped
1	cup sugar	1	cup chocolate chips
2	eggs, beaten	1	teaspoon vanilla
1	stick margarine, melted	1	unbaked pie crust

Preheat oven to 350 degrees. Mix flour and sugar. Add eggs, margarine, nuts, chocolate chips and vanilla. Pour into unbaked pie crust and bake at 350 degrees for 30 minutes.

VARIATION:

Mrs. Herbert Kirsh (Suzanne)

Use 1/2 cup white sugar and 1/2 cup brown sugar. Bake 325 degrees for 1 hour. Cool. Serve with whipped cream.

JOE'S CHOCOLATE PIE

Representative Joe Anderson, Jr.

1-1/2 or 2 squares semi-sweet chocolate		3	egg yolks
1	cup sugar	2	tablespoons butter
3	tablespoons flour	1	teaspoon vanilla
1-1/2 cups scalded milk (bring it to a boil)		1	pie shell, baked
		3	egg whites
		3	tablespoons sugar

Melt chocolate in double boiler. Stir sugar and flour together. Add to chocolate with the hot scalded milk using a wire whip. Separate eggs and reserve the whites for the meringue (remember to put the egg whites in a grease free container). Beat the yolks and add a little of the hot mixture to them gradually. Add this to hot mixture, beating with the wire whip. Cook until very thick. Add the butter and vanilla. Pour into the baked pie shell and top with MERINGUE: Beat egg whites until foamy and add sugar gradually.

WORLD'S FINEST CHOCOLATE PIE

Serves 8   Mrs. James Craven (Beverly)

2	envelopes Dream Whip Topping	1/4	cup Orange Liqueur
2	2-1/2-ounce World's Finest Chocolate bars	1	9-inch pie crust, baked

Prepare Dream Whip according to directions. Whip in melted chocolate and Orange Liqueur. Pour into baked pie shell and chill. Garnish with whipped cream dots and shaved chocolate, if desired. For extra special treat use chocolate cracker crumb crust.

COCONUT PIE

Yield: 1 10-inch pie   Mrs. T. Bruce Smith, II (Dot)

1-1/4	cups sugar	3	eggs
2-1/2	cups sweet milk	1-1/4	cups coconut, frozen variety
3	teaspoons butter	1	10-inch pie shell, unbaked

Beat sugar and eggs until fluffy. Add milk and beat. Stir in coconut. Pour into pie shell and dot the top with butter. Bake in a 400 degree oven until it begins to brown, then turn down to 300 degrees and bake until filling is firm. Don't overbake.

CRUMB PIE

Mrs. Dick Elliott (Anne)

3	egg whites	1	cup Waverly Wafer crumbs
1	cup sugar	1	cup chopped nuts

Beat egg whites until stiff. Gradually beat in sugar, fold in crumbs and nuts. Pour into a greased pie pan. Bake at 325 degrees for 25 minutes. Let cool completely. Put Cool Whip on top, let chill for 2-3 hours. Good served with dry roasted nuts on the side.

CHOCOLATE NUT PIE

Serves 8   Mrs. Thomas F. Hartnett (Bonnie)

1	cup sugar	1	cup pecans
1/2	cup sifted flour	1	6-ounce package chocolate chips
2	eggs, lightly beaten	1	teaspoon vanilla
1	stick butter, melted and cooled	1	pie shell

Mix sugar and flour. Add eggs, butter, vanilla, chocolate chips and pecans. Mix well after each ingredient. Bake one hour at 325 degrees. Do not overbake.

CAKES AND PIES

JAPANESE FRUIT PIE

Mrs. William J. McLeod (Sara)

2/3	stick margarine, room temperature	1	tablespoon vinegar
1	cup sugar	1/2	cup coconut
2	eggs	1/2	cup chopped nuts
1	teaspoon vanilla	1/2	cup white raisins

Combine sugar, vanilla, eggs and vinegar with margarine. Blend. Add coconut, nuts and raisins. Pour into 9-inch pie crust. Bake at 325 degrees for 50 minutes or until done.

BETTY'S FRUIT PIE

Serves 4

Mrs. T. W. Edwards, Jr. (Dottie)

1	cup self-rising flour	3/4	cup buttermilk or sweet milk
1/2	cup sugar		

Mix above ingredients together. Cut up one stick margarine in bottom of pan; pour mixture into pan. Then add desired amount of sweetened fruit of your choice. Bake 350 degrees for 45 minutes.

VERNE'S LEMON MERINGUE PIE

Mrs. Verne Smith (Jean)

1	9-inch baked pie shell	2	tablespoons grated lemon peel
1/3	cup cornstarch or flour	2	tablespoons butter
1-1/2	cups sugar	4	egg whites, room temperature
1/4	teaspoon salt	1/4	teaspoon cream of tartar
4	egg yolks, slightly beaten	1/2	cup sugar
1/2	cup fresh lemon juice		

In small saucepan or double boiler, combine cornstarch, sugar and salt. Gradually add 1-1/2 cups water, stirring until smooth over medium heat. Bring to boil, stirring constantly, boil 1 minute. Remove from heat and quickly stir half of hot mixture into egg yolks, mixing well. Return to saucepan.Bring to boil over medium heat, stirring constantly. Boil 1 minute. Remove from heat and stir in lemon juice, peel and butter. Pour into pie shell. MERINGUE: Preheat oven to 400 degrees. Make meringue by beating egg whites with cream of tartar until soft peaks form. Gradually beat in sugar and beat until stiff peaks form. Spread meringue over hot filling, sealing to edge of crust. Bake about 9 minutes, or until golden. Cool on wire rack at least 1 hour before serving.

"IMPOSSIBLE PIE"

Mrs. Nick Theodore (Emilie)

4 eggs
1/2 stick butter
2 cups milk
1 cup shredded coconut
1/2 teaspoon baking powder

1 cup sugar
1/2 cup flour
1/4 teaspoon salt
1 teaspoon vanilla

Combine all ingredients in blender. Mix until smooth. Pour into a well greased 10-inch pie pan. Bake at 350 degrees for 1 hour and 5 minutes. Crust will form on bottom, custard in middle, and coconut on top.

LIME PIE

Mrs. W. B. Hawkins (Sarah)

1 chocolate pie shell
1 6-ounce can frozen limeade
1 14-ounce can condensed milk

1 carton Cool Whip
4 drops green food coloring

Mix limeade and condensed milk. Add sour cream, Cool Whip and food coloring. Mix well and pour into shell. Top with grated bitter chocolate.

LIME JELLO PIE

Mrs. Jarvis Klapman (Arlene)

2 eggs
1 cup sugar
1-1/2 cups pineapple juice
1 3-ounce package lime gelatin

1 13-ounce can evaporated milk
1 box vanilla wafers
Few drops green food coloring, if desired

Beat eggs, add sugar and beat these together. Add pineapple juice and bring these ingredients to a boil. Remove from heat and dissolve gelatin in the mixture. Cool at room temperature. Whip the milk until very stiff and add the cooled gelatin mixture and food coloring. Pour into 3 small or 2 large pie pans lined with vanilla wafers. Chill for several hours. Serve with a scoop of whipped cream and garnish with a maraschino cherry.

CAROLINA PEACH PIE

Mrs. I. S. Leevy Johnson (Doris)

8	fresh South Carolina peaches, cut in halves	1/4	cup flour
1	9-inch pie shell		Pinch salt
3/4	cup sugar	1/2	pint heavy cream

Combine sugar, flour and salt in a small mixing bowl. Sprinkle half of this mixture on pie shell. Place peach halves on shell. Sprinkle remaining mixture over peaches and pour on cream until covered. Bake at 350 degrees for 45 minutes. Allow enough time in baking for cream and flour mixture to thicken to a sauce like consistency.

OLD TIME PECAN PIE

Representative Lewis Phillips

3	eggs	1	teaspoon vanilla
1	cup white Karo syrup		Dash salt
1/2	cup sugar	1	cup pecans
1/2	stick margarine	1	pie shell

Beat eggs, melt butter and combine with other ingredients. Pour into pie crust and top with pecans. Bake at 275 degrees for 60 minutes.

BRUCE'S FAVORITE POTATO PIE

Mrs. T. Bruce Smith, II (Dot)

2	cups sweet potatoes, cooked and mashed	1/2	stick margarine, melted
1	cup milk	1	teaspoon vanilla
1	egg	1/2	teaspoon allspice
3/4	cup sugar		Pinch salt

Mix together and pour into 2 baked pie shells. Bake at 325 degrees until firm, about 30 minutes. This is an original recipe given to me by my grandmother, Pearl Norwood, many years ago.

SOUR CREAM PUMPKIN PIE

Yields: 1 9-inch pie   Mrs. Robert N. McLellan (Doris)

4	3-ounce packages cream cheese	2	eggs plus 2 egg yolks
3/4	cup sugar	1	cup cooked or canned pumpkin
1-1/2	tablespoons flour	1/8	teaspoon cinnamon
1	teaspoon grated orange peel	1	9-inch graham cracker crust,
1/2	teaspoon grated lemon peel		unbaked

In electric mixer blend together cheese, sugar, flour and grated peels. Add eggs and egg yolks; beat at medium speed until smooth. Mix in pumpkin and cinnamon; continue beating until light and smooth. Pour into prepared crust. Bake at 350 degrees for 40 minutes or until custard is set. Remove and spread with the following mixture: 2 cups sour cream, 3 tablespoons sugar and 1 teaspoon vanilla. Bake 10 minutes longer. Remove from oven, cool and spread with a thin layer of cold sour cream.

STRAWBERRY PIE

Serves 8 - 10   Mrs. Jarvis Klapman (Arlene)

1	3-ounce package Wild Strawberry gelatin	1	pint strawberries, sliced lengthwise
1	cup sugar	2	8-inch pie shells, baked
1	cup boiling water	8	ounces Cool Whip or other topping, optional
3	tablespoons cornstarch		
1	cup cold water		

Dissolve the gelatin and sugar in the boiling water in a saucepan. Stir the cornstarch into the cold water until it has a smooth consistency, then add it to the gelatin mixture and boil to a clear glaze which begins to thicken. Stir constantly, it may require 10-15 minutes. Remove from burner and cool to lukewarm. Place a layer of strawberries in baked pie shells. Pour the gelatin mixture over this and refrigerate for several hours or overnight before serving. Top with whipped topping or ice cream.

SOUTH CAROLINA STRAWBERRY PIE

Serves 8   Mrs. Carroll A. Campbell, Jr. (Iris)

1	9-inch baked pie shell	1	cup sugar
1	3-ounce package cream cheese, softened	3	tablespoons corn starch
1	quart strawberries	1	cup whipping cream

Blend the cheese with a little cream to make it smooth for spreading. Spread mixture over bottom of baked pie shell. Wash and drain strawberries and place half of them over cheese spread with tips up. Mash rest of strawberries and place them in a saucepan; bring to a boil. To this add the sugar and corn starch; stir together well, and cook until thick. Rub mixture through a sieve and pour over berries in pie shell. Refrigerate until well set. Top with whipped cream.

VINEGAR PIE

Yield: 1 pie   Mrs. John I. Rogers (Carolyn)

1	stick margarine, melted and cooled	1	tablespoon vanilla
1-1/2	cups sugar	2	tablespoons vinegar
2	tablespoons flour	3	eggs
		1	9-inch pie shell, unbaked

Combine first 6 ingredients, blending well. Pour into pie shell. Bake at 300 degrees for 45 minutes.

COCONUT CHESS PIE

Yield: 1 pie   Mrs. B. E. Thrailkill, Jr. (Peggy)

1	stick melted margarine	1	teaspoon vanilla
1-1/2	cups sugar	1	can Angel Flake Coconut (1-1/3 cups)
3	large eggs, beaten		Unbaked pie shell
1	tablespoon vinegar		

Combine all ingredients and pour into pie shell and bake at 350 degrees for 1 hour.

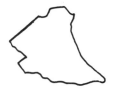

Florence County grew up around the town of Florence, an important trading center for farmers, a train center, and tourist stopover, since it is half-way between New York City and Florida. It took twelve years of debate before the four bordering counties agreed to give up rich portions of their territory to create Florence County in 1888.

The history of the town of Florence might have been much different if Colonel Eli Gregg, a large landowner in Mars Bluff during the 1850s, had not held a strong prejudice against the workers brought in by railroads. He blocked the building of the railroad depot near his store, and the Manchester Railroad had to resort to a virtual pine wilderness seven miles away to erect a station. The place locally referred to as "Wilds" after a local family, became by 1859 the junction of three different railroad lines. The budding metropolis was renamed "Florence" in honor of the infant daughter of General William Harllee who was the head of the first railroad and enthusiastic booster of the young town.

As a railhead, Florence gained in importance during the Civil War. Troops and supplies were channeled through the town and later, the injured and captured filled the hospitals and a prison camp that had been built for their accommodation.

Throughout the political and economic uncertainties of Reconstruction, the railroads remained the mainstay of Florence's economic growth. Today, Florence is one of the fastest growing towns in the state, drawing its strength not only from the surrounding tobacco-producing country, but also from textiles and light manufacturing. It is also the home of Francis Marion College and Florence-Darlington Technical College.

Marion County in the heart of the PeeDee "Swamp Fox" country, was originally part of Craven County, the largest of the first three Carolina counties. During the early colonial period, because of its distance from Charleston, the area was sparsely settled. Local historians credit John Godbold, a former captain in the British West Indian service, with being the first settler.

After the Revolution, Marion was laid out as a county. This center of patriotic sentiment was first named Liberty in 1785, but was later changed to its present name in 1798. The town of Gilesborough, later called Marion, was named the seat of the Marion county judicial district in 1800. The county seat took the name of the county and a courthouse and jail were built on four acres donated by the Godbold family, descendants of the first settler. The commercial life of the county revolved around the days when the men of the surrounding area came to town to handle business affairs, their wives made their seasonal purchases from the numerous peddlers who gathered and formed a fair at the very site of an ancient Indian trading post.

As the rich lands along the many creeks and swamps of the area were drained and put into cotton production, the county prospered until the Civil War. During the war, the Confederate Navy built a shipyard eight miles from the town of Marion on the PeeDee River and built the wooden gunboat, the CSS PeeDee. Not launched until November 1864, the ship had to be burned to prevent its capture by Union forces the next spring.

With the decline of the cotton market and advent of the boll weevil in the state, Marion farmers joined their neighbors in converting their acreage to tobacco. They were so successful that the Marion county town of Mullins enjoys the reputation as the largest tobacco market in the world.

BROWNTOWN

Browntown, five miles south of Johnsonville in Florence County, was a settlement which may be the first industrial site in South Carolina. Its origin can be traced to 1768-69. Of special interest are the hand carved wooden machines which were powered by horses walking in endless circles. Browntown is being restored.

pickles and jellies

CHOW-CHOW

Yields: 12 pints   Mrs. Robert N. McLellan (Doris)

1	gallon green tomatoes	4	big onions
1	small head cabbage	1/2	cup salt
1/2	dozen red peppers	2-1/2	cups white vinegar
1/2	dozen green peppers	1	cup water
	(can be hot pepper and	1/2	cup sugar
	all one color)		

Grind all vegetables. Add salt and let this set overnight. Next morning drain well and add vinegar, water and sugar. Bring all ingredients to a boil, turn to simmer and cook 10 to 12 minutes. Seal in jars.

CRYSTAL PICKLE

Mrs. B. L. Hendricks, Jr. (Carolyn)

Wash 25 cucumbers and put in brine (salt water) strong enough to float an egg. Weight down and let stand 2 weeks. Wash the cucumbers, sliced about 3/8 inch thick. Cover with fresh water and add alum, about the size of a walnut. Let stand overnight; then drain and wash again.

SYRUP

1	quart vinegar	2	sticks cinnamon
2	quarts sugar	1	teaspoon cloves

Boil and pour over the pickle for three mornings in succession. On the fourth morning, heat the pickle and seal while hot. Pickle will become clear and crisp.

PATSY'S FREEZER PICKLES

Mrs. William Cork (Helen)

7	cups thin sliced cucumbers	1/4	cup salt
1	cup thin sliced onions		

Mix above ingredients and let stand for 1 hour; rinse thoroughly and drain. Combine the following:

1	cup vinegar	1	teaspoon mustard seed
2	cups sugar	1	teaspoon celery seed

Bring to a boil and pour over cucumbers and onions and let stand overnight. Make sure pickles are covered in liquid. Put in containers with liquid and freeze.

APRICOT CHUTNEY
Mrs. J. M. Cooper (Melba)

3	pounds peeled and cored apples (weigh after peeling)	1	tablespoon salt
4	ounces green ginger root, scraped and sliced in long thin slivers	1	pound apricots, dried and cut in strips, large enough to see and really taste in chutney
3	pounds sugar	1/2	pound raisins, seeded and cut, not put through blender
1/2	ounce red chili, pounded or almost pulverized	1	pint apple cider vinegar
4	ounces garlic, peeled and sliced the short way of the small clove		

Cook apples into an applesauce. Add sugar, ginger, chili, garlic and salt. Cook down to a jam. Stir from bottom of pot as this mixture will burn easily. Add apricots and raisins: continue cooking about 20 minutes. Add the vinegar and bring to a rolling boil. Pour into jars and seal.

SLICED CUCUMBER PIQUANT
Mrs. Herbert Kirsh (Suzanne)

1/2	cup water	1/4	teaspoon pepper
6	tablespoons sugar	2	large cucumbers, scrubbed and scored
1/2	teaspoon salt	1	cup white vinegar
1	onion, sliced thinly		

Combine water, sugar, salt and pepper in a saucepan. Bring to a boil and remove from heat. Set aside to cool. Slice cucumbers and onions very thin. Add the vinegar to the cooled liquid and pour mixture over the cucumbers in a jar. Cover and store in refrigerator. Let marinate for at least 24 hours. Serve.

SOUTH CAROLINA CUCUMBER PICKLES
Mrs. Horace C. Smith (Dot)

Slice 7 pounds cucumbers and cover with a solution made of 2 cups lime in 2 gallons of water. Let soak 24 hours, then rinse well. Cover with clear water and let soak 3 hours. Drain well, cover with the following mixture:

2	quarts vinegar	1	teaspoon whole cloves
4-1/2	pounds sugar	1	teaspoon celery seed
1	tablespoon salt	1	teaspoon pickling spice

Heat vinegar mixture until sugar melts. Put cucumbers in it and soak overnight, covered. Cook cucumbers in syrup for 35 minutes at boiling stage. Pour in hot jars while syrup is hot. Boil jars to seal for 5 minutes.

PICKLES AND JELLIES

GREEN TOMATO PICKLE

Yields: 14 pints   Mrs. Michael Daniel (Peggy)

7   pounds green tomatoes, sliced

Soak for 24 hours in 2 gallons water in which 3 cups lime (3 bottles) has been dissolved. Drain and soak in fresh cold water, changing every hour for 4 hours. Drain. Place in large pot. Bring to boil 5 pounds sugar, 1 teaspoon each of cloves, ginger, allspice, celery seed, mace, cinnamon, and 3 quarts vinegar and pour over tomatoes. Let stand overnight. Next morning boil 1 hour. Seal in jars.

RIPE TOMATO RELISH

Yields: 14 pints   Mrs. Larry L. Gentry (Barbara)

8 quarts ripe tomatoes, peeled	1/3 cup salt
6 large onions	4 tablespoons mustard seed
4 green peppers, cored	3-1/2 tablespoons cinnamon
1 quart vinegar	2 cups cut-up celery
4 cups brown sugar	

Chop tomatoes coarsely. Put the other vegetables through the coarse knife of food chopper (or chop with knife). Combine all the ingredients and cook slowly, about 2 hours. Ladle into jars and seal.

PICKLED OKRA

Yield 5 pints   Mrs. Herbert Kirsh (Suzanne)

1 quart white vinegar	5 cloves garlic, peeled
1/2 cup water	2 tablespoons salt (do not use Iodized salt)
2 pounds small okra, washed and stems trimmed	1 tablespoon celery salt
5 hot red peppers (or 10 strips jalapeno peppers)	5 teaspoons dill seed (optional)
	5 teaspoon mustard seed (optional)

Sterilize 5 pint jars and keep hot until ready to use. Combine vinegar, water and salt and bring to a boil. Into each jar pack okra in 2 vertical layers. The first layer should be packed with the stems down and the next layer with the stems up. Also add to each jar 1 clove garlic, 1 hot red pepper, (or 2 strips jalapeno peppers), 1 teaspoon dill seed and 1 teaspoon mustard seed. Heat vinegar, water, salt and celery salt until it comes to a boil. Pour hot vinegar mixture over okra and seal as soon as filled. Pour paraffin on top to seal properly. To insure a good seal, process 5 minutes in boiling water bath. Let stand several weeks before opening. If very small okra is used, then half pint jars should be used instead. Let stand several weeks before opening. Very small pickled okra is delicious in a martini.

SQUASH PICKLES

Yields: 5 pints   Mrs. Parker Evatt (Jane)

8	cups squash, thinly sliced	2	teaspoons celery seed
2	cups onions, thinly sliced	2	teaspoons mustard seed
4	bell peppers, thinly sliced	3	cups sugar
2	cups dark vinegar		

Combine squash and onions. Sprinkle top with salt. Cover with ice. Set aside to chill for 1 hour. Drain. Mix remaining ingredients in saucepan. Bring to a boil. Add squash and onions. Bring to boil again. Seal in hot sterilized jars. Zucchini may be substituted for the squash in this recipe.

HOT PEPPER JELLY

Yields: 12 to 14 1/2-pint containers   Mrs. L. Edward Bennet (Peggy)
                                              Mrs. James B. Stephen (Ginger)

6	green bell peppers, seeded and cut up	2-1/2	6-ounce bottles Certo
20	hot green peppers, seeded and cut up (or about 1/2 cup jalapeno peppers)	5	pounds sugar
		3	cups cider vinegar
		10	drops green or red food coloring

Put peppers in the blender with 1/2 cup of vinegar at high speed. Blend well. Pour into a saucepan, rinse blender with remaining vinegar and add to peppers. Add sugar and bring to a rolling boil that you cannot stir down. Remove from heat. Let stand 5 minutes (or boil about 7 to 8 minutes and remove from heat). Skim if necessary. Strain liquid into a second big saucepan. Add Certo and food coloring of your choice. Boil 1 minute. Pour into 12 to 14 sterilized 1/2 pint containers and seal. This is good to serve with cream cheese on crackers, in pepper jelly turnovers and is especially good with lamb.

MAMA LEE'S OLD FASHIONED BLACKBERRY JAM
Mrs. John M. Rucker (Harriet)

Wash berries carefully, drain and carefully remove caps and stems. To each pound of prepared fruit, allow an equal weight of sugar. Crush berries and bring slowly to boiling, stirring constantly. Add sugar and boil until fruit mixture has thickened to jelly like consistency. Stir throughout the cooking process. Pour into hot sterilized jars and seal immediately. OPTIONAL: If berry seeds are objectionable, boil fruit for a few minutes and then put through a fine sieve to remove seeds before weighing fruit and adding the sugar.

STRAWBERRY PRESERVES

Yields: 6-1/2 pints   Mrs. Lloyd I. Hendricks (Sue)

9   cups sugar   1   cup water
2   quarts strawberries

Wash and hull before measuring. Put sugar and water in large pot and stir and boil until sugar dissolves. Add strawberries. Boil 15 minutes (rolling boil). Do not stir, but shake kettle and skim off top. Pour into flat pans and shake occasionally until cold. Put in sterilized jars when cold. Never cook more than 2 quarts at one time.

Around the year 1540 the first European visitors made their way into the Aiken County area. The Spanish Explorer De Soto and a small band of soldiers reportedly stopped at an Indian village located on the banks of the Savannah River near Silver Bluffs.

Two hundred years after De Soto's visit white settlers returned to the spot. It was on this site in 1730 that George Galphin built a home and established an Indian trading post. His success lured other settlers and by the time of the Revolution numerous small farming communities had taken root along the banks of the Savannah.

However, the fortunes of Hamburg, a boom-town, declined almost as quickly as they had risen. Trade patterns in the upstate shifted to Greenville and across the river, Augusta began to capture what was left of the Savannah River traffic. The town of Aiken began to grow and by the beginning of the Civil War Hamburg was virtually abandoned.

During the latter years of the war, Aiken became an important military target. The Graniteville Mill, the first cotton mill built in the state, manufactured cloth for the Confederate government until Sherman's advancing army put it out of commission in 1864.

The county was organized in 1871 by the state's Reconstruction government. Officially named Aiken, after the former president of South Carolina Railroad, William Aiken, the new county became a hot bed of political dissent during the late 1870s. Reacting to the Hamburg riot, county residents began organizing para-military groups known as the Red Shirts. The Red Shirt organizations spread to other sections of the state eventually becoming the major political organization of General Wade Hampton.

During the antebellum period the town of Aiken was a popular resort area for lowcountry planters. After the war many hotels were built in Aiken and by the 1920s the city was one of the South's major resort communities.

Known for its first six years as Winton, Barnwell County was organized by the legislature in 1798. Originally the county boundaries encompassed all of the territory between the South Edisto and Savannah rivers. The first settlers to the region were transplanted Virginians. The rich soil in the area was adaptable to many crops; by the end of the Revolution numerous plantations were prospering in the county.

The county seat, Barnwell, was known during the war as Red Hills. The town's name was officially changed to honor General John Barnwell, noted Revolutionary War leader. On the town square is a Vertical Sundial believed to be the only one of its kind remaining in the country. The clock, given to the city by an eccentric planter, has kept perfect time for over 140 years.

Blackville, named for Alexander Black, an early railroad executive, has played a major role in the development of Barnwell County. The town was an important junction point for the early South Carolina Railroad line.

During the Civil War the county suffered badly. Taken over by Sherman, the town of Barnwell and most of the local plantations were burned. Legend has it that when the Union General Kilpatrick entered the county seat he invited the ladies of Barnwell to dance in celebration of the army's arrival. In mocking acceptance of the General's order the women of Barnwell waltzed in the streets as their homes burned.

In recent years nuclear power has become an important resource of Barnwell. Built in the 1950s in the western portion of the county, the Savannah River Nuclear Plant is one of the largest nuclear power stations in the country. The 250 acre Barnwell State Park with its picnic sites, campgrounds, and hiking trails offers a variety of recreational opportunities.

For the past fifty years Barnwell County has been represented by the Honorable Solomon Blatt in the House of Representatives. His colleagues elected him Speaker for thirty-three years and he was designated Speaker Emeritus upon relinquishing that position. His portrait hangs in the House Chamber, and the House Office Building is named for this distinguished statesman.

Bamberg is a rural and agricultural county carved from the piney hills and plains of Barnwell County in 1897. Two of its borders, the Edisto and Salkehatchie rivers, are noted for their perch, trout and jack while their wooded banks are said to be plentiful with game.

The county lies along the route of the historic Charleston-Hamburg railroad branch made famous in 1831 when the nation's first steam locomotive for passengers, "The Best Friend," zipped riders through the area at the unbelievable speed of 15 m.p.h.! Other, more leisurely and scholarly visitors came to the area in antebellum days to visit "Woodlands," the plantation home of William Gilmore Simms, the most prolific southern writer of the period. The estate and portions of the original house remain today.

The courthouse town and the county itself are named for the founding Bamberg family. A small town atmosphere dominates the county seat which is also the home of a boys' preparatory school, Carlisle Military Academy.

The town of Denmark is one of several in the southwestern part of the state with Scandinavian names. The others in the constellation - Norway, Sweden and Switzerland - are in neighboring counties. Once an important railroad junction, Denmark was named for a family of rail promoters. It is the home of Voorhees, a four year college which began in 1897 as an Industrial and Normal School for Negroes. Voorhees started with one teacher and a half dozen students who paid 10 cents per week to attend. The institution is now supported by the Episcopal Church.

At the southern point of this roughly diamond-shaped county is Rivers Bridge State Park, near Ehrhardt. It stands on the site of a Civil War battle which occurred on February 3, 1865; a small outnumbered Confederate division, forced across the Salkehatchie River, put up a gallant defense which delayed for two days Sherman's march through the State. A historical marker tells the story. Quietly. Proudly.

311

THE CHARLES HAMMOND HOUSE

The Charles Hammond House was built in 1775-1780 and is located in North Augusta, South Carolina.

menus for every occasion

Entries GM refers to recipes in the Governor's Mansion section.

MENUS   **WINE RECOMMENDED**

SUNDAY BRUNCH BUFFET

Melba Grapefruit Sections, p. 54
Cheese Soufflé, p. 159, GM 17
Baked Brisket, p. 173 with Rolls, p. 75
Molded Eggs and Shrimp, p. 102
Cucumbers in Sour Cream
Marinated Asparagus, p. 109
Wheat Muffins, p. 72 with Butter
Pound Cake, p. 287 and Apple Cake, p. 274-75

A red Bordeaux from the Medoc. If white wine is preferred - a Muscadet from the Loire Valley of France. A domestic equivalent would be Fume Blanc.

LADIES GARDEN OR PATIO POOL BRUNCH BUFFET

Fruit Salad with Crème Fraîche, GM 15
Eggs Mornay, GM 17
Sausage Bake, p. 160
Crab or Ham Mousse, p. 44-51 with Toast Points
Green Salad with Palmetto French Dressing, p. 119
Warm Brioches, GM 11 and Croissants
Butter and Strawberry Preserves, p. 308
Rum Nut Cake, p. 289 and Finger Chews, p. 261

It is said that egg dishes give wine a peculiar taste for some people. You might want to experiment. Some suggestions: A Bordeaux white, such as Graves, a dry Rosé such as Tavel, or a Beaujolias Villages.

A BRUNCH FOR WEEKEND GUESTS

Fruit with Raspberry Cream Dressing, p. 108
Turkey Loaf with Mushroom Fondue, p. 199-200
Green Bean Bacon Roll-Ups, p. 128
Thin Slices English Muffin Bread, p. 67 with Sweet Butter
Carolina Cake, p. 287 and Bite Size Fruit Cakes, p. 283

A German Moselle, such as Bernkastel Kabinett or a Johanissbert Riesling from the U. S.

MENUS	WINE RECOMMENDED

A SOUTH CAROLINA GAME BRUNCH

Hot Fruit Compote, p. 246
South Carolina Dove, p. 236-37
Quail on Country Ham, p. 237-185
Brunch Egg Casserole, p. 160
Hash Browns Au Gratin, p. 136
Spinach Casserole, p. 139
Bo J's Biscuits, p. 66 and Butter
Pots of Jams and Jellies, p. 307-08
Orange-Caramel Rolls, p. 74
Sour Cream Coffee Cake, p. 291

A good heavy red wine from the Rhone Valley of France, such as Nuit St. George, a white Rhone or a domestic Pinot Chardonnay.

A LUNCH FOR WEEKEND GUESTS

Thin Slices of Veal Parmigiana, p. 192, Marsalla, p. 192 or Piccata, p. 191
Cold Ratatouille on Half of a Peeled Tomato, p. 138
Green Noodles, p. 150
Rum Nut Cake, p. 289

A light Italian red with Parmigiana, like Bardolino. A heavier red, such as Amarone with Marsalla. Some may prefer white with Piccata. In that case an Italian Frascati.

FORMAL SEATED DINNER FOR ANY OCCASION

la Mousseline de Poisson, GM 15, 59 with Crab Meat Sauce, p. 231
Thin Toast Triangles with Butter
Broccoli Bisque, p. 81
Bibb and Romaine Salad with Palmetto French Dressing, p. 119
Raspberry Sherbet laced with . . . .
Chateaubriand, p. 189 or Standing Rib Roast
Roast Potatoes, p. 137
Fresh Asparagus, Tied and Baked with a Green Onion Leaf
Buttermilk Dinner Rolls, GM 12 and Sweet Butter
Cherries Jubilee, p. 245
Demitasse

A white Bordeaux Graves, such as Chateau Olivier.

Champagne

In order to build the wines with the tastes in the meal, a full bodied Burgundy, such as Hautes Côte-de-Nuit.

A brandy, such as Martells's Cognac V.S.O.P.

A LADIES LUNCHEON

Cantelope Ring Surrounded with
  Fruit Salad, GM 15 with Poppy
  Seed Dressing, p. 119
Cheese Roulade with Spinach
  and Mushrooms, p. 161
Edens Flower, p. 132
Refrigerator Rolls, p. 73 and Butter
Chocolate Roll, p. 281

A Macon white, from the French
Burgundy, or a California Pinot
Chardonnay. (When serving a tradi-
tional roulade wrapped in beef Strips,
then a Macon red from the French
Burgundy, or a California Pinot Noir.)

A POTPOURRI OF SALADS LUNCHEON

Fruit Salad with Crème Fraîche
  in a small Shell, GM 15
Chicken Salad, p. 113-14 in a Small
  Shell
Deviled Crab in a shell, p.
  220-21-22 or
Zesty Rice Salad, p. 116 in a Shell
  (Place rounded edges to outside
  of plate)
Frozen Fruit Sherbet, p. 251 in a
  Parfait Glass or Orange Shell
  Glacé (in middle of plate), p. 250
Thin Melba Toast and Coffee

Any of the fruity white wines of the
Loire Valley of France. It might be an
interesting departure to use a spar-
kling wine, such as an inexpensive
Spanish Champagne.

AN EASTER SUNDAY DINNER

Cauliflower Soup, GM 13
Hearts of Palm Salad, p. 111
Crown Roast of Lamb Filled with
  Mushroom Soufflé, p. 188
Hot Pepper Jelly, p. 307
Cabbage and Shrimp, p. 131
Cold Thick Tomato Slices Piled
  with Ratatouille, p. 138
Hot Rolls, p. 73 and Sweet Butter
Chocolate Roll, p. 281
Demitasse

A Bordeaux red from St. Émilion or a
California Cabernet Sauvignon.

315

MENUS	WINE RECOMMENDED

A SOUTH CAROLINA THANKSGIVING BUFFET DINNER

Beautiful Easy Bisque, p. 82

Roast Turkey with Gravy and
   Cornbread Dressing, p. 199

Wild Rice Casserole, p. 155-56

Edens Flower, p. 132

Spinach and Artichoke Casserole, p. 139

Sweet Potato Surprise, p. 138

Cranberry Sauce and Pickled
   Peaches

Holiday Cranberry Salad, p. 103

Refrigerator Rolls, p. 73-74-75 and
   Butter Curls

Sour Cream Pumpkin Pie, p. 299

Demitasse

A white French burgundy or a California Pinot Chardonnay, or if a light red is preferred, a red Bordeaux from St. Estephe.

A GALA DINNER HONORING A SPECIAL BIRTHDAY

Curried Cardinal Cup, p. 86

Smoked Salmon with Capers,
   Cayenne, Celery Brushes and
   Pickled Onions

A full-bodied white Burgundy or California Pinot Blanc.

Thin Triangle Slices of Rye
   Bread, p. 70 and Butter

Old English Beef Roast, p. 174

A full-bodied red Burgundy or California Pinot Noir.

Potatoes and Onions Chantilly, p.
   135

Sweet and Sour Fingerling Carrots,
   p. 132

Paper Cup Frozen Salad, p. 106

Hot Rolls, p. 73 and Butter

White Pound Cake, p. 288 with
   White Birthday Icing, p. 288 or

Chocolate Pound Cake, p. 288 with
   Chocolate Birthday Icing, p. 288

Demitasse

MENUS	WINE RECOMMENDED

PLANTATION GAME DINNER

Quail, GM 18, 237-39
Roasted Wild Duck, GM 18, 238
Venison Roast, GM 18, 239-40
Wild Rice with Apples, p. 156
Scalloped Oysters, p. 223
Sweet Potato Souffle, GM 18
Tomato Aspic, p. 106, GM 15
Spoon Rolls, GM 12 and Butter
Ambrosia, GM 19 and Date-Nut Cake, GM 20

A good red Bordeaux. A good heavy red from the Rhone Valley of France, such as Chateauneuf-du-Pape or Côte-du-Rhone.

CHRISTMAS DAY DINNER

Consomme, p. 84
Baked Ham, p. 183-185-191
Broccoli Nut Casserole, p. 130
Sweet and Sour Carrots, p. 132
Macaroni Mousse, p. 149 or Red Rice, p. 154
Frozen Fruit Salad, p. 107
Whiskey Cake, p. 290, Christmas
   Cookies, p. 260 and Bite Size
   Fruit Cakes, p. 283 with Ambrosia, GM 19
Christmas Eggnog, p. 26

A fruity white French wine such as Vouvray, or a California Chenin Blanc. A dry Rosé such as Tavel would go well with ham also.

A V.I.P. SUNDAY SUPPER

Cucumber Mousse, p. 103
Seafood Salad, p. 115
Chicken and Artichoke Hearts in
   Wine Sauce, p. 203 or Breast of
   Chicken Gruyère, p. 202
Brown Rice Pilaf, p. 155
Sweet and Sour Carrots, p. 132
Broccoli Casserole, p. 130
Hot Rolls, p. 73 and Butter
Pineapple Icebox Cake, p. 285

A German Riesling Kabinett or a California Gewurztraminer.

MENUS FOR EVERY OCCASION

MENUS	WINE RECOMMENDED

A HARD DAY AT WORK SUPPER

Beef Stew, p. 174-75 or Braised Beef, p. 172 (Cooked day before)	A Mâcon red from the French Burgundy.
White Rice or Rice Pilaf, p. 155	
Very Fine Slaw, p. 117-18	
Warm Buttered Cheese Bread, p. 68	
Lime Jello Pie, p. 297	

A PREPARE YOUR OWN SEAFOOD KITCHEN AND DECK BUFFET

Steamed Oysters and Scallops, p. 224	A medium white burgundy, such as Macon Village.
Remoulade Sauce, p. 55	
Shrimp Scampi, p. 230	
Sautéed Oysters, p. 223, and Sautéed Shrimp, p. 223, Fish Scallopini, p. 218, Herb Stuffed Fish, p. 219 or Fish Fillets Fried in Beer Batter, p. 217, Tartar Sauce, p. 224,	A Bordeaux white like Graves. A white wine from the Loire Valley of France, such as Pouilly-Fume or a California Fumé Blanc.
Caper Sauce, p. 230 and Crab Sauce, p. 231 (Each person preparing his own)	
Shrimp Pie, p. 230 and Seafood Casserole, p. 226	
Rice Salad With Seafood, p. 116	
Slaw, p. 117	
Hush Puppies	
Tipsy Squire, p. 290	

A THEATER OR BENEFIT SUPPER

Country Captain, p. 201 or	An Italian white Frascati.
Chicken Tetrazzini, p. 210	
Spinach Salad with Palmetto French Dressing, p. 119	
Baked Chutney Peach Halves, p. 250	
Butterscotch Cookies, p. 257 Chocolate Coconut Squares, p. 258 Date Bars, p. 260, Cream Puffs with Mocha Filling, GM 21, and Pâté Brisée with Lemon Butter, GM 22	

LATE NIGHT BALL GAME SUPPER

Fruit with Raspberry Cream
  Dressing, p. 108
Sliced Whole Country Ham, p. 185
Sausage and Egg Casserole, p. 160
Cheese Grits, p. 157-58
Marinated Vegetable Salad, p. 112
Buttermilk Biscuits, p. 66 with
  Butter
Sour Cream Coffee Cake, p. 291

With baked ham, a fruity white French wine such as Vouvray, or a California Chenin Blanc. A dry Rosé such as Tavel would go well with ham also.

FOOTBALL GAME SOUP PARTY

Tureens of Oyster Bisque, p. 82
Red Catfish Stew, p. 217-18 or
French Onion Soup, p. 88-89
  (ladled into Mugs)
Beer Cheese Spread, p. 39 with
  Melba Toast
Slices of Fresh Fruit
Raw Vegetables in Ice, p. 56, 112
Southern Popovers, p. 73 and
  Beer Muffins, p. 72 Hot from
  the Oven
Heavenly Brownies, p. 256, Date
  Bars, p. 260 and Lemon Bars, p. 262

Alscatian Riesling with the Oyster Bisque.

A good heavy red, such as a Spanish Rioja.

A HOT HEARTY SOUP FOR A COLD DAY

Senate Bean Soup, p. 82 or
  House Split Pea Soup, p. 81
Three Ring Salad, p. 111
Sour Cream Cornbread, p. 71 or
  Corn Spinach Bread, p. 72 and
  lots of Butter
Apple Pie, p. 293

MENUS	WINE RECOMMENDED

SOUP AND SANDWICH FOR GOOD FRIENDS

Spinach Vichyssoise, p. 89
Egg Salad Sandwich with
  Shrimp Topping, p. 92
Butterscotch Cookies, p. 257 or
  Fat Ladies, p. 282

A CHINESE BUFFET SUPPER FOR GOOD FRIENDS

Egg Rolls, p. 43 with Sweet
  and Sour Sauce, p. 43 and Hot
  Mustard Dip, p. 42
Egg Drop Soup with Chinese
  Noodles, p. 87
Shrimp Curry, p. 229, Sweet and
  Sour Pork, p. 187, Chinese Spare-
  ribs, p. 186, Teriyaki, p. 177, Chinese
  Pepper Steak, p. 170, or Chicken
  Chow Mein with Chow Mein
  Noodles, p. 207
Shrimp Fried Rice, p. 154 and
  Steamed Rice
Three Ring Salad, p. 111 with a
  can of Bean Sprouts and Soy
  Sauce
Orange Shell Glacé with a Paper
  Parasol stuck in top, p. 250

Wines are more available in the U.S. from mainland China. A medium dry white called Dynasty would work well with this supper. If you prefer something tried and true, an Anjou Rosé would match the tastes.

A GREEK SUPPER

Spanakopita (Spinach Triangles), p.
  38
Tiropetes (Cheese Triangles), p. 37
Moussaka, p. 184
"Pastitsio," Greek Macaroni
  Squares, p. 148
Spinach and Artichoke Casserole,
  p. 139-141
Sweet and Sour Carrots, p. 132
Hot Herb Bread
Baklava, p. 245

To go all Greek, White Demestica or Danielis.

A sweet dessert wine from Greece would go well - Mavrodathne

MENUS	WINE RECOMMENDED

AN ITALIAN BUFFET SUPPER

Italian Meal in a Dish, p. 162   Chianti Classico Riserva from Italy.
Lasagna, p. 163, Manicotti, p. 164
    Spaghetti, p. 149, or Italian
    Sausage Zucchini, p. 189
Three Ring Salad, p. 111 with Pepperoni
Crusty Italian Bread and Butter
Irish Coffee Parfait, p. 251 or
    Pious Angel Parfait, p. 251

A FAMILY SUPPER

Chicken Pot Pie, p. 208 or   A German Rhine wine or Domestic
Meat Loaf, p. 178-180-81   Riesling. A Beaujolias Villages, or a
Green Bean Bacon Roll-Ups, p. 128   California Zinfandel.
Slaw, p. 117-18
(Macaroni and Cheese with the
    Meatloaf, p. 151)
Mandaran Orange Cake, p. 285

A TAIL GATE PICNIC

Liver Pate, p. 57 with Melba Toast   A French Pouilly-Fuissé, or Cali-
Fried Chicken, p. 53, 217 or   fornia Pinot Chardonnay.
    Deviled Rock Cornish Hens in Foil,
    p. 200
Rice and Seafood Salad, p. 116 or
Beef and Potato Salad, p. 115 in 4 large
    Sourdough Rolls, p. 115
Deviled Eggs or Hot Swedish Meatballs
    with Sour Cream, p. 58
Buffet Bean Bowl, p. 109
A round loaf of bread hollowed out, p. 91
    and the center filled with Pimento
    Cheese, p. 95 and Ham Sandwiches (Take a
    lot of extra sandwiches for refilling)
Chocolate Coconut Squares, p. 258

MENUS	WINE RECOMMENDED

LABOR DAY PICNIC

Marinated Chicken to Grill, p. 213
Corn on the Cob
Baked Beans, p. 127
Patio Potatoes, p. 137
Taco Salad, p. 118
Hard Rolls with Cheese
Chocolate Eclair Cake, p. 247

Beaujolias Villages or American Gamay Beaujolias.

FOURTH OF JULY PICNIC SUPPER

Charcoal Broiled Flank Steaks, p. 170
Onion Pie, p. 135
Layered Salad, p. 111
Cheese French Bread, p. 68
Fudge Cake, p. 283

A good full bodied red such as Moulin-a-Vent or the Carolina red from the Truluck vineyards near Lake City, S. C.

A DELI PICNIC

Borscht, p. 83 (kept chilled in a thermos bottle)
Platters of cold meats selected at the Delicatessen
Platters of Anchovies, thin-sliced Swiss Cheese, Tomatoes, Sliced Onions, Hard Cooked Eggs, Pickled Corn on the Cob, Okra, pickles and lettuce
Crocks of Mustards, sour cream, cream cheese and butter
Bagels, Rye Bread and French Bread from the bakery
Apple Cake, p. 274 and Fresh Fruit Slices

A German Mosel, Italian Soave, Champagne or a domestic Green Hungarian (kept well chilled).

MENUS	WINE RECOMMENDED

A SUMMER POOLSIDE PATIO PARTY

Marinated Shrimp, GM 11
  la Mousseline de poisson
  (Salmon Mousse) with Herbed
  Mayonnaise, GM 15
Cold Pasta Salad, GM 14
Buttermilk Dinner Rolls, GM 12
Cream Puffs filled with Mocha
  Filling, GM 21
Pâté Brisee filled with Lemon
  Butter, GM 22

An Italian Verdicchio or a California Gewurztraminer.

A white Bordeaux Graves, such as Château Olivier would go with the Salmon Mousse.

BARBECUE BUFFET PARTY

Barbecue Pig, p. 186
Barbecue Beef, p. 172
Baked Bean Bash, p. 127
White Rice
Slaw, p. 117-18
Rolls and Butter

A dry red or white jug wine from France, Italy or the U.S. will match Southern tradition in taste and the price. The French are heavier, the Italian lighter, the domestics in between.

HAMBURGER AND HOT DOG COOK-OUT

Carterburgers, p. 183 and Hot Dogs
Hot Dog Chili, p. 183
Baked Beans, p. 127
Hash Browns au Gratin, p. 136
Buns, Catsup, Mustard, Mayonnaise
Tomatoes, Onions and Pickles
Fat Ladies, p. 282

With hamburgers, a hearty red Burgundy, Macon red or the Carolina red from the Truluck vineyards near Lake City, S. C.

A DOCKSIDE PARTY

Barbecued Beef on Buns, p. 172
Beef and Potato Salad, p. 115 in a Hollowed
  out Round Sandwich Loaf, p. 91
Ranch Baked Beans, p. 127
Corn on the Cob
Slaw, p. 117-18
Jalapeño Dip, p. 48 with Fritos and Doritos
$1,000,000 Chocolate Cake, p. 280

MENUS	WINE RECOMMENDED

WINE AND CHEESE PARTY

Cheese:

Wine:

Cream Tilsit (Denmark) or
Graddost (Sweden)

Muscadet De Sevre Et. Maine from Loire Valley of France. A less expensive light white would be an Italian jug wine.

Port du Salut (France)

Margues De Riscal Reserva Limousin (A hearty white from Spain)
A substitute at the same price would be a California Fume Blanc. A less expensive selection, if red is preferred, would be a jug of French Burgundy.

Brie (France)

California Zinfadel from a small vineyard or boutique. There's only one Zinfadel and it's all USA.

Aged Gouda (Holland)
Garnished with bunches of grapes, orange segments, fingers of melon, apples and pears, cherries, radishes and celery. Unsalted or very lightly salted crackers, crusty French Bread, crisp rolls and lots of butter. Brie Quiche or a Quiche Lorraine would be appreciated.
Tiny hot mince pies and bite-size fruit cakes, p. 283

A good heavy red Gigondas from the Rhone Valley of France.
A substitute, but not less expensive, would be a California Pinot Noir. The jug of French Burgundy would be the less expensive route.

A TEEN-AGE PARTY

Barbecue Beef on Buns, p. 172
Taco Dip, p. 48 and Dorito Chips
1-Inch Corn on the Cob Rings
    with Picks (Attach them onto
    a grapefruit)
Slaw, p. 117-18
Dr. Pepper Chocolate Cake, p. 280

MENUS   WINE RECOMMENDED

A COKE PARTY

Jalapeño Dip, p. 48 in Fondue Pot
Fritos and Doritos
Bite Pizzas, p. 95
Sloppy Joes on Buns, p. 96
Fat Ladies, p. 282 and
    Peanut Butter Cup Tarts, p. 263

CREOLE OR SEAFOOD RAGOUT PARTY

Shrimp Creole, p. 227-28 or   A good heavy red wine such as a Cote-
    Seafood Ragout, p. 226   du Rhone, or a California Pinot Noir.
Plenty of White Rice
Make-your-Own Salad
Small Hot Buttered Rolls, p. 73-74-75
Chocolate Mousse, p. 249

COCKTAILS AND COCKTAIL BUFFETS

Baked Barbecue Brisket with Rolls, p. 173
Buffet Drummettes, p. 53
Liver Pâté with Bite-Size Pita
   Bread, p. 57
Chutney Sausage Balls, p. 50
Tiropetes (Cheese Triangles), p. 37
Deviled Eggs with Green Herb Dressing
Marinated Shrimp, GM 11
Smoked Oyster Log, GM 10
Ham Mousse with Rice Crackers, p. 44
Stuffed Mushrooms, p. 46
Vegetable Basket, p. 56 with Dips, p. 47-48-58
Butter Nut Brie, p. 10
Cheese Ball with Assorted Crackers, p. 40
Chocolate Coconut Squares, p. 258 and
   Finger Chews, p. 261

Marinated Roast Tenderloin with Rolls, p. 174
Caviar Dip with Toast Points, p. 10
Brie Quiche in Tart Shells
Seafood Mold with Crackers, p. 50
Marinated Mushrooms, p. 46
Meatballs, p. 52-58

MENUS	WINE RECOMMENDED

Scallops Ramaki, p. 45
Artichoke Spread with Triscuits, p. 39
Spanakopita Triangles, p. 38
Marinated Vegetables, p. 112
Merry Christmas Cookies, p. 260, Bite Size Fruit
  Cakes, p. 283, Almond Christmas Cookies, p. 259,
  Christmas Balls, p. 259 and Fruit Nut Bars with
  Ornamental Icing, p. 261

Oysters Rockefeller with Crackers, p. 45 or
  Spanakopita (Spinach Triangles), p. 38
Fried Chicken, p. 53, 217
Deviled S. C. Crab in Shells, p. 220-21-22
  or Seafood Casserole, p. 224-25-26
Baked Ham on Hot Biscuits
Rice Salad with Seafood, p. 116
Marinated Asparagus, p. 109
Buffet Bean Bowl, p. 109
Hot Rolls, p. 73 and Butter
Slices of White and Chocolate
  Pound Cake, p. 288
Watermelon Basket, p. 57 or
  Fruit with Raspberry Cream Dressing, p. 108

LADIES GATHER FOR A MID-DAY CHAT

Crab au Gratin, p. 221
Cold Chicken in Aspic, p. 201
Asparagus Vinaigrette, p. 109
Assorted Rolls, GM 11-12, 73-74-75
Strawberry and Raspberry Compote, p. 247
Petits Fours
Coffee

Without question one of the fine whites of French Loire Valley-Pouilly Fumé. A less expensive selection would be California's Fumé Blanc.

MEDWAY PLANTATION HOUSE

Medway Plantation House was built by Jan Van Arrsens in 1686 and is probably the oldest house in South Carolina. Its Dutch stepped gable ends are built of bricks made of clay from the banks of the Black River. The house is dwarfed by great oaks hung with typical Carolina plantation moss.

Berkeley County, which is in area the largest of the state's counties, was created in 1882, but the name dates back to 1682.

It was in Berkeley County that the plantation system found its finest expression. Rice, cotton, and indigo thrived and supported large plantations with classic homes, many of which remain in the families of the original owners. Mulberry, Silk Hope, Liberty Hall, and Stoney Landing are among the more historic and successful plantations.

The county seat of Moncks Corner was originally a trading post on Mitten Plantation that had been bought by Thomas Monck in 1735. When the railroad lines were built a mile away from the old outpost in 1865, the town relocated to gain this new commercial advantage.

The long-abandoned Santee Canal is the result of another Depression during 1770 when inland planters petitioned the legislature to build a passageway from the Santee to the Cooper River that they might more easily get their crops to the Charleston market. The canal, finished in 1800, was 22 miles long and operated until 1850 when the railroad provided a more economical alternative. It was a success in that the wages paid the planter for the use of their slaves during the construction phase were put into circulation and provided a needed boost to the post-war economy.

Berkeley retains the beauty that Herbert Ravenel Sass and Archibald Rutledge described in their stories of the South. Every type of tree, flower, fruit or shrub native to this latitude may be found in this county. Hunters and fishermen find it a heaven boasting of wild turkey, deer, doves, ducks, and streams with black bass, bream, and perch.

Berkeley (pronounced Barkley after the British fashion until around the time of the Revolution) was the name of the first three counties laid out by the Lord Proprietors and encompassed the town of Charleston.

CHARLESTON COUNTY

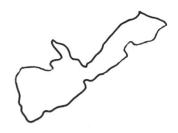

Extending from the South Santee River to the mouth of the South Edisto River, Charleston County enjoys 91 miles of coast line and beaches. The first settlement in the county was at Oyster Point in 1670, now the site of Charles Towne Landing. In 1680, the colony populated by settlers from England, Barbados, Virginia, and later France, moved across the Ashley River to the current location of Charleston, where the harbor permitted large vessels to enter more easily.

One of the five largest cities in America at the eve of the Revolution, Charleston developed a sophisticated and cultured way of life. The first public library in the colonies was founded in 1698. Among Charleston's other "firsts" are the first newspaper in the South, The South Carolina Gazette, (1702), first commercial cultivation of rice (1680), first theatrical performance in North America (1702), first school for blacks on the continent (1743), and the first city college in America (1770).

Prosperous and strategically located, Charleston was an inviting target for the British during the Revolution. Although William Moultrie's forces fighting from their Palmetto log fort on Sullivan's Island repulsed the first attack in 1776, the British finally occupied the city in 1780. It was the last spot in the state evacuated in 1782.

In 1790, the capitol was relocated in Columbia, a more centrally located site. With the decline of the rice and indigo trade, and the depletion of the cotton growing soils, Charleston's fortunes began to wane during the 1820s.

Today, Charleston County has managed to blend respect and preservation for the past with a progressive and optimistic vision of the future.

Drayton Hall, built in 1738, is the finest example of Georgian Palladian architecture extant in the United States and may be viewed by the public. Nearby is Magnolia Gardens, still owned by members of the Drayton family. Three hundred years old, this plantation includes the oldest surviving colonial estate garden.

The development of the phosphate industry and the location of the U. S. Navy Yard in North Charleston helped the city begin the twentieth century.

Arrival of Scots and South Germans in the eighteenth century, and North Germans and Irish in the nineteenth have given the town a Cosmopolitan nature.

BAKED BEANS: 2-1/2 gallons
BREAD: 5 loaves
BUTTER: 1 pound
CABBAGE FOR SLAW: 10 pounds
CAKE: 3 of any kind (18 to 20 slices per cake)
CANDY: 1 pound
CHICKEN FOR CHICKEN PIE: 20 pounds
CHICKEN SALAD: 2-1/2 gallons (1 5-pound hen yields 1 quart cooked meat)
CHOPPED NUTS: 2 cups (2 teaspoons per serving)
COFFEE: 1 pound will yield 50 cups
COFFEE CREAM: 4 cups
COFFEE SUGAR: 1 pound granulated
COOKIES: 12 dozen (3 per person)
CORN CHIPS: 8 9-1/4-ounce packages
CRACKERS: 2 pounds
DIPS AND SPREADS: 5 cups
FUDGE SAUCE: 48 ounces (1 ounce per serving)
HAM: 16 to 18 pounds
HAMBURGER: 15 pounds
ICE CREAM: 2 gallons (using a No. 12 dipper)
ICED TEA: 3 gallons
ICED TEA SUGAR: 3/4 pound granulated
LETTUCE: 10 heads
MAYONNAISE: 2 quarts
MEATS: 12-1/2 pounds (4 ounces per person)
MEAT LOAF: 12 pounds
NUTS: 3 pounds
PICKLES: 1 quart
PIES: 9 (6 slices per pie)
POTATO CHIPS: 8 6-ounce packages
POTATOES: 17-1/2 pounds
POTATO SALAD: 6 quarts
PUNCH: 2 gallons
ROLLS: 100
SALAD DRESSING: 1-1/2 quarts
SPAGHETTI: 5 pounds and about 26 and 2/3 cups sauce
TURKEY: 2 18 to 20 pounds
VEGETABLES: 6 quarts cooked (fresh or canned)
WEINERS: 12-1/2 pounds
WHIPPING CREAM: 1 quart whipped (2 tablespoons per serving)

Food	Amount Before Preparation	Approximate Measure After Preparation
CEREALS		
MACARONI	1 cup (3-1/2 oz.)	2-1/2 cups cooked
NOODLES	3 cups (4 oz.)	3 cups cooked
SPAGHETTI	8 oz.	4 cups cooked
LONG GRAIN RICE	1 cup (7 oz.)	3 cups cooked
QUICK-COOKING RICE	1 cup (3 oz.)	2 cups cooked
POPCORN	1/4 cup	5 cups popped
BREAD	1 slice	3/4 cup soft or 1/4 cup fine dry crumbs
SALTINE CRACKERS	28 squares	1 cup finely crushed
RICH ROUND CRACKERS	24 crackers	1 cup finely crushed
GRAHAM CRACKERS	14 squares	1 cup finely crushed
VANILLA WAFERS	22 cookies	1 cup finely crushed
GINGERSNAPS	15 cookies	1 cup finely crushed
CHOCOLATE WAFERS	19 cookies	1 cup finely crushed
VEGETABLES		
BEANS AND PEAS, DRIED	1 lb. (2-1/2 cups)	6 cups cooked
CABBAGE	1 lb. (1 small)	5 cups shredded
CARROTS, WITHOUT TOPS	1 lb. (6 medium)	3 cups shredded
CELERY	1 medium bunch	4-1/2 cups chopped
CORN	1 medium ear	1/2 cup cut from cob
GREEN BEANS	1 lb. (3 cups)	2-1/2 cups cooked
GREEN ONIONS	1 bunch (7)	1/2 cup sliced
GREEN PEPPERS	1 large	1 cup diced
MUSHROOMS	1 lb. (6 cups)	6 cups sliced or 2 cups cooked
ONIONS	1 medium	1/2 cup chopped
POTATOES	1 medium	2/3 cup cubed or 1/2 cup mashed
RADISHES	1 bunch	1 cup sliced
TOMATOES	1 medium	1/2 cup cooked
ZUCCHINI	1 medium	1 cup sliced
FRUITS		
APPLES	1 medium	1 cup sliced
LEMONS	1 medium	3 Tbsp. juice; 2 tsp. peel
ORANGES	1 medium	1/4 to 1/3 cup juice; 4 tsp. peel

MIDDLEBURG PLANTATION HOUSE

Middleburg Plantation House was built by Benjamin Simons about twenty five miles north of Charleston in 1699. This is the oldest known wooden house still standing in South Carolina.

INDEX

EGGS, CHEESE AND GRAIN

FISH AND SHELLFISH

337

338

339

SANDWICHES

SAUCES, DESSERT

SAUCES FOR MEAT, FISH, ETC.

ORDER FORM

Sandlapper Publishing Co., Inc.
PO Box 730
Orangeburg, SC 29116-0730

A Taste of South Carolina

_____ copies @ **$16.95** ea. _____

Postage/handling ($2.50*) _____
*first book, $1.00 ea. additional
Sales tax ($.85 ea.**) _____
**South Carolina residents only
TOTAL _____

Make checks payable to Sandlapper.

Name_____

Address_____

_____

City_____

State_____ Zip_____

Charge my Visa ☐   MasterCard ☐

Card #_____

Expiration Date_____

Name on card_____

Signature_____

Credit card orders may be placed by phone. Call 1-800-849-7263.

Shipments are made from our warehouse within 48 working hours after receipt of order.

☐ Please send me a listing of other cookbooks you have available.

Prices listed good through 1996. After that time, call 1-800-849-7263 for price change information.
NOV 1995

ORDER FORM

Sandlapper Publishing Co., Inc.
PO Box 730
Orangeburg, SC 29116-0730

A Taste of South Carolina

_____ copies @ **$16.95** ea. _____

Postage/handling ($2.50*) _____
*first book, $1.00 ea. additional
Sales tax ($.85 ea.**) _____
**South Carolina residents only
TOTAL _____

Make checks payable to Sandlapper.

Name_____

Address_____

_____

City_____

State_____ Zip_____

Charge my Visa ☐   MasterCard ☐

Card #_____

Expiration Date_____

Name on card_____

Signature_____

Credit card orders may be placed by phone. Call 1-800-849-7263.

Shipments are made from our warehouse within 48 working hours after receipt of order.

☐ Please send me a listing of other cookbooks you have available.

Prices listed good through 1996. After that time, call 1-800-849-7263 for price change information.
NOV 1995

ORDER FORM

Sandlapper Publishing Co., Inc.
PO Box 730
Orangeburg, SC 29116-0730

A Taste of South Carolina

____ copies @ **$16.95** ea. _____

Postage/handling ($2.50*) _____
*first book, $1.00 ea. additional
Sales tax ($.85 ea.**) _____
**South Carolina residents only
TOTAL _____

Make checks payable to Sandlapper.

Name_____

Address_____

_____

City_____

State_____ Zip_____

Charge my Visa ☐   MasterCard ☐

Card #_____

Expiration Date_____

Name on card_____

Signature_____

Credit card orders may be placed by phone. Call 1-800-849-7263.

Shipments are made from our warehouse within 48 working hours after receipt of order.

☐ Please send me a listing of other cookbooks you have available.

Prices listed good through 1996. After that time, call 1-800-849-7263 for price change information.   **NOV 1995**

ORDER FORM

Sandlapper Publishing Co., Inc.
PO Box 730
Orangeburg, SC 29116-0730

A Taste of South Carolina

____ copies @ **$16.95** ea. _____

Postage/handling ($2.50*) _____
*first book, $1.00 ea. additional
Sales tax ($.85 ea.**) _____
**South Carolina residents only
TOTAL _____

Make checks payable to Sandlapper.

Name_____

Address_____

_____

City_____

State_____ Zip_____

Charge my Visa ☐   MasterCard ☐

Card #_____

Expiration Date_____

Name on card_____

Signature_____

Credit card orders may be placed by phone. Call 1-800-849-7263.

Shipments are made from our warehouse within 48 working hours after receipt of order.

☐ Please send me a listing of other cookbooks you have available.

Prices listed good through 1996. After that time, call 1-800-849-7263 for price change information.   **NOV 1995**